ISLANDS IN THE DESERT

ISLANDS IN THE DESERT

A History of the Uplands of Southeastern Arizona

John P. Wilson

Foreword by Patricia M. Spoerl

Published in cooperation with the Historical Society of New Mexico

University of New Mexico Press
Albuquerque

Library of Congress Cataloging-in-Publication Data

Wilson, John P. (John Philip), 1935– .
Islands in the Desert: a history of the uplands of southeastern Arizona /
John P. Wilson.
p. cm.
"Published in cooperation with the Historical Society of New Mexico."
Includes bibliographical references and index.
ISBN 0-8263-1615-8.
1. Mountains—Arizona—History.
2. Mountains—Coronado National Forest (Arizona and N.M.)—History.
3. Arizona—History, Local.
4. Coronado National Forest (Ariz. and N.M.)—History.
I. Historical Society of New Mexico.
II. Title.
F811.w76 1995
979.1'5—dc20
95–7557
CIP

First edition

CONTENTS

ILLUSTRATIONS

MAPS

FOREWORD

Islands are found in the desert as well as in the sea. The forest-covered mountains that rise from the arid Sonoran Desert of southern Arizona form such islands. Although separated by land instead of water, these isolated mountain ranges are unique, as different from their lowlying surroundings as they are from each other. They contain some of the most rugged and remote lands in the American Southwest and comprise one of the most ecologically diverse regions in the United States.

Just as the sky islands of southern Arizona are environmentally diverse, so are the stories to be told about human use of them. The relationship between people and the mountains has been a vital one for thousands of years. Knowledge of these relationships is essential to understanding the history of settlement, ranching and mining ventures, and Indian relations in the American Southwest. Certain time periods and events, such as the era of Spanish exploration and the Apache Wars, also were important in the creation and development of our nation.

Numerous books have been written describing the major events in Arizona's history, however, few have placed these events in the overall context of the surrounding environment and exploitation of needed or valued resources. Histories of southern Arizona usually only mention the mountains and focus instead on settlement and use of the river valleys. While the drainage networks are essential for survival, the forested uplands also were critically important to successful settlement.

Seldom does one receive a realistic view of human use of the mountains; they remain merely vague geographic areas on the fringes of the valleys. The mountains do, however, contain a rich history and are the actual locales for numerous incidents known throughout the country. Apaches, led by Cochise and later Geronimo, camped in the stronghold canyons of the Dragoons and in the high elevations of the Chiricahuas; miners searched for gold and silver in remote ranges such as the Galiuros, or the Santa Ritas and Tumacacoris where Spanish treasure was supposedly hidden; the U.S. Army established camps in the Chiricahuas to track renegade Indians, and built a hospital on Mt. Graham for ill and wounded soldiers; ranchers moved large herds of cattle from higher to lower pastures depending upon the season;

desert residents developed roads to the top of the Santa Catalinas so they could build summer retreats in newly created forest reserves; the Civilian Conservation Corps established summer camps in the Pinaleños and other ranges, and constructed fire lookouts and logging roads. The Apache, Pima, and Tohono O'odham used the mountains for hundreds of years, each leaving distinctive material remains.

This book summarizes, evaluates, and makes accessible to a wide audience numerous disparate, scattered, and often unpublished studies. It began as a Forest Service history overview of the Coronado National Forest, to be written primarily with published materials as the main sources. It soon became evident, however, that primary sources were essential to providing more than a cursory historical review. Forest Service files, newspaper accounts, land status reports, mining records, and archival sources have been used extensively to gain a better understanding of southern Arizona history.

Attempting to synthesize and interpret history in a geographically disjointed area is difficult. The purpose here is not a general history of southern Arizona, but rather to present substantive historical background of interest to persons in a variety of fields. Major historical themes that transcend regional issues are considered although their coverage varies. The emphasis is placed on providing new information, thus topics such as railroad history and Forest Service administrative history, both of which are readily available in other publications, receive little treatment here.

The volume also serves to explain the past rather than just chronicle events. This is particularly evident in the mining chapter where mining activities are viewed as driven by market forces where the many on-again off-again ventures reflect the availability of capital and prices for various metals. A similar situation still exists today. Another example is the alternative view presented for the 1890s transition from an open-range cattle industry to the type of ranching operations still in place today, an account which dispels in part the popular romantic notions of cowboys and the cattle industry.

Islands in the Desert is important both for its synthesis of historical information (much from unpublished sources,) and for its focus on the uplands. In providing a more complete picture of southern Arizona history, the book is intended to be of value to all persons interested in Southwestern history.

Patricia M. Spoerl
U.S. Forest Service

PREFACE

Recorded history in southeastern Arizona dates back four and a half centuries to the days of the first Spanish explorers. They found one or more of the principal river valleys settled by Piman-speaking natives. Many years later, Jesuit fathers arrived to convert these natives and to establish missions. Still later came the miners to pry silver from the reluctant hills, and ranchers seeking lands for their cattle. Today, winter visitors from northern states bask in the sunshine and warm temperatures while they enjoy the rugged beauty of this land.

This is not intended to be a general history of southeastern Arizona, and readers will quickly notice the absence of a single unifying theme. The concern here is with the scattered mountain ranges that form units of Coronado National Forest and with the human use of these desert islands, with some attention to the intervening basins and valleys. The focus is upon places and activities rather than on natural history or environmental changes. The geographic limits are Tucson and Arivaca on the west, New Mexico on the east, and from the Gila River south to the boundary with Mexico.

One central purpose is to offer new information to Spanish-colonial and military historians, to students of mining, rangelands, and recreational history and others while attracting a broader audience with a variety of topics and fresh explanations. The chapters on the Spanish era, the mining frontier, and the U.S. Army and Indian affairs are drawn from a diversity of little-known as well as standard sources. The sections on forest homesteads and summer colonies are built around primary references. With ranching and lumbering, I hope to show how these industries developed initially and then either changed to meet new circumstances or, in the case of lumbering, virtually disappeared. Five of William A. Bell's southeastern Arizona photographs from 1867 are published here for the first time. Fifteen more of his photos taken in southeastern Arizona or southwestern New Mexico unfortunately lack specific identifications.

Another goal is explanations: how the mountains were named, where Coronado's troops entered Arizona, why silver mines were so sought-after in the 1850s, how two major stage lines managed their contemporary operations across southern Arizona, what circumstances led to the creation of Cochise's reservation in 1872 and to its later dissolution, why and how the cattle industry changed in the 1890s, what made forest homesteads so attractive (to certain ranchers), and how distant markets and suppliers influenced the development of southern Arizona's mineral, lumber, and livestock resources. The chapter on mining history is the first extensive attempt to evaluate the significance of mining districts objectively through their records of production since James Tenney's 1927–29 study.

Accuracy, which requires close analysis, has also received priority. This can lead to better explanations, which may in turn provide a basis for future studies. Historical research is a continuing process, with a beginning but no end, one wherein every discovery points in a new direction. For example, the calculated distance between Coronado's Chichilticalli and Corazones III is only fifty leagues. If Chichilticalli lay along the Gila River, as seems likely, then Corazones III must have been in southern Arizona rather than in northern Sonora. Again, Sergeant Neil Erickson's claim that Loco's band of Apaches was literally pushed into an ambush in April of 1882 differs from official versions of this pursuit. Erickson's explanation has implications for Army tactics as well as the creditability of other sources. Buffalo Bill evidently bought some worked-out gold mines at Campo Bonito, surely not the first person to be victimized in this way.

In the Southwest, a chronological outline works well into the Civil War period. By this time, information begins to overload the old framework and some new organizational scheme must be sought. We change to a topical approach, with topics that represent the breadth of this region's history but do not exhaust it; more can always be found. The cities, railroads, and many of the leading figures from southeastern Arizona's early days have already found their historians.

Outsiders first glimpsed this land in 1539 when the viceroy of New Spain sent a Franciscan priest, Marcos de Niza, and two companions northward on a mission of discovery. Their hasty trip took them as far as Cibola, near modern Zuni Pueblo in western New Mexico, and Fray Marcos returned telling of kingdoms that counted their treasure in turquoises and gold. The next year Francisco Vásquez de Coronado led his army of adventurers across southeastern Arizona searching for this imagined wealth, only to return to Mexico emptyhanded. For the next century and a half, little is know about this land.

In the 1690s Father Eusebio Kino arrived to proselytize the villages of the native Pimans and establish a chain of missions. Other Spaniards made occasional military campaigns against more nomadic natives, who were beginning to raid towards the south. A few borderlands settlers took up ranches and mines and founded small communities, but in 1848 only Tucson and the scattered Pima and Tohono O'odham settlements remained. Until the 1870s Apache Indian bands controlled the country east of the Santa Cruz River.

Through the Gadsden Treaty with Mexico, the United States acquired present-day Arizona south of the Gila River in 1856. Newcomers from the eastern U.S. reopened the old silver mines, only to see them close with the onset of the Civil War. An Apache war at the same time drove most of the miners and settlers away. Although the military returned in 1862, Indian raids continued for another ten years.

Peace arrived in 1872 when much of southeastern Arizona became a huge Chiricahua Apache Indian Reservation. Four years later the Chiricahuas were moved to San Carlos on the Gila River and their lands reverted to public domain. In these newly opened spaces, prospectors and cattlemen staked their claims to silver and copper discoveries and to the desert grasslands. The railroads arrived, new towns sprang up, and the mountains assumed a new importance because of their wealth in timber and minerals. The Army's frontier military posts disappeared except for Fort Huachuca.

By the early twentieth century ranching had peaked, declined, and recovered; saw timber and fuelwood had largely been cut out; and the increased mineral production came from ever-fewer mines. Livestock grazed in the mountains where homesteaders had stayed long enough to prove-up and sell out, and where summer visitors now sought relief from the season's heat. In the 1920s and through the Depression years dude ranches flourished, introducing a winter resort tradition. Today, while ranching and mining continue, thousands of visitors and residents alike share an appreciation of this region's abundant natural beauty and its colorful past.

ACKNOWLEDGMENTS

I am indebted most of all to Dr. Patricia M. Spoerl, the Recreation Staff Officer of Coronado National Forest, for her patience, guidance, and encouragement during the research and writing of this study, beginning with the original version in 1987 and continuing through final publication. Dr. Spoerl located and made available historical files and older administrative records at the Forest Supervisor's office in Tucson, provided unpublished manuscripts and photographs, suggested many references, and oversaw preparation of the maps. The Forest Service records, among them transcripts of the Camp John A. Rucker post records and the recently completed Rucker Canyon Archeological District National Register nomination, proved to be rich sources of information.

Elsewhere in the Tucson area I used the ephemera files and Frederick Winn Collection at the Arizona Historical Society; the Faraway Ranch Papers at the National Park Service's Western Archeological and Conservation Center; and many journals, theses, and early twentieth-century promotional periodicals at the University of Arizona library. The Arizona Bureau of Geology and Mineral Technology Library made available elusive geological titles, including James B. Tenney's manuscript *History of Mining in Arizona.* Colleagues in Tucson who contributed their knowledge included Drs. Bernard L. Fontana and Thomas Naylor of the University of Arizona; the Extension Agent at the University of Arizona Animal Sciences Department; Mr. Don Bufkin; and Miss Gloria Fenner and Mr. Richard Y. Murray of the Western Archeological and Conservation Center. At Fort Huachuca I was assisted by Messrs. Conrad McCormick, Wayne Fordham, Michael Shaughnessey, and Mike Granger.

Within the Forest Service Mr. Robert B. Tippeconnic, formerly the Forest Supervisor of Coronado National Forest; Dr. Dennis Roth, Chief, History Section, U.S. Forest Service; Mr. Robert Schiowitz of Gila National Forest, and Mr. John Irish of Flagstaff, Arizona, all aided with the research. Mr. James McDonald, Coronado National Forest archeologist, and Dr. David Gillio, Southwestern Regional historian, arranged for prints of the Forest Service photos included as illustrations. Charles Sternberg, Debby Kriegel, and Stan

Helin of Coronado National Forest performed the immense task of drafting the maps. To everyone in the Forest Service, I can only say that you deserve much of the credit for whatever merit this work may have.

In New Mexico I am obligated to my wife Cheryl, who endured the many months of my research and writing and also discovered a valuable map; to Drs. Russell E. Clemons and Robert H. Weber for their geologic knowledge; to Dr. Darlis Miller at New Mexico State University for the use of her notes on the 1864 Apache Expedition; to historians John L. Kessell and Rick Hendricks of the University of New Mexico; and most particularly to the New Mexico State University Library's Interlibrary Loan staff for their persistent efforts to borrow numerous newspaper microfilms and journal articles.

The National Archives in Washington D.C. identified and provided photocopies of many early maps and documents. Microfilms of their records were indispensable, and assistance given by the Military Reference Branch is most sincerely appreciated. The U.S. Army History Institute at Carlisle Barracks, Pennsylvania, furnished all of the bibliographic citations known to them relating to the period of the Mexican border troubles, 1910–1920. The Bancroft Library at the University of California sent a photocopy of an eighteenth-century Spanish campaign diary and a microfilm of Army questionnaires, completed in 1874, on the Indians of southern Arizona. As in other projects, I have called upon Mr. David A. Clary, formerly Chief of the History Section, U.S. Forest Service, for help with difficult questions on nearly any subject. The title *Islands in the Desert* was suggested by Dr. Spoerl.

JOHN P. WILSON
Las Cruces, N.M.

CHRONOLOGY OF EVENTS, 1539–1946

1539 Fray Marcos de Niza is the first European to see and report on southeastern Arizona.

1540–42 Francisco Vásquez de Coronado leads a Spanish expedition across southeastern Arizona and explores the Southwest.

1691 Father Eusebio Kino's first visit to southern Arizona; first Spanish campaign against the Apaches in southeastern Arizona.

1692 Father Kino's first visit to the Sobaipuris of the San Pedro River.

1695 General Juan Fernández de la Fuente leads a campaign across southeastern Arizona.

1700 Father Kino establishes the first church at San Xavier del Bac.

1701 Kino founds a mission at Guevavi.

c. 1715 Apaches occupy the pass of the Rio Gila, blocking visits between the Sobaipuris and the Hopis.

1720s Spanish settlers arrive in southern Arizona and establish ranches in the San Luis Valley.

1736 Rich silver deposit discovered at Planchas de Plata, just below the present U.S.-Mexico boundary; silver mining in southern Arizona begins not long after this.

1748 The Spanish viceroy approves a declaration of war against the Apaches.

1751 Pima Indians revolt in southern Arizona.

1752 Lieutenant Bernardo Urrea defeats the Pimas in an epic battle at Arivaca, January 5, 1752.

1753 First permanent Spanish garrison, or *presidio,* in southern Arizona, at Tubac.

1762 Sobaipuri Indians abandon the San Pedro Valley.

1767 The King of Spain orders the Jesuits expelled from New Spain and assigns the Franciscans to replace them as missionaries.

1775 Modern Tucson is founded; presidio is moved from Tubac to Tucson.

1775–80 Presidio of Santa Cruz de Terrenate is moved to the San Pedro Valley; Fronteras presidio is relocated to the San Bernardino Valley. Both are withdrawn in 1780.

c. 1783 Construction begins on the present San Xavier del Bac mission; it is completed by 1797.

1786–93 Beginning of the Apache peace establishments; Apache Indians are generally peaceful until 1831.

c. 1803 Construction of the present Tumacácori mission begins.

1821–33 Land grants are made for cattle ranching in southeastern Arizona.

1831 Apache raids resume and soon devastate southern Arizona and Sonora.

1843 Apaches force abandonment of last Mexican ranches in southern Arizona.

1846 The Mexican War begins; the Mormon Battalion and other U.S. Army forces cross southern Arizona.

1848 The Treaty of Guadalupe Hidalgo cedes former Mexican territory north of the Gila River to the United States.

1849 Forty-niners cross southern Arizona bound for the California goldfields.

1850s Boundary surveys and explorations are carried out for a southern transcontinental railroad route.

1854 The Gadsden Purchase is ratified; the United States acquires Mexican territory south of the Gila River.

1856 The United States takes formal possession of the Gadsden Purchase; the first U.S. Army garrison in southern Arizona and the first pinery are established.

1857 Silver mines are rediscovered in southern Arizona; the San Antonio and San Diego Mail Line begins regular stage runs between Texas and California, across southern Arizona.

1858 The Butterfield Overland Mail is established and operates until early 1861.

1861 War breaks out with the Apaches. The Civil War begins and the U.S. Army is withdrawn from Arizona.

1862 Confederates occupy Tucson for two months; later a federal army called the California Column occupies southern Arizona and New Mexico; Fort Bowie is established.

1863 The Territory of Arizona is organized, December 29, 1863.

1864 Brigadier General James H. Carleton carries out his Apache expedition; the first good descriptions of southeastern Arizona are made; the Apache wars continue.

1868 Purebred cattle are introduced into soutern Arizona.

1869 The first steam sawmill in southern Arizona is constructed, in the Santa Rita Mountains.

1871 The Camp Grant massacre occurs, April 30, 1871.

1872 Brigadier General O. O. Howard negotiates peace with the Chiricahua Apache chief Cochise; Cochise agrees to go onto a reservation, and the Apaches are now peaceful.

1873 Sierra Bonita Cattle Co. is founded.

1875 Placer gold is discovered at Greaterville; a mining boom develops.

1876 The Chiricahua Apache Reservation is terminated in June, and the Indians are transferred to San Carlos; Geronimo flees instead.

1877 Silver is discovered at Tombstone; a major mining boom begins there in 1878; the first copper mine is located at Bisbee; Fort Huachuca is established.

1878 The first steam-powered circular sawmill is established in the Huachuca Mountains; Camp Supply, renamed Camp John A. Rucker is founded on April 4.

1879 Commercial lumbering and the earliest steam sawmill begin in the Chiricahua Mountains.

1880 The Southern Pacific Railroad is laid across southern Arizona; Camp Rucker is abandoned in November 1880.

1880–81 Short-lived silver booms occur at the mining towns of Harshaw and Galeyville.

1880–85 The open-range cattle industry enjoys its peak years.

1881–86 Sporadic raids are made by off-reservation Apaches until the summer of 1886.

1882 The first sawmill and commercial lumber production take place in the Pinaleños.

1883 The price of copper drops, and many copper mines close.

1886 Geronimo surrenders on September 4, 1886; the Indian wars are over.

1893 The price of silver drops, and many silver mines close; cattle prices are also low.

1894 Fort Bowie in Apache Pass is abandoned.

1899–01 Copper prices peak and mining booms; prices and mining activity fluctuate in later years.

1902 The first forest reserves in southern Arizona are proclaimed.

1905 The U.S. Forest Service is created and charged with administering the forest reserves; the Santa Catalinas become Tucson's summer resort.

1906 The Forest Service adopts a schedule of grazing fees; the Forest Homestead Act becomes law on June 11, 1906.

1907 A financial panic occurs in the United States this year; many mines close.

1908 Coronado National Forest is established by presidential proclamation; the first modern summer cabin (Huntsman) is built on Mt. Lemmon.

1909 The peak year for goat ranching in southern Arizona.

1910 The Mexican Revolution begins; U.S. Army units move to the Mexican border; Tucsonians reported "rusticating" for the summer at Soldier Camp and Mt. Lemmon in the Santa Catalinas and at Madera Canyon in the Santa Ritas.

1912 The state of Arizona is admitted to the union on February 14, 1912.

1913 The Chiricahua Apaches who surrendered in 1886 are finally given their freedom; many choose to live at the Mescalero Apache Reservation in New Mexico.

1915 Congress authorizes the leasing of national forest lands for summer homes, lodges, and other recreation-related facilities.

1916 Pancho Villa raids Columbus, N.M., and Brigadier General John J. Pershing leads Regular Army units into Mexico; the National Guard patrols the border in Arizona.

1920 The Control Road to Mt. Lemmon is opened; many summer cabins are built at Soldier Camp and Summerhaven in the Santa Catalinas.

1921 Cattle prices tumble, drought strikes, ranchers face bankruptcy.

c. 1924 Dude ranching begins in southern Arizona.

1933 The Army abandons its last border posts in Arizona; Congress approves the Emergency Conservation Work Act, which becomes the Civilian Conservation Corps (CCC); CCC camps are established in southern Arizona.

1946 The General Hitchcock Forest Highway is completed in the Santa Catalinas.

ISLANDS IN THE DESERT

MAP 1

Mountains of Southeastern Arizona.

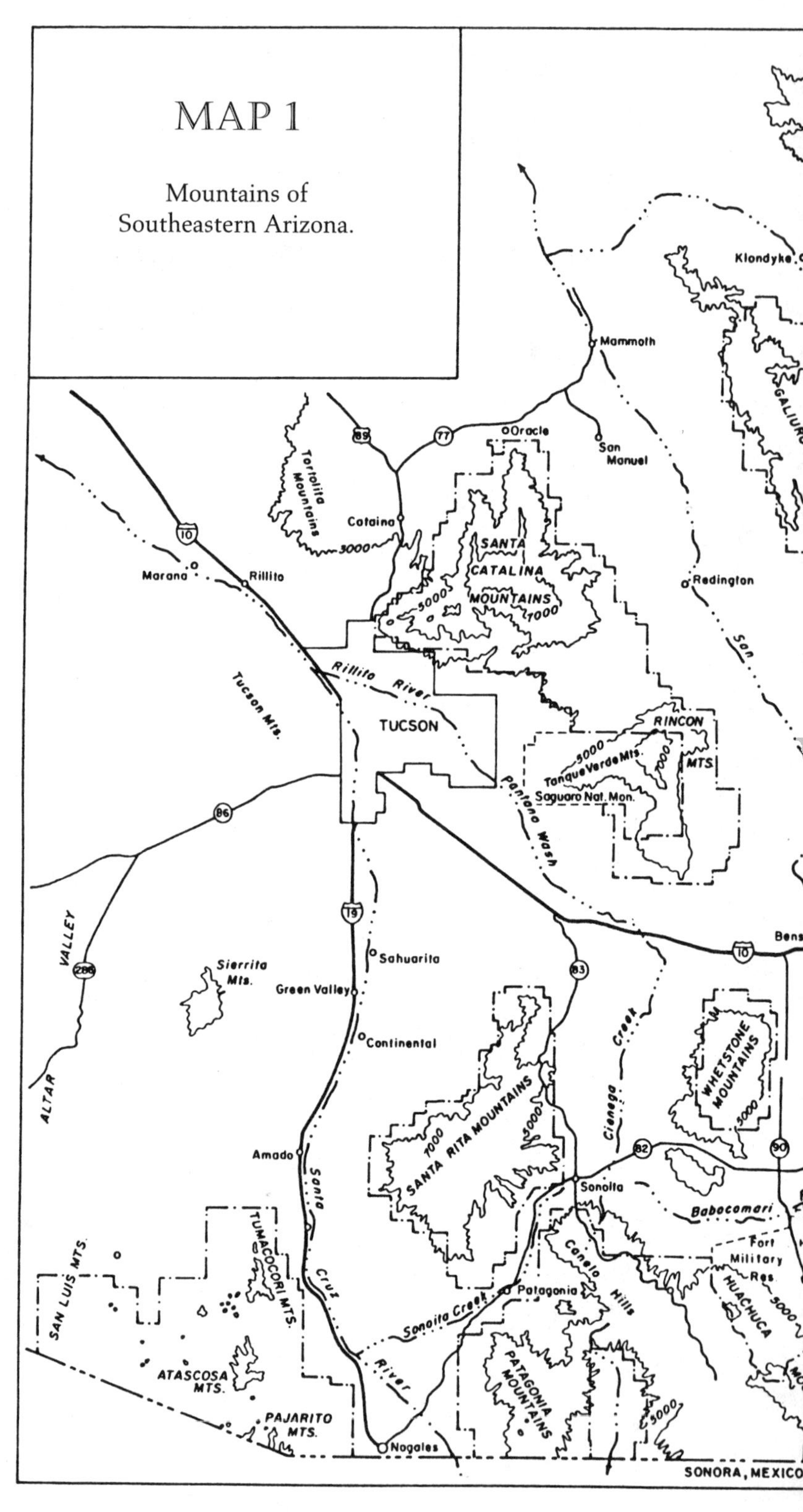

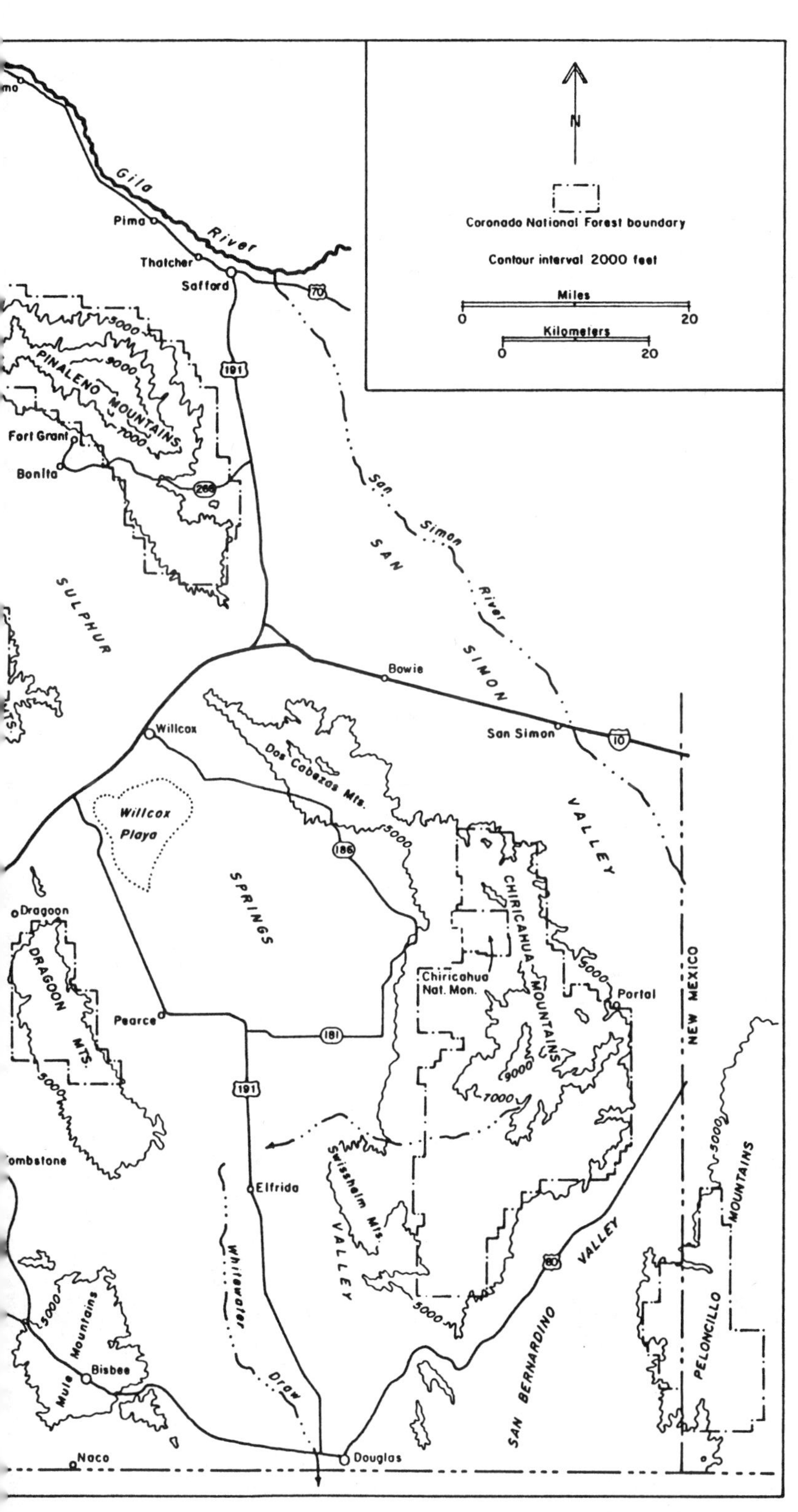

N
Coronado National Forest boundary
Contour interval 2000 feet
Miles
0
20
Kilometers
0
20
Gila
River
Pima
Thatcher
Safford
70
191
PINALENO MOUNTAINS
5000
9000
7000
Fort Grant
Bonita
266
San
Simon
River
SAN
SIMON
VALLEY
SULPHUR
SPRINGS
Bowie
San Simon
10
Willcox
Dos Cabezas Mts.
5000
Willcox
Playa
186
CHIRICAHUA MOUNTAINS
Chiricahua
Nat. Mon.
5000
Portal
9000
7000
NEW MEXICO
Dragoon
DRAGOON
MTS.
5000
Pearce
181
191
Tombstone
Elfrida
Swisshelm Mts.
VALLEY
Whitewater
Draw
80
VALLEY
SAN BERNARDINO
5000
5000
MOUNTAINS
PELONCILLO
5000
Mule
Mountains
Bisbee
Naco
Douglas

1
THE NATURAL LANDSCAPE

The plains and uplands of southeastern Arizona form part of the Basin and Range physiographic province, a region that spans the southern Southwest and extends well beyond it. Each basin range is typically less than thirty miles in length, often much less, and has a single crest line that trends north-south or northwest-southeast. The Chiricahua, Huachuca, Santa Rita and Santa Catalina mountains rise more than 5,000 feet above the adjacent valley floors to elevations exceeding 9,000 feet, while Mt. Graham is the highest point in southern Arizona, at more than 10,700 feet (map 1).

West of the Santa Cruz River and south of Arivaca, we find a complex composed of the Tumacácori, Atascosa, Pajarito, and San Luis mountain ranges and their interconnecting ridges. East of the river and south of Sonoita Creek lie the Patagonia Mountains, and beyond them the Canelo Hills stretch to the north and east. Still farther east the Huachuca Mountains dominate the skyline. North of Sonoita Creek in the direction of Tucson are the Santa Ritas. Around Tucson the mountains include the Santa Catalinas to the north and the Rincons and Tanque Verdes on the east.

The Whetstones are an isolated and relatively small range southwest from Benson, Arizona, while the Dragoons loom up fifteen miles to the east. Farther north the Galiuro and Winchester mountains constitute a rugged divide between the San Pedro River and the Aravaipa and Sulphur Springs valleys. North and east of Sulphur Springs Valley is the great mountain mass of the Pinaleños, also known as Mt. Graham. The remote Santa Teresa Mountains lie northwest from the Pinaleños. Another major range, the Chiricahua Mountains, dominates the landscape in far southeastern Arizona. Straddling the border between Arizona and New Mexico is the easternmost crest, the Peloncillo Mountains. Many of these ranges contain deposits of silver, copper, and other minerals. They are administered in whole or in part by Coronado National Forest.

This landscape began to take its present form during the Laramide orogeny, a period of intense folding and faulting of the earth's crust that spanned the late Cretaceous—early Tertiary eras, about 70 to 40 million years ago.[1] This widespread volcanic and intrusive igneous activity was of prime importance in the implacement of major ore bodies as well, such as the great porphyry copper deposits. More recently, in the middle to late Tertiary, some 30 to 25 million years ago, the Basin and Range disturbance uplifted most of the present ranges by block faulting, both locally and along faults that cut across earlier structural trends.

Structural deformations, volcanism, and sedimentation have left a complex structural history in these basin ranges. The identification of some rock units remains controversial, such as the Tertiary granitic rocks and the much older Precambrian gneisses that compose much of the Santa Catalinas. The Rincons were a consequence of doming, which caused the Tertiary-age cover rocks there to crack and slide away, exposing the Precambrian core. Mountains of this type are called metamorphic-core complexes. The many fault-block ranges exhibit rocks that range in age from the more than 1.5 billion-year-old Precambrian schist and granites of the Pinaleños to the Laramide intrusives of the Santa Teresa, Galiuro, and Winchester mountains, with exposures from intermediate periods and more recent volcanics as well. East from the mountain chain bordering the San Pedro Valley are the broad alluvial basins of the Sulphur Springs, San Simon, and San Bernardino valleys, surrounded in part by mountains.

There are only two major watercourses, the Santa Cruz and San Pedro rivers; both drain northward through elongated intermontane depressions. Two smaller streams, the Babocomari River and Aravaipa Creek, join the middle and lower segments of the San Pedro. None of these has a perennial flow throughout its length. Springs and intermittent mountain streams furnished water elsewhere.

In the same way that geologic history determined subsequent mining activity, natural vegetation has conditioned uses of the land surface. The mountain ranges except for the Santa Teresas supported a woodland with evergreen oaks, junipers, the Mexican piñón, relictual Arizona cypress and *Pinus* species such as the Apache pine, Chihuahua pine, and Arizona pine. Higher elevations in the Pinaleños, Chiricahuas, Huachucas, Santa Ritas, and Santa Catalinas exhibited a montane conifer forest with ponderosa pine dominant, commonly in association with Douglas fir, Mexican white pine, white fir, and quaking aspen. Engelmann spruce and corkbark fir were found on the summits and higher slopes of the Pinaleño and Chiricahua mountains. Shrub live oak and other brush of the interior chaparral community sustained herds of angora goats on the Santa Teresas at one time.[2]

The landscape has the appearance of a desert in many places, but prior to settlement the lower-lying areas were a semidesert grassland, with black grama in the more gravelly areas and tobosa grass on the heavier soils. Yuccas, agaves, sotol, and woody shrubs grew on the rockier slopes. The Sonoita-

Elgin area and the San Rafael Valley supported true plains grasslands that made these areas unusually attractive to stockraisers.[3]

Desert or desert-scrub areas in southeastern Arizona were quite restricted in extent. Chihuahuan desert scrub, typified by creosote bush, tarbush, whitethorn acacia, sandpaper bush, scrub mesquite, and a variety of yuccas and low-growing cacti, was limited to the San Simon Valley north of Portal and the San Pedro Valley south of Cascabel. More recently Chihuahuan Desert flora has expanded into former semidesert grassland habitats. The picturesque Sonoran Desert, with its tree-sized mesquite, palo verde, catclaw acacia, and saguaro cactus, is found only in the Tucson Basin, the lower San Pedro Valley, and along the Gila River below Clifton.[4]

2
WHO NAMED THE MOUNTAINS?

Place-names have a history of their own. While mountains are a permanent part of the landscape, their names are not, and over the course of time many of southeastern Arizona's mountains have been called by different names, often in the language of new residents. The result is that the names by which we know some mountain ranges are quite recent in origin, while others are much older.

The Spaniards with Coronado's *entrada* of the 1540s left no permanent place-names, so our earliest records are from Spanish expeditions in the late seventeenth century. Spaniards generally followed definite priorities in assigning names; they first identified the settlements and springs, then the valleys and rivers, and eventually the *sierras,* or mountain ranges. Eighty years after these first explorations, Nicolás de Lafora, an engineer who accompanied the Marqués de Rubí through northern New Spain in 1766–68, could still write that "in every direction were a number of nameless sierras."[1] It happens also that what we perceive to be adjoining ranges might once have been known by a single name, while through time a single sierra could receive several names. Spanish-period terms include Native American words as well as Spanish ones, suggesting that native guides provided some of the identifications.

The earliest known reference from this part of Arizona was to the Sierra de Huachuca, south and west of present-day Sierra Vista. Captain Juan Mateo Manje, a frequent companion of Father Eusebio Kino, made a passing mention of this range in his journal for June 1694, citing a campaign that had taken place there some six years before.[2] Huachuca, or Guachuca as it was often spelled, had been the name of a *ranchería* farther to the south, occupied in 1680,[3] while a 1695 expedition referred to the *valley* of Guachuca, probably in the vicinity of the old ranch.[4] A few of the territorial-period maps after 1863 labeled the peaks the Sierra Espuela ("Spur Range"); otherwise they have always been known as the Huachuca Mountains.

The Chiricahua Mountains are a prominent chain near the southeastern corner of Arizona. A Jesuit missionary claimed that Chiricahua was an Opata Indian word meaning mountain of the *guajolotes,* or wild turkeys, and that this and other Opata names "would indicate that this was land of the Opata nation."[5] The first recorded use of this name dates to the Suma revolt in

1684, when a group of the rebellious natives reportedly took refuge in the sierra de *Cuchicagua*, almost surely the Chiricahuas.[6] Eleven years later General Juan Fernández de la Fuente, commander of the Janos presidio, led a military expedition to these mountains and encountered various Native American groups.[7] Not until the 1770s did *Chiricahua Apache* come to designate a particular band living in this range. Until then the natives had simply been called the Apaches of the Sierra de Chiricahua. Their native name for themselves, "Chokonens," is often used by modern writers.

The Spaniards left a number of place-names during their 1695 campaign across southeastern Arizona. At one point their guides said that a mountain range ahead was the "sierra that they call the *cerro* of Dos Cavesas [Cabezas]." The general or his secretary evidently misunderstood and applied the name *Dos Cavesas* to some part of the Sierra de Santa Rosa (that is, the Pinaleño Mountains), while they identified the range at the northern end of the Chiricahuas as the Animas Mountains.[8] The latter name was quickly forgotten, and *Dos Cavesas* has designated the sierra adjoining the Chiricahuas for almost three centuries. Between these two mountain masses lies Apache Pass, called the Puerto del Dado until the early 1850s. The 1695 campaign journal labeled it San Felipe Pass.[9]

East of theChiricahuas on the Arizona–New Mexico border is a string of ranges now called the Peloncillo Mountains. The Spanish name *peloncillo* ("little sugarloaf") dates from the early 1850s. Until then traveler's journals had generally followed the identifications shown on a 1784 map, which divided the chain into four segments; from north to south, the Sierra San Marcial, Sierra San Vicente, Sierra de Nochebuena, and the Sierra Sarampeón.[10]

North of Willcox are the Pinaleño Mountains, or Mt. Graham, the highest mountain range in southeastern Arizona. As of 1695 these peaks were known as the Sierra de Santa Rosa. Two years later Captain Manje referred to them as the Sierra de Santa Rosa de la Florida.[11] By the 1780s this name had been shortened to Sierra de la Florida, while on one nineteenth-century map, these same mountains are identified as the Sierra Bonita. When Brigadier General Stephen W. Kearny's Army of the West marched through southern Arizona along the Gila River valley, Lieutenant William Emory called the highest peak in the old Florida range Mount Graham, evidently in honor of Lieutenant Colonel James Duncan Graham, a senior officer in Emory's own unit, the U.S. Army Corps of Topographical Engineers. On his map Emory showed the heights that included Mount Graham as the "Pinon Llano," whereas his journal mentioned a "Piñon Lano" range on the north side of the Gila. At the same time (1846), the lieutenant identified a small band of Apaches along the middle Gila as "Piñon Lanos."[12] A few years later another officer referred to the Pinal Leñas Apaches and to the Pinal Leño mountains north of the Gila River.[13] By the middle 1850s these inconsistencies in spelling and location were gone, with Pinaleño and Mount Graham designating the range, south of the Gila, that bears these names today.

When in September 1695 General Fernández's troopers crossed the Río de Terrenate (the San Pedro River) during their return march, they continued eastward and camped at a canyon in a *sierra mui peñascosa,* probably at Middlemarch Pass in the Dragoon Mountains.[14] Their name, "S. de la Peñascosa," meaning a very rugged range, remained in use; a Spanish map from 1780 shows it clearly. One hundred years later, a Hispanic resident still claimed that "the northern part of the Sierra del Dragón is thus called, and on account of a Mexican dragoon who died there," while the southern part bore the name Sierra Peñascosa.[15] Since the late 1860s, maps have labeled the entire range the Dragoon Mountains. The Dragoon Springs stage station and Cochise Stronghold, two prominent landmarks in western American history, lie near the northern end of these mountains.

The remote Galiuro Mountains, along the eastern side of the lower San Pedro River, have borne many names through the centuries. Two Spanish campaign journals from the 1780s referred to the Galiuros as the Sierra de Santa Teresa, while Spanish maps from this same period identified the range as the Sierra del Arivaypa. The name *Aravaipa,* which one scholar says is a Hispanicized form of *ali* ("small") and *waxia* ("water"),[16] continued in use as recently as the 1850s, although maps were already representing the Galiuro-Winchester chain as the San Calisto Mountains or the Sierra Calitro.[17] The transformation of Calisto/Calitro into Galiuro probably took place within the next few years.

North and somewhat east of the Galiuros lies the Sierra de Santa Teresa, known by that name for at least two centuries. Spanish maps from 1780 and 1784 placed these mountains at their present location, but a 1789 campaign diary labeled this chain the Sierra de San Calistro, "in which were found many abandoned rancherías."[18] For awhile in the nineteenth century, the Santa Teresas were considered a part of the Pinaleño Mountains, but they subsequently regained their own identity.

Two smaller ranges in southeastern Arizona, the Whetstone and the Winchester mountains, have English names. The Whetstones allegedly contain a deposit of novaculite, a hard, fine-grained rock used for whetstones. Colonel B. L. E. Bonneville toured southern Arizona in May of 1859, and his report used the name *Whetstones* repeatedly. Spanish maps of the 1780s had identified them as the Sierra del Babocomari.[19]

The Winchester Mountains were recognized as a separate range around the end of the nineteenth century. The name may derive from the Winchester mining district and a small community called Winchester, both identified with a Henry D. Winchester in 1882. Immediately south of the Winchesters lies Nugent's Pass, once a prominent feature on the southern overland route, named for John Nugent, a forty-niner. Travelers who passed between Sulphur Springs and the San Pedro valleys via Nugent's Pass followed the route of the modern Cascabel Road and Tres Alamos Wash. During the 1850s surveyors favored Nugent's Pass for a wagon road and a transcontinental railroad, but it gained neither and was eventually forgotten.[20]

Western slope of the Dragoon Mountains, from Middlemarch Pass. The absence of trees is probably because of fuelwood cutting. (Courtesy, U.S. Forest Service, Southwestern Region. C. Leavitt, photographer, c. 1906.)

There is no real evidence that Father Eusebio Kino named the Santa Catalina or the Santa Rita mountains. Whether these ranges even had names in Kino's time is not known; the earliest specific references to them came in the aftermath of the 1751 Pima Revolt. Father Kino did visit an Indian ranchería called Santa Catherina de Cuytoabucam northwest of modern Tucson, and this village may be the namesake of the Santa Catalina Mountains; until around 1880 the name was usually spelled Catarina, or even Catherina.[21]

The pass of La Cebadilla, now called Redington Pass, separates the Santa Catalinas from the Rincon Mountains. In the late 1700s, the Rincons were called the Sierra de Tres Alamos, after their proximity to a Sobaipuri Indian

Probably the Whetstone Mountains, with slopes partially covered with oaks, c. 1914–15. (Courtesy, U.S. Forest Service, Coronado National Forest.)

community and a prominent arroyo, both known as Tres Alamos. By the midnineteenth century, the range had become the Sierra Colorado, a name used by the army into the 1880s. Maps for the last hundred years have shown these peaks as the Rincon Mountains. In Spanish, a *rincón* is a physiographic feature, the inside of an angle or a cul-de-sac in the landscape.[22]

West of the Santa Cruz River is a series of rugged hills and ridges—the Sierrita, Cerro Colorado, Tumacácori, San Luis, Atascosa, and Pajarito mountains. Most of these names are Spanish. How they came to be applied here is not known, but they seem to date from the eighteenth and nineteenth centuries. *Pajarito* means little bird, while *Atascosa* is Spanish for bogged down or miry. In the nineteenth century, these two ranges were sometimes mapped as the Arizona Mountains. The Tumacácori Mountains share their name with the former Sobaipuri village of San Cayetano de Tumacácori, first visited by

Atascosa Mountains looking northwest from Summit Motorway. (Courtesy, U.S. Forest Service, Coronado National Forest. Bailey F. kerr, photographer, November 7, 1941.)

Jesuit missionaries in 1691 and situated near the more recent Tumacácori mission. A later Jesuit, Father Pfefferkorn, wrote that Tumacácori meant "pepper bush, place where the little round pepper [the *chile tepín*] is found in abundance."[23]

East of the Santa Cruz and south of the Santa Ritas lie the Patagonia Mountains. In the late eighteenth century, they were called the Sierra de Chihuahuilla. Then in 1787 the Spanish presidio of Santa Cruz de Terrenate was relocated to a spot along the river just south of present Lochiel, and both the watercourse and the nearby mountains assumed the name Santa Cruz. As recently as the 1870s, the name Sierra de Santa Cruz applied both to this range and to the adjoining mountains south of San Antonio Pass, in Mexico.[24]

Patagonia dates back to 1858, when a group of army officers bought a new silver strike and called it the Patagonia Mine. The property changed

Canelo Hills and Canelo Ranger Station, c. 1930. (Courtesy, U.S. Forest Service, Coronado National Forest.)

owners several times, until Sylvester Mowry bought the holdings in 1860 and renamed them the Mowry Mine. The surrounding mountains and later the town on Sonoita Creek retained the distinctive name, *Patagonia.* [25]

The Canelo Hills, sandwiched between the Patagonia and Huachuca ranges, were first identified as the Canille Mountains on maps printed toward the end of the nineteenth century. At the southern edge of these hills, bordering the San Rafael Valley, is Canelo Pass. Both names were in use by 1915. *Canelo* in Spanish means cinnamon-colored, perhaps in reference to the color of the hills.

While we often do not know who named the mountains, we can sometimes estimate when this was done and perhaps say a bit about the circumstances. Several ranges have had three to four names over the past three centuries, and while some names are relatively recent, others are much older. Huachuca and Chiricahua may even be aboriginal. Most or all of these ranges have borne names in Southwestern native languages as well, these usages being little-known except to the native speakers themselves. The place-names familiar from history not only identify the settings for southeastern Arizona's colorful past but also remind us of the series of peoples who have lived here.

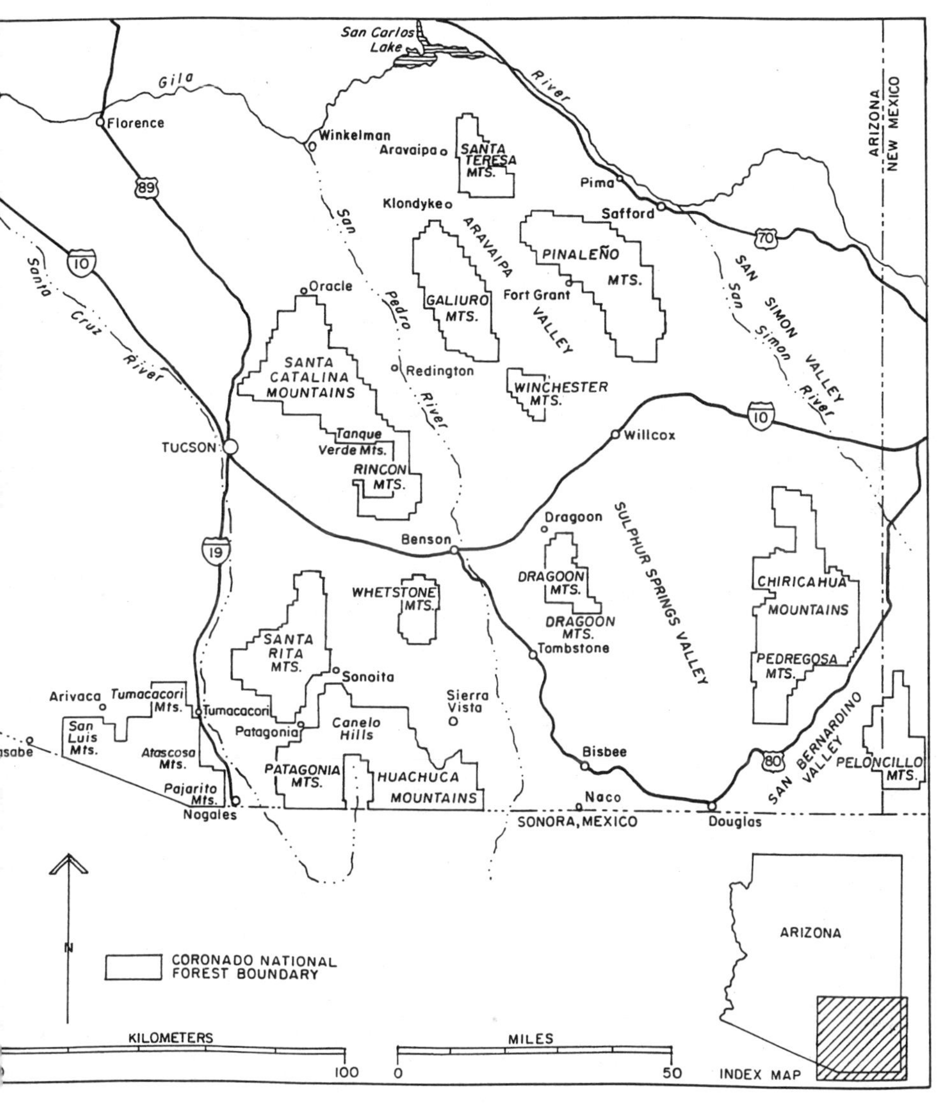

Map 2

Mountain ranges of Coronado National Forest.
(Map by Coronado National Forest.)

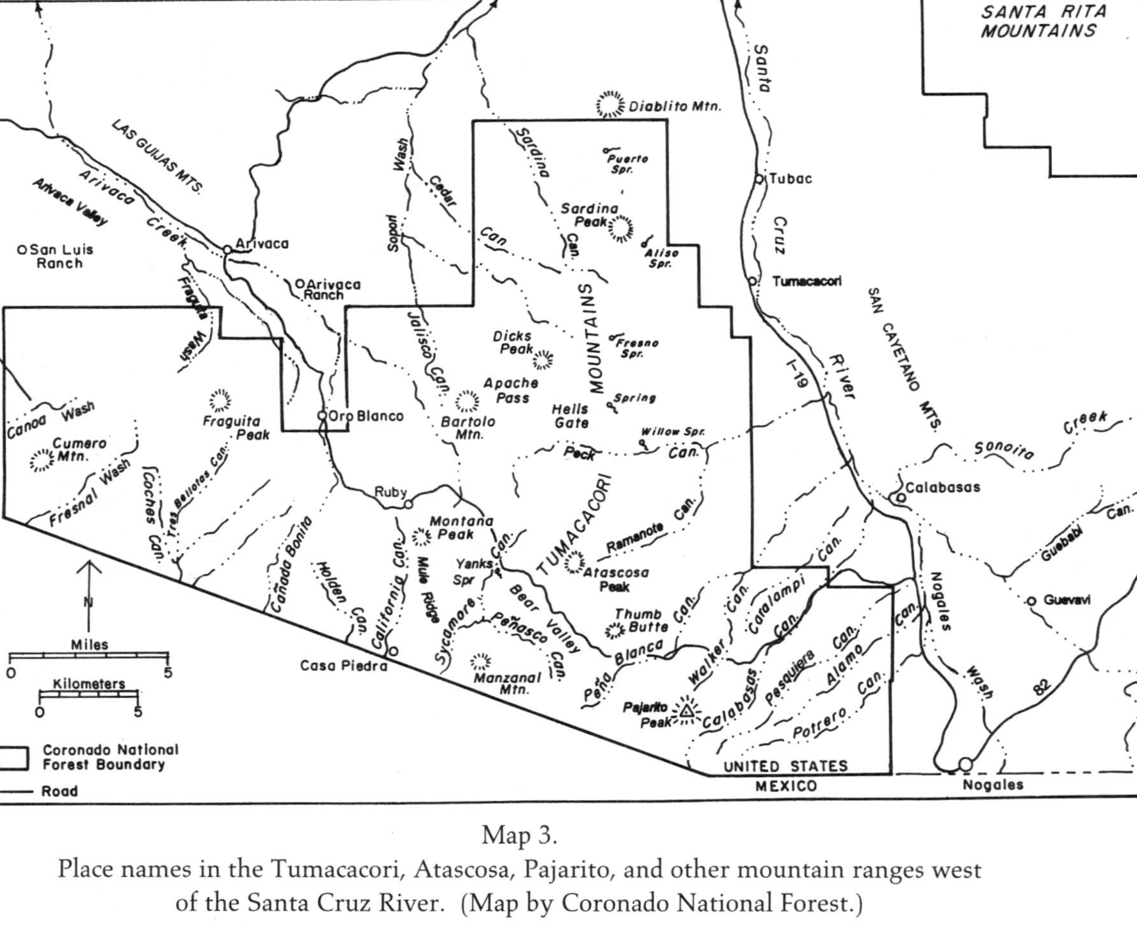

Map 3.
Place names in the Tumacacori, Atascosa, Pajarito, and other mountain ranges west of the Santa Cruz River. (Map by Coronado National Forest.)

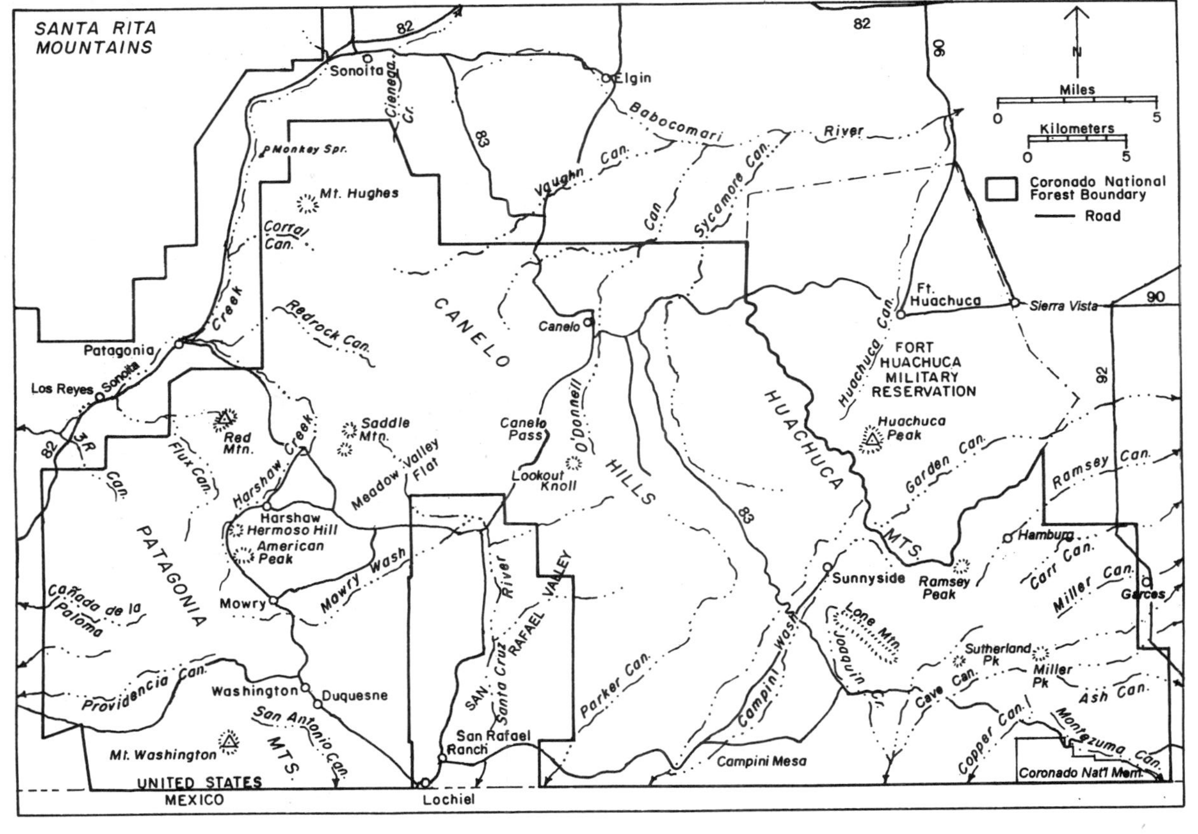

Map 4.
Places in the Patagonia and Huachuca mountains, Canelo Hills, and San Rafael Valley. (Map by Coronado National Forest.)

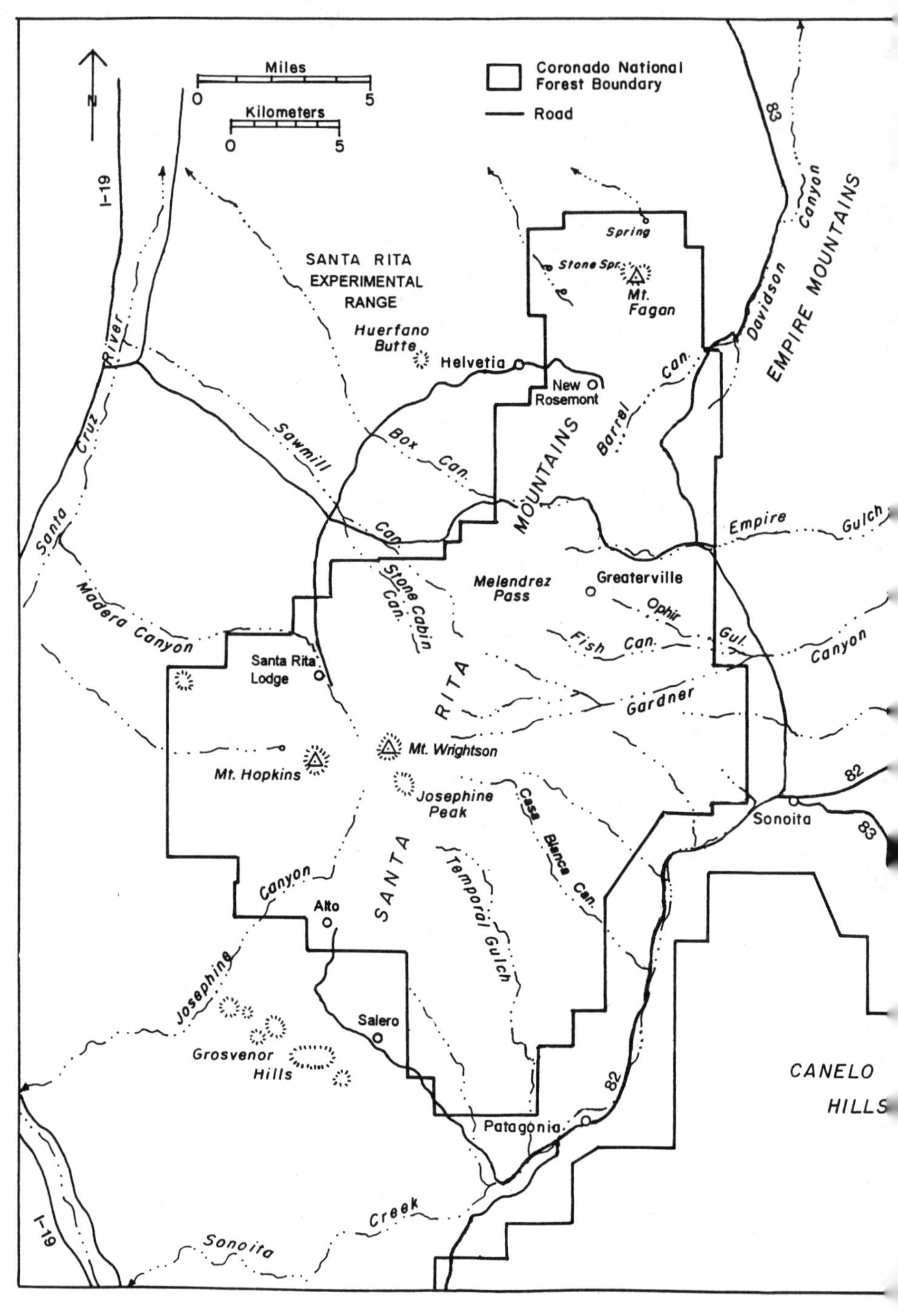

Map 5.
Principal places in the Santa Rita Mountains.
(Map by Coronado National Forest.)

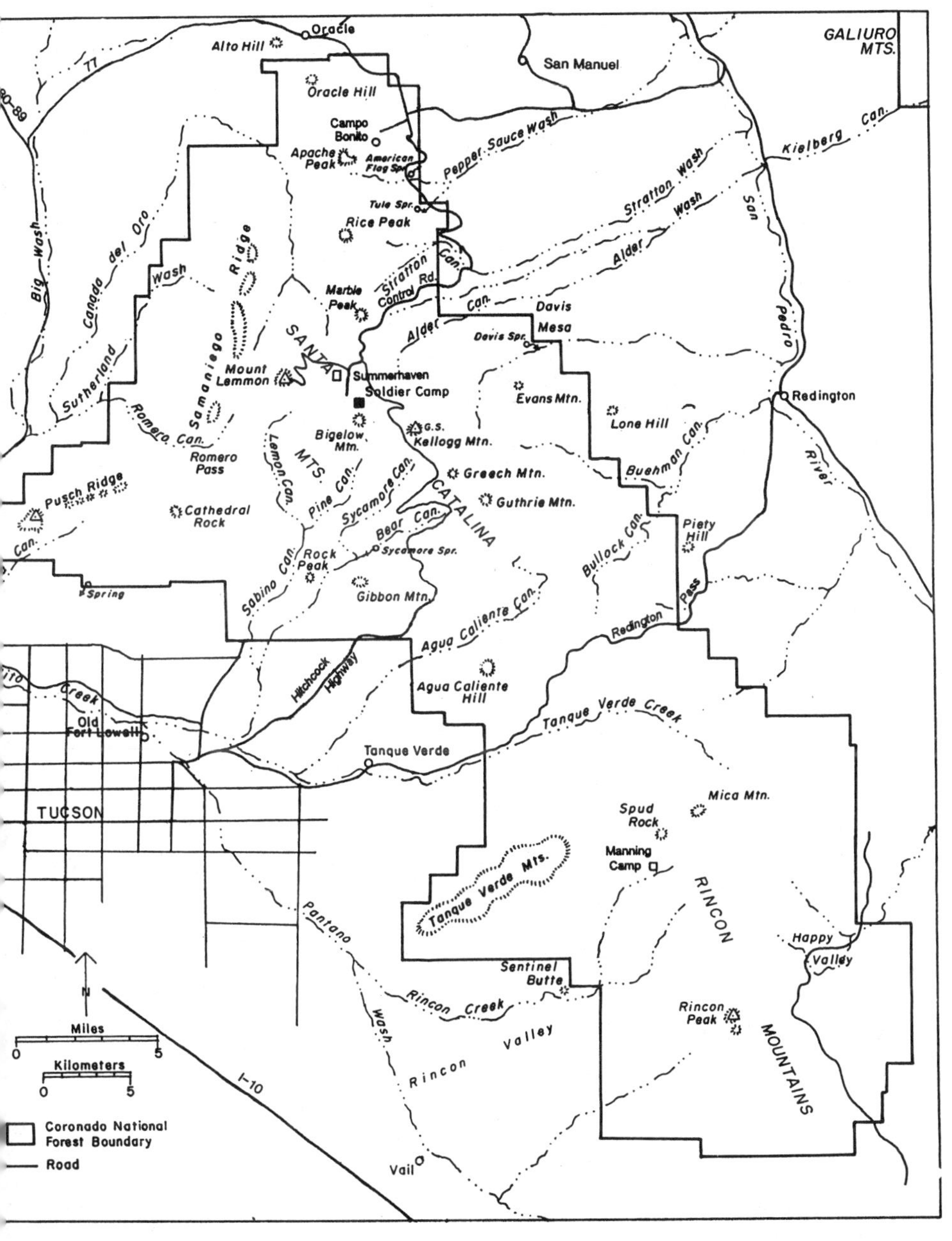

Map 6.
Place locations in the Santa Catalina and Rincon mountains.
(Map by Coronado National Forest.)

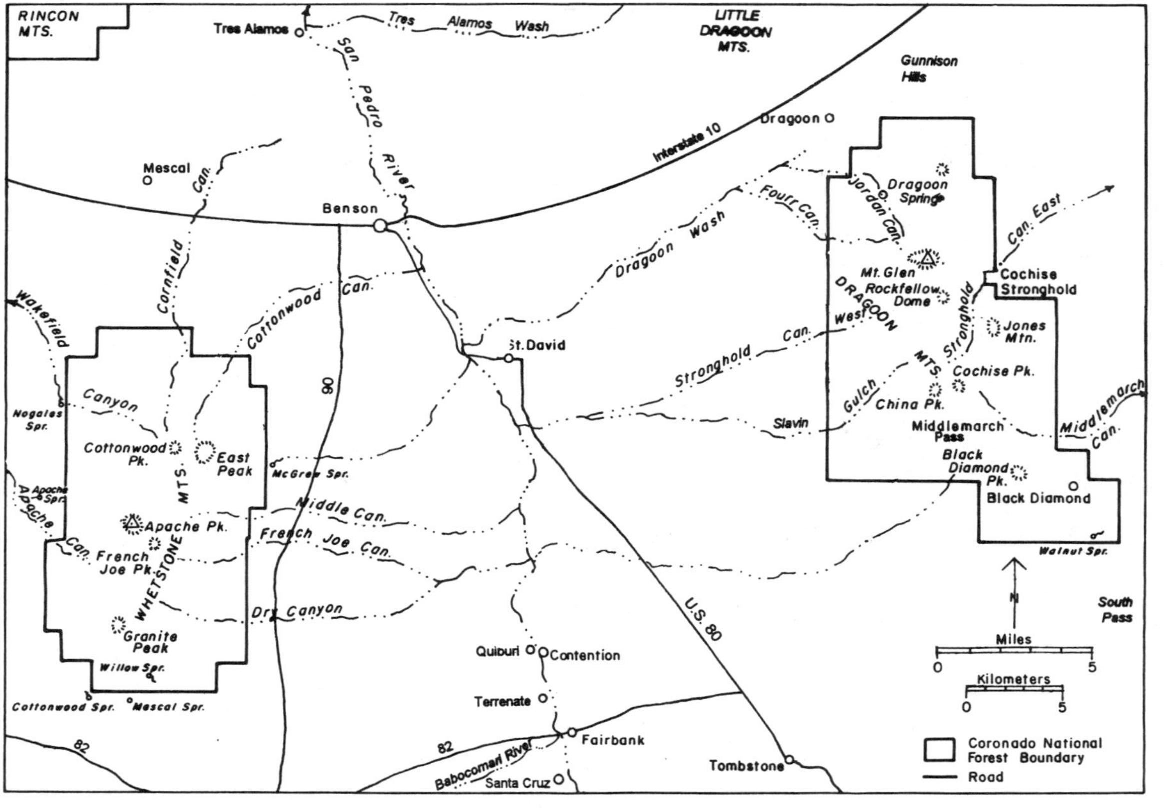

Map 7.
Historical and natural features in the middle San Pedro River Valley and the Whetstone and Dragoon mountains. (Map by Coronado National Forest.)

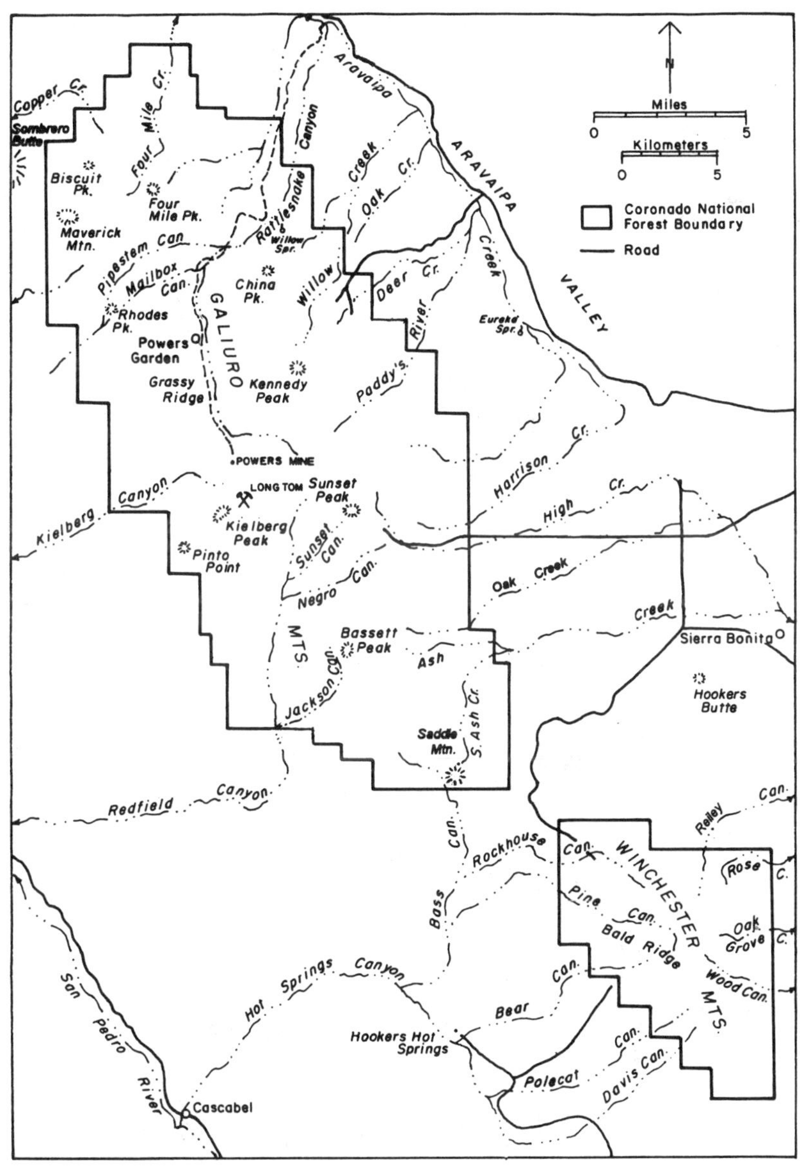

Map 8.
Names of places in the Winchester and Galiuro mountains.
(Map by Coronado National Forest.)

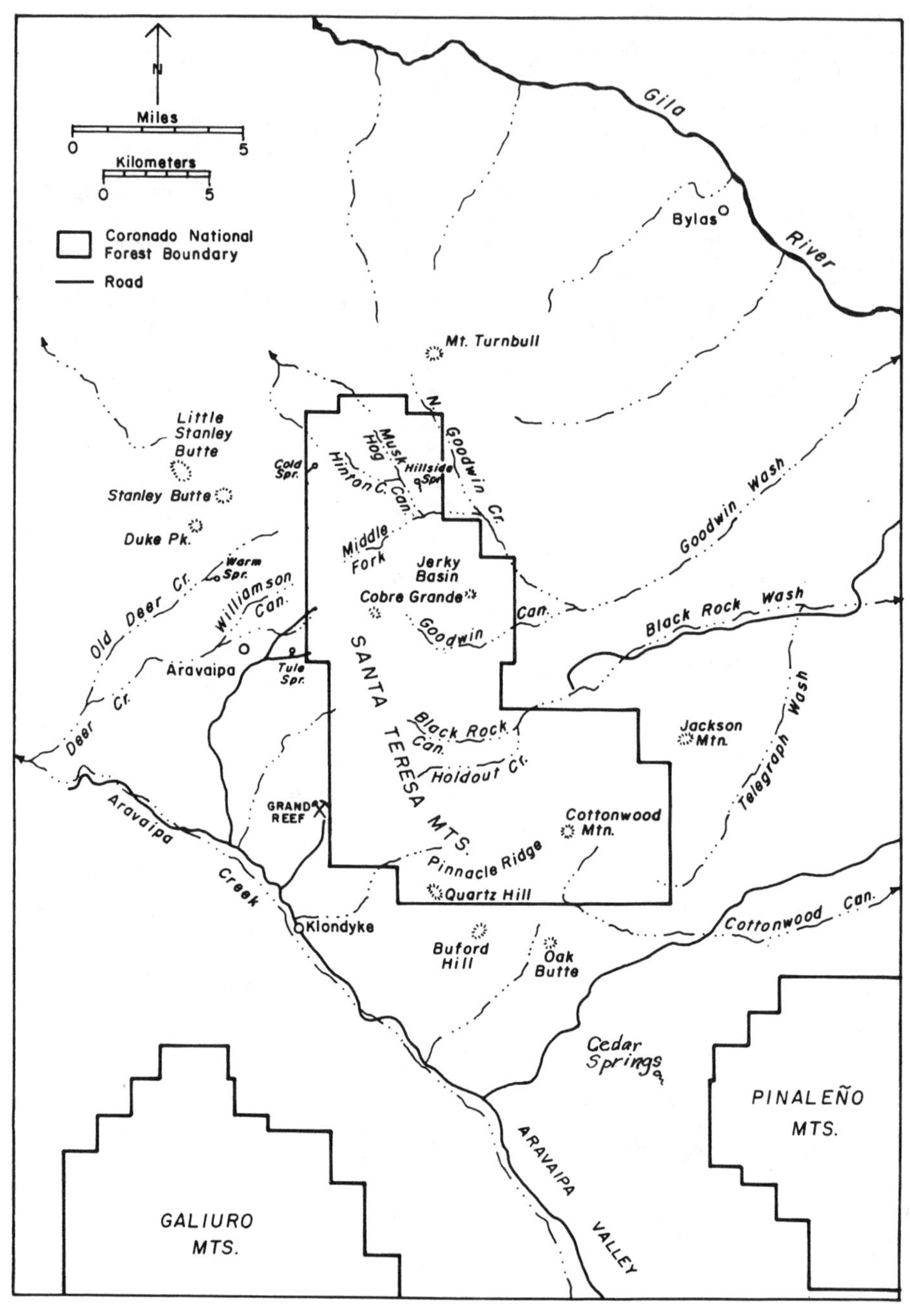

Map 9.
Place names and locations in the Santa Teresa Mountains.
(Map by Coronado National Forest.)

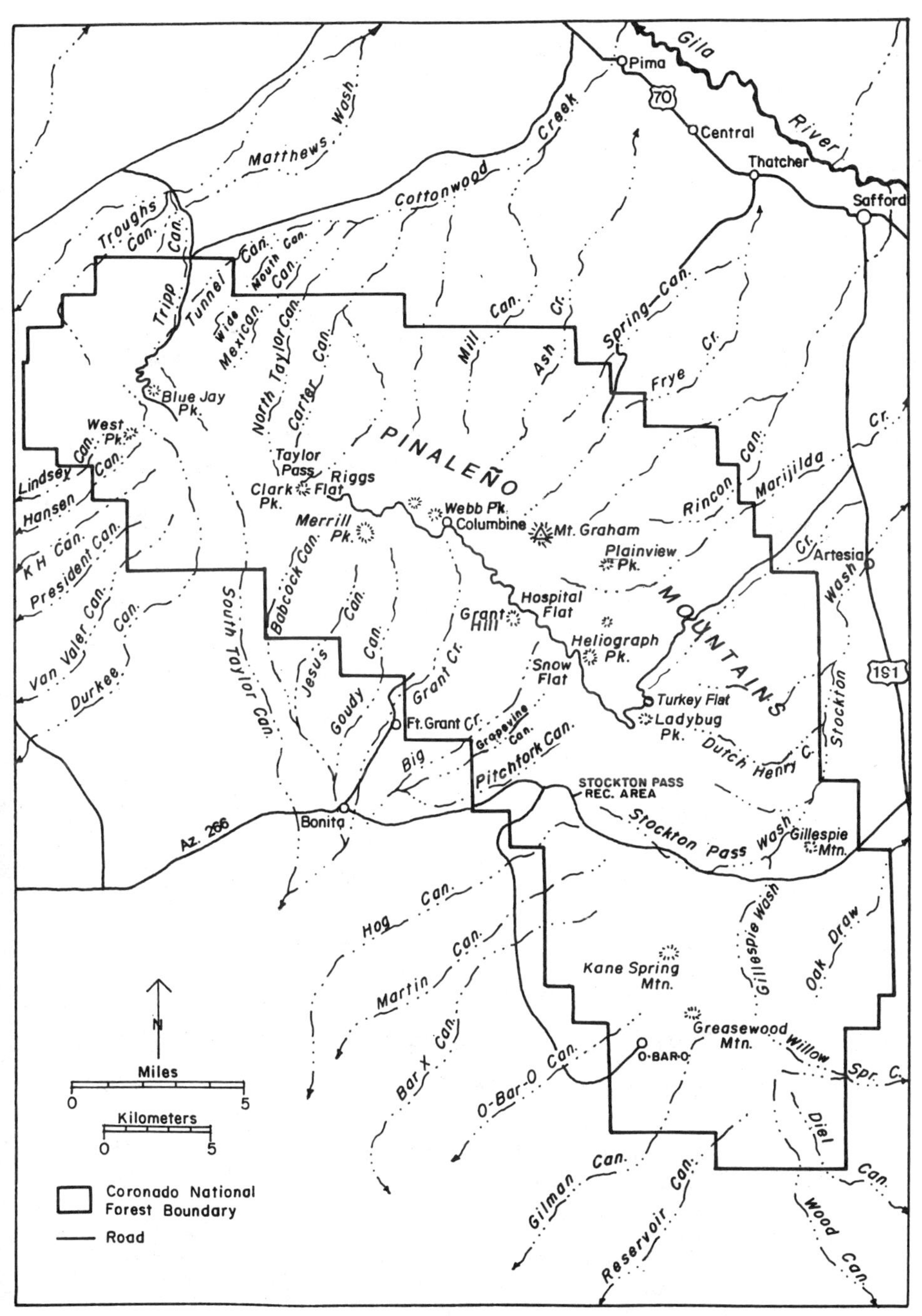

Map 10.
Place name locations in the Pinaleño Mountains.
(Map by Coronado National Forest.)

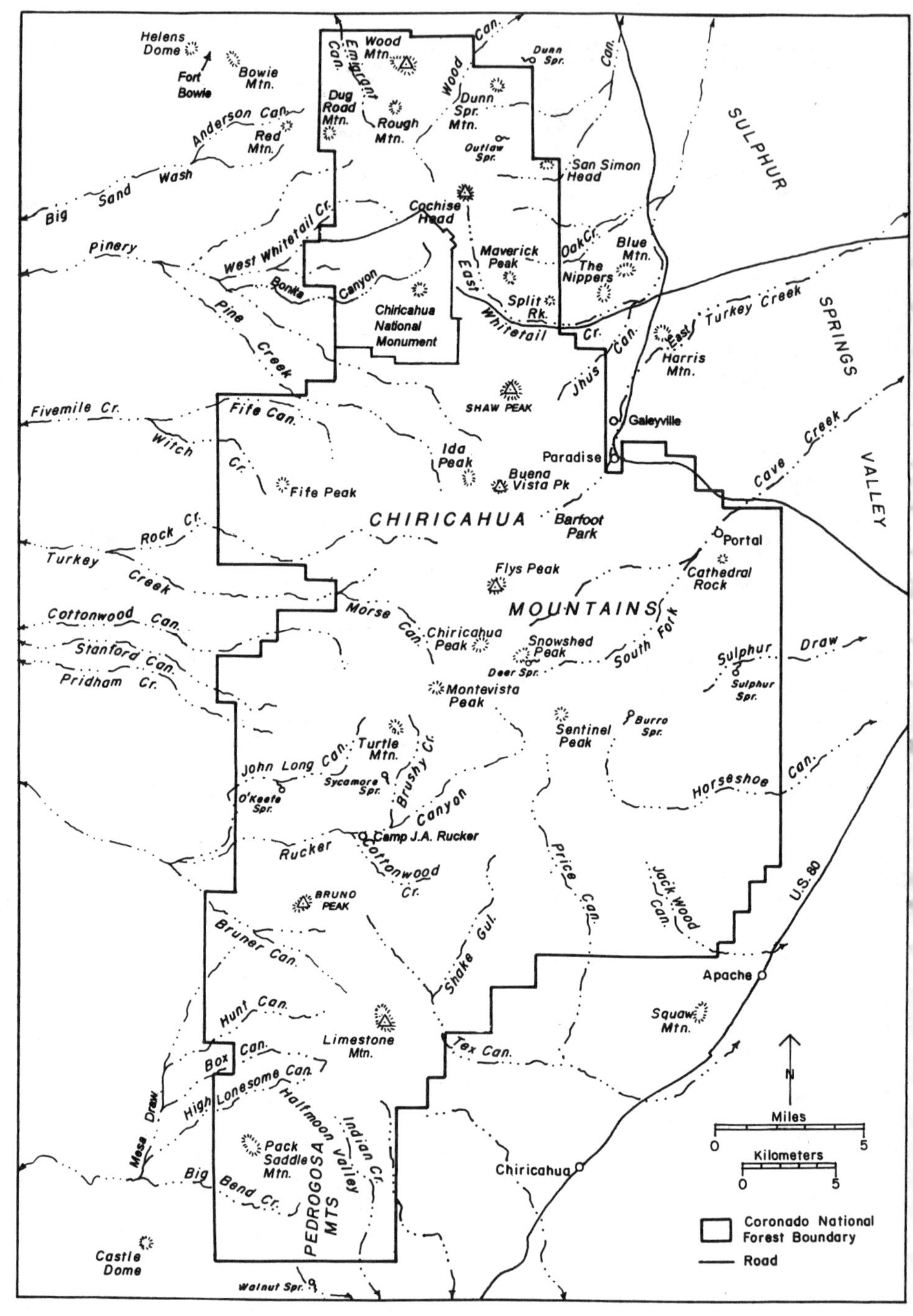

Map 11.
Natural and historical places in the Chiricahua Mountains.
(Map by Coronado National Forest.)

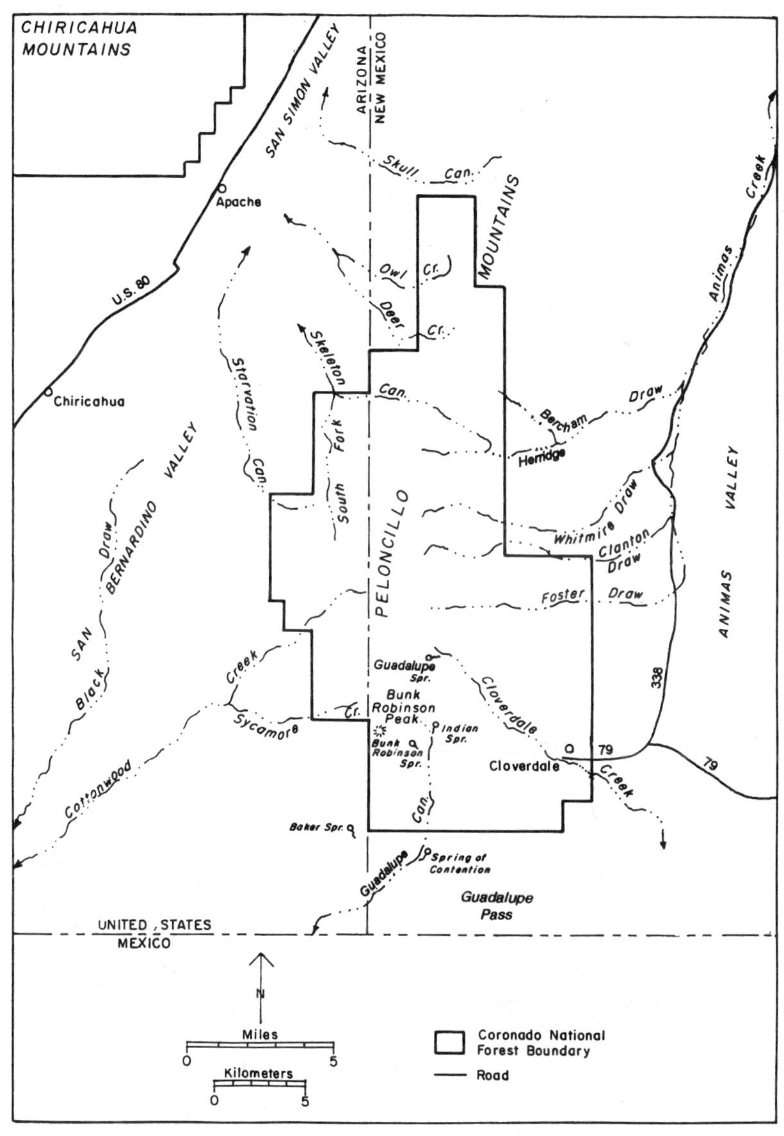

Map 12.
Some place names in and around the Peloncillo Mountains.
(Map by Coronado National Forest.)

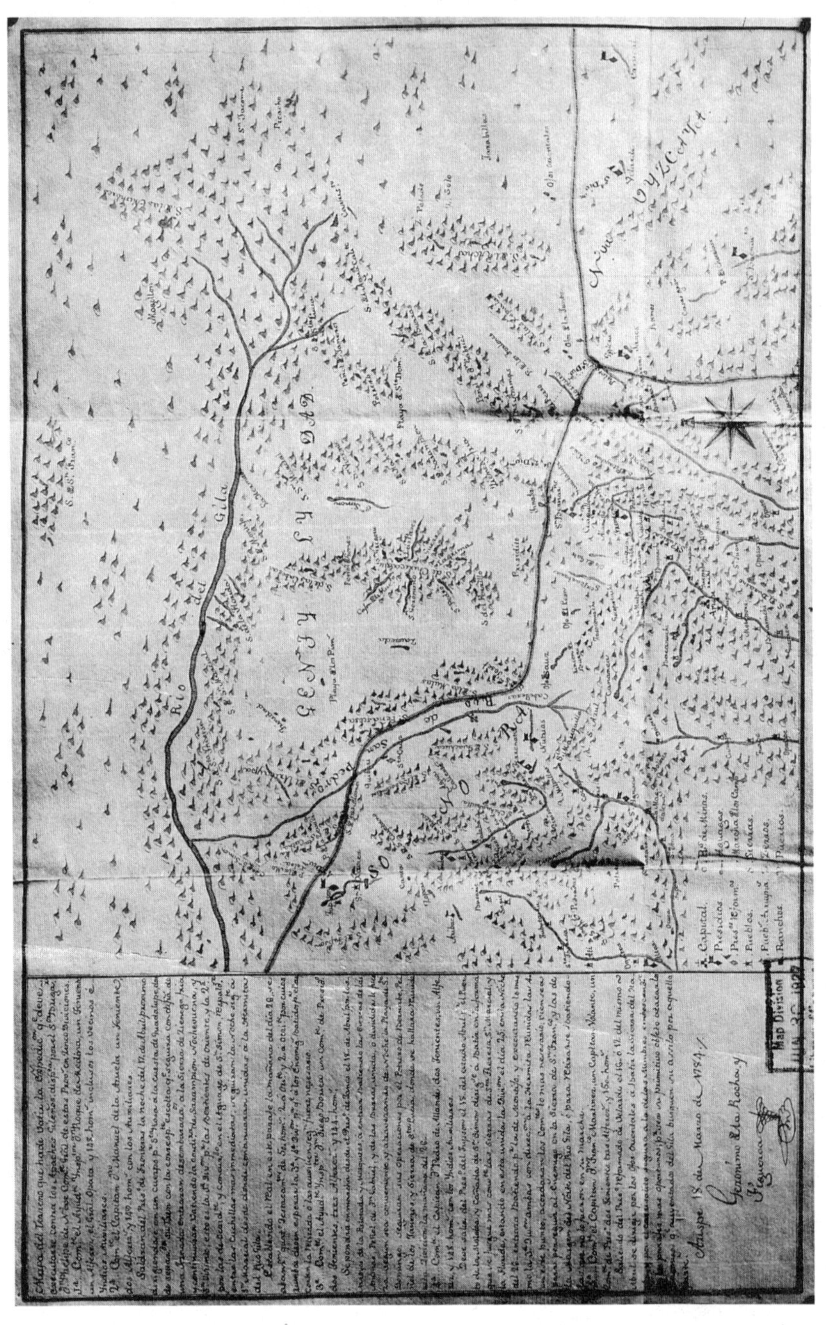

Map 13.
Gerónimo de la Rocha's map of the Gila River region, 1784.
(Courtesy, The Library of Congress.)

3
THE SPANISH ERA

The Earliest Explorers

In November of 1528, eighty shipwrecked survivors from Pánfilo de Narváez's ill-fated colonizing expedition in Florida were swept up on the Texas gulf coast. Four of these castaways survived eight years of wandering across Texas and northern Mexico until, in 1536, they finally wandered into the frontier outpost of Culiacán, almost on the Pacific Ocean in New Spain. The route that Alvar Núñez Cabeza de Vaca and his three companions had followed, described vaguely in Vaca's narrative, probably lay somewhat south of Arizona and New Mexico. His report mentioned extensive signs of gold and silver, without giving these much emphasis.[1]

The viceroy of New Spain felt his interest stirred nonetheless and commissioned a Franciscan friar, Fray Marcos de Niza, to explore northward and discover new lands and peoples beyond the limits of Spanish settlement. As a guide the viceroy sent along a dark-skinned slave named Esteban, one of the men who had returned with Vaca. The small party set out on March 7, 1539, and after hearing of a great country called Cibola, pushed on in search of it. Esteban went in advance and reached Cibola, the country of the Zuni Indians in western New Mexico; the natives there killed him soon after his arrival. Fray Marcos came ahead anyway but dared not go beyond where he could see what "appears to be a very beautiful city, the best that I have seen in these parts," before he beat a hasty retreat in fear for his own life.[2]

The good friar and Esteban were the first nonnatives to see what is now southeastern Arizona. In his report to the viceroy, Fray Marcos described Cibola as the first of seven cities, greater than the city of Mexico, its people wealthy in cattle and turquoises. Within months his stories swept across New Spain. The Seven Cities grew with each retelling until they became a land of gold and silver, a new El Dorado. As one contemporary put it, ". . . the land was so stirred up by the news which the friar had brought from the Seven Cities that nothing else was thought about . . . He exaggerated things so much, that everybody was for going there and leaving Mexico depopulated."[3]

As a result of these stories the Viceroy organized a much larger expedition, under the command of Francisco Vásquez de Coronado. Coronado's army of about three hundred Spaniards and thirteen hundred Indians left

Mexico in the spring of 1540 and traveled north to the Seven Cities along the route of Fray Marcos. Their hopes turned to bitter disappointment when the army found no golden treasures or jeweled cities, at Cibola or elsewhere. They explored New Mexico for two years and discovered the Hopi Indian towns, the Grand Canyon, and the Colorado River.[4] After their return to Mexico, it was another hundred years before the Spaniards ventured into southern Arizona again.

Fray Marcos's report and the various accounts from the Coronado expedition included the first descriptions of southeastern Arizona. There is no daily journal, and few of their landmarks are readily identifiable, which makes a determination of their actual route uncertain; attempts to do so have resulted in numerous interpretations.[5] However, by comparing distances and geographical references in the explorers' narratives with later travelers' accounts for the same country, the journeys of the friar and Coronado's army can be retraced with reasonable accuracy.

The Spaniards entered southern Arizona by way of the upper Santa Cruz River, passed north across the San Rafael Valley, and continued over the Canelo Hills via Canelo Pass into the upper Babocomari River valley, then followed the Babocomari downstream to its junction with the San Pedro River. Others who passed north-south through this part of Arizona, including the Jesuit missionary Father Eusebio Kino in the 1690s and a series of travelers in the nineteenth century, also crossed the Canelo Hills. So far as is known, not one of them chose to follow the upper San Pedro River.

The San Rafael Valley, with its excellent grasslands and adjacent springs, made this the desirable route for a horse-borne army with thousands of head of livestock. By contrast the upper San Pedro in 1850, and presumably long before, was a narrow stream that flowed between steep banks eight to ten feet in height, difficult of access for livestock, its valley filled with mesquite; it would have been an altogether poor choice.[6]

Through northern Sonora, Coronado's army probably marched by way of the San Miguel Valley or that of the Río Sonora, the only valleys that in 1540 would have allowed them to remain among natives speaking the same language all the way to the Valley of Suya in southern Arizona.[7] Either the Río San Miguel or the western branch of the Río Sonora above Arispe would have led them directly toward the San Rafael Valley. Along one of these rivers, Coronado attempted to found a town he named San Hierónimo de los Corazones. Its two earliest locations, now called Corazones I and II, were short-lived. Forty leagues to the north lay the Valley of Suya, the country of the Sobaipuri Indians, and it was here, "on a little river," that Coronado's men tried for a third time to establish their settlement, Corazones III.[8] The distances listed in the Coronado narratives conform with this route, and the identification of Corazones III with a site on the Babocomari River would all but end the controversy over the explorers' trail to that point.

The army then made its way down the San Pedro Valley, perhaps to the vicinity of Tres Alamos, then turned off toward the northeast on a journey that crossed the northern end of the Sulphur Springs Valley or the upper Aravaipa region. Five days' travel from the San Pedro, they encountered Chichilticalli, the famous 'red house' of the Coronado expedition. This landmark, near a defile called the pass of Chichilticalli, has yet to be identified. It lay somewhere along the Gila River valley, probably between present-day Safford and Geronimo.[9] Cibola was another fifteen days' march ahead of them.[10]

The only settled Indians whom Coronado met in Arizona were ancestral Sobaipuris. Then, as later, they lived in villages along the Babocomari and the middle and lower San Pedro rivers. Their lands were well-populated and all under irrigation; food was plentiful, and the people went about dressed in skin clothing and strands of turquoise. Fray Marcos did not give this country a name, but Coronado's chroniclers called it the Valley of Suya.[11]

The first village of Suya lay at the northern end of a *despoblado,* or uninhabited country, the crossing of which normally required four days. Fray Marcos noted that the despoblado was twenty-eight leagues across—just two leagues more than the distance Captain Juan Mateo Manje recorded in 1697 from the mission of Cocóspera in northern Sonora to San Joaquín de Baosuca, the first Sobaipuri settlement on the Babocomari River.[12] San Joaquín, so named by Father Kino in the 1690s, was quite possibly the same site as the first village of Suya, the despoblado having vanished in the intervening 150 years with the founding of two small settlements at San Lázaro and Santa María on the upper Santa Cruz River.

Coronado had sought to leave a permanent Spanish garrison along his route. At the unsuccessful location of Corazones II, the natives revolted and killed seventeen Spanish soldiers, whereupon that site was abandoned. The colony, relocated in the Valley of Suya, witnessed the same fate in the late summer of 1541, when the local Indians (the Sobaipuris) rebelled, killing the Spanish captain and a number of other people at Corazones III. The surviving Spaniards fled all the way back to Culiacán in western Mexico, where the expedition had begun. At Culiacán another of Coronado's captains, Juan Gallego, collected twenty-two men and stormed northward like some avenging spirit, putting now-rebellious villages to the fire and sword all the way to Corazones. There, "where the town of Hearts had been," he killed and hanged a large number of natives, effectively ending the revolt.[13]

The forty leagues between Corazones II and III is nearly identical with the distance (39 leagues) to San Joaquín on the Babocomari from Father Kino's home mission of Nuestra Señora de los Dolores on the upper Río San Miguel in Sonora.[14] These two communities or their near vicinities may have been the locations of Corazones III and II.

The Sonora Frontier in the Seventeenth Century

In the century and a half after the earliest explorers, occasional visitors passed through southeastern Arizona, en route to somewhere else. In the spring of 1638, Governor Luis de Rosas of New Mexico led five Franciscan friars and forty soldiers into the Ypotlapigua country of northern Sonora. The governor, a hard-driving type with an insatiable appetite for wealth, reportedly forced these Opata-speaking people to bring him hides and feathers, robbed them of their clothing, and threatened to burn their villages. His extortions caused the natives to flee to the mountains. The friars' missionary efforts not surprisingly bore no fruit, and Rosas's troop soon went back to New Mexico.[15]

Seven years later the Franciscan fathers came again from New Mexico and established a short-lived chain of missions among the Opatas. Jesuit missionaries, already established to the south, responded quickly to this perceived threat by expanding into the same area. For another eight years, the two religious orders competed for souls, the rivalry ending when the Jesuits obtained an order for the Franciscans to abandon northern Sonora.[16]

Southern Arizona, at that time a part of northern Sonora, undoubtedly witnessed traffic back and forth as a result of these activities. Indeed Father Kino said he had reports that before the Pueblo Revolt (in 1680) the Spaniards of New Mexico ". . . used to come by way of Apachería to these our most remote Pimas Sobaiporis to barter hatchets, cloth, sackcloth, blankets, *chomita* [a kind of coarsely woven cloth], knives, etc., for maize."[17]

These comings and goings imply that whoever lived east of the San Pedro River was peaceful. The first glimpse of these natives dates from about 1649, when large numbers of Suma Indians assaulted the Opata pueblos in far northeastern Sonora, about thirty miles south of modern Douglas, Arizona. It was 1651 before a Jesuit priest could restore peace. Two years later thirty chiefs, evidently from the northern Sumas, came to the Opata mission at Teuricachi to ask for a missionary. Most Sumas lived farther east, however, some as distant as present-day Casas Grandes and El Paso.[18] After 1651 the far northern frontier remained generally quiet until after 1678.

The Suma Indians, usually mentioned in association with the Janos and Jocomes, ranged into southeastern Arizona. How long any of these groups had lived there is unknown. Perhaps ancestral Sumas or a closely related group were the natives whom a Coronado chronicler described as "the most barbarous people thus far encountered";[19] people who were not agricultural, relying instead upon *tunas* (prickly-pear fruit), agave, mesquite, and seeds. The Sumas evidently had no permanent settlements or much in the way of material goods. Their way of life differed little from that of the Apaches, who evidently absorbed them.[20]

Soon after 1680 rumblings from the Pueblo Revolt in New Mexico reached northeastern Sonora, where discontent already simmered among the dominant Opatas. Then in the space of a few days during July of 1681, *alcalde mayor* Lázaro Verdugo squelched an uprising before it started and hanged its ringleaders. The numerous testimonies coerced from the conspirators implicated most of the Opata pueblos. Their plan was simple: one group of intriguers would raise a false alarm to drawn the attention of the Spaniards and surprise them, while other Indians pretending to be Apaches would attack the towns.

The depositions revealed that these Apache impersonators would actually be christianized Sumas and Janos, together with unconverted Jocomes. The Apaches at this time may even have been peaceful, but they did have some understandable reasons for rebelling—padres who whipped them and a captain who was hanging them. Where these abuses were taking place is not stated; the Opatas obviously sought to capitalize on them and draw the Apaches into the conspiracy. Witnesses claimed that the Apaches had been storing up arrows in the mountains and would come at night by way of the range between Cumpas and Nacosari as far as the *real,* or mining town, of San Juan Bautista. They clearly were a minority at the time. The same documents also made the first reference to the natives of the Valley of Quiburi, the Sobaipuris, who dwelt along the Río Terrenate, a few leagues to the north.[21]

For whatever causes, in March 1682 Apaches made their first recorded raid into Mexico, striking a ranch far to the south near Casas Grandes in what is now Chihuahua. The frontiers of Sonora then began to suffer heavy losses of horses and other livestock. The attackers included many "Apaches of the plains," some two hundred leagues distant from their own territory. Before the Pueblo Revolt, these Plains Apaches had entered New Mexico to trade, but after 1680 they penetrated farther west, to seek horses among the Gila Apaches.[22] Fifteen years later Captain Manje described the Apaches who lived in the Pinaleño Mountains (his Sierra de Santa Rosa de la Florida) as dressed in fringed buckskin clothing with feather headdresses, living in movable tepees and using large dogs for transport.[23] They were still plains Indians.

This relatively recent origin of Apaches in southeastern Arizona finds support among anthropologists, who point to greater similarity between the Mescaleros of eastern New Mexico and the Chiricahua Apaches in Arizona than of either group with the Western Apaches.[24] Inclusion of the Mimbres and other Apache groups in New Mexico with the Chiricahuas may reflect an alliance reported in 1769 between the latter and the upper Gileño Apaches. The lower Gileños near the confluence of the Gila and San Pedro rivers had distanced themselves from others and presumably became the Aravaipa Apaches.[25]

Spanish Campaigns on the Northern Frontier, 1686–1695

The Franciscan fathers, followed by the Jesuits, had missions at the northeastern Opata villages beginning in 1646. There are also hints of Spanish ranches as far north as the San Bernardino Valley in the seventeenth century. This frontier advance ended by 1686, when the Jano, Jocome, and Suma Indians began serious raiding on the Sonoran settlements. Jocome is a Piman word meaning "them" or "those," which leaves uncertain the identity of Indians called by this name.[26] The Apaches, Chinarras, and other peoples soon joined in spreading death and destruction. Two years later the Pimas and Sobaipuris rose up, when a corporal of the Sinaloa garrison invaded a peaceful ranchería and put fifty Pimas to the sword, taking the women and children away as prisoners. The frontier blazed, with Opata villages being the most frequent victims of assaults.[27]

Out of this violence came two of the greatest frontier fighters of northern New Spain, Francisco Ramírez de Salazar and Juan Fernández de la Fuente. These captains led their companies forth to do battle many times during the 1680s and 1690s. At one point the viceroy of New Spain, fitting new tactics to the increased threat, ordered the newly appointed governor of New Mexico, Don Diego de Vargas, to march west from El Paso sixty leagues to Janos, combine his forces with Fernández's soldiers at the Janos presidio, and then turn northwards into Apache country. The two contingents left Janos on October 22, 1691, and joined forces with Captain Ramírez's Flying Company of Sonora somewhere north of the Opata towns, continuing on and eventually reaching a river (the Gila) that flowed westward toward the lands of the Pimas and Sobaipuris. On its banks they found some Apache rancherías and attacked them, capturing twenty-five Indians. Snow and cold weather caught the Spaniards a hundred leagues beyond the frontier, whereupon they split up and returned to their various posts. All in all it was not considered a successful expedition.[28]

Ramírez was back the next spring, attempting to drive a diplomatic wedge between the Pimas and Sobaipuris on the one hand and the Janos, Jocomes, Sumas, and Apaches on the other. His success was a major turning point in the history of this frontier, since the Sobaipuris and other Pimas subsequently became a significant force in the defense of Sonora. Captain Ramírez's trip, in which he ventured down the San Pedro River as far as "The Narrows," about ten miles north of modern Benson, was the first recorded visit to the Sobaipuris since Coronado's time.[29] Then the captain died unexpectedly, on December 31 of that year.

The Spaniards by the 1690s were becoming familiar with the country of their common enemies, as they called them, and had developed a place-name terminology, as we saw earlier. For example Captain Ramírez's diplomatic feat separated the Sobaipuris from the Apaches of the Sierra of Chiguicagui [Chiricahua]. Manje's 1697 reference to the Sierra de Santa Rosa de la Florida, "where many Apaches have their habitations," denoted the modern Pinaleño Mountains. General Fernández de la Fuente reiterated the importance of these ranges: "We have seen how the Janos, Jocomes, Mansos, Sumas, Chinarras, and Apaches have united. We have seen their great numbers and how they always travel together and how they never leave the rugged sierras where they always have their habitations."[30]

Apart from references to mountainous country, the Spaniards were usually quite vague in specifying where these roving Indians lived when not raiding.[31] The best insight prior to the nineteenth century comes from the journal of a June-thru-September 1695 expedition headed by that inveterate campaigner, General Juan Fernández de la Fuente. He and other captains led the largest Spanish force to take the field in northern New Spain up to that time—the troops from four presidios and their Indian allies—against the warring Janos, Jocomes, Mansos, Sumas, Chinarras, and Apaches.

This army departed from General Fernández's own Janos presidio in early June and wended its way towards the San Bernardino Valley. In a skirmish the troops captured several Indians and from them learned about Suma and Jocome camps in the Chiricahua Mountains. The Spaniards accordingly marched toward the eastern side of the Chiricahuas. They arrived in the vicinity of Sulphur Draw, went on to Cave Creek, and finally to the mouth of Turkey Creek, near modern Paradise, Arizona. They found the Janos, Jocome, Suma, Chinarra and Manso Indian captains waiting, with their people scattered in the mountains. The army had come prepared either to fight or

Grand Cañon (Cave Creek Canyon), Chiricahua Mountains, from a sketch by Charles Schuchard, 1854. (Courtesy, Rio Grande Historical Collections, New Mexico State University Library.)

negotiate for the release of Opata captives and to make peace. After two days of fruitless talks, the generals (there were two of them on the expedition) told the hostile captains that "... they were telling two thousand lies. If they wanted to fight, we were ready here." Another five days of stalling ensued, after which the army packed up and moved on to suppress a Pima rebellion in western Sonora.[32]

Fernández left the Pimas at peace and returned to southeastern Arizona to settle affairs there. The Spaniards camped on the western side of the Chiricahuas, then moved up near Apache Pass, which they called the pass of San Felipe. Several captured Indians told them that the Janos, Jocomes, Sumas, Chinarras, Mansos, and many Apaches were living in the woods along the Gila River and on the slopes of the Santa Rosa (Pinaleño) Mountains. The army's earlier visit apparently caused the Indians to leave the Chiricahua range.

At their camp many of the soldiers became seriously ill, allegedly from the water in poisoned springs, but Lieutenant Antonio de Solís set off with sixty-four picked men and Indian auxiliaries to find the Jocome governor and attack his ranchería. Mostly by luck they found the village, on a flat probably near the Winchester Mountains. Solís' men surrounded the fleeing Jocomes, then killed the governor and twelve others as they tried to fight their way out. Forty-three people were made captives. The army was now mostly too sick to continue campaigning, so after a final council at San Simon Springs, the troops split up and made their ways back to their garrisons.[33]

The Sonoran frontier continued to be a cauldron of raids and retributions through the 1690s, as the thin line of presidial troops, citizens, and Indian allies fought to hold back an amalgam of hostile tribes. The Janos had the leading role for awhile, often joining with the Jocomes and Sumas. The Sonorans, led now by General Don Domingo Jirónza Petris de Cruzate, finally prevailed and forced these three tribes to segregate themselves from the Apaches and seek peace. Their request was granted and they settled close to the presidios of Janos and El Paso. After 1700 these non-Apache peoples were mentioned less and less frequently until by the 1730s only the Apaches survived outside the areas of Spanish settlement.[34]

Father Kino and Early Missionary Efforts

Father Eusebio Kino, the Jesuit missionary whose name became synonymous with Pimería Alta, arrived in this land in March of 1687. He took up his permanent mission at Nuestra Señora de los Dolores, a Pima village on the upper Río San Miguel, southeast from present-day Magdalena, Sonora. This continued to be his home until he died in 1711.

Father Kino began a series of visits to the unconverted natives farther to the north and west. Initially he journeyed to the Sobaipuri villages along the Santa Cruz and San Pedro rivers, but very soon he went as far as the Gila River and among the more scattered Pimans living in northwestern Sonora. On his first visit in January of 1691, a number of Sobaipuri messengers met Kino and Father Visitor Juan María de Salvatierra at El Tucubavia and asked the two fathers to visit their own villages, more than forty leagues distant.

The padres departed from El Tucubavia, which lay at the headwaters of the Río Altar, a few miles south of the present Arizona line, and proceeded probably by way of Sycamore Canyon and Bear Valley to the ranchería of San Cayetano del Tumacácori, on the Santa Cruz River near the later mission with that name. They continued up the river to a second ranchería at Guevavi, where Guebabi Canyon joins the Santa Cruz, before concluding their trip.[35]

Father Kino returned a year and a half later, in late August and early September of 1692. On that visit he saw the ranchería of San Xavier del Bac for the first time and met its eight hundred people. From there he passed east on a brief journey among the Sobaipuris of the Río de San Joseph de Terrenate, today known as the San Pedro River. Lieutenant Antonio de Solís made the same trip, in reverse order, looking for some stolen horses in May of 1694.[36]

Kino's missionary journeys are chronicled in his own historical memoir as well as in the diaries of Captain Manje, his frequent escort. In mid-December of 1696, Father Kino took a few head of livestock to San Pablo de Quiburi, on the middle San Pedro River, "on the frontier of the Hocomes." By then the Sobaipuris along the San Pedro had split into two groups, one along the middle section of the river around the mouth of the Babocomari River, and a second below "The Narrows."[37] Kino returned to Quiburi in March of 1697 for his first serious effort to convert the Sobaipuris of the San Pedro, in the meantime having started small ranches in the Santa Cruz Valley in preparation for founding missions at San Xavier and San Cayetano. Kino visited Quiburi again in November of 1697 and found the villagers dancing over the scalps of thirteen enemies killed in a battle a few days earlier.[38]

This skirmish was a prelude to the events of March 30, 1698, when some 600 Jocomes, Sumas, Mansos, Janos, and Apaches attacked the new Sobaipuri ranchería at Santa Cruz, a league and a half from Quiburi. The people from Quiburi and other Pimas came to the rescue and eventually sent the enemy fleeing. On the ground 54 of the attackers lay dead, and 168 reportedly died later from the effects of the Pimas' poisoned arrows.[39]

The victory at Santa Cruz proved to be a hollow one. Later that year the Sobaipuri captain Coro led his people west from Quiburi to Sonoita Creek, where they established a new settlement alled Los Reyes de Sonoita, about four or five leagues east of the ranchería at Guevavi. How many Indians removed from the San Pedro Valley is not known, but by 1700 more than 500 people lived at Los Reyes, somewhere near modern Patagonia, Arizona. Many of them, including Captain Coro and his followers, subsequently returned to their village at Santa Cruz. Both Guevavi and Sonoita in time became dependent missions, or *visitas.*

By 1703 the situation in Pimería Alta had improved as a result of a campaign by the Pimas, ". . . the result being that through some good victories by our Pimas the hostile Apaches were greatly restrained."[40] Father Kino had established a church at San Xavier del Bac in 1700; in 1701 he laid the foundations for a large church and house at Guevavi. Both villages received their first resident priests at that time, but the fathers became sick within a year and had to leave. They were not replaced, and indeed Father Kino's mission program was faltering at the time of his death in 1711.

For twenty years following Kino's demise, three Jesuit fathers periodically visited the upper Pima settlements from the home missions of Dolores, San Ignacio, and Caborca, all in northern Mexico.[41] After nearly forty years of efforts to Christianize the natives, southern Arizona was still a land of missionaries and neophytes—and Apaches. It was 1732 before the Sobaipuri communities along the Santa Cruz and the San Pedro saw resident missionaries again.

Native Settlements in the Eighteenth Century

The frontiers of settlement remained at the Indian villages along the Santa Cruz and San Pedro rivers, where they had been since Coronado's time; beyond lay Apache Indian country. For most of the eighteenth century, the San Pedro Valley was a frontier region that attracted little interest. A new missionary, Father Ignacio Keller, passed that way in May of 1732 and mentioned a half-dozen villages "in which there must be over 1,800 souls," on the way to his mission at Santa María de Soamca, on the upper Santa Cruz. Fourteen years later the San Pedro Valley reportedly had six settlements—Quiburi, Tres Alamos, Naideni, Bacoachi, Santa Cruz, and La Azequia Grande—all of which Father Keller ministered to by visitations.

One of these communities, sometimes called Naidenibacatri or Naidembacachi ("land of the beautiful reeds" in Opata), was far to the east of the others. With reference to twentieth-century landmarks, this village lay south of the old Forrest siding on the El Paso and Southwestern Railroad, a few miles west of Douglas. A Sobaipuri village remained on the Babocomari River until sometime between 1743 and 1751, when a tribal leader persuaded the people to move elsewhere.[42]

Soamca's padre served the Sobaipuris in the San Pedro Valley as well as his own flock until two more German Jesuits, Francisco Hlava and Miguel Gerstner, arrived in the first days of 1757 to begin their labors of conversion. They hoped to go to the San Pedro Sobaipuris, but when they rode out there in company with Father Keller, the Indians threatened to kill any missionary sent to live with them and made it clear that they would accept only their minister at Soamca. These Pimans had been able to keep Christianity at arm's length and had no wish to change. The disappointed fathers returned to Father Keller's home mission and from there went to other stations.[43] None of the San Pedro villages received a resident priest.

In the first months of 1762, the interim governor of Sonora ordered the commander of the Terrenate presidio to remove the Sobaipuris of the San Pedro from their exposed frontier to the settlements of their kinsmen on the Santa Cruz River and Sonoita Creek. By now these easternmost Sobaipuris had grown weary and much reduced in numbers, from warring with the Apaches. Contemporary sources gave the number of refugees as about 400 souls in all, rather less than the figure of 2,000 sometimes cited. Of these 400, some 250 relocated at Tucson, 30 more at Santa María, and an unspecified number at Guevavi and other visitas.[44] This order proved to be a tragic error, because it removed a major barrier to the Apache plundering of the missions and towns farther south. The settlement on the Sonoita endured until Apache raids extinguished it in 1773 or early 1774. To the west, beyond the Santa Cruz, lay many other Piman rancherías.

No Spaniards lived in Pimería Alta as of 1723, but settlers began taking up ranches in the San Luis Valley, along the Santa Cruz south of Guevavi, later in the 1720s.[45] In another decade or so, miners were exploring the desert ranges of southern Arizona. These newcomers found that Apache bands lived "in the high hills toward the north" or had pastures and encampments near the Santa Rita silver mines. While they made only limited use of the region between the San Pedro and Santa Cruz, the Apache considered the country east of the San Pedro Valley and especially the forested uplands to be their domain.[46] From these mountains they raided across the northern frontier, running off livestock and sometimes destroying ranches, mining camps, and towns. The war with the Apache that began "officially" in 1748 had been going on unofficially in northern Sonora for decades.[47] Pima villagers continued to visit the foothills during this time, making mescal, collecting wild fruits, and occasionally seeking refuge from their enemies.[48]

Spanish Mining in the Upper Santa Cruz Valley

For Spaniards the attraction of any new country was in direct proportion to its prospects of mineral wealth. They discovered gold and silver in southern Arizona but had limited success in exploiting their finds. One bit of irony is that the Coronado expedition probably passed within a dozen miles of what became one of southern Arizona's richest silver-mining areas. Had Coronado's men known this, however, they might not even have cared, since their quest was for gold.

The appearance of Bartolomé de Medina's *patio* process in the mid-1550s made possible the tremendous boom in silver mining in New Spain. A century later silver was being mined at various places in the Opata-speaking regions of northern Sonora. Captain Manje saw what appeared to be a piece of silver ore at San Xavier del Bac during his 1697 visit there. However, Fathers Luis Velarde and Jacobo Sedelmayr made it quite clear that mines were not actively worked in Pimería Alta during the first twenty years of missionary endeavors there.[49]

Missionaries had a low opinion of miners. Their complaints were based upon more than moral grounds, since the two sides competed for the same native labor. Father Sedelmayr, writing at a later time, had seen some of the mineral prospects and mining camps in northern New Spain. He was not unsympathetic to ". . . the deficiencies and needs of those poor miners. Today they have no lead, tomorrow no mercury, another day they have no steel and iron. Then they may need a house or they have no clothes to cover the nakedness of their peons. Then they need a blacksmith. Sometimes they lack everything, sometimes only a few things. There is always something wanting . . ."[50] Padre Philipp Segesser was a little less generous: "Everywhere there are people who seek metal up hill and down dale, but there are few persons who wish to work. . . . these fellows move from house to house with their bare-boned nags and somehow earn a right to sponge and lounge about."[51]

Father Ignaz Pfefferkorn had learned quite a lot about the relations between Indians and miners:

> It was principally the Spanish miners who stood in the way of the propagation of religion and the improvement of customs among the Sonorans. Most of these miners were people who, failing to make their livelihood in the cities, were forced to seek their fortune in the Sonora mines. . . . No aim was farther from their hearts than the conversion and promoting of the good conduct of the Christian Indians. All they desired was to lay hold of gold and silver.[52]

Another Jesuit, Father Juan Nentvig, saw the wayward (and sometimes all-too-willing) Indians as doomed to perdition quite as much as the miners themselves: "The worst is that those who taste the licentious life seldom return to their villages. If they do, they become the devil's own leaven, . ." As for the goldseekers who led the natives down this path,

> So great is the laziness and love of idleness of most of these people that in spite of the abundance of gold in more than twenty different places, most of the people remain poor. They do not persevere at any one place, and when they hear of another spot, they leave what they have to ride the trail of doubtful hopes. They are much like the mastiff that, letting the piece of meat he carried in his mouth drop, ran after its own image reflected in the water.[53]

Mining contributed to the padres' burdens in another way, after stories began to circulate about buried treasures in the missions. This was beginning even before the Jesuits were exiled from New Spain, in 1767.[54]

Southern Arizona witnessed limited activity in gold mining during the Spanish period. The garrison at Coronado's Corazones III had discovered veins of gold that they were unable to work because the country was at war.[55] In the 1770s gold placers ten or fifteen miles beyond Arivaca attracted the Tubac settlers. This find may have been either the Arivaca placers or the Oro Blanco placer district, both of which saw renewed working in the nineteenth century.[56] The placer deposits along Guebabi Canyon seem to have been known as well.

Spanish mining was predominately for silver. A mining camp called the *Real de Arizonac* came into existence about 1730, some ten leagues southwest from the mission at Guevavi, south of the present U.S.-Mexico border. A Yaqui Indian made the first real strike, two leagues north of Arizonac, when he found large nuggets of silver along an arroyo. His discovery, in October of 1736, became famous almost overnight, as the Bolas ("balls") or Planchas de Plata ("slabs of silver"). The word spread like wildfire or, as Father Pfefferkorn put it, "The circumstance became notorious, and everything in and out of Sonora that had legs ran to the spot hoping to get rich quickly."[57]

The most spectacular find was a huge slab of silver estimated to weigh 2,500 pounds. By the time the presidio captain from Fronteras, Juan Bautista de Anza, rode in to investigate whether this was a mine or a buried treasure, most of the riches had disappeared. Planchas de Plata was something of an enigma; there were no veins and the silver lay within a few feet of the surface. The king of Spain subsequently claimed it as a treasure trove, which meant that it was declared a crown property; but the nuggets and slab had long since vanished. The most enduring legacy from this episode was to permanently fasten the name of Arizona onto the region.[58]

Prospectors soon made other silver discoveries. These were less well-documented and became the stuff from which legends are born. Twelve years after the reestablishment of missions at Guevavi, Santa María, and San Xavier del Bac, in 1732, Father Sedelmayr claimed that various mines had been found nearby, but he did not elaborate.[59] Twenty years later Father Juan Nentvig observed that there were several silver mines and one gold prospect in the vicinity of Guevavi mission, but these were not being worked.[60]

Greater activity centered around the garrison town of Tubac, one league north of Tumacácori along the Santa Cruz. Mining was being carried on near the old Sopori ranch, about three leagues northwest from Tubac.[61] As of

1777 three settlers of Tubac claimed that the ore from two silver mines in the Santa Rita Mountains had been reduced by smelting and that silver was extracted at three other mines with quicksilver (using the patio process, or amalgamation). Local Apaches prevented the Tubac citizens from operating these mines continuously.[62]

When the Marqués de Rubí passed just south of the Huachuca Mountains in December of 1766, he noted that the mines there "are now producing good silver, notwithstanding the scarcity of people and the excessive risk."[63] The risk referred to Apache depredations. These workings, in Cave Creek Canyon on the south side of the Huachucas, created brief excitement at the time of their rediscovery late in 1879. The smelting furnaces lay to the south, just inside Mexico.[64]

Arivaca, or La Aribac, is a valley about seven leagues west of Tumacácori. With the refounding of the Guevavi mission in 1732, the native settlement at Arivaca became a visita. Don Antonio de Rivera maintained an *estancia,* or stock ranch, near Arivaca from about 1740, until the Pima uprising in November of 1751 reduced both his ranch and the mission to smoldering ruins.[65] Captain Juan Bautista de Anza, son and namesake of the captain who investigated the Planchas de Plata bonanza, passed by Arivaca in January 1774 and commented on the circumstances of its destruction: "It was inhabited by Spaniards until the end of 1751, the year of the uprising of the Pima tribe, which massacred many of the inhabitants of the place and finally despoiled the ranch of all kinds of stock which they possessed."[66]

At the time of Anza's visit, the Aribaca valley was under consideration as the site for a presidio. Although Anza was impressed with the abundant pasturage and a large spring near the site of the former settlement,[67] a royal inspector considered this to be a *ciénega,* or swamp, and rejected the location:

> This valley is large, but swampy and unhealthy. It has no more water than that of La Cieneguilla, which dampens everything. The horse herds will enjoy good pastures, but the soldiers no health, and the only good which this transmigration will produce will be that the rich mines of silver called Longoreña, La Duri, and others will be worked.[68]

Arivaca harbored "many mines of very rich metals," three of them especially productive, so the Tubac settlers claimed. Anza said that people worked both gold placers and silver mines until 1767, when Apache harassment forced them to leave. Left unclear was whether mining resumed at Arivaca or was taken up initially following the destruction in 1751. Whichever the case, the

Arivaca Valley, from a sketch by Charles Schuchard, c. 1857. (Courtesy, Rio Grande Historical Collections, New Mexico State University Library.)

Marqués de Rubí found the La Ciénega silver mine abandoned when he passed there in January of 1767, while "Neither is working being done in the little camp of El Aribaca, which lies a league to the right of the road and another league from La Ciénega, from where its ruins can be seen."[69] Only in the nineteenth century were these mines worked again and the valley resettled. In 1893 the older residents, when asked to locate the original Spanish settlement of Arivaca, placed it 1.5 miles northwest of the modern town.[70]

The marqués had mentioned a place called La Longoreña, a league and a half beyond La Ciénega. The royal inspector called Longoreña a rich silver mine. The old Longoreña mining claim, one of an alleged twenty-five silver mines in the Arivaca district, lies in a rocky canyon known as Fraguita Wash, about three miles south of present-day Arivaca. The names and rough locations for some of the other properties have survived, because they were reopened in the late 1850s.[71]

How the Spaniards Mined

Spanish mining technologies changed little during the colonial era and were carried over into the early American period. Ore from a mine first had to be crushed. This could be done by hand or, more efficiently, with a *molino,* or stamp mill. Next came grinding in an *arrastra,* which was a circular pit lined on the sides and bottom with flat stones carefully fitted together. One or more heavy stones were attached to a boom set on a revolving post placed in the center of the arrastra. Rotating the boom caused the drag-stones to crush the ore that had been placed in the pit, grinding it to a powder.

With the addition of water and mercury to the powder, the arrastra became an amalgamator, a small-scale version of the patio process, wherein mercury was used to combine with and extract silver or gold from its finely ground ore.[72] After retorting or boiling away the mercury, the miner was left with a sponge of precious metal. Captain Anza mentioned that the use of quicksilver was "not established in this province of Sonora," to everyone's detriment. Since arrastras are a concomitant of the amalgamation process, we could specify when these were introduced into southern Arizona if we knew when mercury was first employed there.[73]

In northern Sonora the more usual method of extracting silver was to smelt the ore. To accomplish this, the silver-bearing rock had to be reduced to nut-sized chunks, then hand-sorted to select the higher-grade pieces. These in turn were added to a smelting furnace, or *vaso,* together with a quantity of lead or lead ore, plus charcoal as fuel. These crude blast furnaces were largely constructed of adobe and, as with the arrastras, built by the miners themselves. A 1910 newspaper article briefly described the little smelters seen near the Tumacácori mission and the Patagonia Mine:

> These furnaces were built on a pattern of the Mexican vasa, practically a combination of a reverberatory and a shaft furnace, and were adapted to the treatment of comparatively small quantities of high-grade silver ores in mixture with silver-bearing lead ores. The resulting metallic-lead, rich in silver, was cupelled with the formation of lithage [*sic;* litharge] and pure silver. Charcoal was used for fuel.[74]

For the separation of argentiferous lead to take place, the furnace charge might require ores from more than a single mine. Such furnaces were high-maintenance and relatively low-production facilities that burned enormous amounts of fuel. The charcoal for even a modest smelting operation could leave the adjacent landscape denuded of trees. The advantages of these home-built smelting furnaces were simplicity and low cost. Samuel P. Heintzelman, the president of one mining company in the early territorial period, left a rather biting account of the construction of one such furnace.[75]

Most of the mines in New Spain, including some of those in southern Arizona, were evidently worked out by the earliest operators.[76] Exhaustion of the mineable ores led to the mines being abandoned or closed. This is probably what happened in the Huachucas. One mining engineer wrote that ". . . the old workings I have run across in Mexico . . . offered very little inducement for exploitation. I have examined many of the old mines and have found that they invariably were abandoned because they had been exhausted, or, to use a modern phrase, did no longer produce pay ores."[77]

Raphael Pumpelly, a young mining engineer in early territorial Arizona, said that the old mines his company sought to reopen had only thin, albeit rich, veins of ore. The silver from these did not meet expenses.[78] Apaches no doubt caused some mines to be abandoned, perhaps because of the perceived threat more than by actual depredations; aside from an occasional spectacular victory, hostile natives killed relatively few miners or settlers in Pimería Alta.[79]

If the veins were not exhausted, and if unfriendly Indians stayed away, another problem arose when, as often happened, the nature of the ore changed as a mine was developed. Similarly an ore that might be unsuited for reduction by itself could be mixed with other ingredients and successfully smelted.[80] The company that bought the old mines at Cerro Colorado and Arivaca prior to the Civil War met this problem and sought to resolve it by importing lead ore from other mines.[81] The Spaniards a century earlier would probably have sought out argentiferous copper and galena ores, because these could be easily reduced by smelting.[82]

The Pima Revolts, 1734–1760

Apaches were not the only natives who harassed the mines, missions, and ranches of early Arizona. After the establishment of three new missions in 1732, the neophytes sometimes became as much a danger as the roving tribes. Father Juan Grazhofer died scarcely a year after coming to Guevavi, almost surely a victim of poison. Father Philipp Segesser succeeded him and also became very sick. In the summer of 1734, the Pima converts at all three of the missions (San Xavier del Bac, Guevavi, and Santa María de Soamca) abruptly took to the hills, after first doing considerable damage to the mission property at San Xavier. The fathers talked the fugitives into returning.[83]

The spring of 1737 witnessed a more serious disturbance, this one around the mission of Tecoripa, several hundred miles to the south. Juan Bautista de Anza (senior) quashed this uprising, but fell a victim himself two years later, in an Apache ambush not far from Soamca.[84] It was his son who grew up to carve out a distinguished career as a frontier officer and eventually to serve as governor of New Mexico for ten years.

Luis Oacpicagigua was a Pima Indian who lived at the mission of Sáric in northwestern Sonora, where he held the rank of native governor and captain general of the Pimas. Luis led the most serious Pima uprising, which broke out on the night of November 20, 1751. This time the Indians murdered two padres and reduced the missions at Sáric and Tubutama to ashes. At least one hundred settlers and peaceful Indians fell in this bloodletting. Fathers Sedelmayr and Nentvig, besieged for two days at Tubutama, finally escaped through the mountains at night.[85]

The Pimas coordinated their assaults and attacked Arivaca the same night they struck Sáric. At Arivaca they massacred the mission foreman and several families, before reducing both the visita and Don Antonio de Rivera's estancia to rubble. Don Antonio had been at Guevavi at the time looking over a gold mine, but when the news arrived, he collected a dozen citizens from the San Luis Valley and set off for Arivaca to bury the dead. Instead they were met by some two hundred Pima warriors and had to fight their way back to Guevavi.[86]

Just months before this uprising, Pimería Alta had received four new Jesuit fathers. Now two of them were dead and the other two fled from their missions, lest they suffer the same fate. The new missionary at San Xavier del Bac escaped even as the rebels burned his temporary chapel, or *capilla.* At Sonoita they torched the house that served as a church. The Tubac natives set fire to their church and the father's house, while at Guevavi the villagers dashed off to join the other apostates, despite their padre's pleadings. The priests from San Xavier and Guevavi joined the stream of refugees that flowed south through the San Luis Valley and up the Santa Cruz River to Santa María de Soamca. Five leagues beyond, they found asylum at the presidio of San Phelipe de Terrenate. Meanwhile a band of natives sacked the church at Guevavi; "Unhinging the doors of the Father's house they ransacked it, then began in the church, tearing, throwing down, and abusing the few santos that remained."[87]

Within a week of the outbreak, Don Diego Ortiz Parrilla, Sonora's newly installed governor, gathered what troops he could collect and marched north. Ortiz Parrilla, who "seldom faced danger with a stout heart" according to a modern historian, had evidently won his spurs in the War of Jenkins' Ear.[88] He was reluctant to wage war against Luis, whom he held in high esteem.

Once in northern Sonora, he set about issuing reprimands, sending out peace missions, blaming the Jesuits for the insurrection, and generally behaving like a martinet. The rebellious Pimas sat watching in the hills.

Within a month Don Diego had two hundred troops at hand, but Luis and his followers remained as intractable as ever. In late December a reconnaissance party reported that the rebels had plundered the houses in the San Luis Valley. Then on January 4, 1752, Luis led some two thousand warriors out of his camp in the Baboquivari Mountains. Early on the following morning, they fell upon Lieutenant Bernardo Urrea and his troop of eighty-six soldiers, camped at Arivaca. Urrea had been alerted and in the face of these incredible odds the valorous lieutenant thundered into the enemy's ranks with sixty-three mounted men! With a great effort the Spaniards managed to turn the tables, and by sunrise that day the Pimas had been routed, leaving forty-three dead on the field. Several hours later the Indians renewed their attack, only to lose three more killed, including the son of Luis. Spanish casualties were two men wounded.[89] Arivaca, scene of the bloody beginning of the Pima Revolt, also witnessed its last battle.

This campaign then dissolved into a wrangle between Ortiz Parrilla and the Jesuits. The shooting war stopped, and a paper war of accusations and investigations began. Luis meanwhile was willing to surrender, on the condition that Father Ignacio Keller, now a twenty-year veteran at Soamca, be removed from Pimería Alta. After parleys in the Santa Catalina Mountains, Luis came alone to Tubac and received the governor's amnesty. More than one hundred of his followers left the Santa Ritas and made their appearance at Sonoita, once more swearing obedience to God and king. As many more rebels reappeared at Tubac and Guevavi, Father Keller left for a year, but then he returned to Soamca and served there until his death.

Luis escaped punishment at the time, but he was taken into custody later, after the governor decided that jail was the safest place for this troublemaker. He languished there for more than a year and then died. In the words of a coconspirator, Luis justified the 1751 revolt in his own mind as revenge for the slaughter of Pimas at El Tupo back in 1695, a purposeless massacre ordered by Lieutenant Antonio de Solís of the Flying Company of Sonora. These slayings had led to the Pima uprising that General Fernández de la Fuente quieted between trips into southeastern Arizona that summer. Luis of Sáric either had a long memory or a convenient fund of grievances for venting his malice.

Five years of official investigations failed to find any cause for the 1751 rebellion other than the desire of the Indians to be free from Spanish control. From the point of view of colonial officials, this last was wishful thinking! Eventually the whole matter was remanded to perpetual silence, with approval of the pacification measures already taken.[90]

Missionaries, settlers, and repentant natives returned to southern Arizona, but peace remained elusive. Apostate Pimas drove off hundreds of head of livestock and harassed both settlers and the Indians living at the missions. The next explosion came in the fall of 1756, when the priest at San Xavier del Bac apparently tried to suppress a native festival. A band of Gila River Pimas, aided by some of the Indians at San Xavier, fell upon the mission and sacked both the father's house and the houses of loyal Indians; Father Alonso Espinosa fled and thereby saved his life. An ensign from the newly founded Tubac presidio rode to the rescue with fifteen soldiers. He met the rebels and routed them in a fury of fighting, killing fifteen in the process.[91]

The new governor of Sonora, Colonel Don Juan Antonio de Mendoza, was no faint heart in dealing with rebellions. He organized a punitive expedition and rode north, collecting Father Bernard Middendorff en route to serve as the military chaplain. The troops pushed on through Guevavi and San Xavier, tracking the enemy to the banks of the Gila River. There on a hill near the confluence of the Gila and the Salt, Father Middendorff became a war correspondent: "The Lord Governor springs to his steed, calling upon Saints James and Joachim is the first to attack foe and mountain. He came, he conquered—Since, indeed, the heathen at once flinging their weapons from them, flung themselves down from the top of the mountain into the river stretched out below, . . ."[92] The battle was actually inconclusive, since the enemy escaped.

As the decade wore on, die-hard Pimas continued raiding at will. Their end came early in 1760, when young Juan Bautista de Anza with a squadron from his new command, the Tubac presidio, tracked a rebel band and found them standing over the body of a dead soldier, not only caught red-handed but in the process of removing the murdered man's scalp. Anza and his men attacked with a vengeance and in the ensuing fight killed nine of the malefactors, including Luis's son Cipriáno. The setting for this melee was south of the old visita of Arivaca, "in the Sierra de la Horca."[93] From this time on the Apaches were the only ones who challenged Spanish control of Pimería Alta.

Defending the Frontier: Presidial vs. Apache

Two groups of native defenders sought to protect the frontier from Apache incursions. The Sobaipuris and other Pimas often fought the Apaches unaided, even launching forays into Apachería. At other times the Pimans acted as auxiliaries to the frontier regulars, the presidial troops. The Sobaipuris of the San Pedro Valley acted as a first line of defense until 1762, when the Spaniards evacuated them to villages along the Santa Cruz River and Sonoita Creek. This native militia was formalized in 1782, with the organization of an eighty-man Pima Indian infantry company, modeled after the Opata company at Bavispe in eastern Sonora, created just a year earlier. This Pima garrison occupied Tubac in 1787 and stayed for half a century.[94]

The presidio at Janos, thirty miles south of the border with New Mexico in what is now northern Chihuahua, had been an active post since its establishment around 1690. Since Janos lay east of the Sierra Madre, it was too remote to offer much protection to northern Sonora. To remedy this situation, the viceroy created the Flying Company for the frontiers of Sonora. The first captains of this company, Francisco Ramírez de Salazar and Don Domingo Jironza Petriz de Cruzate, were a couple of tough, frontier Indian fighters. The latter had served a term as governor of New Mexico.

In 1692 this Compañía Volante was designated a presidial company, based at the Opata village of Santa Rosa de Corodeguachi, about twenty-seven miles south of modern Douglas. For the first quarter of the eighteenth century, official corruption rendered the troops at Corodeguachi mostly ineffective, but reforms made in consequence of General Pedro de Rivera's 1726 inspection saw the whole presidio system straightened out and made a fighting force again. A first-rate soldier, Captain Juan Bautista de Anza (the elder), received the command at Corodeguachi, which was now being called Fronteras.[95]

The defense of Sonora in the mid-1730s rested mainly upon the troops at Fronteras, aided by a rather weak militia and native auxiliaries. For a five-year period, 1775–80, the Fronteras garrison was relocated at a site in the San Bernardino Valley, just one mile south of the present U.S.-Mexico boundary. This proved to be a bad idea, because it ". . . served . . . only to increase the number of the king's vassals who might be victims of the cruelty of the Apache, to fatten the latter's robberies among the horse herds and mule trains bringing provisions, to keep the troop eternally employed in weak maneuvers for their own defense, . . ."[96] The troops returned to their old post at Fronteras in 1780. Following the reorganization of border administration in 1786, Fronteras became the location of one of the Apache peace establishments.

To bolster Sonora's defenses, the viceroy authorized the creation of a new presidio, originally intended to be near the mission of Guevavi. Instead it was established at San Mateo de Terrenate, on the headwaters of the San Pedro River. This garrison was expected to protect the *vecinos*, or citizens,

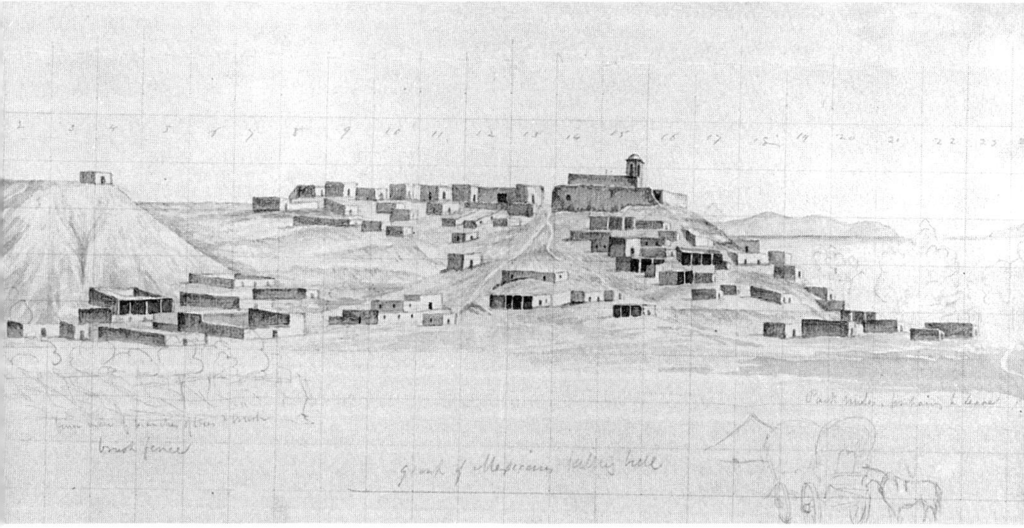

Fronteras, Sonora—sepia wash by John R. Bartlett, 1851. (Courtesy, the John Carter Brown Library at Brown University.)

and the peaceful Indians of Primería Alta, to chastise the Apaches, curb recurrent restlessness among the Pimas, and also protect the Spanish miners in three valleys! The formal founding of Terrenate was June 1, 1742.[97] Scarcely twenty years later, Father Juan Nentvig wrote that ". . . since the establishment of the presidio, the Apache enemy has caused more destruction in the province of Sonora than ever before."[98]

Even the location was bad. The garrison and their families suffered from an unhealthy climate, bad water, and a lack of nearby farmland, which meant a dangerous trip to the San Pedro Valley, five leagues away, to plant on its banks.[99] Terrenate's horse herd proved to be a powerful temptation for the Apaches. Early in the winter of 1767, leather-jacketed Apaches swooped down on this herd, killed two soldiers, and caused the others to take flight. The following autumn two hundred raiders struck the unsuspecting presidio and within an hour carried off the entire horse herd, leaving the defenders afoot. Terrenate's horses had a reputation for fleetness; on November 15, 1772, the enemy requisitioned another 257 head.[100]

Late in 1775 the entire garrison was transferred some twenty-five leagues north, to a point on the terrace overlooking the western side of the San Pedro Valley near present Fairbank. The new establishment was called Santa Cruz de Terrenate. Although one inspector made Santa Cruz sound like a valley of happy farmers, the presidials found duty there more like a sentence of death. The company proved unable to defend itself, much less to prevent Apache raiders from passing south to the interior settlements. Attacks came daily, and by 1776 "already the troops were becoming possessed with the terror of panic," That year Captain Francisco Tovar and thirty of his men perished at the hands of their foes.[101]

This was all-out war, and the natives were winning. One engagement between thirty-four presidials of Santa Cruz and sixty Apaches took place on an open plain. The troops made a fighting retreat, losing their captain with nineteen soldiers and settlers. Then in the course of carrying the monthly mail to San Bernardino, eight more men were killed. Horses disappeared, as did the mule train transporting provisions. Altogether two captains and more than eighty men died at the hands of the enemy within a short distance of the post, all in the space of five years. By 1780 the troops were starving.[102]

For the garrison to continue was suicidal. Finally the order came to pull out. The survivors limped back up the San Pedro, bringing little more than the name Santa Cruz. At a place on the arroyo of Las Nutrias, just two leagues east of their old quarters at Terrenate, the men began building temporary barracks for a new presidio. While stationed at Las Nutrias the captain, Don Joseph Antonio de Vildosola, led some two hundred regulars and Opata auxiliaries on a campaign to the Chiricahua Mountains and the San Simon Valley. One party scouted up the west side of the Chiricahuas and found a walled cave. They opened it, ". . . revealing in it various things for the use of the Apaches, hides, leather, mescal, maize, and seeds which they gather for their sustenance and many things which they steal."[103] The troops took what they could carry and left the rest. Two days later they caught up with an Apache ranchería, probably in the northern Peloncillos, and dislodged the Indians in a hard-fought battle that lasted until nightfall.

In 1787 the Terrenate company moved from Las Nutrias to what another inspector called an ideal site for a permanent presidio—the abandoned mission of Santa María de Soamca, about eight miles south of present-day Lochiel. Here the garrison of Santa Cruz did find a permanent home. The name Santa Cruz soon became attached to the adjacent river, to the mountains just to the northwest, and to the community itself.[104]

Meanwhile the creation of a fifty-man presidio farther west, at Tubac, was expected to block any repetition of the 1751 Pima revolt. Tubac, a small ranchería on the west side of the Santa Cruz River, became a garrison town in March of 1753, when it received the formal name San Ignacio de Tubac. It lay about one league north of a new settlement and visita called San Joseph de Tumacácori. The soldiers and their dependents preempted the good land, while the dispossessed natives were gathered in at Tumacácori.[105]

For twenty-two years the Tubac soldiers waged a campaign against enemies in several directions; primarily with the Apaches but also fighting the Seri Indians and the Lower Pimas far to the south. From 1760 to 1777 the presidio captain was that model soldier, Juan Bautista de Anza. He won some individual battles, but the northern frontier actually retracted. First came the withdrawal of the Sobaipuris from the San Pedro Valley early in 1762. Then in late 1763 or early 1764, the vecinos of the San Luis Valley petitioned Captain Anza for permission to abandon their homes. The captain approved. After forty years these descendants of the first Spanish settlers in Arizona had given up, in the face of near-certain death at the hands of the Apaches if they stayed.[106]

In the fall of 1768, these enemies launched a major offensive in place of their routine plundering. After rounding up San Xavier's horses and mules, the raiders set off toward Redington Pass. Two soldiers and some of the local Pimas gave chase and engaged the Apaches in a running battle. At the pass another band of hostiles set an ambush and carried away the two soldiers. On November 19 the Apaches descended on Soamca, riding horses recently stolen at the Terrenate presidio only five leagues to the east. In a ten-hour assault, they turned Santa María de Soamca into smouldering ruin, destroying the mission residence and ravaging the church. The town at that time had no garrison, and the thirteen Pima families fought from a makeshift fortress. The following February the few remaining Pimas at Soamca abandoned their village.[107] At San Xavier the raiders returned at least twice in 1769 to replenish their supplies, on one occasion riding right through Tucson.

The situation deteriorated still more the following summer, when the attackers devastated the visita of Sonoita, slaughtering nineteen women and children. Guevavi was deserted in 1774, its people beaten into submission "because of the furious hostility of the Apaches."[108] Emboldened by such successes, these enemies extended their depredations to the horse herds at Tubac. Their crowning achievement came on September 7, 1775, when they rounded up and drove off the entire Tubac *caballada,* five hundred head of horses. By that time the decision had already been taken to move the garrison of Tubac to a new site at San Agustín del Tucson, eighteen leagues to the north.[109] Tucson remained a military post from 1776 until the last Mexican soldiers marched away on March 10, 1856.

Battered as they were, the presidial soldiers and their allies carried the war to the enemy's land. As one commander put it, "There really is no means other than offensive war for restraining them."[110] The frontier forces struck into the mountain ranges between Janos and Terrenate and north from there, including the Chiricahua Mountains, "where there are always many Apaches villages."[111]

The troops who carried out this offensive sometimes found a curious feature in the mountains—scattered corrals. These were part of the Apache strategy. Horses taken during raids on Terrenate and cattle from ranchos in Sonora were divided up and kept in these hidden corrals, allowing the Indians to have fresh mounts and also a commissary while they continued depredations, until eventually they returned to their homeland. Indeed the rugged sierras where the Chiricahua, Mimbres, and Gileño Apaches lived included such places as the Corral de Piedra, Corral de Pícora, and Corral de San Augustín.[112]

Captain Juan Bautista de Anza's résumé gives a fair summary of what the men in his commands accomplished. While still a lieutenant at Fronteras during the late 1750s, he followed his captain in five general campaigns against the Apaches:

> I was entrusted with the most arduous and dangerous patrols. We killed forty of the enemy and captured more than 200. . . . During the last of these campaigns I was under orders to lead a detachment of soldiers and Indian allies to take a stronghold in the Chiricahua Mountains, garrisoned with 180 of the enemy. I stormed the stronghold and retreated with six of their stolen cattle . . .

Anza went on to explain that he captured the enemy captain single-handedly, making this an unqualified victory. As a lieutenant he later led two forays that left 29 Apaches slain and 114 of their family members captured, with 500 head of stolen livestock recovered.[113]

Diaries, journals, and other accounts tell us that the garrisons at Tubac and Tucson were not lax at chasing raiders—when the troops had horses with which to do so. At the end of February 1766, Anza and his troopers searched through the Sierra Florida (Pinaleños), where they found twenty Apache men, whereupon he tempted them into attacking him. When they did, he fired on them from the flank, apparently wounding a number. On the same campaign, he attacked another group "on the summit of a very tall hill" somewhere north of San Simon and took the hill in an inconclusive engagement. In August of 1771 he again rode out of Tubac towards the Sierra Florida. This time the presidials and Pima auxiliaries surprised an Apache ranchería and scattered the enemy, killing nine and taking eight prisoners.[114]

Anza's successor and the first captain of the Tucson presidio was a no-nonsense disciplinarian, Don Pedro de Allande y Saavedra. Allande arrived for duty on June 12, 1777. Unloved by his own troops, he was ruthless towards the enemy. He launched one assault into the Santa Catalina Mountains in 1779 and destroyed two Apache rancherías, killing many and taking six prisoners. The Indians retaliated and on two occasions attacked Tucson with up to five hundred warriors. The troops beat them off, and the second time the soldiers sent in pursuit overtook the raiders, putting seventeen of them to the sword. In 1782 Allande made three expeditions into Apachería. His December trip "between the Santa Teresa and La Florida Mountains" saw eleven Apache men killed and nine taken prisoner, in an action that began in midafternoon and lasted into the night.

In 1784 and 1785 Allande was relentless. He took to the field in April 1784, on the third campaign that year, ". . . into the mountains of La Florida, Santa Teresa, La Piedad, Dos Cabezas, and Babocomari. Nine braves were killed, together with three women and four children, . . ." During September he led an expedition to the lofty and rugged Sierra del Arivaipa, where his troops killed three women and an Apache shaman. March and April of 1785 saw him fighting in the Babocomari, Peñascosa, Huachuca, Santa Catalina, and Santa Rita mountains, burning rancherías and slaying any warriors who got in the way. He claimed to have killed one man in hand-to-hand combat on this occasion, "to inspire his troops." He also supervised construction of the palisade wall around the Tucson presidio and instituted a particularly grisly type of trophy-taking to embellish it: "Lines of countless Apache heads have crowned the palisade."[115]

The Apache Peace Establishments

Allande was transferred away in 1788, but the officers at other garrisons had begun to employ his search-and-destroy tactics, with equal results. The year 1788 was a particularly active and successful one for the frontier military, and perhaps for the first time the enemy was beginning to be significantly affected. This coincided with the Spanish viceroy's adoption of a new pacification policy, part of the innovative Gálvaz reforms of 1786. As a result of the unceasing war against them, the Apaches would be led to see the wisdom of accepting the viceroy's offer of peace treaties. They would then settle in rancherías near the presidios, where they would be taught to farm, receive rations, and otherwise engage in peaceful activities, all under military supervision.[116]

The new strategy worked surprisingly well. Some Chiricahua Apache

Tubac and the Santa Rita Mountains, from a sketch by Charles Schuchard, c. 1857. (Courtesy, Rio Grande Historical Collections, New Mexico State University Library.)

bands sued for peace as early as September 1786 and moved to Bacoachi on the upper Río Sonora, about halfway between Fronteras and Arispe. Others followed until by March of 1787 more than 250 Chiricahuas were settled there. The Mimbreño Apaches appeared at Janos presidio. Farther to the east, the Mescalero bands congregated at El Paso del Norte and San Elizario. By 1793 Fronteras became the setting for one of these peace establishments, as they were called. The first settlement of "Apaches de paz" at the San Agustín del Tucson presidio took place in January of 1793, when the principal chief of the Aravaipa band induced 107 of his followers to move there and settle down. They built their wickiups downstream from the presidio.[117]

Rationing was at the heart of this reservation system. Once a week the Apaches living within a four-league radius of a presidio were eligible to receive corn or wheat, beef, brown sugar, salt, and even cigarettes. They were not missionized and retained considerable freedom of movement. Any plans to educate or make peaceful agriculturalists out of them fell by the wayside, but the men served effectively as auxiliaries in combatting still-hostile bands. The Sonoran frontier entered a period of relative peace and prosperity during the 1790s that endured for nearly forty years.[118]

A contingent of 235 Pinal Apaches was admitted to peace at the Tucson establishment in the summer of 1819. How many remained is uncertain, since a report a few years later listed a total of only 144 Apaches at that presidio. The peace-establishment system ended in 1831, when the military commandants of Chihuahua and Sonora decreed that weekly rations would be discontinued because of insufficient resources. The Indians began to abandon the presidios and resumed their old life of raiding.[119] However, not all of the Apaches returned to the mountains.

Tubac, which had been garrisoned by the Compañía de Pimas since 1787, reported almost 170 Apaches de paz camped outside the presidio in 1842. The State of Sonora evidently paid for rationing this group as well as for a larger one at Tucson. A devastating raid in December of 1848 prompted the abandonment of Tubac, but the survivors returned in the summer of 1853. In a very short time the peaceful Apaches were back too and accepting their rations. Two years later a lieutenant with the U.S.-Mexico boundary survey noted "some Mexicans and tame Apaches" dwelling near Calabasas, a rancho and old mission visita at the mouth of Sonoita Creek. As recently as 1870, some thirty 'tame' Apache families lived at Tucson, the men serving as scouts for the army.[120]

Population Changes in Pimería Alta

Until the 1790s northern Sonora continued as a mission frontier. A few Spaniards presided over the neophyte Piman Indians—the Sobaipuris, Pimas, and Papagos—in both civil and ecclesiastical matters. Present in increasing numbers were settlers called *gente de razón,* a generic term for people who were culturally Hispanic but racially mixed, neither wholly Indian nor Spanish.[121] The peace establishments introduced still another population element, the Apaches, into the settled areas of Pimería Alta.

In 1767 King Carlos III expelled the Jesuits from New Spain and assigned friars of the Franciscan order in their place. The new fathers faced an overwhelming challenge. For years the missions had been in decline, suffering severe population losses from diseases more than from Apache arrows. The original Pimas and Sobaipuris had either died off, moved north to villages on the Gila River, or fled to their heathen cousins, the Papagos. One padre wrote in 1817 that there was hardly a legitimate Pima left.[122]

To maintain their congregations, the priests were forced to recruit desert-dwelling Papagos to come and settle at the missions. After 1800 the mission populations finally stabilized and the number of people increased overall, due to more gente de razón moving into Pimería Alta. The leaders among them took advantage of the prevailing peace with the Apaches to build up these frontier lands.[123]

4
THE LATE SPANISH AND MEXICAN PERIOD, 1800–1846

The Revival of Mining

The birth of a new century ushered in an era of modest economic growth. Mining resumed around 1804, primarily at gold placers instead of in the old silver-mining districts. One placer district lay "in the sierrita" (Tumacacori Mountains?) between the Tubac presidio and the old rancho of Arivaca. Gold was discovered in the gravels near Quitobac in northwestern Sonora and at other locations in Papago Indian country.[1] A gold mine in the mountains about one-half mile south of the old Guevavi mission had been worked before the 1751 Pima uprising. This mine was revived in 1814 with Yaqui Indian labor and continued until 1849, when Apache threats brought production to a halt.[2] Then in 1864 a rolling stone named W. Claude Jones filed a notice on what, with dubious clarity, he described as

> the old shaft of the abandoned gold mine formerly worked by the Jesuit and San Franciscan Fathers known as the 'Padres Mine' . . . situated to the southwest of the mines of the ancient mission of Huevavi in the side of the mountain range in front of a mesquite tree near an old forge to the left of the main ravine leading from the Santa Cruz river opposite to and south of the ruins of the mission church, within one mile thereof more or less.[3]

When an old Spanish (before 1821) or Mexican silver-lead mine west of there was reopened in 1875, the discoverers found the scene of a tragedy:

> The Old Mine, supposed to be the old Tumacacori, has recently been re-opened and its shafts and tunnels cleaned out. This is one of the numerous mines worked by the Mexicans many years since.
>
> Already, in cleaning out the mine, Mr. Darrah has found two sacks of silver-ore worth at the rate of $7,000 per ton. He finds the old drill-holes to be 4 inches square, proving that the work was done very many years ago. He also found skeletons in the old works, leading to the belief that the workmen staid by the mine until they were murdered by Indians, and this theory is strengthened by the very rich ore found on the dump, which in case of abandonment, would very likely have been taken along. The Old Mine is in the Ostrich Mountain range, and is about 75 miles southward from Tucson.[4]

The Missions in the Nineteenth Century

One measure of economic expansion in Arizona during the Apache peace was a surge in church construction. The great mission church at San Xavier del Bac was begun about 1783 with the seven thousand pesos that Father Juan Velderrain borrowed against his mission's wheat futures. Velderrain died in 1789 or 1790, and his successor, Juan Bautista Llorens, supervised most of the construction. This inspiring monument, reportedly built at a cost of more than thirty thousand pesos, was finished in 1797 and was regarded even then as a wonder; yet it served a congregation that dwindled from 167 persons in 1783 to only 119 in 1801.[5]

Father Llorens built more than one church. It was later claimed that some of the peaceful Apaches helped him to erect a large, box-shaped two-story adobe convento and chapel at San Agustín del Tucson (also known as San José), following completion of the San Xavier church.[6] The padre's final project was a chapel dedicated to Santa Ana, built at Cuiquiburitac in Papago country, less than fifty miles northwest of Tucson. The Cuiquiburitac mission, founded about 1812, lasted but a few years.[7]

Upstream along the Santa Cruz, the resident priest at Tumacácori sold most of his mission's cattle (four thousand head) in order to build a new church for his flock. His replacement, Father Ramón Liberós, continued construction of the San José church at Tumacácori, using the proceeds of this sale. Work began about 1803 and was still not quite finished in 1828, when Mexico banished all *peninsulares, or* peninsular-born Spaniards, a sweep that included Father Liberós.[8] No resident priest replaced him. Twenty years later the last twenty-five or thirty Indians at Tumacácori abandoned their homes and retreated down the Santa Cruz Valley to San Xavier del Bac.

Land Grants and Ranches in Southern Arizona

Spanish ranches had existed in the San Luis Valley since the 1720s, whenever the Apaches allowed them. Ranches also flourished at Arivaca and El Sopori before the Pima Revolt of 1751. The owners held their properties by simple occupancy, without specific titles; sooner or later all were abandoned. With the coming of the Apache peace in the 1790s, stockmen could at last hope that the lush grasslands of southern Arizona would reward them.

By 1800 stock raising had become a major enterprise. Sheep and cattle formed the mainstay of this industry, with lesser numbers of horses and mules.[9] Cattle were the principal source of meat, usually prepared as jerked

Ruins of the mission of Tumacácori, from a sketch by Charles Schuchard, 1854. (Courtesy, Rio Grande Historical Collections, New Mexico State University Library.)

or dried beef, while the commercial value of these animals derived mainly from the sale of hides and tallow. The cattle roamed freely and were rounded up chiefly for slaughter or for sale.[10]

The basis for the livestock industry was land grants. In southern Arizona there were nine such grants issued between 1821 and 1833, two of them partially within Mexico, that eventually went to patent. Most of these claims lay along major river valleys and were acquired by their landowners at public auctions, following the laws of the period. The U.S. Court of Private Land Claims rejected eight additional claims.

With one exception these grants were expressed as *sitios de ganado mayor,* or livestock ranges. Each *sitio* measured one square league, a fraction over 4,338 acres, with the average claim consisting of four sitios, or more than twenty-seven square miles. Ranchers were allowed to occupy surrounding "overplus" lands as well.

In accordance with Spanish law, each grant originated with a petition directed to an official called *the intendente.* After independence, the treasurer general of each Mexican state exercised this authority. If he approved, the

Tucson, Arizona, with the chapel and mission house of San Agustín del Tucson in the middle distance. Pencil and sepia wash by John R. Bartlett, 1852. (Courtesy, the John Carter Brown Library at Brown University.)

land then had to be measured, appraised, and auctioned. The successful bidder, usually the person who submitted the original petition, received title to the land. If abandoned for more than three years, a grant reverted back to the government, unless Indian encroachments had caused the occupants to leave.[11] Ignacio Pérez, the man who bought the four thousand cattle from the Tumacácori mission, acquired the San Bernardino grant east of present-day Douglas as his new range.[12]

The Arivaca Grant: A Rejected Claim

One of the earliest claims was the Arivaca grant, which Agustín Ortiz purchased in 1812. His two sons, having no title documents, petitioned for two sitios at Arivaca in 1833. Their witnesses claimed that the ranch had been occupied since 1812, but they could specify only vague boundaries. The Ortiz rights passed through a series of owners until the claim landed before the U.S. Court of Private Land Claims, which rejected it because of the indefinite location. The U.S. Supreme Court affirmed the lower court decision in 1902, and the land was returned to public domain.[13]

San Rafael de la Zanja

Several of the confirmed grants in the Santa Cruz, San Pedro, and Babocomari river valleys intruded marginally into upland areas. One such was the San Rafael de la Zanja claim. On July 19, 1821, cattleman Manuel Bustillo petitioned for four sitios in the lush plains grassland of the San Rafael Valley, bounded in part by the Patagonia Mountains and the Canelo Hills. At the auction, Don Ramón Romero and other residents of nearby Santa Cruz outbid Bustillo and received the tract. Ranchers from Santa Cruz then used the San Rafael Valley until sometime in 1843, when Apache raiding finally drove them out. Romero himself escaped and continued to hold title until he died, in 1873. A number of claimants vied for control of the grant, until it came into the possession of Colin Cameron, who sought to make it a cattle barony. In 1902 the U.S. Supreme Court confirmed the original grant size of four square leagues and let stand the Court of Private Land Claims decision awarding title to Cameron's San Rafael Cattle Company. A year later ownership passed to a colorful promoter, William C. Greene, whose heirs still operate San Rafael de la Zanja.[14]

Baca Float No. 3

Quite different in origin was the Baca Float No. 3, in the Santa Cruz Valley south of Tubac. In 1860 Congress confirmed an 1821 land grant in the vicinity of present-day Las Vegas, New Mexico, but in lieu of granting title, allowed the heirs of Don Luis María Baca to select five unoccupied and nonmineral tracts, each of one hundred thousand acres. Three years after this act became law, an attorney for the heirs selected a huge, square area that included part of the Santa Cruz Valley and a mineralized section on the western slope of the Santa Rita Mountains.

In 1866 the same attorney alleged that a mistake had been made and asked for a corrected location farther to the north and east, effectively covering the central Santa Rita Mountains. For the next thirty-three years, assignees of the Baca interests claimed this amended selection, while squatters and others took up land within both locations. The 1866 amended claim was eventually denied. In 1905 this grant was surveyed in accordance with the 1863 description and subsequently confirmed to the claimants; many homesteaders then had to be evicted. There are still large grazing tracts within the Baca Float, although most of the lands have been subdivided and sold to various owners, including the Rio Rico real-estate development.[15]

San José de Sonoita

Along either side of Sonoita Creek was the smallest land grant in Arizona—San José de Sonoita. This began as a petition for two sitios, reduced to one and three-quarter sitios before title was issued in 1825. The old mission of San José de Sonoita, probably the one that had been called the New Church in 1754, was the center of the survey. The land changed hands several times in the territorial period, until the courts confirmed the title for some 5,123 acres, following complex litigation. The grant remained intact and was managed as a cattle ranch until recent years.[16]

As a result of the Apache peace establishments an estimated one-half to two-thirds of the Chiricahuas and Mescaleros stopped raiding and resettled near presidios. With the military watching them, the Indians were not likely to be running off livestock.[17] When rationing stopped in 1831, they went back to plundering until, by the time of the Mexican War in 1846, the stock ranges established during the years of relative peace had been abandoned. However, the ruins of these ranches at San Bernardino and along the San Pedro and Babocomari rivers were still very much in evidence.[18]

Later writers regarded the early nineteenth century as a golden age for the cattleman in southern Arizona.[19] Rancher Colin Cameron, writing in the 1890s, characterized conditions at this earlier time as follows:

> From the Rio Grande this route of the emigrants to California followed the line of the most northern of Mexican settlements. It traversed the very heart of the best cattle ranges of today. The grass was unquestionably the best. For years it had been impossible to hold cattle on the ranges because of the depredations of hostile Apaches.
>
> At the military post of Santa Cruz there were a few cattle (20 or 30 head all told) that were watched all day by herders and at night driven within the adobe walls that surrounded the town. At Tucson there were no cattle.
>
> The emigrants saw the ruins of extensive haciendas and signs of where there had been large corrals. They were told that in the years 1820 to 1830 the country had been stocked with many thousands of cattle and horses, but that in the year 1830 and up to 1843 the Apaches were so numerous and raided so frequently, driving away so many of their stock, killing and carrying into captivity so many of their people, that in the latter year all haciendas had to be abandoned, the people seeking refuge in the walled towns in order to save their lives. Stock raising was impossible when two or three armed men kept the Apaches away from the one at work in the field.

Ruins of the Babocomari Ranch on the Babocomari River, from a sketch by Charles Schuchard, 1854. (Courtesy, Rio Grande Historical Collections, New Mexico State University Library.)

> This condition of affairs continued to grow worse. The Apaches, having broken up all the haciendas in what is now Arizona and northern Sonora, having driven off and destroyed all the stock, every year raided farther, going into Sonora as far as Hermosillo, overrunning towards the west the whole of the Altar district, it being a matter of history as well as of tradition and in the recollection of old Mexican citizens now living that the settlements in the lower and upper San Simon Valley, respectively at San Bernardino and at Pueblo Viejo; in what is now the Sulphur Springs Valley, at Agua Prieta, in the south, and Sierra Bonita (Hookers Ranch), in the north, where was located the largest hacienda in the country; at Tres Alamos, at San Pedro, at the Babacomori, at San Rafael de la Zanja, at Sonoyta, and at Tubac, were all abandoned, and that Santa Cruz and Tucson were the only towns on the frontier that were not entirely destroyed and the people driven away by the Apaches. Tucson had no cattle left. Santa Cruz was reduced to 3 oxen and 1 cow.[20]

Cameron stated the situation quite accurately, except that no ranches existed then in the Sulphur Springs or San Simon valleys, nor at the Sierra

Bonita or Tres Alamos. In some years during both Spanish and Mexican times, settlers from Tucson had planted crops at Tres Alamos under the protection of presidial soldiers. This location on the San Pedro River twice became the setting for grant requests, but the terms were never fulfilled, and no title was given.[21]

Renewal of the Apache Threat

Deteriorating economic and political conditions in Mexico led to the discontinuation of rations at the Apache peace establishments. The disappointed Indians left and soon resumed raiding. Some peaceful Apaches continued to live at Tucson and Tubac, where the state of Sonora still fed them. Their less peaceful cousins drove out the ranchers in southern Arizona and then plunged deep into Sonora and Chihuahua along a series of well-defined plunder trails. An American army officer called one such trail "the great stealing road of the Apaches." He described it as ". . . hard beaten, and in places many yards wide, filled with horses' and mules' and cattle tracks, the latter all going one way—from Sonora."[22]

From north to south this trail crossed the Gila River near modern Eden, traversed the pass between the Pinaleño and Santa Teresa mountains, continued across the lower Sulphur Springs Valley, and then ran south along the San Pedro Valley to enter Sonora northwest of Fronteras presidio. Another route crossed the Gila River farther upstream, paralleled San Simon Creek, and continued south past the old ranch at San Bernardino. Other trails led westward through the San Cayetano and Santa Rita mountains to the settlements in the Santa Cruz Valley, with Consumidero Pass (probably modern Melendrez Pass in the Santa Ritas), said to be "much used by the enemies."[23]

The inability of Mexican officials to mount an effective military defense against these depredations led to more desperate measures. Sonora in 1835 and Chihuahua in 1849 decreed a bounty on Apaches. This attracted scalphunters, including some renegade Americans who preyed upon Mexican citizens as well as on the Indians. The level of violence escalated as Apaches, mostly Pinals, increased their own attacks, until in 1848 settlers felt compelled to abandon the Santa Cruz River valley between Santa Cruz in Sonora and the pueblos of San Xavier del Bac and Tucson. Apache attacks drove the settlers from Fronteras as well, though only for a few months.[24]

Citizen militias lightened this near state of siege by a few victories, as in early June of 1832, when two hundred volunteers claimed twenty-one Apache warriors slain after a four-hour battle in the gorge of Aravaipa Creek. There were other brief campaigns in the 1840s and at least one more battle in Aravaipa Canyon. An affair near Calabasas in 1853 saw sixty Mexican lancers and forty peaceful Apaches from Tucson rush upon two hundred hostile Indians. With a blast from their bugle,

> The Mexican cavalry charged right into the herd of Indians and it was almost all over, so suddenly were they routed, the savages having been taken completely by surprise. We rushed over to pay our friends the little grudge we owed them, but by the time we ran the 500 yards the Mexican cavalry were a half mile beyond us, lancing and killing the rascals, . . . Their allies, the Tucson Apaches, were butchering and mutilating those who were left wounded behind. . . .The carnage was awful.[25]

Such a complete rout was exceptional, and the Apaches occasionally evened the score, as at the water hole called Las Mestenas, where they cut down fifteen Tucson soldiers.[26] U.S. Army parties who crossed southeastern Arizona in 1846–48 found an impoverished population with few resources for its defense, fearful that the next Apache assault might be the final one.

5
THE EARLY UNITED STATES PERIOD, 1846–1863

The mountain man James Ohio Pattie, together with his father Sylvester and five companions, may have been the first Americans to trap along the Gila River and, incidentally, to visit Arizona. Although forced to leave their beaver pelts behind, the stories they brought back to Santa Fe in the spring of 1826 started a stampede. At least four different groups of trappers invaded the Gila country that fall. James Pattie returned with the party led by Michel Robidoux, all but three of whom were massacred by the Papago Indians. Two well-known mountain men, "Old Bill" Williams and Ceran St. Vrain, led another party of sixteen trappers.

These fur hunters marked the beginning of Anglo-American penetration into southern Arizona. Over the next thirty years trappers and traders, followed by bounty hunters, then by *filibusteros* promoting revolution in Mexico, paraded through the Gila and Santa Cruz valleys. The Mexican grip on this country grew weaker.[1]

The Mexican War and the Forty-Niners

In May of 1846 the United States recognized itself at war with Mexico. The Mexican War and its aftermath were to have profound effects on southeastern Arizona. During the first summer, Brigadier General Stephen Watts Kearny led his fifteen-hundred-man Army of the West down the Santa Fe Trail to Santa Fe, New Mexico. There he proclaimed U.S. sovereignty over New Mexico, which at that time included all of Arizona north of the Gila River. Kearny and one hundred picked troops then started for California, guided by the former mountain man Kit Carson. They headed down the Rio Grande and turned westward toward the headwaters of the Gila River, along a trail suitable only for pack animals. This column made a rapid march down the Gila, meeting only Indians and a party of Mexican couriers along the way. The two mountain howitzers with Kearny became the first wheeled vehicles to cross Arizona. On November 25, 1846, his dragoons forded the Colorado River and entered California, having taken just a month to traverse southern Arizona.[2]

Five days after Kearny had crossed the Colorado, Lieutenant Colonel Philip St. George Cooke led his Mormon Battalion into the southeastern corner of Arizona via Guadalupe Pass. These soldiers, volunteers who had been recruited among the Mormon camps in Iowa, were emigrants as well, who hoped to find a land where their brethren could come and settle. Two widely-known mountain men, Pauline Weaver and Antoine Leroux, accompanied these 340 men and thirty wagons. They pioneered a wagon road across New Mexico and southern Arizona closely parallel to the present international boundary as far as the San Pedro River, in fact following the old *camino real* between the former Spanish provinces of Nueva Vizcaya and Sonora.

At the San Pedro, Colonel Cooke turned north and marched downstream to the vicinity of the later town of Charleston, where the battalion fought its only engagement, the so-called Battle of the Bulls. This involved an estimated sixty to eighty wild bulls, huge animals owned by the now-departed Mexican *rancheros* of the San Pedro Valley. The soldiers' muskets decided that encounter, after a wild free-for-all in which the bulls charged men, mules, and wagons alike. The Mormon Battalion then passed on to Tucson, where the Mexican commander had diplomatically marched his troops out of town.[3]

Late in 1848 Major Lawrence P. Graham led a column of troops from Monterrey in Mexico to Los Angeles, California, crossing Arizona by still another route. They paralleled Cooke's trail from Guadalupe Pass west to the San Pedro, but instead of turning north, the soldiers continued west to Santa Cruz, Sonora, then followed the Santa Cruz Valley by way of Tumacácori, Tubac, and San Xavier to Tucson. Since the United States and Mexico were now at peace, the Mexican *comandante* at Tucson made Graham's troops welcome. Shortly after this expedition passed, the Apaches forced everyone south of San Xavier to leave the valley.[4]

The Treaty of Guadalupe Hidalgo, signed on February 2, 1848, and approved in July, ended the Mexican War and ceded more than a half million square miles of former Mexican territory to the United States. These lands included all of Arizona north of the Gila River; everything south of the Gila remained part of the Mexican state of Sonora.

With the ink scarcely dry on the treaty, the discovery of gold in California sent many parties of forty-niners from the eastern United States westward along the so-called southern or Gila route to the goldfields. As one contemporary explained it, "[t]he emigrants from Arkansas and Texas all take the southern route, by way of El Paso; while those from the more northern States go by way of Independence and the Great Salt Lake."[5] Some of the emigrants followed Kearny's trail down the Gila, but the most popular route was Cooke's wagon road. The goldseekers traveled this road as far as the San

"Pass at the Pitoncillo," probably Stein's Pass, with the Chiricahua Mountains in the distance. Watercolor by Seth Eastman, 1851. (Courtesy, the Museum of Art, Rhode Island School of Design. Gift of the RISD Library.)

Pedro River crossing and from there continued west to the Santa Cruz River in the path of Major Graham's column.[6]

One party of forty-niners may have pioneered what soon became the thirty-second parallel or Overland Mail route. The self-styled Frémont Association entered Arizona through Stein's Pass in the Peloncillo Mountains just east of modern San Simon, Arizona, headed west across the San Simon Valley to the old Puerto del Dado [Apache Pass] that separated the Chiricahua and Dos Cabesas ranges, crossed the Willcox basin to Nugent's Pass between the Winchester Mountains and the Steele Hills, then passed down Tres Alamos Wash to the San Pedro River and on into Tucson.[7]

These parties traveled well-armed and alert for Apache attacks, but none of them met serious trouble. The Indians kept their distance. The gold hunters did not always employ guides or bother to learn many of the place-names, so their journals often give little information about the country. The southern routes to California continued in use through the 1850s.

The Great Surveys

The Treaty of Guadalupe Hidalgo provided for a Joint Boundary Commission, charged with determining and marking the boundary between the United States and Mexico. Mexico sent General Pedro García Condé as its commissioner. U.S. President Zachary Taylor selected the scholarly John Russell Bartlett from Rhode Island, a man with solid Whig political credentials, as the United States representative.

John R. Bartlett and the Boundary Controversy

The Rio Grande formed the boundary between Mexico and Texas, but the Disturnell map attached to the treaty specified the initial point for beginning a survey westward toward California. This map, although probably the best of its time, had placed the entire Southwest too far to the north and west with respect to longitude and latitude. Bartlett and his Mexican counterpart negotiated an agreement that put the initial point forty-two miles north of El Paso, Texas, nearly opposite Doña Ana, New Mexico.

This compromise, reached on April 24, 1851, lost the United States a strip of land some 35 miles in width and over 175 miles in length. The official surveyor for the United States, A. B. Gray, refused to endorse the Bartlett-Condé understanding on the initial point. Gray argued that the land lost to the United States contained the only practical route for a southern transcontinental railroad. The technical staff on the commission supported Gray. It was their protests that ultimately doomed this attempt to agree upon a boundary.

Bartlett rode out the political storm that broke over the boundary controversy and stayed in office even after Congress refused to recognize his unpopular agreement with Condé. For a year and a half, while the U.S. commissioner was in the field, he dashed about with his military escort and civilian retinue, examining Indian ruins, viewing the natives, inspecting geologic formations, flora and fauna, and even rescuing a hapless maiden, Señorita Inez Gonzales, from the local Apaches.

While the survey was well-financed, it eventually ran out of money and had to halt work. By the end of 1852, the waste, mismanagement, and use of public funds for personal junkets gave the outgoing administration in Wash-

Guadalupe Pass, Cooke's Road, Sonora—sepia wash by John R. Bartlett, 1851. (Courtesy, the John Carter Brown Library at Brown University.)

ington ample cause to dismiss their commissioner. What Bartlett accomplished during most of 1851 and 1852 was to collect enough material for a two-volume study that became a classic travelogue, one of the most fascinating compilations about the Southwest ever published.

Bartlett's entourage first entered Arizona through Guadalupe Pass, then turned south to visit the old presidio town of Fronteras in Sonora, before wending its way on to the former capital of Sonora at Arispe. The party made a leisurely return to its base in southwestern New Mexico, to find the monotony there broken by the arrival of the beautiful fourteen-year-old Inez Gonzales, whom the Apaches had abducted from her home in Mexico. The infatuated Bartlett purchased the girl from her captors and then deemed it his duty to restore her to her parents. After meeting again with General Condé to put the survey back on track, Bartlett set off on a forty-four-day odyssey through southeastern Arizona that eventually found his party lost along the San Pedro. Here his chief astronomer, Colonel J. D. Graham, came to the rescue. The troop then proceeded up the Babocomari River, south across the Canelo Hills, and into Santa Cruz, Sonora, to a tear-filled reunion with Inez's family. These adventures all transpired by late September of 1851. Meanwhile commission members actually involved with marking the boundary had proceeded along the Gila River, quite remote from the scenes of knight-errantry.

Bartlett came down with typhoid fever and spent the winter of 1851–52 in California. By the following May, he was ready for the field again. This time the official party entered Arizona from the west and worked its way up the Gila River, visiting both Indian villages and prehistoric settlements. At Casa Grande they turned south to Tucson and then followed the Santa Cruz River to Tubac, where the New England puritan was shocked to find Inez now living with the captain of the garrison. Commissioner Bartlett and his retinue continued on to Santa Cruz, Sonora, again, then wandered across northern Mexico to arrive in El Paso on August 17, 1851.

By this time the commission had expended over $200,000 of public money and had accomplished little beyond the survey of the Gila River portion of the boundary. Two years later the publication of Bartlett's *Personal Narrative* atoned for much of this earlier extravagance.[8]

The Gadsden Purchase

In the summer of 1853, the new Democratic administration in Washington sought to purchase enough of the lands in dispute to provide a good southern route to California. Colonel James Gadsden went to Mexico as the American negotiator. His efforts met with success, and the signatories put their names to the Gadsden Treaty (known as the Treaty of Mesilla in Mexico) on December 30, 1853. Four months later the U.S. Senate ratified the treaty.

In Arizona the Gadsden Purchase added 27,305 square miles of land south of the Gila River to the United States. The commissioner chosen to mark the new boundary was Major William H. Emory. Emory had first seen Arizona as a lieutenant with General Kearny, and he was already known as an enthusiastic supporter of a southern transcontinental railroad. He began the boundary survey in December 1854 and completed it without incident or interruption in October of the following year. Emory's work marked the boundary as it is today, with durable monuments of stone and iron, and also resulted in a three-volume report composed mainly of scientific papers on the new country.

The last formalities were completed on June 25, 1856. By this time the last Mexican soldiers had already left Tucson. That November several companies of the 1st U.S. Dragoons arrived and set up a temporary post at Camp Moore, on the Santa Cruz River near the old settlement of Calabasas. There they raised the American flag and took possession of the settled portions of Arizona.[9]

Lieutenant Parke's Railroad Survey

Hardly had the Gadsden Treaty been signed when the U.S. Army's Corps of Topographical Engineers began its most ambitious project yet: a series of surveys across the western United States to identify routes for a railroad to the Pacific coast. Major Emory himself was a member of the Topographical Engineers, the army's smallest and most elite corps, which consisted of thirty-six officers skilled as engineers, scientists, and geographers. Lieutenant John G. Parke of the corps was selected to investigate a possible railroad line between the Pima Indian villages on the Gila River and El Paso, Texas. By January of 1854 Parke's expedition was underway.

The lieutenant set off with orders to obtain information on the grades, roadbeds, passes, and extent of the resources that could support construction of a railroad. During February and March, he followed a cut-off version of the Thirty-second Parallel route called Nugent's Wagon Road. This led from the Pima Villages to Tucson along the approximate alignment of the Southern Pacific Railroad today. Parke's people continued from Tucson to the southeast, paralleling Pantano Wash, then bore east to strike the San Pedro River near Tres Alamos. From Tres Alamos their trail led eastward through Nugent's Pass between the Winchester Mountains and the Steele Hills, thence across the Willcox basin and through the passage (still being called the Puerto del Dado) between the Chiricahua and Dos Cabesas ranges. After crossing the San Simon Valley, they headed into New Mexico through Stein's Pass, the route of both the Southern Pacific and Interstate 10 today.

Parke returned to southern Arizona in the summer of 1855 and discovered two alternative routes, both with advantages over his original choice. One of these skirted the slopes of the Pinaleños and followed the valley of Aravaipa Creek to the San Pedro, continuing down that river to the Gila. The second went through Nugent's Pass to the San Pedro, then north along that stream to the Gila River. Parke's major achievement was locating what he called Railroad Pass, the gap between the bases of Mount Graham and the Dos Cabesas range. When a railroad was built across southern Arizona, twenty-five years later, it ran through Railroad Pass.[10]

A. B. Gray and the Texas Western Railroad

Private interests were at work as well. Early in 1854 the Texas Western Railroad Company sent A. B. Gray, the surveyor on Bartlett's boundary com-

First camping-ground in Aravaipa Canyon—photo by William A. Bell, Kansas Pacific Railroad survey, November 22, 1867. (Courtesy, Colorado Historical Society, Negative No. F-28149.)

mission, to locate a proposed rail line across southern Arizona. Gray accomplished this and also produced another interesting and well-illustrated travelogue, with supporting technical data. His artist's sketches survive only as engravings, the originals unfortunately having been lost in a fire.

The survey recommended two alternatives, one essentially the same as Parke's 1854 route. The second alternative crossed the southern end of the Chiricahua range at what Gray called the Pass of the Dome, which was probably Silver Creek gap, between the Perillo and Pedregosa mountains. In the twentieth century this became the route of the El Paso and Southwestern Railroad. Gray's survey continued westward across the Sulphur Springs Valley and reached the San Pedro River by Mule Pass, thence via the valleys of the Babocomari River and Sonoita Creek to Tubac. From Tubac the line led down the Santa Cruz to Tucson and on to the Pima Villages. Although

Aravaipa Canyon, southern Arizona—photo by William A. Bell, Kansas Pacific Railroad survey, 1867. (Courtesy, Colorado Historical Society, Negative No. F-7315.)

the Texas Western never laid a mile of track, most of Gray's second alternative was subsequently used by segments of three railroads.[11]

William A. Bell and the Kansas Pacific Railway

Another private survey, this one for the Kansas Pacific Railway Company, took place a decade later, but the principal report followed the style of Bartlett's *Personal Narrative.* Indeed William Bell subtitled his book "A Journal of Travel and Adventure." In any event this survey party saw a lot of southern Arizona in November and December of 1867 and established distances for a number of prospective rail lines. Bell was the expedition's photographer, and he took some of the earliest photographs of that country.

The choice for a Kansas Pacific route was to use Runk's Pass, located twelve

Saguaro cacti in Aravaipa Canyon, southern Arizona—photo by William A. Bell, Kansas Pacific Railroad survey, 1867. (Courtesy, Colorado Historical Society, Negative No. F-7314.)

miles south of Stein's Pass in the Peloncillos, and Railroad Pass, which Bell found to be the highway for Apaches living north of the Gila River when they set off to pillage Sonora. From Railroad Pass one reconnaissance party pushed west through Nugent's Pass and then down the San Pedro; another examined Aravaipa Canyon to its junction with the San Pedro Valley. The surveyors next removed to Tucson and explored routes south into Mexico.[12] Only the Railroad Pass segment was eventually used for a rail line.

James Leach and the El Paso and Fort Yuma Wagon Road

Long before a railroad crossed southern Arizona, the U.S. Congress paid for the construction of a wagon road. Early in 1857 Congress put the Department of

The cañada of the Aravaipa, southern Arizona—photo by William A. Bell, Kansas Pacific Railroad survey, 1867. (Courtesy, Colorado Historical Society, Negative No. F-7313.)

the Interior into the business of building roads for California-bound emigrants. One such route was the Leach, or the El Paso and Fort Yuma, Wagon Road, surveyed and built between late October 1857 and October 1, 1858.

James B. Leach, the superintendent of construction, entered Arizona through Doubtful Canyon in the Peloncillos, about eight miles north of present-day Interstate 10. His route went across the San Simon Valley, through Railroad Pass, and traversed the Sulphur Springs Valley to Nugent's Pass. West of there it descended to the San Pedro, some thirteen miles below where Parke's survey had struck the river, and proceeded downstream along the east bank to the mouth of Aravaipa Creek. At that point travelers forded the San Pedro and continued west for another forty-seven miles to the Gila River.

Construction consisted of side-hill cuttings and embankments in the hilly areas, with simple grading and clearing of brush, boulders, and timber elsewhere. The result was a road eighteen feet wide on the straight sections and twenty-five feet wide on the curves. Wells, tanks, and a reservoir were constructed to reduce the length of the waterless stretches. The Leach road was completed just in time for sections of it to be used by John Butterfield's Overland Mail Company. The El Paso and Fort Yuma project nearly dissolved in financial chaos, and Leach himself, an experienced contractor, was indicted later for falsifying vouchers to defraud the government. The outbreak of the Civil War saved him from prosecution.[13]

Stage Lines Across Southern Arizona

The San Antonio and San Diego Mail Line

On June 22, 1857 James E. Birch of the California Stage Company contracted with the Post Office Department to carry the mail between San Antonio, Texas, and San Diego, California, a distance of 1,476 miles. For this he was to receive an annual subsidy of $149,800. Within days Birch set about organizing the San Antonio and San Diego Mail Line, more popularly known as "The Jackass Mail."

The new express line was required to run on a thirty-day schedule twice a month between its terminal points in Texas and California. The first mails left San Antonio on July 9 and 24, 1857, and arrived in San Diego together on August 31st. Thereafter the dispatches were made bimonthly from both ends. The earliest record of eastbound passenger service dates to the first week of November 1857, while the sixth mail from San Antonio brought four through passengers to San Diego on October 19th. The fare from San Antonio to San Diego was $200. Provisions for the passengers were erratic, and the firm used a variety of conveyances, including Concord stages, light-covered wagons called ambulances, and a type of light stage with a wood-framed canvas top known as a mud-wagon or celerity wagon.

Birch died at sea very early in the line's operation. Control of the firm passed to George H. Giddings, who already operated a San Antonio–to–Santa Fe stage line, and to Robert Doyle, who had been Birch's chief agent in California. Initially the company maintained regular stations only at San Antonio, El Paso, and San Diego, with a brush hut and corral at Maricopa Wells, Arizona, for a resident agent and cook. Elsewhere they used established military posts and civilian towns or ranches as additional stops. The operation was a flexible one, and if traffic warranted, a mail dispatch might consist of two or three coaches or wagons, accompanied by armed escorts riding alongside. Until intermediate stations were added, a herd of mules driven in company with the vehicles allowed teams to be switched with this *caballada* from time to time. The stages carried food for the passengers, and at night everyone stopped and camped. The diary of Phocion Way gives a graphic view of this enterprise in operation.[14]

According to Silas St. John, who worked for the San Antonio and San Diego line during its first year, their stages went from Tucson via the San Xavier mission to the north point of the Whetstone range, thence to the San Pedro about seven miles above present-day Benson, and on to Dragoon Springs. East of Dragoon Springs the drivers dodged from water hole to water hole to Apache Pass and from there across the San Simon Valley to Doubtful Canyon.[15]

Passengers at the end of their journey were likely to be weary and out of sorts. Phocion Way, tortured by a long ride from San Antonio, instantly labeled Tucson "this God forsaken town." Nor was he any more pleased with the mail company's service: "The mail company do not run their stages farther than here, and those who paid their passage through must ride over a sandy waste on mule back and furnish the mule themselves, or stay here and get the fever and ague. This is a most rascally imposition and the company will very likely have to pay for it."[16]

The San Antonio and San Diego Mail Line was the first transcontinental venture in staging. It began in haste, and the proprietors never quite worked out the kinks in their operation. In October of 1858 the postmaster general terminated Gidding's contract for the section between El Paso and Fort Yuma, at the same time increasing the subsidy to $196,488 a year for a weekly mail run over the two segments between San Antonio and El Paso and from Fort Yuma to San Diego. The line continued to carry passengers across Arizona. In the spring of 1861 an effort to reestablish service over the entire distance met with the spectacular disaster recounted at the end of the next section.[17]

The Butterfield Overland Mail

Few ventures were as well-publicized at the time or have captured the public imagination more than the Overland Mail Company, usually called the Butterfield Overland Mail. John Butterfield, one of the founders of the American Express Company, was a successful promoter and the owner of express firms in New York state. On September 16, 1857, Butterfield and his associates signed a six-year contract with the postmaster general to provide a semiweekly mail service between St. Louis, Missouri, and San Francisco, for $600,000 per year. They had one year in which to begin operations. The distance as of 1860–61 was some 2,888 miles, almost twice the length of Birch's line.[18]

During the year following the award of the contract, the company built 141 stations (and subsequently added about 60 more), purchased a hundred coaches, a thousand horses, five hundred mules, and recruited nearly eight hundred men. The first eastbound stage left San Francisco on September 15, 1858, and the first mail west departed St. Louis on September 16. Trips averaged from twenty-one to twenty-three days, with some requiring only nineteen. Through passengers heading east paid $100 in gold at San Francisco, while the fare for westbound travelers was $200. Meals came extra. Letters sent by way of the Overland Mail cost 10¢ per half-ounce.

This well-financed ($2 million) and well-organized operation established stations at average intervals of eighteen to twenty miles. In 1860 the company advertised this table of distances across southeastern Arizona:

Tucson to Cienega	30 miles
Cienega to San Pedro	25
San Pedro to Dragoon Springs	21
Dragoon Springs to Ewell Station	25
Ewell Station to Apache Pass	15
Apache Pass to San Cimona [Simon]	18
San Cimona to Steen's [Steins] Peak[19]	13

Early in the line's operation, one eastbound traveler observed that "[t]he stations, after leaving Tucson, are large square enclosures, with adobe walls. Rifles, shot-guns, revolvers and muskets, heavily charged, and at convenient places, are the objects that first strike attention, upon entering them; and the four or five men who are in attendance, appear always on the alert against the attacks of Indians."[20]

Not all of the stations were built of adobe; at Dragoon Springs a postal inspector found a stone enclosure measuring 45 by 55 feet. Silas St. John, head of the construction crew for the Tucson-to–El Paso division, nearly lost his life there when he and six assistants remained to complete the structure, roofing the storeroom and residence portion. At midnight on September 8, 1858, St. John changed the guard, then returned to his room. About 1:00 A.M. he heard a commotion; his three Mexican laborers attacked the other three assistants and killed them, leaving St. John with his arm severed at the elbow and a deep cut in his thigh. For three days there was no help or water, until:

> Mr. Archibald, correspondent for the *Memphis Avalanche,* arrived on [the San Antonio and San Diego] mail stage on way from Tucson to Rio Grande. He was left with St. John. Soon after three wagons of the Leach party approached from the east. Col. Leach, Maj. Hutton and some other veterans. They dressed the wounds and started an express for Ft. Buchanan by way of Tucson. They reached the fort on Wednesday following. Dr. B. J. D. Irwin started with escort and reached Dragoon, Friday, the 9th day after St. John was wounded. Arm was amputated at socket. Six days later St. John got into a wagon and rode to the fort.[21]

Newspapers at the time gave the incident wide publicity. Silas St. John's days with the construction crew were over, but he had an active and productive life for another sixty-one years.

"Home" stations on the Butterfield route furnished meals and did necessary maintenance, while the smaller "swing" stations provided a change of teams only. Four and six-mule teams pulled celerity wagons through the mountains. Elsewhere Spanish horses from California, wild but with great endurance, drew the coaches at speeds of up to fourteen miles per hour. The average pace was five miles an hour, with the teams being changed at every station. The stages rolled around the clock.[22]

In Arizona the only significant difference between the San Antonio–to–-San Diego and the Butterfield routes was the latter's elimination of a stop at San Xavier. For almost two and a half years, both lines crossed Arizona; a Butterfield passenger even commented upon the novel method that the San Diego firm used to collect its mules (sounding a gong) when both stages happened to be at the San Simon station.[23]

Officially the Overland Mail Company service ended on March 2, 1861, when Congress authorized the postmaster general to discontinue the southern route and make a new contract to carry the mail over the central route through Denver, Salt Lake City, and Sacramento. Three days later Texas withdrew from the Union. The last mail to the east was made up at Tucson and left there on March 6; the last mail from the east left for San Francisco early in April. Company personnel were still moving stock and equipment to California as late as June of that year.[24]

In April and May of 1861, George Giddings made an attempt to restore service over the southern route. He had received a contract for his San Antonio and San Diego Mail Line to carry mail once again from San Antonio to California. As he recalled it later, this was part of an elaborate scheme to restore Texas to the Union. The plan fell apart, but until his mail contract was canceled, Giddings made a serious effort to reorganize the Butterfield network and acquire its remaining unsold property and stock. In the course of all this, his brother, James Giddings, and three Butterfield hands made an opening run with both the San Antonio and St. Louis mail bags. They left Mesilla, New Mexico, heading west, late in April of 1861. *The Mesilla Times* of May 11 gave a full account of what happened after they pulled out of Barney's ("Tanks") Station, east of present Lordsburg, New Mexico, on April 27:

> On the 27th a coach left the Tanks for the West, in which were five persons—Mr. J. J. Giddings, Superintendent of the San Antonio and San Diego Mail Company, Michael Nies, Road Agent, and Anthony Aldar, Samuel Neely, and Mr. Briggs, employees of the Overland Mail Company. Two of the mules which left [with] the coach returned to the Tanks Station badly bruised, and had evidently been in a severe struggle. This circumstance aroused the suspicions of all, and our informant the next day went to Fort McLane and applied for an escort of troops to investigate the matter.

Near Stein's peak the soldiers met a train of freight wagons and heard a grisly tale from the teamsters, who had just survived a running fight with the Apaches:

> They found scattered along the ravine, newspapers and other mail matter, pieces of harness, etc. The roof of the station (which was some time since abandoned) had been burnt, the corral wall had been thrown down, and the Indians had formed a breast work of it around the spring. Near the station the bodies of two men were found, tied by the feet in trees, their heads reaching within 18 inches of the ground, their arms extended and fastened to pickets, and the evidences of a slow fire under their heads. The bodies had been pierced with arrows and lances.[25]

The Stein's peak station lay along Doubtful Canyon, barely one mile east of the present Arizona line. When the army arrived, they found the remains of the stagecoach in a canyon half a mile from Stein's Peak Spring, with three bodies sprawled near it. A prominent gravestone later marked the spot, about one-third of a mile inside Arizona. The soldiers continued west and removed the livestock at the San Simon and Apache Pass stations to Dragoon Springs and the San Pedro River. Apaches followed and absconded with forty-four head of Overland Mail Company mules. Either the Indians or the mail company itself set the San Simon, Apache Pass, Dragoon Springs, and San Pedro station buildings ablaze, ending stage operations in Arizona until after the Civil War.[26]

Stein's Peak from below the stage station, Butterfield Trail in the foreground. Vegetation along the roadside is probably Apache plume, with yucca and mesquite in the middle distance. Photo by William A. Bell, Kansas Pacific Railroad survey, November 3, 1867. (Courtesy, Colorado Historical Society, Negative No. F-40600.)

Settlements and Garrisons, 1846–1861

The Overland Mail Company had a tremendous economic impact during its short life, both in drawing people to Arizona and as an employer. The firm kept about fifty people busy in Tucson alone. One traveler said that the Anglo-American population there was either connected in some way with the mining companies or employed by the Overland Mail Company.[27] Indian and Mexican residents followed more traditional occupations by farming and raising livestock.

The stage stations did not become the nuclei for settlements, however, and Arizona's frontiers during the late 1850s remained close to where they had been for the previous century. Miners and others had reoccupied the old towns of Tubac, Tumacácori, and Calabasas on the upper Santa Cruz. There were mining camps at Arivaca, Cerro Colorado, Santa Rita, and the Mowry Mine. Ranchers and farmers had scattered out along Sonoita Creek, and by 1861 there were farmers in the San Pedro Valley as well, but "not over fifty persons" according to one newspaper correspondent.[28] Nearly everyone lived in the valleys, and settlers often stayed but a short time at any one place. As one historian wrote later, "This restless, almost nomadic, life was characteristic of the time and reminds us of the story of [William] Kirkland, another pioneer of that day, of whom it was said that after he had lived a short time in one place his chickens would come up and suggest another move by turning over on their backs to have their legs tied!"[29]

When the United States established its authority over the Arizona portion of the Gadsden Purchase, the army sent Major Enoch Steen with four companies of the 1st U.S. Dragoons. The major and his troops arrived in November 1856 and set up a temporary camp near Calabasas on the Santa Cruz River. This spot, which they named Camp Moore, offered superior grazing, an abundance of water, proximity to timber, and ready access to flour, corn, and other foodstuffs from nearby Sonora. During their six-months stay, the soldiers lived in tents and in *jacales,* the latter being shanties made of logs set upright in the ground and roofed with dirt. Food was cheap and abundant. Even London ale and champagne were to be had at $6 per dozen, until an American filibustering expedition met a disastrous finale in western Sonora and most trade with the United States ceased for awhile. Indians at this time were not troublesome.

Captain Richard S. "Baldy" Ewell, later a Confederate general but at the time commanding one of the dragoon companies at Camp Moore, was ordered to find a more suitable location for a military post. He recommended a site on Sonoita Creek, about 3.5 miles west of modern Sonoita, Arizona, where the garrison would be in a better position to protect settlers. Major Steen approved Ewell's selection and began removing his camp to the new site, named Fort Buchanan, during the first week in June 1857.[30]

Fort Buchanan lay on a small plateau with a marsh, or *ciénega,* around it on three sides. The troops there sought to protect both settlers and miners, but scarcely a year had passed before one official said that "its present location is the very worst which could have been chosen."[31] The post surgeon agreed; Fort Buchanan had become a fever pit. Since its occupation, nearly every person at the post had contracted malaria.[32]

The garrison stayed nonetheless. Storerooms, workshops, laundresses' quarters, and most of the structures occupied by officers and men were built of upright logs chinked with mud and covered by flat, earth-covered roofs. The hospital and two sets of officers' quarters were of adobe. To protect his horses, Captain Ewell had an adobe corral 100 feet square erected. These buildings lay scattered over a distance of half a mile. When the department commander inspected Fort Buchanan, he was not impressed: "The post is built more like a village than a military post."[33]

This fort had an active life of little more than four years. During most of that time, Indian affairs were quiet, except for depredations on livestock. Captain Ewell and his three companies of the 1st Dragoons did figure prominently when Colonel B. L. E. Bonneville launched his Gila River Expedition, even though Ewell confessed in a private letter that he would rather be raising potatoes and cabbages than chasing Indians at the orders of men who didn't know what to do. On June 27, 1857, Ewell's dragoons led the charge when Bonneville's two columns fell upon an unsuspecting camp of Coyotero Apaches, slaying an estimated thirty-seven or thirty-eight warriors and taking twenty-seven women and children captive. The camp lay on the Gila River, thirty-five miles north of Mount Graham. At least one officer thought these Indians had been guilty of nothing more than getting in the way, but it was subsequently learned that they had attacked parties on the road to California.[34]

To overawe the Indians into staying peaceful, the Buchanan garrison would go on patrols and respond to any raids or other provocations. Occasionally a scouting party got into a fight, as on March 11, 1858, when thirty troopers of Company G, 1st Dragoons, clashed with an Apache band in the Huachuca Mountains and left one Indian dead.[35] Ten months later three discharged sergeants and their wives were traveling east from Fort Buchanan when a Pinal Apache war party attacked them at Whetstone Springs, eighteen miles from the fort. Two soldiers were soon killed, while the third one made his escape; the wives, however, seized their husbands' revolvers and fought off the attackers, until another party of travelers "arrived at the scene opportunely enough to save them."[36]

There was a Pinal campaign out of Fort Buchanan later in 1859, with "Baldy" Ewell and two companies of his 1st Dragoons forming part of the sweep. On December 24 his men had a battle in the Pinal Mountains that left six Apaches slain, while Captain W. L. Elliott's company of the Regiment of Mounted Riflemen got into one fight north of Dragoon Springs on December 3 and a second one fifteen days later, some thirty miles northwest of the springs. On December 18 the Indians scattered when they heard the soldiers coming, but lost two warriors and the livestock they were driving back from Sonora. Pressure of this kind persuaded the Pinal Apaches to come in to Fort Buchanan and make peace.[37]

In March 1860 the Tonto Apaches raided a lumber camp at Madera Canyon in the Santa Ritas, abducting a woman and a ten-year-old girl. "Baldy" Ewell rode to the rescue, only to find that the raiders had escaped. He recovered the little girl through negotiations, even as the woman, Mrs. Larcena Page, was driven along by her captors until she grew exhausted and lagged behind. The Apaches thrust at her with their lances, then threw her over a ledge and pelted her with rocks, leaving her for dead in the hills just east of modern-day Helvetia, Arizona. She revived and in a fourteen-day ordeal managed to crawl back through the mountains to the lumber camp.[38]

The pace of Apache depredations picked up in the fall of 1860 and soon became a reign of terror (a very nearly successful one) to drive the settlers out of southern Arizona and southwestern New Mexico. These hostilities grew out of a complex background. In northwestern New Mexico the army had been pushing the Navajos south and west from their homeland; their displacement in turn put pressure on the Pinal and Coyotero Apaches to the south. Meanwhile gold discoveries in southwestern New Mexico during the summer of 1860 caused miners to flood into that country and disturb the native Apaches there. Water to work the placers was scarce that fall, and out-of-work miners formed one or more "ranger" companies to go on Indian hunts. Tucson periodically had "ranger" companies as well. The activities of these vigilante groups were inciting the southern Apaches even before the Bascom Affair.[39]

The most notorious single incident in pre–Civil War Arizona was the Bascom Affair, the "Sixteen Days at Apache Pass" between February 3 and 19, 1861. The episode began when raiders of the Pinal band abducted a young Mexican boy from a ranch in the Sonoita Valley. The army's efforts to recover him led to a confrontation at the Butterfield station in Apache Pass, with five hundred Chiricahua and Coyotero Apache warriors under Cochise, acknowledged leader of the Chokonen band of the Chiricahuas, and Francisco, the Coyotero chief, facing second Lieutenant George Bascom and his company of infantrymen. Both sides took hostages, and Bascom sought to hold the great Chiricahua leader as well, but Cochise rushed past the guards. Negotiations proved fruitless, and the Apaches murdered their prisoners before withdrawing. The army retaliated by hanging six Indian captives. The whole affair received wide publicity in the newspapers and helped to launch a decade-long Indian war.[40]

Soon after the Bascom Affair, the Overland Mail Company began aban-

Apache Pass from Fort Bowie—photo by William A. Bell, Kansas Pacific Railroad survey, 1867. (Courtesy, Colorado Historical Society, Negative Nos. F-7016, F-28151.)

doning its route through the Southwest by order of the government. The Apaches saw the affair at Apache Pass and the departure of the mail line as cause and effect instead of coincidence. Sensing victory they began a campaign to kill or push out all of the settlers in southern Arizona. Stage stations came under increasing attack as the only points of settlement between the San Pedro River in Arizona and the Mimbres Valley in southwestern New Mexico.

At Fort Buchanan the climax came on June 22, 1861, when Cochise led upwards of a hundred men and ran off a herd grazing about a mile south of the post. The Apaches killed two guards and drove the mule herd toward Mexico, turning the cattle in the direction of the Whetstone Mountains. Lieutenant Bascom with a few troopers and two citizens set off after Cochise and the cattle. Near the Whetstones reinforcements joined Cochise's raiders, who then turned and skirmished with the outnumbered soldiers. Bascom and his men held their ground, and the Indians eventually withdrew, suffering four killed and several wounded to one soldier wounded.[41]

Eight days later Special Orders No. 97 from the Department of New Mexico directed the abandonment of Fort Buchanan. The threat of a Confederate invasion had prompted the Military Department commander to pull his scattered garrisons together to mount a defense. The situation around the posts was little short of chaos, as many local citizens proclaimed their Southern sympathies and others looked for opportunities to plunder. On July 23, 1861, Fort Buchanan lay abandoned and burned.[42] Just nine days before this, the Canoa Hotel, scarcely twenty miles distant, had been the scene of a spectacular fight, when about eighty Coyotero Apaches attacked the house and left the bodies of its four defenders strewn about the yard, the building itself in ruins. William Roods, a rancher, happened by, and the Apaches took after him until he found cover in a *charco,* or mudhole, where he fought them off, leaving twelve Indians killed or wounded.[43]

As of August 8, all of the ranches, mines, and settlements in southern Arizona stood deserted, except for the Mowry Mine and Tucson.[44] The last cry for help, in the August 10, 1861 issue of the *Arizonian,* went unheeded. In the face of bandit raids, a ferocious Indian war, and an imminent Confederate invasion, the citizens were now entirely on their own.[45]

The Civil War in Arizona

By the summer of 1861 Charles D. Poston, adventurer, director of the Sonora Exploring and Mining Company, and "Father of Arizona," had been in Arizona for almost five years. He left for California about a week after the army marched out of Fort Buchanan. In Los Angeles he told a newspaper that affairs in Arizona were "deplorable in the extreme," with Apaches raiding everywhere, no security for life or property, bands of Mexican guerillas plundering the country, and all of the mining interests abandoned. Anyone who chanced to read the stark descriptions and statistics in the *Arizonian* for August 10 might have concluded that Poston even understated the situation.[46]

The Civil War itself was not an immediate concern in Arizona. Lieutenant Colonel John R. Baylor and his Texas Confederates had captured the U.S. forces in the Mesilla Valley of southern New Mexico late in July. On August 1, 1861, Baylor proclaimed a Confederate "Territory of Arizona," with himself as the governor. People around Tucson knew little of this, until veteran expressman Henry Skillman began carrying the mail west from Mesilla to San Diego under a contract with the Confederate Post Office Department. On his last trip, Skillman arrived at Tucson early in September escorted by fifteen men from the San Elizario Spy Company, a unit raised among Southern sympathizers in the El Paso area. These were the first Confederate troops that Arizonians had seen. For at least another two months, the citizens of Tucson heard only silence from the east.[47]

In mid-December Brigadier General Henry Hopkins Sibley, C.S.A., arrived in the Mesilla Valley with his Army of New Mexico, after a long march from San Antonio, Texas. There he joined his forces with the troops already at hand, under Lieutenant Colonel Baylor. These now included Captain Sherod Hunter's locally raised company of Arizona volunteers, many of whom had worked for the Overland Mail Company or had lived in the Tucson area. Hunter himself was a Tennessee native, but he had been in southern New Mexico at least since 1857.[48]

Sibley marched up the Rio Grande Valley in New Mexico to victory at Valverde and then to defeat at Glorieta. At the same time, he sent Captain Hunter and his men west to take post "at some point near Tucson." The citizens there were believed to be pro-Southern, and the mineral wealth of that country was well known. Hunter also had instructions to open communications with southern California and to watch for an invasion from the west. During the march to Tucson, snowstorms buffeted his company and one man, Benjamin Mays, died at the San Simon crossing. When his command reached Tucson on February 28, 1862, the people hailed its arrival.[49]

Hunter tarried only briefly before going on to the Pima Villages on the Gila River. There he captured a captain of the California Volunteers with nine of his men, a Federal scouting party that had ventured east from Fort Yuma on the Colorado River, where a Union army was being assembled to retake the Southwest. Some of the Confederates pushed west down the Gila River to the old Butterfield stop at Stanwix Station and exchanged shots with two Union pickets in the westernmost skirmish of the Civil War.[50]

Out in Los Angeles, Colonel James H. Carleton heard about Hunter's Confederates entering Tucson. Scarcely two weeks after their arrival, Carleton ordered the first units of his twenty-three-hundred-man California Column east from Fort Yuma. On April 15 the Californians' advance guard ran into a Confederate picket post at Picacho Peak, northwest of Tucson, losing an officer and two men in the skirmish known as the Battle of Picacho Pass. Rumors flew on both sides about the strength of the opposition.

The California troops pulled back and two weeks later resumed a cautious advance. This time they selected a route up the Gila River to the San Pedro, where they reoccupied old Fort Breckenridge, a short-lived post on the lower course of this river, renaming it Fort Stanford. They continued into Tucson via the Cañada del Oro and arrived on May 20, 1862, more than two weeks after Hunter's men had left.[51]

The retreating Confederates had to fight their way past Dragoon Springs, where the Apaches attacked them and reportedly caused the loss of forty horses, thirty-five mules, and all of the wagons.[52] One prolific correspondent in the California Column described what he saw at Dragoon Springs as of June 23:

> 23d.—At Dragoon Springs found water scarce, but sufficient by using with care and patience. At night the surrounding mountains were alive with Indian fires. Near the stage station are the graves of Hunter's men, killed by the Apaches. On the graves were these inscriptions, neatly cut in rough stone, executed by one of the Union prisoners they had along: "S. Ford, May 5th, 1862" "Ricardo". Ford was a Sergeant, and Ricardo was a poor Mexican boy the Texans had forced into service at Tucson.[53]

Carleton, now a brigadier general, pushed east again toward the Rio Grande and New Mexico. His columns never caught up with the retreating Confederates but found themselves opposed by hostile Indians at Apache Pass. In a confusing incident on June 25, some sixty Apaches managed to kill, scalp, and mutilate three soldiers, hold a parley with the lieutenant colonel in command, and then flee when shooting broke out again.[54]

The Californians kept on toward the Rio Grande, crossing the southern deserts by detachments in consequence of the scarcity of water. On July 15 Captain Thomas Roberts led his contingent of 126 California Volunteers into the west entrance of Apache Pass, where an unknown number of Indians under the chiefs Mangas Colorado and Cochise lay in wait behind rock breastworks overlooking the approaches to a spring. As Roberts's troops advanced, the Apaches fired down on them. The Californians had brought a section (two guns) of mountain howitzers along. They now moved these guns up and commenced bombarding the Apache fortifications. The soldiers advanced under cover of the exploding shells and chased them away. The next day, as Roberts put it, he "[h]ad to repeat the performance of yesterday to obtain water." Once again his men drove the Indians out, then secured the spring and forced their way through Apache Pass. Ten Indians were reported killed, while two soldiers died and two were wounded. Carleton left a military post in the pass, naming it Fort Bowie.[55]

Once arrived in Santa Fe, General Carleton assumed command of the Military Department of New Mexico and appointed Brigadier General Joseph West to head a district that included Arizona. Desperadoes and suspected Confederate sympathizers, including Sylvester Mowry, proprietor of the Mowry silver mine, and a Tucson merchant named Palatine Robinson, were hauled before a military commission for examination. California Volunteers and civilian expeditions chased Apaches in a continuation of the blow-for-blow fighting that left peace as elusive as ever. For several more years, the Indians ruled southern Arizona outside of Tucson. A single rancher, Pete Kitchen, stayed on in his fortified house on Potrero Creek in the upper Santa Cruz Valley.[56] As of 1864, the writer J. Ross Browne described the Mowry Mine as the sole mine still in operation.[57]

The Territory of Arizona

Changes were about to take place. No longer would citizens have reason to complain, as had Charles D. Poston back in 1857, that there was ". . . no government . . . no law . . . We are living in a perfect state of nature." Nor would visitors write home that "[t]he knife is the law, and the revolver justice," as did one Butterfield passenger in 1858.[58] Squatter sovereignty, on the other hand, still reigned supreme and even received official encouragement. This concept held that "Every man squats where he pleases, and uses what timber is necessary for his purposes. Each mining district has its own laws, and it is astonishing how the people quietly and peaceably obey them."[59]

In 1863 prospectors discovered gold around present-day Prescott and near Wickenburg, in north-central Arizona. The inevitable rush followed, and suddenly Arizona was no longer just the Santa Cruz Valley. This happened virtually as President Abraham Lincoln signed a bill to establish a Territory of Arizona, on February 23, 1863.[60] Eleven months later newly appointed Governor John Goodwin and a set of territorial officials reached a new post, Fort Whipple, after a long ride from Washington, D.C. Fort Whipple became the temporary seat of government until a townsite almost twenty miles to the south had been selected as the territorial capital. The new territory with its wilderness capital, Prescott, was in business.[61]

A Land of Many Frontiers

As a territory Arizona received benefits considerably more substantial than just the federal appointees who were sent to govern it. Nearly all of the territorial expenses were met by federal appropriations, including the cost of the constitutional convention in 1910.[62] Government purchases for Indian reservations and army supplies injected large amounts of money into the economy; for example, the cost to keep a single cavalry regiment in the field for a year was estimated at $1.5 million in 1865, exclusive of the original cost of the horses and arms or pay for the men.[63]

With a stable government after 1863 and hostile Indians slowly coming under control, the citizens could turn to developing the country. The opportunities lay mainly with mining and livestock raising, but to take advantage of these the mine owners and ranchers needed both financing and markets. Capital to underwrite the mining industry, for the range cattle business and eventually for railroad building came from investors outside of the territory. As for markets the federal government remonetized silver in 1878 and thereby guaranteed to purchase the output of silver mines. Mining boomed. Other post–Civil War developments in Arizona included farming, lumbering, and the expansion of transportation and commerce, so that the economic arena became much wider than it had ever been before.

For virtually the first time, the mountains of southeastern Arizona were seen as possessing resources that might be exploited. Miners, ranchers, lumbermen, farmers, and eventually recreation seekers all probed the upland areas and began viewing them as potential assets rather than as obstacles for travelers or a refuge for the Apaches. The desert ranges all displayed a broad similarity in appearance, yet they had important differences in mineralization, timber cover, and grazing prospects.

After the Civil War, it is reasonable to follow a thematic or topical approach to the history of southeastern Arizona. The topics are closely linked to the expansion of economic opportunities and are also related in some degree to the mountains. Information is uneven while certain mountain ranges are better known than others. Additional possibilities (homesteading, transportation, the important role of federal agencies in a country still sparsely populated) invite the attention of future scholars.

6
MILITARY AND INDIAN AFFAIRS, 1863–1896

The Indian wars in Arizona continued intermittently through September of 1886, when the last Chiricahua Apaches surrendered and were shipped off to Florida. Even then army patrols occasionally skirmished with off-reservation parties for another ten years. As miners and settlers arrived, the old military posts were abandoned, until today only one (Fort Huachuca) is still active.

Less than two weeks after Captain Thomas Roberts's howitzers blasted the Apaches out of the rocks overlooking Apache Pass, General Carleton found it "indispensably necessary" to establish a fort at that location. One hundred men of the 5th Infantry, California Volunteers, were left to build the new post, which was named after the colonel of their regiment, George Washington Bowie. Besides doing all of the construction, the small garrison was expected to control access to the water supplies and to the pass itself, to provide escorts for couriers and supply trains, and to attack hostile Indians whenever opportunities arose.[1]

The first Fort Bowie was a set of breastworks around a hill overlooking the spring. The soldiers lived in tents until these were blown to tatters, after which they burrowed into the hillside and sheltered themselves in huts. By 1864 an inspector described the post as "arranged without order, and so to speak, a kind of rookery." He also recommended that it be relocated to a flat, some 700 yards to the east.[2] Four years later the garrison finally moved to its new, and permanent, location.

Tucson had not been a military post since the last Mexican troops marched away in 1856. After 1862 garrisons came and went several times until July of 1866, when a troop of the 1st U.S. Cavalry arrived and established Fort Lowell. The fort itself, known as Camp Lowell after 1866, served mostly as a supply depot.[3] Down on Sonoita Creek, old Fort Buchanan was reoccupied for a time in 1865 as a vedette station, a change-over place for army express riders. On February 17 the six soldiers there had a furious battle, when a large band of Apaches attacked and soon managed to set the station house on fire. The surrounded troopers fought until the roof began to collapse, then shot their way past the Indians and escaped to Santa Rita. Fort Buchanan was subsequently abandoned.[4] Other short-lived posts along Sonoita Creek and in the upper Santa Cruz and Babocomari valleys included Fort Mason, Camp Cameron, Camp Crittenden, and Camp Wallen.

Fort Bowie, in Apache Pass—photo by William A. Bell, Kansas Pacific Railroad survey, 1867. (Courtesy, Colorado Historical Society, Negative No. F-6667.

When the California Column occupied southern Arizona, the Union troopers found themselves in the midst of an Indian war; Apache depredations continued without letup for another ten years. Until 1872 no settlers dared to live beyond the San Pedro Valley, while those who dwelt in the upper Santa Cruz and Sonoita Valleys paid a heavy price in livestock and human lives. The understrength garrisons at Fort Bowie and other army posts took to the field many times, but when peace finally came it was a result of negotiations, not of military actions.

Until 1863 only the Apaches and a few of the army's civilian scouts knew anything about southeastern Arizona away from the Overland Mail route. As one result of the renewed scouting, officers and men began to learn more about the country, and until mining boomed in the late 1870s and 1880s, army reports continued to be the main sources of information about this part of Arizona.

Captain T. T. Tidball led twenty-five California Volunteers and some citizens from Tucson in one early expedition. They marched for five days, guided by six "tame" Apaches, and at dawn on May 7, 1863, they surprised the principal ranchería of the Aravaipa Apaches in lower Aravaipa Canyon. Their assault left more than fifty Indians dead, with virtually no loss among the attackers.[5] That same year Indians ran off all of the horses at Fort Bowie and skirmished with the soldiers even in sight of the fort. Another fight took place at the San Pedro River crossing.[6]

Less than a year after Captain Tidball's success, Captain James Whitlock and sixty California Volunteers from Camp Mimbres, New Mexico, trailed a band of Indians "supposed to be the Chiricahua tribe" west into Arizona. This trail eventually led to the south end of the Pinaleño Mountains, about thirty-five miles northwest of Fort Bowie. At dawn on April 7, Whitlock charged the Indian camp, estimated at upwards of 250 people, and in an hour-long firefight, the troopers sent their adversaries fleeing. The Apaches left twenty-one dead, while the soldiers suffered no losses. The Captain wrote that he captured everything they possessed, including perhaps a ton of dried mescal and as much dried mule meat. Some of the loot from the camp was more curious, such as the copper slugs used as bullets and "arrow points enough (like these) to fill a peck measure."[7]

The Apache Expedition: Summer 1864

While Whitlock was pursuing the Chiricahuas, General Carleton sat in Santa Fe planning the last and perhaps the least-known of four major expeditions that he launched against the Apache and Navajo Indians in the years 1862–64. Expectations of mineral wealth may have motivated Carleton in this particular effort. Whatever the reasons he proposed to send a force of about five hundred men to southern Arizona to punish the Indians "who are not only very numerous but very hostile."[8]

From a new post (Fort Goodwin) situated on the Gila River about midway between the present-day cities of Safford and Globe, columns were to be sent in every direction. At the same time, troops from northwestern and southwestern New Mexico would converge on the Apaches in southeastern Arizona. Other detachments would be ordered north from Tucson and south to the Chiricahua Mountains from Fort Bowie. The idea was to harass the Apaches to such an extent that they would have nowhere to run. Then by removing them to a reservation or by exterminating the men, the country would gain a lasting peace.[9] So went the reasoning.

Carleton launched his Gila or Apache Expedition during the summer of

1864. Large numbers of troops penetrated Apache country adjoining the Gila River and to the north of it, very much along the lines envisioned, destroying corn and wheat fields and clashing several times with the Indians. Captain Julius Shaw thought that his troops reduced not less than 375 or 400 acres of corn and other crops. Captain Tidball was out again, and he reported slaying fifty-one Apaches and ruining the crops at the Indian farms as well. The Indians, however, sought to stay out of the way, and the army considered the overall results disappointing. Reports by the commanders of the several columns provided the first really good look at the upper Gila River Valley and the country north of it.[10]

Captain Tidball, just back at Fort Bowie from a month-long sortie along the Gila, set off again in early July. Scarcely a month before, one of the columns converging on Fort Goodwin had noted "many Indian fires burning in the Chiricahua Range."[11] Tidball now marched toward the Chiricahuas and spent ten days exploring the northern reaches of these mountains, gradually working his way down the eastern side. He found timber in abundance and the finest stock range that he had seen in the territory, but only two small bands of Apaches. Eventually he crossed the mountains, probably ascending Tex Canyon and then descending via Rucker Canyon. According to his guide, the Apache name for the latter translated as Alder Canyon.

Tidball's troopers continued down the western front of the Swisshelm Mountains, turned west across Sulphur Springs Valley, and eventually traversed Mule Pass to reach the San Pedro Valley. After following the San Pedro downstream for awhile, they turned and made their way through the Dragoon Mountains, probably by way of Middlemarch Pass, and returned to Fort Bowie without further incident. Captain Tidball's report on this expedition gave an unparalleled description of the Chiricahua Mountains.[12]

Had General Carleton been able to continue his Apache Expedition, he might have resolved southern Arizona's Indian problems the same way he dealt with the Navajo Indians—by removing them to a distant reservation. The Apaches were actually quite vulnerable, since they depended more upon their farm crops than anyone realized, and the columns out of Fort Goodwin had destroyed the ripening fields. Two released captives even testified about the Indians' tight food situation.[13] Their condition grew desperate, but when four hundred hungry Apaches did surrender at Fort Goodwin in March of 1865, the post commander believed he lacked the authority to issue rations and told the Indians to return to their mountains![14]

Carleton's resources were too thin either to keep up this campaign or to provide for the Indians if they surrendered; and the enlistments of his California Volunteers were expiring, which meant that he had many fewer sol-

Cave Creek Basin from Centella Point, Chiricahua Mountains. (Courtesy, U.S. Forest Service, Coronado National Forest, July 8, 1939.)

diers.[15] At the same time, thousands of Navajos were pouring into the Bosque Redondo reservation in eastern New Mexico and creating a huge drain on available supplies and manpower. The Apache Expedition faded away, and the old familiar pattern of raid and retribution resumed.

Campaigning in the Apache Country, 1865–1872

From the arrival of the California Column in 1862 until early 1866, the army garrisons in Arizona were drawn from California and New Mexico volunteer troops. When the volunteer regiments mustered out of service, regular army units took their place. In January 1865 jurisdiction over southern Arizona passed from the Military Department of New Mexico to the more remote Department of the Pacific, where Apache problems were much more dimly perceived. For the period 1866–70, the army tallied 137 small-unit actions with Indians in Arizona and claimed 649 Indians killed, at a cost of 26 soldiers dead and 58 wounded.[16] Administrative disruptions and the accompanying uncertainties, together with a parade of openings, closings, and relocations of military posts, had much to do with the instability of Indian-military-settler relations during the latter half of the 1860s.

Sometimes even the grimmest of situations had an element of humor. Sam Drachman, a pioneering Tucson merchant, left California for Arizona in the late summer of 1867. The stage driver filled Drachman's young ears with tales of Apache cruelties and particularly the dangers of Picacho Pass, "where many a man had been laid low by the ruthless hand of the Apache." They started through the pass late in the day, and then one of their mules was snake-bitten, requiring a halt. Consternation soon reigned, and to their eyes every bush became an Indian with a scalping knife. They pulled off the road and awaited the inevitable attack, prepared to sell their lives dearly.

About 11 P.M. they heard a murmuring sound, then the tread of horses, and finally human voices. They clutched their rifles, ready to open fire, but were astonished when out of the night came the melody: "Hang Jeff Davis on a sour apple tree." The would-be victims raised their heads, to witness the arrival of Charles T. Hayden and another early Tucsonian, Charles A. Shibell. After a round of Arizona "bug juice," Hayden, the father of the late Senator Carl Hayden, and his companion journeyed on, while the next morning Drachman and his stage driver rode safely into Tucson.[17]

For their part neither the army nor the Indians were 100 percent bent on mayhem. John Spring was with the first regular army units to return to Arizona in 1866. In retrospect he realized that:

> The manner of scouting in those days, before Generals Crook and Miles . . . was far from effective. . . . Some Apaches who gave themselves up later on at Fort Goodwin related that they followed that big scout [an unsuccessful one] from day to day at a safe distance, enjoying the scraps of food, etc. scattered in its wake. They hugely enjoyed the bugle calls, large campfires and general hubbub attending that enterprise, and continually expected that a band with a bass drum would turn up somewhere . . . perhaps to render the soldiers even more conspicuous.[18]

John Spring was stationed at Camp Wallen on Babocomari Creek. While there he took part in two scouts to the Chiricahua Mountains, where he saw how the Apaches lived: "These mountains are of such a nature as to afford almost everywhere a natural and in some places impregnable fortification; in such places Cochise would establish his rancherias . . . when he desired to rest awhile from his nomadic life and depredatory excursions. . . As a rule the Apaches would establish their rancherias in a hollow between two mountain cliffs, near a spring or small stream, known only to them."[19]

Captain Reuben F. Bernard, 1st Cavalry, said much the same a few years later, in explaining why Indian casualties were less than they might have been, "owing to the rocky condition of the country, the Rancheria being scattered over many rocky hills as Cochis [sic] always does."[20]

Again Spring described one "temporary rancheria" that they surprised and captured in the Chiricahua Mountains:

> It consisted of about a dozen huts put together very indifferently with dry sticks of decayed giant cactus, the thorny branches of the candlewood (*Fouquiera spinosa*), some scrub-oak and willow branches, all covered in a slouchy manner with the long, coarse bunch grass called here *sacaton* grass. We found two small hollows excavated from the hillside in which we discovered quite a lot of jerked deer meat, cut in long strips and tied into bundles, several dried but untanned deer and antelope skins, and several nets or bags woven from the fiber of the agave plant, containing roasted agave heads (roasted mescal), dried hard for future use as we dry apples or peaches. The men picked up two old blankets, two lances, four bows, eight arrows, several baskets of very crude make, and the head of a deer with antlers prepared for hunting purposes.[21]

Many army reports described rancherías. One officer who entered the country with General Kearny observed that "a tenement of a few hours' work is the home of a family for years or a day."[22] Some aspects of Apache home life were less wholesome; namely, the animal carcasses strewn around their campsites. The Indians themselves acknowledged an association between bones or cattle carcasses and livestock thefts. One Pinal Apache chief even cited the absence of any bones scattered around their homes as evidence that the Indians on Pinal Creek were not thieves.[23]

By the late 1860s, the army was becoming more knowledgeable as to the ranges of Indian bands. For example Inspector-General Nelson Davis claimed that "Cuchais' [Cochise's] band is about the only one that lives south of the Gila."[24] Davis was essentially correct, but a few years later another officer refined this somewhat by referring to "the band of Cochees [Cochise], whose haunts properly are the Chiricahua mountains, southern Arizona and northern Sonora."[25] The Dragoons on the other hand were said to be a small mountain range "[w]here Indians seldom live."[26]

The country south of the Gila River and east of the mountains fringing the San Pedro Valley remained relatively quiet until October 5, 1869, when an Apache band attacked a stagecoach several miles east of Dragoon Springs.

Four soldiers, the driver, and a passenger all died in the ambush. The passenger was Colonel John Finkle Stone, president of the newly reorganized Apache Pass Mining Company.[27] The raiders struck again the next morning, capturing and driving off a trail herd of 250 cattle.

First Lieutenant W. H. Winters and twenty-five men from Camp Bowie took up the Indians' trail and pursued them over what was then called Chiricahua Pass, the low divide between Tex and Rucker canyons in the Chiricahua Mountains. In a running fight with some fifty of Cochise's well-armed warriors, Winters killed twelve of them near the mouth of Tex Canyon and recovered the entire herd of cattle.[28] On October 16 Captain Reuben Bernard left Camp Bowie with sixty-one men, riding down the eastern side of the Chiricahuas. Four days later he picked up a trail and followed it through the mountains until heavy gunfire crashed out from the slopes of a mesa. The captain tried a flanking movement to either side, but the Indians easily held him off, until he withdrew. Cochise had killed two of Bernard's men and wounded three; an estimated eighteen Apaches were slain.[29] Thirty-one of Bernard's troopers received Congressional Medals of Honor for gallantry or bravery in action.

The site of this battle has recently been identified, thanks to a panorama drawing made soon afterwards, as the rocky mesa at the confluence of Rucker and Red Rock canyons.[30] Bernard returned to Camp Bowie and collected supplies, then hurried south again to bury the dead soldiers and continue the campaign. Early on the morning of October 27 he advanced up a canyon, when the Indians tried to surround him. The two sides traded long-distance rifle fire for awhile, and the soldiers then pulled back, making camp. Reinforcements arrived on October 29, boosting the captain's strength to 118 men. The following day after leaving a strong guard to protect their camp and animals, the troops climbed to the top of the mountains.

> I moved at 2 o'clock A.M. with the remaining men (93) reaching the top of the mountain where we had seen the Indians just at daylight. This march was very fatiguing and many of the men became exhausted. The top of this mountain showed signs of having been occupied by Indians for several days and was fortified to some extent by the building of Rifle pits, formed of stones placed on each other and loop holes through which to fire. Little work was required to make these so that fifty men could whip five times that number . . .[31]

Bernard's command then descended into a deep canyon. When the troops reached the canyon bottom, intent upon capturing some of the Indians' horses, warriors posted on the slopes above opened fire and then held off the army men by rolling huge stones down on them. Bernard broke off this fight and returned to Camp Bowie, claiming two more Indians dead, but a few days later he was back in the field with 156 men, including a troop of Mexican cavalry.[32] Now with the odds clearly against them, Cochise's men led the soldiers on a merry chase through the Chiricahuas, until the troopers and their mounts had been worn down and forced to give up the pursuit. By November 14 they were back at Camp Bowie.[33]

Reuben Bernard was a seasoned officer, but his adversary outmatched him. His contemporary in the 3d Cavalry, Captain "Jerry" Russell, had very much the same experience, fighting the same Indians.[34] Bernard admitted, following his first battle, that "[i]n contending with *Cochis* I do not think I will exaggerate the fact to say that we are contending with one of the most intelligent Indians on the continent."[35] This 1st Cavalryman was persistent, and on January 28, 1870, he surprised Cochise's band in the Dragoon Mountains. There he killed thirteen Indians and captured two, while destroying their camp equipage, as he called it. The amounts of their possessions astonished him: "Their Camp Equipage consisted of large quantities of Buckskins, Hides, Robes, Pots, Pans, Kettles, Buckets, Bags, Baskets, Blankets, Knives, Canvass, Saddles, Bridles, Holsters, Lariats, Needles, Matches, Awls, Salt, Sugar, Axes, Hatchets, Hammers, Paints, Bows & Arrows and about 3000 pounds of corn &c &c." "&c &c" included thirteen horses, one mule, one burro, and two revolvers. Most of this was burned. Almost all of the huts at this ranchería "were covered with canvass in such a manner as to astonish all who saw them."[36] Matters then quieted for a time.

In April of 1870 the army created a Military Department of Arizona, which was to endure for another twenty-three years.[37] The year 1871 saw more skirmishing in the Peloncillos, Huachucas, Chiricahua, and Dragoon mountains.[38] One of the ugliest incidents in Arizona's history took place that spring, an affair that President U. S. Grant called "purely murder." In February an Aravaipa Apache chief had taken his people to Camp Grant, near the junction of Aravaipa Creek with the San Pedro, and asked that they be allowed to live along the creek in peace. The post commander, Lieutenant Royal E. Whitman, granted this request and began to issue rations. Soon he had five hundred or more Indians at hand, living in a ranchería about five miles up Aravaipa Creek from the garrison. Whitman had just learned what other young officers in the process of becoming Indian agents were discovering; that the quickest way to settle Apaches was to allow them a decent location and begin issuing rations. Especially the rations. Indians would come from everywhere for rations.

Civilians might favor these so-called feeding stations for a time, because they reduced marauding. If peace led to smaller army garrisons, however, this was not good, because prosperity depended upon contracts to provide all manner of commissary and quartermaster supplies to the troops. Whatever lay behind their actions, Tucson citizens soon began to blame the Aravaipas for renewed depredations and to raise a punitive expedition for settling accounts. On April 28, 1871, a party of Anglo-Americans, Hispanics, and Papago Indians slipped out of Tucson and made their way toward the ranchería on Aravaipa Creek. They surrounded the encampment and at daybreak on April 30 commenced to pour gunfire into the unsuspecting Indians. The attackers followed this up by clubbing the wounded and stripping the bodies, leaving an estimated 85 to 125 corpses strewn around the burning camp, all but 8 of the dead Apaches being women and children. This assault, the Camp Grant Massacre, caused a nationwide sensation. The perpetrators were eventually brought to trial, whereupon a jury reported all 104 of the accused "not guilty" in a record time of nineteen minutes. Apaches later came back to Aravaipa Creek, which turned out to be a sickly location.[39]

At the time of the Camp Grant Massacre, the military commander in Arizona thought that Tonto and Pinal Apaches had caused most of the recent depredations.[40] Whoever were to blame, the spring of 1871 was a particularly bloody period in southern Arizona.[41] Less than a week after the Camp Grant Massacre, another band of Apaches succeeded in killing Lieutenant Howard B. Cushing.

Cushing was one of a rather elite corps of young officers who breathed new life into a military effort that had begun to lag in Arizona. His success was such that in August of 1870 he received a roving command to seek out, capture, or kill Apaches wherever he found them. Accompanied by Sergeant John Mott and about twenty men of Troop F, 3d U.S. Cavalry, he took to the field. Cushing's troopers fought one skirmish in the Pinal Mountains in October and another one at Mount Turnbull in December. February 1871 saw two fights in the Galiuro Mountains, neither with casualties. In April Cushing fought three engagements, one in the Sierra Aniba and two in the Apache Mountains, leaving a total of thirty-two Apaches slain.[42] Then his luck ran out.

On April 27 Cushing rode out from his field headquarters near Tucson, in company with Sergeant Mott and sixteen privates. By May 2 they were scouting the eastern side of the Huachuca Mountains. The cavalrymen continued north, and about two miles beyond old Camp Wallen they struck an Indian trail. This soon led into a canyon or deep arroyo that turned into a trap. The Apaches, led by the Nednhi chieftain, Juh, opened fire and rushed down from all sides. The soldiers were getting the worst of this when Lieutenant Cushing fell, mortally wounded. The rest of the troops fought their way out of the entrapment, leaving behind the bodies of their lieutenant, one soldier and a civilian.[43]

Cushing was eulogized as a fallen hero. At the time his antagonist was assumed to have been the Chiricahua chief Cochise, but Juh's son clarified this many years later, when he alluded to the healthy respect earned by the young officer in only a couple of years: "My father was afraid that the old sergeant might warn Cushing, and he may have; but Cushing was so sure of himself and had killed so many Apaches that he must have thought he knew more than Ussen Himself. At any rate, he walked into the trap Juh set for him."[44]

Although army records place the fight in the Whetstone Mountains, the times and distances in Sergeant Mott's report would have it farther south, somewhere on the eastern slopes of the Mustang Mountains. The sergeant and four of his men received Congressional Medals of Honor for their actions.[45]

The Pinal and Chiricahua Apaches continued raiding in southern Arizona, with the army at their heels. Captains Jerry Russell and Reuben Bernard were both busy; Russell and his troop rode out of Camp Bowie on October 21, 1871, in response to an attack on two civilians. Three days later they turned into Horseshoe Canyon, on the eastern side of the Chiricahuas. When the men had gone three miles into the canyon, rifles cracked from both slopes. The soldiers scrambled for cover and traded gunfire with the Indians from 3 P.M. until nightfall. The only casualty was Bob Whitney, a volunteer guide. After dark the command withdrew and worked its way back out of the canyon.[46]

Whoever led the Apaches in Horseshoe Canyon, it was not Cochise. At the time he was in New Mexico, camped on upper Cuchillo Negro creek in what is now western Sierra County. His family was enjoying the rations at the Southern Apache Agency, while Cochise himself prepared for an interview with a newspaperman! Chief Cochise had visited New Mexico at least twice since the autumn of 1870, drawn by a liberal rations policy at the Southern Apache Agency in Cañada Alamosa (now Monticello), a town about fifty miles southwest of Socorro.[47]

The Apaches and Reservations, 1870–1876

The pace of the Apache wars began to slow after 1871, until by the spring of 1873 fighting was only sporadic. There were fewer Indians now, and they were kept on the run, literally being worn down. Cochise had been reduced to harassing mail parties and travelers. Peace now became an alternative.

Never again did warfare approach the intensity of the earlier years, despite the widespread newspaper coverage given to the later campaigns.

Food eventually proved to be the solution to Arizona's Indian problem. The idea of reserves where the Indians could receive rations and protection had been around since 1865, but proved to be premature.[48] In the summer of 1869, Lieutenant Colonel John Green came back from a visit to the country of the Coyotero, or White Mountain, Apaches, much impressed with their land. He was also struck by the poverty of these Indians and their wish for a reservation, recommending in his report that they be fed, clothed, and placed on a reservation. Green's suggestions found favor in the War Department, which in January of 1870 set aside an extensive area in the White Mountain region of eastern Arizona as a proposed Indian reservation. The first census of the Indians there, taken on July 1, 1871, enumerated 1,043 men, women, and children, with an estimated 400 to 500 more people scattered through the mountains.[49]

In the meantime Congress, dissatisfied with the Office of Indian Affairs, had authorized President Grant to organize a Board of Indian Commissioners. For several years the commission members were a dominant force in determining government policy toward the Indians. The secretary of the commission, Vincent Colyer, arrived at the new post of Camp Apache, Arizona, on September 1, 1871, where he quickly endorsed the army's designation of a White Mountain Indian reservation. Colyer continued on to Camp Grant, still located on the lower San Pedro, and proclaimed the Camp Grant reservation there. The latter was an area that extended east-west from the base of Mount Turnbull to a line ten miles west of the San Pedro, and from the Gila River south to the vicinity of present-day Mammoth, Arizona, set aside for the use of Aravaipa, Pinal, "and other roving bands of Apache Indians."[50]

Colyer left much undone. A newly appointed special commissioner of Indian affairs with plenary powers, Brigadier General O. O. Howard, arrived in the spring of 1872, "to take such action as, in my judgment should be deemed best for the purpose of preserving peace with the Indians of those [Arizona and New Mexico] Territories."[51] In southern Arizona Howard simultaneously abolished the "pestilential region" of the Camp Grant reserve and attached what he called the San Carlos division to the White Mountain Apache reservation. By the end of 1872, he had moved the thousand or so Apaches from Camp Grant to San Carlos. The general also established peace between the Indians living at Camp Grant and the Pimas, Papagos, and citizens of southern Arizona. All in all it was a good beginning, and after a quick trip to Washington, D.C., he came back to continue his peace making.[52]

General Howard Meets Cochise

Brigadier General George Crook, commanding the Department of Arizona since early June, 1871, had been waiting to turn his troops loose in the expectation that Howard's peace negotiations would fail.[53] Cochise had been conferring with other officers and civilian officials since 1869 and indicating a willingness to make peace. To him this meant being left alone, and he had been holding out for the best terms he could get. The Apache leader recognized that times were changing; by 1872 his Chokonens were the last Apaches not assigned to a reservation. General Howard had not met him during his first trip to Arizona, and he viewed a settlement with the legendary chieftain as a matter of unfinished business, the last step in implementing President Grant's peace policy in Arizona.

At this point Thomas J. Jeffords, a friend of Cochise and an unusual individual in whom the Indians placed special confidence, stepped in and agreed to guide the special commissioner and his aide-de-camp and two Indians to meet the famous Apache leader. Jeffords's price for this service was his appointment as Indian agent at the yet-to-be-established "Cochise reservation," which everyone assumed would lie near Cañada Alamosa in southwestern New Mexico. Howard gave Jeffords his appointment, and three days later they set off from Cañada Alamosa for Arizona, to find the Chiricahuas.[54]

Howard's journey has been portrayed as a near-odyssey, a step into the unknown, with the general traveling almost unescorted across hostile country to meet with the great chief at his stronghold in the Dragoon Mountains. The truth was not quite so dramatic, but the results were still highly important.

The president's representative and his small escort arrived in Arizona at the end of September 1872. Howard and Cochise met for the first time on October 1, in a natural amphitheater at the head of West Stronghold Canyon in the Dragoons. The two men talked all day and then split up, agreeing to meet again in a few days, after Cochise had gathered his people. Howard then rode over to Camp Bowie, to collect a wagon load of stores and cloth. When he arrived back on October 3, everyone camped in East Stronghold Canyon to wait while Cochise's captains gradually came in. By October 10 they were ready to parley. The actual meeting saw Cochise and several of his more important men sitting with General Howard, Jeffords, the general's aide, and the interpreters beneath the shade of a broad spreading tree, while other Chiricahuas gathered outside in circle after circle around the conferees.

Eventually they reached an agreement, although it was an unwritten one and some confusion arose later over the terms. A New Mexico reservation

Fort Bowie, c. 1874. (Courtesy, The National Archives.)

was unacceptable; it would be in southeastern Arizona instead. Cochise had not succeeded in negotiating an abandonment of Camp Bowie within the new reserve, but to ensure that the troops there knew the conditions for peace, he insisted upon meeting with Major Sumner and the other officers from that post at Dragoon Springs on October 12. At this last session Howard, who had thought everything was settled, found himself giving the Chiricahuas all of the land between the Peloncillo and Dragoon ranges—four times as much land as what he thought they had agreed upon.[55]

Cochise clearly entered these talks with the intention of gaining a reservation, and he succeeded wonderfully well. As soon as everyone was in accord, Howard issued orders setting forth the reservation boundaries and affirming Jeffords as agent, then departed with his mission accomplished.[56] In less than a year, the special commissioner had settled the great majority of Apaches in Arizona and New Mexico on reservations, without resorting to troops. For his part General Crook eventually got an Indian campaign, but it was against Yavapai bands and Apaches in the Tonto Basin, where he broke their resistance during a winter offensive in 1872–73. After this all of the Indians in Arizona were for the first time theoretically at peace.[57]

The Chiricahua Reservation

General Howard spelled out the terms of his oral agreement with Cochise in two letters to the impatient Crook. The Indians confirmed that if they received the Chiricahua Mountains for a reservation, they would cease from war and be contented. For the future they promised emphatically to seize any stock or other property stolen from citizens and deliver it to the Indian Agent. The agent was Tom Jeffords and the agency itself an independent one, to be headquartered at Sulphur Springs. Nothing was said about the Apaches desisting from raids into Mexico, although Cochise did guarantee the safety of the Tucson road and of all roads in Arizona and New Mexico insofar as his people were concerned. He also asked for as few troops as possible on the Chiricahua reservation, which comprised all of southeastern Arizona from the western base of the Dragoon range east to the New Mexico line, south of a diagonal from Dragoon Springs to the high point on the Peloncillo Mountains. In November the Chiricahua agency was assigned to the Arizona Superintendency of Indian Affairs.[58] A Presidential Executive Order set aside the reservation on December 14, 1872.

Thomas Jeffords was the only agent the Chiricahua reservation had during nearly four years of existence. He found it necessary to move the agency headquarters three times, beginning on September 1, 1873, when he relocated from a rented adobe hut at Sulphur Springs to the San Simon ciénega. Scarcely two months later, malaria and whooping-cough forced abandonment of this sickly location in favor of Pinery Canyon, on the west side of the Chiricahua Mountains. Then on May 14, 1874, he shifted to Apache Pass, actually to a place in Siphon Canyon below Camp Bowie. From Apache Pass Jeffords hoped that he might be able to check "the rapacity of the white vultures" coming onto the reservation, as one contemporary put it.[59]

Initially it appeared that Cochise had done well by his people. They gained a large reservation and were subject only to loose civilian controls, while they received rations of corn and beef. Little or nothing had been surrendered in return, although the younger men had to be deterred from raiding. Cochise's people, the Chokonens, numbered between six and seven hundred individuals, but their vast reservation attracted about four hundred recalcitrants from other Apache reserves, and these visitors had to be fed as well.

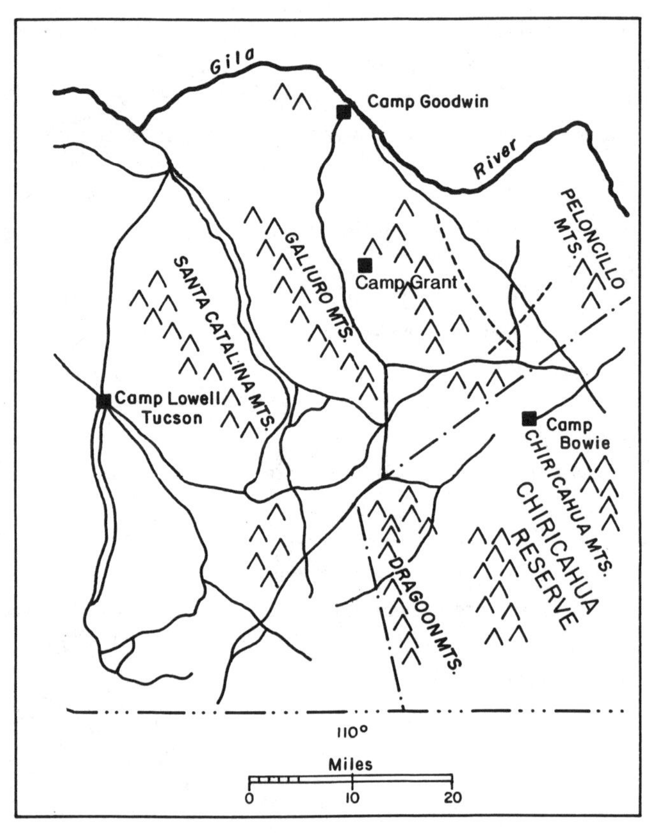

Map 14.
Location of the Chiricahua Reservation agreed upon by Cochise and General Howard, 1872. (Map by Coronado National Forest.)

Problems at the Chiricahua reservation stemmed partly from these other groups raiding into Mexico, as well as from Jeffords's informal management style. There were plenty of undesirable citizens around as well, only too willing to exchange whiskey and firearms for livestock with no questions asked.[60]

Cochise died at his stronghold in the Dragoon Mountains on June 8, 1874. Tom Jeffords later told pioneer settler John Rockfellow that the chief's burial place was a grassy mesa just north of the canyon (the East Stronghold) and overlooking Sulphur Springs Valley.[61] Already outside of Arizona an idea was afoot to vacate the reservation and move the Indians to another one.

The Chiricahua reservation was an expedient solution, not a long-term one. The largest cloud hanging over it was a new Federal Indian policy soon to be adopted in the name of efficiency and economy. This policy was concentration. For the Apaches it meant that as many of the different Apache bands as possible should be collected at the White Mountain and San Carlos reservations.[62] Agent Jeffords and his charges had no way to know what was coming.

The incident that spelled the end for the Chiricahua reservation came in January of 1876. For more than three years, the Indian Bureau had first been parsimonious, then generous, and again reverted to economy in its support of Jeffords, finally cutting the agency's beef quota to less than three-quarters of what it had been.[63] Through all of this the Indians themselves had stayed peaceful. To compensate for reduced rations, Jeffords let some of the Chiricahuas hunt in the Dragoon Mountains.

While hunting they fell to quarreling. Most of the Indians returned to the agency. Two who stayed, Skinya and his brother Pionsenay, joined a raid into Mexico and returned with gold dust and silver; they converted these into whiskey at the Sulphur Springs mail station–turned–groggery. On the following day, April 7, 1876, Pionsenay watched for his chance, then shot both Rogers, the station manager, and his cook, a man named Spense. The murderer and his cohorts stole some horses, ammunition, and whiskey, and the next day rode over to the San Pedro Valley, where they killed another citizen and took four horses. Jeffords and Lieutenant Austin Henely's troop from Camp Bowie took the trail of the renegades, whom they found posted in the crags of the San Jose Mountains near the Mexican border. After exchanging a few shots, the troops withdrew.[64]

In 1866 the murders of two men would have created little excitement. Ten years later, the territory went into a panic. When the commander of the military department wrote six months after the fact that "The killing of these men created great alarm in the southeastern portion of the Territory, great excitement prevailed, and the outrages were greatly exaggerated," he may even have understated things.[65] Territorial Governor Anson Safford fired off a telegram in which he claimed that the "Chiricahuas have undoubtedly all broken out." All available cavalry was ordered to scout for hostiles and protect the settlements. Actually the Indians except for the alleged murderers had returned to the reservation by April 23. Army patrols found only trails leading toward the agency. The sole additional deaths reported that summer were of two prospectors killed early in July, about twenty-five miles south of Camp Bowie.[66]

The uproar in Arizona spurred the U.S. Congress into acting with lightning-like speed in helping to finance a movement already under way to abolish the Chiricahua reservation. On May 9, 1876, Congress enacted a law that provided $50,000 for two months of subsistence supplies for the Apache Indians of Arizona, with any surplus to be used "to defray the expenses incident to the removal of the Indians of the Chiricahua Agency to the San Carlos reservation." Passage of this act was evidently a foregone conclusion: the day *previous* to passage, the acting commissioner of Indian affairs had suggested calling upon the secretary of war to order troops to stand by for aiding in the removal "of the Chiricahua Indians who have recently been engaged in a serious outbreak."[67]

Removal to San Carlos

The Indian agent at San Carlos, John P. Clum, effected the removal of the Chiricahuas; a regiment of cavalry backed him up, just in case. The Indians had consented to move, and the transfer went smoothly. Three hundred and twenty-five of them made the trip and arrived at San Carlos on June 18, after a six-day journey. One small band of twenty-five or thirty Southern Chiricahuas under Juh, Geronimo, and Naiche originally agreed to go but instead fled from the Chiricahua reserve on the night of June 7–8. They spent the next year roaming and raiding.[68]

Agent Tom Jeffords was now out of a job. His last report, dated October 3, 1876, claimed that Indians formerly belonging to the Chiricahua agency had killed twenty men and women and had stolen over 170 head of stock since the agency was discontinued. The department commander, Brevet Major General August V. Kautz, emphatically disagreed, citing the deaths of only the two prospectors and losses of a few animals.[69]

Actually the ranchers in southwestern New Mexico experienced a rash of stock stealing during the early fall. On September 14 Captain Henry Carroll caught up with a band said to be Chiricahuas about thirty-five miles out of Fort Cummings, New Mexico. The Indians were on their way toward the

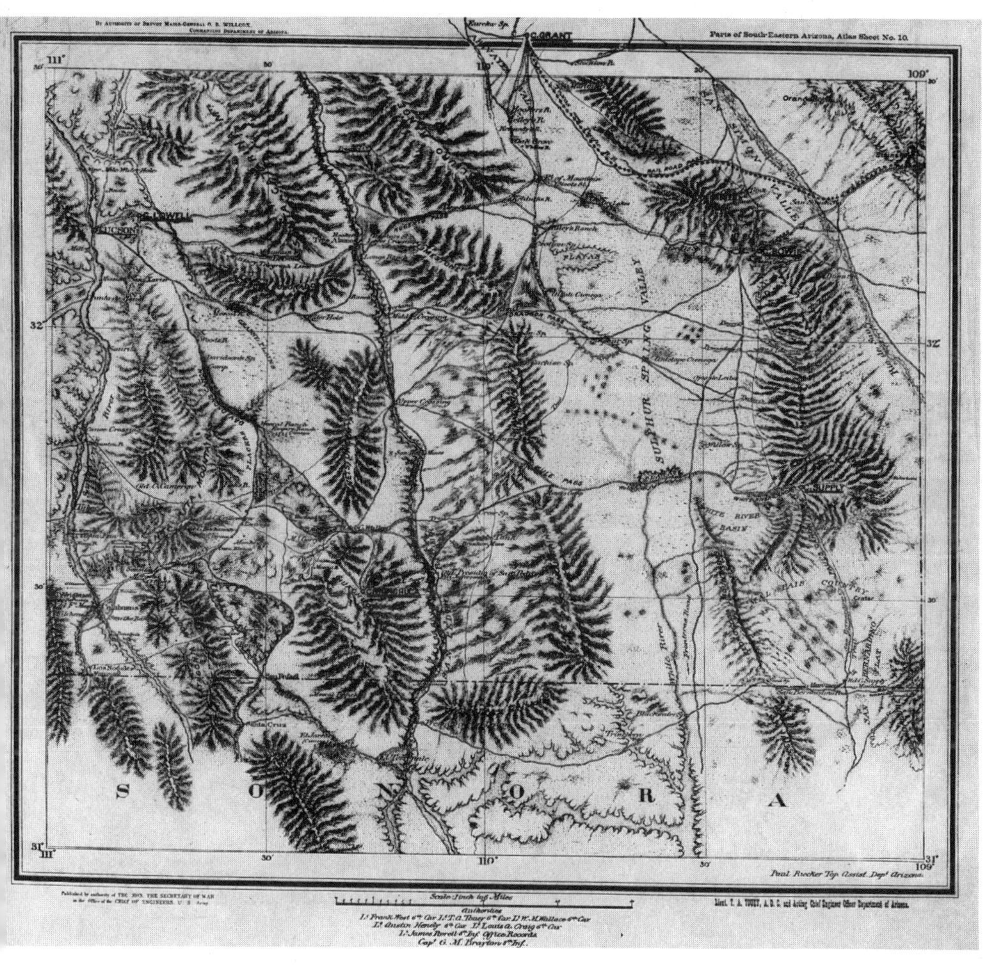

Military Department of Arizona, atlas sheet of southeastern Arizona, 1878. (Courtesy, The National Archives.)

Florida Mountains when the soldiers surprised them. A desperate fight ensued, the Apaches scattering into the mesquite. Carroll reported one Indian killed and one of his own men wounded, with eleven head of stock captured.[70] While such incidents stirred New Mexico, southeastern Arizona seems to have been quiet until December.[71]

The San Carlos Agency, which very soon became the San Carlos reservation, came into existence in 1872 as a division or enlargement of the White Mountain Apache reservation. When John P. Clum arrived on August 8, 1874, as the new agent at San Carlos, he found about 1,000 Pinal and Aravaipa Apaches and Tontos present, people who had been removed from the old Camp Grant reserve. In March 1875 another 1,400 Indians were conducted to San Carlos from the Rio Verde reservation east of Prescott. Then in July of that year the Interior Department ordered Clum to move the Indians, mostly Coyotero Apaches, from the Camp Apache Agency down to San Carlos. This influx augmented the rolls at San Carlos by another 1,800 souls, about half of whom were anxious to go, since they regarded the Gila as their old home and planting grounds. The other half had to be persuaded to move.[72]

Abolishment of the Chiricahua reservation added 325 Chiricahua Apaches to the growing potpourri of people at San Carlos. By now the government's concentration policy was in full effect. Finally in May of 1877 Clum acted under orders from the Interior Department to oversee the transfer of 453 Southern Apaches to San Carlos from the Ojo Caliente, or Warm Springs, reservation in New Mexico.[73] By that summer the agent had approximately 5,000 Apaches under his charge.

The enforced association among so many unrelated and mutually unfriendly bands of Apache Indians created much unrest at San Carlos. For the most part the Indians behaved well enough toward outsiders; the problems stemmed from marauders off the reservation. There were more of these individuals than General Kautz had thought, and army patrols continued actively scouting through 1877 and 1878. Lieutenant "Tony" Rucker and his company of Indian Scouts had several brief, fierce clashes with renegade Chiricahuas. Apart from these, the level of violence by Indians stayed remarkably low in southeastern Arizona for the balance of the decade.

Camp John A. Rucker, an Indian Wars Outpost

The story of one post on the western side of the Chiricahua Mountains well illustrates the role of many such garrisons at this point in Arizona's history, a time when the Apaches had been placed on reservations, but before the country was taken up by ranchers and miners. Camp John A. Rucker

Lt. John A. (Tony) Rucker and Company C—Indian Scouts in a photograph probably taken in 1877 or 1878. (Courtesy, Sharlot Hall Museum Library/Archives, Prescott, Arizona.)

has been the subject of many articles, most of them factually quite accurate.[74] Several post buildings survive, and the military records are readily available, while an association with several frontier personalities has helped to perpetuate interest. The camp had a short life (less than three years), and those who served there found life largely routine, although several episodes drew wide attention.

When the old Chiricahua reserve was terminated and a small band under Geronimo, Juh, and Naiche fled rather than go to San Carlos, this was the earliest reference to any of these three leaders. Many other Chiricahua Apaches avoided San Carlos and showed up instead at the Southern Apache agency at the Warm Springs, or Ojo Caliente, reservation in New Mexico. These off-reservation Indians were quickly termed renegades.[75]

Citizen complaints about Indian depredations began coming in. The army made a series of sweeps through southeastern Arizona, with the patrols having little success at finding the missing Chiricahuas or any other Indians until January of 1877. On January 9, Second Lieutenant John A. "Tony" Rucker at the head of his Company C, Indian Scouts, and a small detachment from the 6th Cavalry surprised Geronimo's camp in the Animas Mountains, about forty miles south of Ralston [Shakespeare], New Mexico. The soldiers killed ten Indians and scattered the rest, capturing all of their property.[76] Rucker and his company of Apache Scouts, recruited at the San Carlos reservation, had a number of other successful skirmishes that year, most of them in the same part of New Mexico.[77]

To stay in the field, these patrols had to be resupplied. In late March of 1878, Captain Daniel Madden, 6th Cavalry, received orders to set up a supply camp at the San Bernardino Ranch, just north of the U.S.-Mexico boundary. He reported on April 4 that he had established his camp that day about one-half mile from the old San Bernardino Ranch. By coincidence, Lieutenant Rucker was ordered out from Camp Bowie that same day, in still another pursuit of Indians.[78]

Madden's new post, known as Camp Supply, was poorly situated for grazing. The governor of Sonora protested its nearness to the border. After three weeks the captain received orders to move his camp "to a point near the junction of the main creeks in White River Cañon" on the western side of the Chiricahua range. He did so and arrived at the new site of Camp Supply on April 28, 1878.[79]

For two and one-half months, Second Lieutenant Rucker with his company of Indian Scouts and First Lieutenant Austin Henely, newly assigned to the command of Company D, Indian Scouts, ranged out of Camp Supply. Henely was evidently a contentious sort and also defensive about the men in his command. One night in early June his Indian soldiers disturbed the rest of the camp with their chanting. The post commander, Captain Madden, directed Henely to cause all noises after taps to cease. The lieutenant shot back that he considered this order "meddlesome and presumptive." The situation verged on a confrontation, after Henely threatened to meet with "the armed resistance of the entire force under my command" any effort to make arrests for singing. Rather than ask for a general court martial, the post commander bucked this "case of mutinous insubordination" up to Department of Arizona headquarters. Back came a telegram that directed Henely, in unmistakable language, to move his camp at least three-quarters of a mile from Camp Supply. He presumably complied since the story ended at that point.[80]

Scarcely a month later, Henely and Lieutenant Rucker died in a double tragedy at Camp Supply. The post commander described what happened in two telegrams:

> I have the honor to report the deaths by drowning of Lieutenants Henely and Rucker 6th Cavalry—at about (7) seven o'clock yesterday afternoon—in a flood suddenly coming down the canyon here—Lieut. Rucker's body was only recovered by (10) ten o'clock last night and Lieut. Henely's this morning at daylight—The whole command of the camp and the two Indian companies of the deceased officers, were ceaseless in searching for the remains until they were found . . .
>
> There are but few more particulars concerning Lt. Rucker's noble death that my telegram just sent you embodies—high water, rather a torrent, pouring down the cañon in which we are camped, came suddenly between us and Capt. Madden's camp here—in which while attempting to cross Lieut. Henely was swept to his death. Tony instantly plunged in after him mounted—but it was hopeless without almost a miracle from the moment Henely was washed off his horse—the flood came down with the usual roar—full of driftwood, making it very hazardous to attempt crossing—and was of such violence that large boulders in the ordinarily nearly dry bed of the creek, were distinctly heard heaving against each other. Henely's head shows the effect of a blow or snag that if received before drowning, would doubtless have rendered him senseless. Tony simply drowned. . . . We are crushed with grief. Tony's Indians seem awe struck. They are perfectly devoted to him. I know of no one more universally liked and esteemed. . . .[81]

Rucker, the son of a prominent general, and the Irish-born Henely both received tributes that emphasized the high regard in which they were held. In October of the same year Captain Madden issued a post order changing the name of the camp to Camp J. A. Rucker, subject to approval by the Department Commander. The change was approved and Post Orders no. 78, dated December 9, 1878, proclaimed that "[t]his Camp will hereafter be known and designated as Camp John A. Rucker."[82]

Camp Rucker began as a tent community, and it remained largely a tent camp throughout its existence. A diagram and description of the post com-

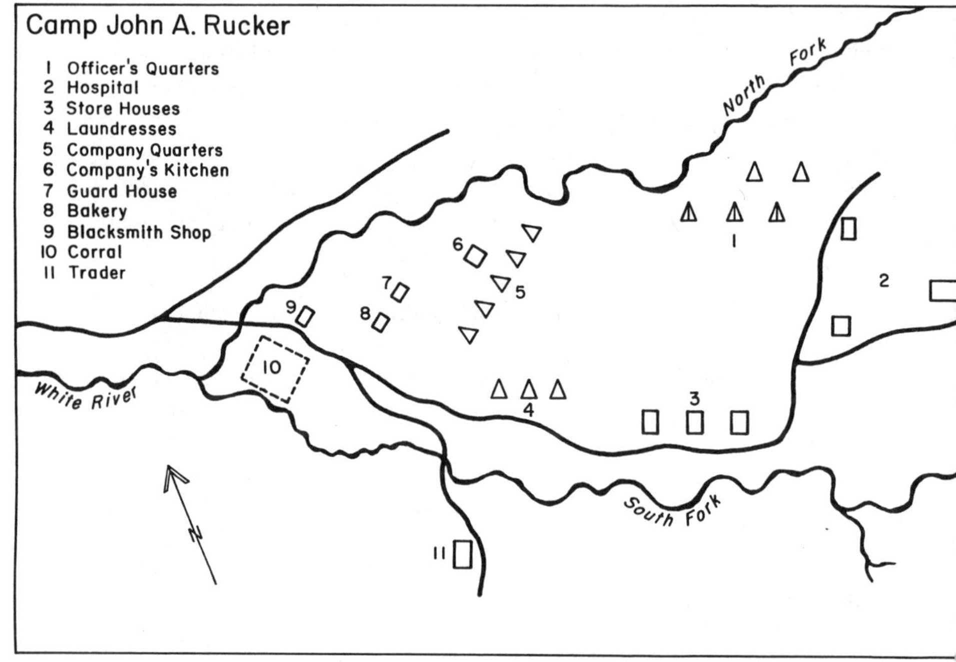

Map 15.
Plan of Camp Rucker, redrawn from Major General Irvin McDowell's *Outline Descriptions of Military Posts . . .* (1879).
(Map by Coronado National Forest.)

piled in May of 1879 showed the layout of the quarters, storehouses and other buildings. The post also received a comprehensive inspection of all of its facilities in January of the same year. These and other sources allow for tracing the evolution of the post's buildings.

The army inspection report found the garrison (Company E, 12th U.S. Infantry) living in stockaded tents with a chimney in the rear of each, two men to a tent. By a stockaded tent was meant one that had been walled with vertical logs set side by side in the ground, in the manner of a Hispanic *jacal*, then roofed over by a canvas tent. At Camp Rucker these were described as comfortable and made by the men themselves. The two officers and the post surgeon also lived in tents, while the guard and prisoners (if any) found similar shelter. A company mess room, stockaded and with a dirt floor, was in fair condition. It at least exceeded the blacksmith shop, noted as a "bad stockade." The only other buildings listed specifically in the inspection were the quartermaster and subsistence storehouses, both of these being stockaded log structures with canvas covers. Nothing was said about a hospital.

The slack discipline and careless appearance of this isolated post were causes for criticism. The inspecting officer attributed these faults mainly to the attitude of First Lieutenant James Halloran, the post commander, "who appeared to be a person habituated to the use of liquor." Less than a month later, Halloran found himself reassigned to Camp Grant. The brightest spot was the food situation, with both the mess arrangements and the cooking listed as "good," the bread as "very good," and the quality of the fresh beef as "excellent."[83]

By May of that year a 14 by 14 foot log building with an earth roof had been added as the post bakery, and a 12 by 12 foot structure of similar construction served as a guardhouse. The hospital was a slightly larger log building, augmented by three hospital tents, while the garrison remained in their tents. A diagram showed the camp layout as an irregular quadrangle within the angle formed by two creeks (map 15). Across the south fork lay the post trader's establishment.[84] Sometime in the summer or early fall of 1879, construction began on another stockade-walled structure, this one intended as a company kitchen, mess, and reading room.

In May of 1880 a permanent building program finally got underway. Extra-duty men made adobes for a subsistence storehouse and a post hospital, then began erecting the storehouse. By July this structure, also known as the commissary building, had essentially been completed. It had adobe walls, a commodious stone-walled cellar, and a shingled roof. Like the mess building, it never received doors or windows and so had to have a guard posted to protect its contents. By November an adobe bake house had been added, but only the foundation was laid for the hospital. This was the situation as of November 10, 1880, just twelve days before the post commander relinquished command for the last time and marched away.[85]

To relieve boredom at such isolated posts, the men sought diversions at the post trader's store. As early as May of 1878, Captain Madden had to order the trader to sell liquor only by the drink and under no circumstances to intoxicated people. In August Madden tightened this to a maximum of three drinks a day to any enlisted man, with at least two hours between each drink. The drinking problem evidently worsened, and in February 1879 the commander banned the sale of liquor altogether. However, ten days later came still another order, this one prohibiting enlisted men from loitering at the post trader's store or from going in the back door![86] The post traders had their own troubles, with the clerk being "drunk as an owl" and creating trouble in the camp. Another order followed, this one closing the store as of about July 1, 1880.[87]

One incident that did *not* take place at Camp John A. Rucker was Geronimo's surrender in December 1879, despite contemporary newspaper claims to the contrary. What did happen was best explained by First Lieutenant H. L. Haskell, at that time aide-de-camp to the department commander, Brigadier General Orlando Willcox. Haskell had just negotiated the surrender of Juh's band of Chiricahuas. Second Lieutenant Augustus Blocksom was Tony Rucker's successor in command of Company C, Indian Scouts:

> Rucker, December 14, 1879
>
> (To) A.A. General, Prescott
>
> Hoo, Geronimo and other Chihuahua [sic] Indians about 80 have come in and ask General Willcox to be their friend. I was with Lieutenant Blocksom's scout on the night of the 12th instant at San Bernado when they sent a runner for me to go to their camp alone without soldier(s). The runner and Blocksom's interpreter went out to show the way, and I met the Indians at McIntosh Spring in the Guadalupe mountain, 40 miles east of this post where the surrender took place. . . .
>
> Haskell A.D.C.[88]

The balance of Haskell's report gave the substance of their negotiations. Juh, Geronimo, and 80 to 105 other Chiricahuas were escorted from McIntosh Spring by way of Camp Rucker to the San Carlos reservation.

The need for an outpost at Camp Rucker ended in October of 1880, when the Mexican army killed the great Mimbres Apache chief Victorio and many of his followers in the mountains of northern Mexico. At that time Juh, Geronimo, and other Chiricahua leaders were on the San Carlos reservation. The formal termination of Camp John A. Rucker came on November 22, 1880, when the post commander, Captain A. B. McGowan, signed Post Orders no. 66: "The undersigned hereby relinquished Command of this post to date Nov. 22, 1880."[89]

The military role of this site still was not quite over. From May through September of 1886, various troops of the 4th Cavalry and one or more companies of Indian Scouts camped here during the Geronimo campaign. Troops also took station at Power's ranch in the Swisshelm Mountains and at other ranches, flashing messages to one another by heliographs (signalling devices that used reflected sunlight). In September Geronimo and Naiche surrendered for the last time, at Skeleton Canyon on the west side of the

Peloncillo Mountains, and Camp Rucker finally relinquished its role as a military post. The property thereafter served as the headquarters for a succession of ranches.[90]

Renewed Hostilities, 1878–1882

What is now called the Victorio campaign began in the summer of 1878. The name of Victorio, a Mimbres Apache chieftain and veteran of reservation life in New Mexico, struck fear into the hearts of every rancher and miner in the Southwest. This terror-filled period witnessed the bloodiest toll of lives in the history of Indian wars in the Southwest. The fighting was entirely in New Mexico, west Texas, and northern Mexico, with Arizona largely unaffected. Between his final break with the Whites in August of 1879 and his death in Mexico fourteen months later, Victorio left a path strewn with between 250 and 500 bodies of his victims.[91]

Indian affairs in Arizona were in fact largely peaceful during the 1880s, at least south of the Gila River. There were substantial problems with corruption in management of the San Carlos Agency, however, and continuing frictions between the army and the Indian agents. Geronimo lived quietly at San Carlos after his capture at Ojo Caliente in 1877, until he finally tired of reservation life and rode off on April 4, 1878, in the company of several other malcontents. At some point the renegades joined up with Juh and Naiche, but they created so little stir until their surrender at McIntosh Spring that Geronimo completely skipped this interval in his autobiography![92]

After a year and nine months back on the reservation, rumors reached the Chiricahuas on the night of September 30, 1881, that soldiers were about to raid them. The Indians became so alarmed that Juh, Naiche, Geronimo, and some seventy-one others decamped once more, heading toward their old haunts in Mexico. Four U.S. Army columns soon followed, but none of these caught up with the fleeing Apaches until after they had killed thirteen people and destroyed a large wagon train.

This flight marked a dramatic new round in Arizona's Indian wars. About one mile east of Cedar Springs, Arizona, between the Pinaleño and Santa Teresa mountains, the teamsters from the ambushed wagon train made a stubborn fight for their lives. The Indians killed five of them and two other people as well, scattering flour around the wagons. A Mrs. Moulds and several men forted up in the army telegraph station at Cedar Springs, where they stood off the Indians for more than three hours. Mrs. Moulds' husband, the telegraph operator, and several soldiers were shot there, while the Indians had "a good time generally." No less than three troops of cavalry and a company of Indian Scouts joined the fray, led by Brigadier General Willcox, still the departmental commander. The Chiricahuas, lying concealed in the brush, commenced firing on the new arrivees and kept it up until after dark, killing a sergeant and two soldiers, while wounding as many more. During the evening the Indians attacked the soldiers' positions, to draw attention from the escape of their own women and children.

The warriors all slipped away that same night (October 2) and crossed the Sulphur Springs Valley. They passed near Tombstone, where Mayor John P. Clum and a posse of the town's gunmen set off on a chase that Clum later called "brief and eventless." General Willcox caught up with the Indians again at the South Pass of the Dragoon Mountains, but after a skirmish the Chiricahuas headed for Mexico, leaving five more civilians slain and driving off six hundred head of stolen livestock.[93]

Loco, one of the most famous Mimbres Apache war chiefs, had remained at San Carlos when Juh and Geronimo made their break. In the spring of 1882 these marauders rode north to recruit Loco and the others who had come from the old Ojo Caliente reservation. The hostiles struck San Carlos on April 18 and so stirred up his people that Loco agreed to go on the warpath. This band left a trail of plundered livestock and two dozen murdered civilians as they rode east, barely missing General William T. Sherman, commander of the entire U.S. Army, then en route to Fort Grant. By the end of the first week, a total of fifty citizens lay dead.

As the Apaches plunged eastward toward the Peloncillos, Lieutenant Colonel George A. Forsyth was patrolling along the Southern Pacific Railroad near Lordsburg, New Mexico. Forsyth met the raiders at Horseshoe Canyon in the northern Peloncillos, practically on the Arizona—New Mexico line. On April 23 a drawn-out skirmish left one soldier killed and seven wounded. One day before First Lieutenant David McDonald with a part of Forsyth's command had lost four men killed. The colonel clearly had the worst of this, but his troopers followed the escaping hostiles as they headed south into Mexico. There the soldiers pushed the estimated 150 Indians into an ambush laid by Colonel Lorenzo Garcia and the Sixth Mexican Infantry near the Janos River. The Mexicans killed 78 Apaches, mostly women and children, while losing two officers and 19 men of their own. The surviving Indians, including Loco, fled into the Sierra Madre.[94]

The Army vs. Geronimo, 1883–1886

Much has been written about the next four years, the time when Geronimo became famous. The number of off-reservation Apaches was now relatively few, and they had to carry out quick, slashing attacks. These raids earned immense publicity and put new pressures on the army. Reservation problems at San Carlos increased as well. Periodic campaigns were made through southwestern New Mexico and northern Mexico, but southeastern Arizona remained on the sidelines during most of this period. Brigadier General George Crook had resumed command of the Department of Arizona in September of 1882 and directed the military efforts there until late spring 1886.

It was eleven months after Geronimo's escape until the next major raid. In March 1883 about twenty-six Chiricahuas crossed north from Mexico, led by Chihuahua, Chatto, and Bonito. They killed four men at a charcoal camp at Charleston, Arizona, then swirled on to the Total Wreck camp and left three dead there. The raiders cut a bloody path across southern Arizona into western New Mexico, before racing south into Mexico. Chihuahua's party was credited with murdering Judge and Mrs. McComas and kidnapping their young son, Charlie, along the road between Silver City and Lordsburg, New Mexico, on March 28th. This famous incident and the prolonged, unsuccessful search for little Charlie McComas drew nationwide attention. In their whirlwind campaign, the Indians killed twenty-six people and escaped without being sighted by a single soldier. The newspapers began to castigate the army for allowing the Apaches to carry out annual invasions.[95]

General Crook determined to take the war to the enemy. He mounted an expedition that set off from Willcox, Arizona, on April 23, 1883, with one company of cavalry and almost 200 enlisted Indian scouts. Eight days later, he crossed the border into Mexico at San Bernardino Springs. From that point, as far as the outside world was concerned, Crook's expeditionary force lost itself in the wilds of northern Mexico.

In mid-May Crook's men surprised a ranchería that belonged to Chatto and Bonito, but the Apaches scattered with few casualties. One by one the renegade leaders—Chihuahua, Chatto, Naiche, Geronimo, Nana, Bonito, Loco—came in and conferred with the general. By the end of May the Indians had agreed to surrender. One of Crook's officers, Captain Emmett Crawford, escorted a total of 325 Chiricahuas and other Apaches back to San Carlos, where they arrived on June 23. Naiche, with 93 followers, came in that fall, while Chatto and Mangas followed in February 1884, with about 60 people.[96]

Geronimo finally arrived at the border in early March of 1884, accompanied by more than 80 followers and 350 cattle. Lieutenant Britton Davis, assigned to the command of the Apache Scouts at San Carlos, was ordered to escort Geronimo and his livestock back to the reservation via the Sulphur Springs ranch, the site of Tom Jeffords's first agency and later of the murders of Rogers and Spense. While the Indians and their escort were lying over at this old ranch, two men claiming to be a U.S. marshal and a collector of customs rode up late in the day to arrest Geronimo and seize his cattle. Davis, now in a tight spot between the demands of these civilian authorities and Geronimo's belligerence, was saved when another officer rode in from Fort Bowie, carrying a quart of Scotch whiskey. The two of them helped the marshal and the collector to drain most of the bottle and then fall asleep, whereupon the other officer led Davis's own men, Geronimo, and his cattle off toward San Carlos, while Davis remained to 'explain' when the two civilians awoke, ten hours later! The Apaches and their stock arrived safely at San Carlos.[97]

The following spring Geronimo, Naiche, Mangas, Nana, and Chihuahua led the last serious outbreak at San Carlos. Some 134 Indians broke out on the night of May 17, 1885, with the cavalry and Indian Scouts soon on their trail. This break had been prompted by reservation discipline and a division of authority between the army and the Indian agency. In the next year and a half, seventy-three settlers, two officers, and eight regular soldiers, plus twelve reservation Indians lost their lives, as the hostiles brought death and destruction to the ranches in southwestern New Mexico.[98] Chihuahua and his followers captured Captain Henry W. Lawton's supply camp at Guadalupe Canyon, then scoured the Chiricahua Mountains for stock and attacked ranches south of present-day Bowie, Arizona, before heading south into Mexico.[99]

Most of the campaigning took place in Mexico. In early November, 1885, came a brutal raid that slashed across New Mexico and eastern Arizona. Two small bands of Chiricahuas, their leader said to be a younger brother of Chihuahua named Josanie, slipped over the border into New Mexico. With about ten warriors, Josanie descended on the White Mountain reservation, slaying anyone they could catch, sweeping off Bonito's horses, and then pounding southward through the Santa Teresas and Aravaipa Canyon before doubling back to the Gila. The Southwest was in a panic once again, as the raiders spent December plundering and murdering through the San Francisco River and Upper Gila country of western New Mexico. By December 27 they had vanished into the Chiricahua range, after killing several people near the former mining camp of Galeyville. They blithely rode back into old Mexico, leaving a trail of thirty-eight deaths for one Apache killed.[100]

People who survived such a raid might be badly frightened, but after c. 1880, the effects on actual settlement were probably nil. What Chihuahua and Josanie, and in New Mexico, Nana, had demonstrated was that Indians could no longer live in their old homeland, except on a reservation. Fewer and fewer Apaches were involved in these lightning raids, and their only place of refuge now was in Mexico.

General Crook eventually met with the renegades in Mexico on March 25–27, 1886, at the Cañon de los Embudos. Once again the Chiricahuas surrendered. Lieutenant Marion Maus escorted Chihuahua, Nana, Josanie, and their women to Fort Bowie. As of April 7 all of the Chiricahua prisoners there, a total of seventy-seven, were put on a train and sent to Fort Marion, Florida. Geronimo and Naiche bolted just short of the border and were off again with a band now reduced to thirty-six people. Crook, criticized for this escape and faced with what he thought were impossible orders, asked to be relieved rather than change his strategy to a defensive one. He was reassigned and Brigadier General Nelson A. Miles became the new commander of the Department of Arizona.[101]

The Last Campaign: General Miles and Geronimo

Geronimo and Naiche now struck north from Mexico into the Santa Cruz Valley, an area that had been free of Apache raids for almost fifteen years. Early on the morning of April 27, 1886, an estimated thirty to forty raiders swept down the Santa Cruz past Nogales and Calabasas, attacking ranches and wounding several people. Trains with armed volunteers from Nogales followed at a respectful distance. After passing Calabasas the Apaches divided into two bands.[102]

At Arthur Peck's ranch, west of the Santa Cruz near Nogales, one band murdered Peck's wife and their baby son. Peck himself and an assistant, Charles Owen, were about two miles up the canyon above the house at the time. Details of their ordeal were published a few days later:

> Both [men] were unarmed, Mr. Peck's horse was shot under him at the first fire, and he was captured, tied and kept under guard for half an hour or more. Young Owen made a dash for his life, being mounted on a fine animal. Turning into a side ravine he met a shower of bullets from the red devils in concealment on the banks. His horse was shot but ran several steps before falling. While thus flying a shot broke the young man's neck and another broke an arm. He fell upon his face, dead, . . .
>
> At the house, with Mrs. Peck, was her little niece, Jennie, twelve years of age, and an unusually bright little girl. She was taken into captivity. Old Geronimo finally came up and had a brief

> conversation with Mr. Peck, saying that he (Peck) was a good man and he would not kill him. The old fiend then released the prisoner, took his boots away from him, gave him thirty-five cents in money and told him go—but not to go to the house. . . . Mr. Peck went directly to his house, and there found his wife and child lying dead by the door.[103]

The other band of raiders apparently split into smaller parties and proceeded to pillage ranches in the vicinity of Oro Blanco. Early on the afternoon of April 28, Mr. J. Shanahan had just passed 'Yank' Bartlett's ranch on the way to his own ranch three miles away. Ten minutes later Yank's young son Johnny heard three shots. Shanahan soon came stumbling toward the Bartlett house, shot through the body. He had been attacked by three Indians and had tried to defend himself with rocks.

Yank's ranch in Bear Valley was nine miles southeast from Oro Blanco. Yank had Johnny saddle his mare and ride for help, but after two miles the boy saw three more Indians ahead of him and turned to ride back. This group had apparently found some liquor, and Johnny escaped their notice. He made it back safely, only to find the Indians firing on his father inside the house. Shanahan's ten-year-old son Phil had run into the house in the meantime, and Yank sent him off to find his mother and sisters. Little Phil accomplished this, and the women hid in the rocks that night, reaching the Bartlett house safely the next morning.

A shot from the Indians wounded Bartlett slightly; the firing continued until nearly sundown. After dark Yank told Johnny to slip out quietly and try again to reach Oro Blanco. This time the boy was successful. The citizens there raised a party and rode to Yank's relief the next morning, to find the Indians gone. Later that day they attacked Juan Elias's ranch on the Sopori, driving off many of his horses and mules.[104]

General Miles had anticipated such raids and had planned for them by scattering company-sized detachments at camps throughout southern Arizona. One experienced officer, Captain Thomas Lebo, quickly took up a trail with his Troop K, 10th Cavalry. On May 3 Geronimo sought to ambush these pursuers in the Pinito Mountains southeast of Nogales, Sonora. In an afternoon of intense fighting, Lebo lost one man killed and Corporal Edward Scott wounded. The Chiricahuas were in an impregnable position, and eventually the soldiers withdrew. Western artist Frederick Remington's famous drawing *The Rescue of Corporal Scott* portrays an act of bravery during this battle.[105]

Twelve days later another band ambushed Captain Charles Hatfield, Troop D, 4th Cavalry, in the mountains near Santa Cruz, Sonora. Hatfield lost two men killed and two wounded. The Indians then turned north and began raid-

"The Rescue of Corporal Scott (by Lt. Powhatan Clarke)." An incident in the fight with Geronimo, May 3, 1886, drawn by Frederick Remington. Originally published in *Harper's Weekly*, August 21, 1886.

ing in the Dragoon Mountains. Detachments of the 10th Cavalry kept at their heels, intercepting them near Fort Apache and driving them back toward Mexico.[106]

General Miles sent a column into Mexico to continue the pursuit. In a summer-long campaign, the troops wore themselves out, with little to show for it. Another small party under Lieutenant Charles Gatewood did find Geronimo and explained to him Miles's proposal that the Indians surrender and be sent to Florida to join the rest of their people. After a day-long conference, punctuated by a long recitation of grievances and many questions, Geronimo agreed to surrender to Miles. Word of this went out, and Miles designated Skeleton Canyon, about sixty miles southeast of Fort Bowie, as the site where they should meet. The Indians then numbered twenty-four men and fourteen women and children.

Gatewood's scouts and Geronimo's people packed up and began moving north toward the appointed rendezvous with Miles. They camped briefly at Guadalupe Canyon and at Cottonwood Springs, arriving at Skeleton Canyon on September 2. Miles appeared on the afternoon of the next day and had a long talk with Geronimo and some of the other Indians. Geronimo surrendered then, for the fourth time as he said, and on September 4 Naiche placed himself and the rest of the band in Miles's hands. Soldiers and Indians wended their way to Fort Bowie.

Early on the afternoon of September 8, everyone arrived at Bowie station on the Southern Pacific Railroad, where Miles had arranged for a train to transport the Indians. The Chiricahuas climbed on board, took a last look at Arizona, and set off to join their families already in exile in Florida. The Indian wars in the Southwest were almost over.[107]

Massai, Apache Kid, and Other 'Last Apaches'

After 1886 individual Indians continued to roam as outlaws through southeastern Arizona and New Mexico. The two best-known were Massai ("Big Foot") and the Apache Kid. Massai had escaped from one of the trains bearing the Chiricahuas to Florida; the Apache Kid broke away while being escorted to the territorial prison at Yuma, Arizona. Both men were real, but the robberies and murders attributed to them are mostly legendary. One murder, that of Robert Hardie, took place in Rucker Canyon near old Camp Rucker. Hardie was ambushed by Say-es, who was later taken into custody at San Carlos. At the time (May 1890), Say-es had been traveling with the Apache Kid. The Kid stayed in the mountains and evaded all pursuers, with the result that his later years and eventual death are shrouded in uncertainty. Massai was killed around 1911 by a posse in the San Mateo Mountains of southern New Mexico.[108]

As recently as 1896 southeastern Arizona experienced a final round of Indian raids and army campaigning. The murders of several citizens spurred the 7th Cavalry into the field, accompanied by Indian Scouts. News reports had claimed that up to eight Indians killed Alfred Hand in the Cave Creek area of the Chiricahua Mountains on March 28, 1896. Troop F under Lieutenant Sedgwick Rice set off in pursuit but could not catch the murderers.

In early May of 1896, a citizen hunting horses in the mountains found a recently deserted ranchería of ten or more wickiups in a small canyon. Word was sent to Lieutenant N. K. Averill, then in the vicinity of old Camp Rucker. Averill set off with a detachment from the 7th Cavalry and Indian Scouts, following the trail for some eighty-six miles to the Indians' new camp on a high, rocky hill near Cajón Bonito, south of the Mexican border and southeast of Cloverdale, New Mexico. Averill attempted to surround this hill, but fifteen Indians took flight. The soldiers wounded one warrior and captured all of the horses, camp equipage, and provisions. One week later there was another skirmish near Guadalupe Canyon.

During June of 1896, Lieutenant William Yates and an expedition out of Fort Huachuca came upon an Apache band camped in the mountains fifty miles or so south of San Bernardino. The soldiers attacked, but after desultory fighting the Indians broke contact. This skirmish proved to be the last in the long series of conflicts between the army and the Apaches.[109]

The nature of Apache raiding and the relationship of the people to the land changed dramatically between the Civil War years and Geronimo's final surrender. Earlier attacks were often livestock raids; later ones deliberately took lives. In the course of a quarter of a century, incidents grew less frequent and briefer in duration, even as the fighting became very bloody, with the actual losses frequently enhanced by screaming newspaper headlines. Indians were virtually confined to their reservations from about 1880, and they rarely threatened settlements elsewhere. The few Apaches who remained out and continued raiding were forced to operate as guerrillas, moving rapidly and living in Mexico between raids. Eventually their numbers were so reduced that they could threaten only individual ranches and army patrols. The last warriors include the most famous ones, and their feats are among the best known of any from the Indian Wars period.

7
THE MINING FRONTIER

American adventurers began exploring southern Arizona even before the United States took possession of the Gadsden Purchase. The rediscovery of old Spanish and Mexican mines led to a brief mining boom, cut short by the Civil War. Mineral interests between 1857 and 1861 centered on the silver-lead prospects in the upper Santa Cruz and Arivaca valleys. After the Mowry mine closed in 1862, Arizona south of the Gila River saw only limited development until the late 1870s. Mining resumed around 1878 and prospered for fifteen years, spurred by the remonetization of silver. Activity in the twentieth century has been greatest in times of high metal prices and has emphasized the base metals—copper, lead, zinc. By the 1970s increasing costs and the depletion of ore bodies had caused the suspension of most mining, although several major copper producers are still in operation today.

How to Promote a Mine

Any history of mining has several inherent problems. For one thing the usual practice of relying upon contemporary or primary sources turns topsy-turvy. Such sources are often suspect, since mine owners and other interested parties deliberately sought to enhance the value of their properties, promoting them to raise capital for their development or to attract a purchaser. Without capital there could be no development or production. The brightest prospects were understandably the most attractive to investors.

Would-be mining magnates practiced the art of raising money by writing flattering newspaper accounts, advertisements, and brochures; by enticing well-known people to become company directors; and through the collection of expert testimonies and the publication of favorable assays on ore samples, all for the purpose of separating East and West Coast investors from their dollars. Promotion typically had little regard for accuracy; fact and fiction became so intertwined that separation of the two may now be almost impossible.

Heavy promotion did not always lead to development, nor was a lack of capital the only reason why mining properties might fail to be developed or might be shut down after brief runs. Sometimes the price of metal dropped, as with silver after 1893, so that an operation was no longer profitable. If a mine had refractory ores difficult to reduce, or veins and ore bodies too low-grade to work economically, or if the mine had already been worked out, the owners were not likely to advertise such details to prospective buyers.

To do so would have gone against another fact of frontier life, which was that profits were most commonly sought through buying and selling mining properties, rather than by developing them. This was especially true in the early history of a mining district or where ores were of low value. "Booming" a claim or district in an attempt to increase its value and lure purchasers would enable the claimants to sell out at a profit or perhaps float more stock. This kind of promotion was easier and more profitable than actual development, since little capital was required, and the risks attending development were eliminated.

Studies of territorial mining have given little attention to the pivotal role of capital, to the purchase and sale of mines as a business that frequently outpaced mining itself, or to the necessity for cheap, long-distance transportation in order to carry ores to processing plants. As a result, the romance of mining overshadows its realities. An important negative factor in pioneer mining was sheer incompetence and the waste of both capital and resources. As early as 1859 a correspondent from Tubac complained that the great need was for "men who understand extracting silver from its various ores."[1] Writing in 1868, J. Ross Browne concluded that

> In many cases the whole capital of the owners has been frittered away in unnecessary buildings, improper machinery, and large remuneration to unworthy agents, men who, next to the Apache, have by their recklessness obstructed the progress of the country, and prejudiced capitalists against further investment in it.
>
> Thus far it may be truthfully asserted that there have been more failures in superintendents than in mines in Arizona. . . .[2]

The only really major mining developments in southeastern Arizona were the Lavender Pit, Copper Queen, and other properties at Bisbee, also known as the Warren mining district, and since the 1950s, the San Manuel Mine at Mammoth and the various ore bodies of the Pima district south of Tucson. The Tombstone, Harshaw, Patagonia, Cochise (Johnson Camp), Helvetia, and Oro Blanco districts operated on more modest scales, still in multimillions of dollars, often active only for short periods followed by long closures. Many prospects failed to develop at all.

The most reliable sources for evaluating the significance of mining are actual production statistics, where these exist, and relevant geologic literature. The reports by territorial and state geologists and by U.S. Geological

Survey personnel are valuable as well, because these people had technical knowledge and were able to exercise independent judgments. Their findings and statistical compilations are scattered through the mining literature.

Much of the mining in southeastern Arizona has been in our mountain islands in the desert, and the framework chosen here is the various mountain ranges and their mining districts. Mining-district terminology has been stable for a century or more, until a number of new districts were added in the 1980s and the older ones realigned or renamed.[3] Use of the older names is retained here except where, as in the Rincon and Pinaleño ranges, some recently named locations and districts have no older precedents.

Occasionally in older writings one sees the term "chloriders" used in an offhand way. In the late nineteenth century chlorination mills enjoyed a brief popularity as the poor miner's path to riches. The operating principal was the use of gaseous chlorine or bleaching powder to combine with gold or silver (as from low-grade ores) and the subsequent reduction of the precious metal chlorides with a base metal. Chlorination proved to be highly dangerous and technically inefficient; the process was soon dropped.[4]

Mountains West of the Santa Cruz Valley

West of the upper Santa Cruz Valley lies a complex of mountain ranges. The easternmost of these (the Tumacacoris, Atascosas and Pajaritos) have seen little mining activity at any period. Farther west is a mineralized belt consisting of the Cerro Colorados, Las Guijas, San Luis, and Oro Blanco Mountains, Montana Peak, and adjoining ridge systems. Within these ranges are a total of four mining districts.

The Arivaca district includes the Las Guijas and San Luis mountains, northwest and southwest from the old settlement of Arivaca. The Cerro Colorado district lies on the southwestern flank of the Cerro Colorado Mountains. On the north slope of the Pajarito Mountains, between Pajarito Peak and Castle Rock, is the Pajarito mining district. The Oro Blanco district comprises all mining activities in western Santa Cruz County.[5]

Cerro Colorado and Arivaca Mining Districts

In late June of 1855, Lieutenant N. Michler led his section of the U.S.-Mexico boundary survey party south from Tucson and soon picked up rumors of rich mines. Then he reached the ruins of the old ranch at Arivaca, where "[w]ithin four miles, and south of the deserted rancho, are to be found

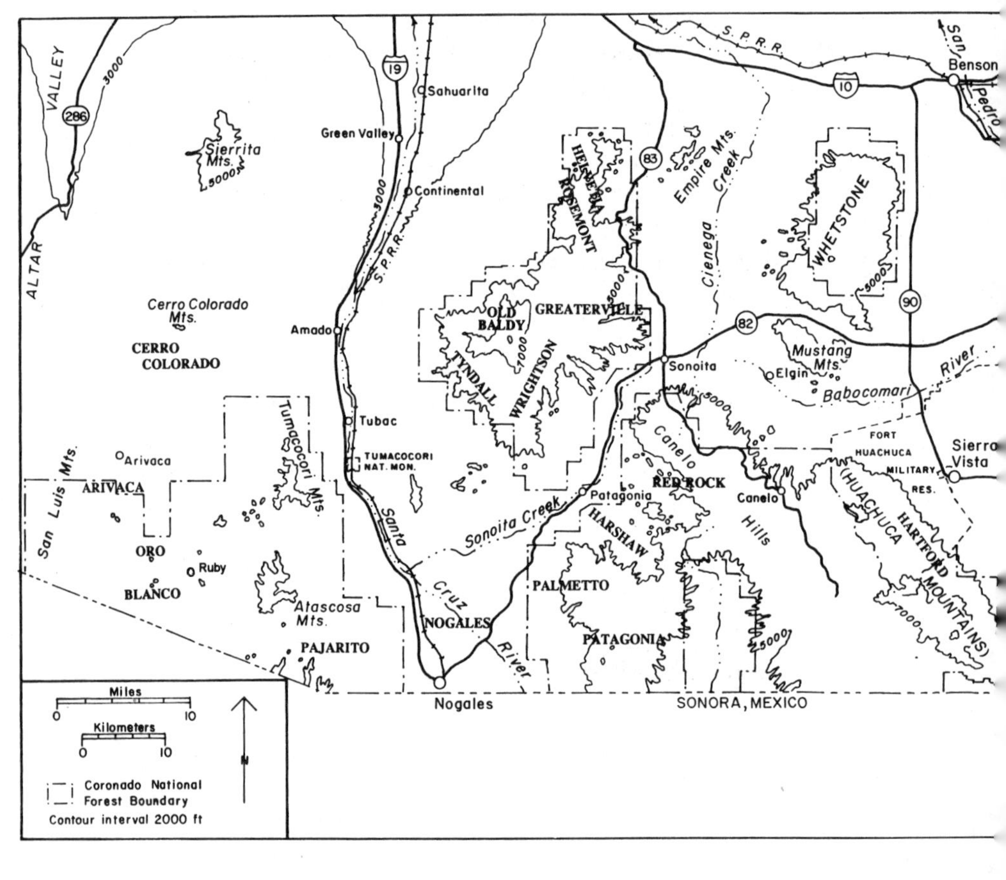

Map 16.
Mining districts between the Santa Cruz and San Pedro rivers, and west of the Santa Cruz River. (Map by Coronado National Forest.)

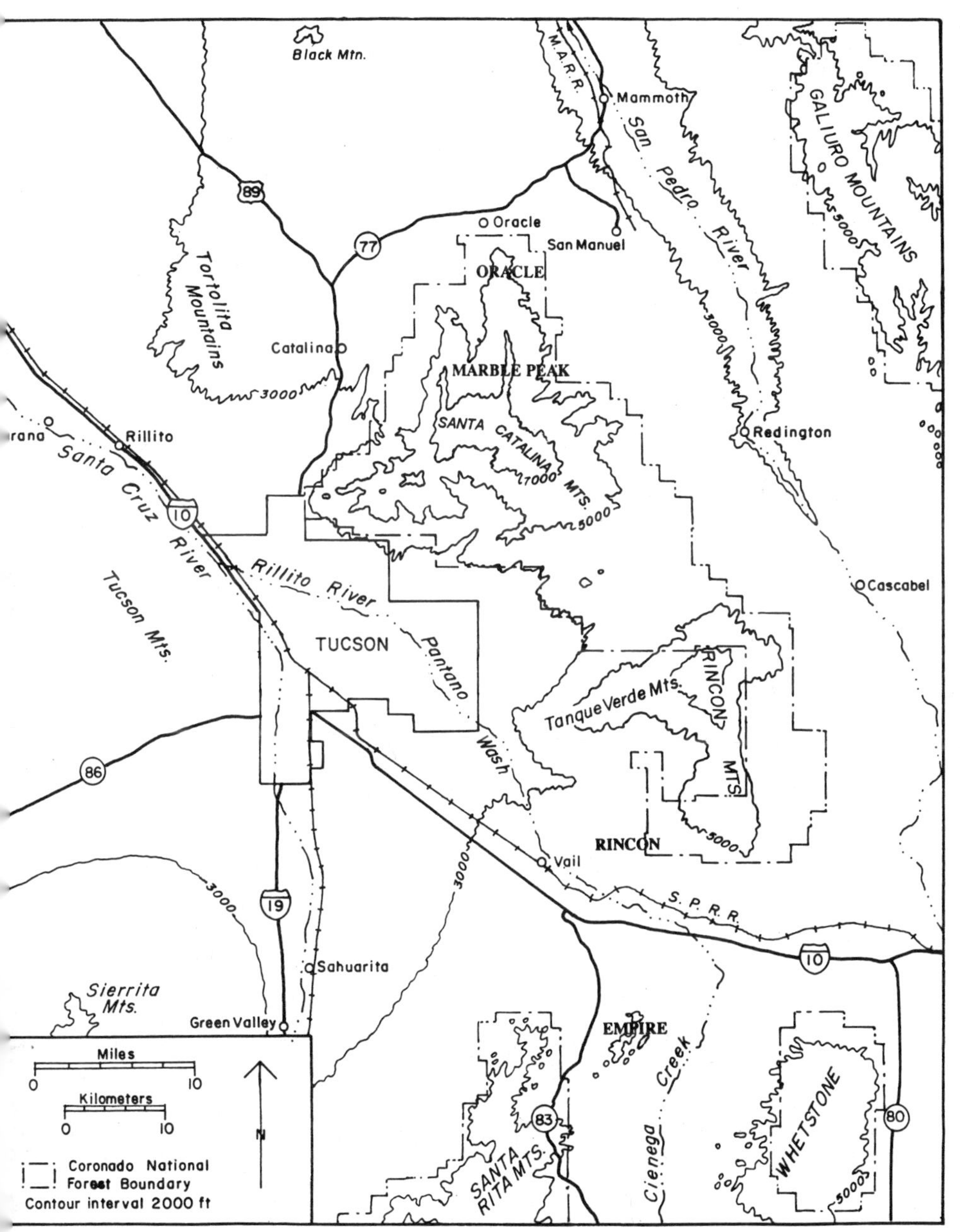

Map 17.
Historical mining districts near Tucson, Arizona.
(Map by Coronado National Forest.)

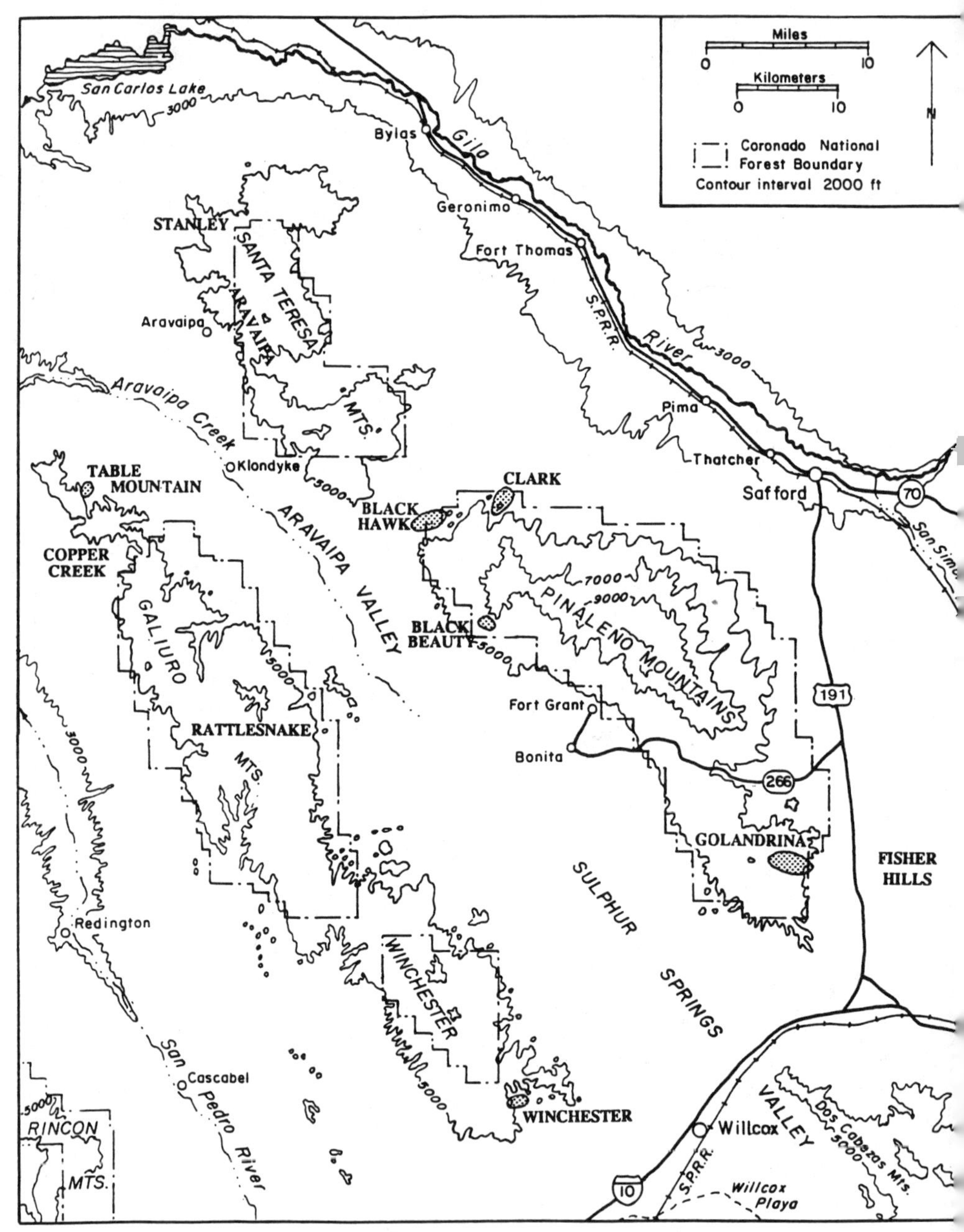

Map 18.
Mining districts between the San Pedro and Gila rivers.
(Map by Coronado National Forest.)

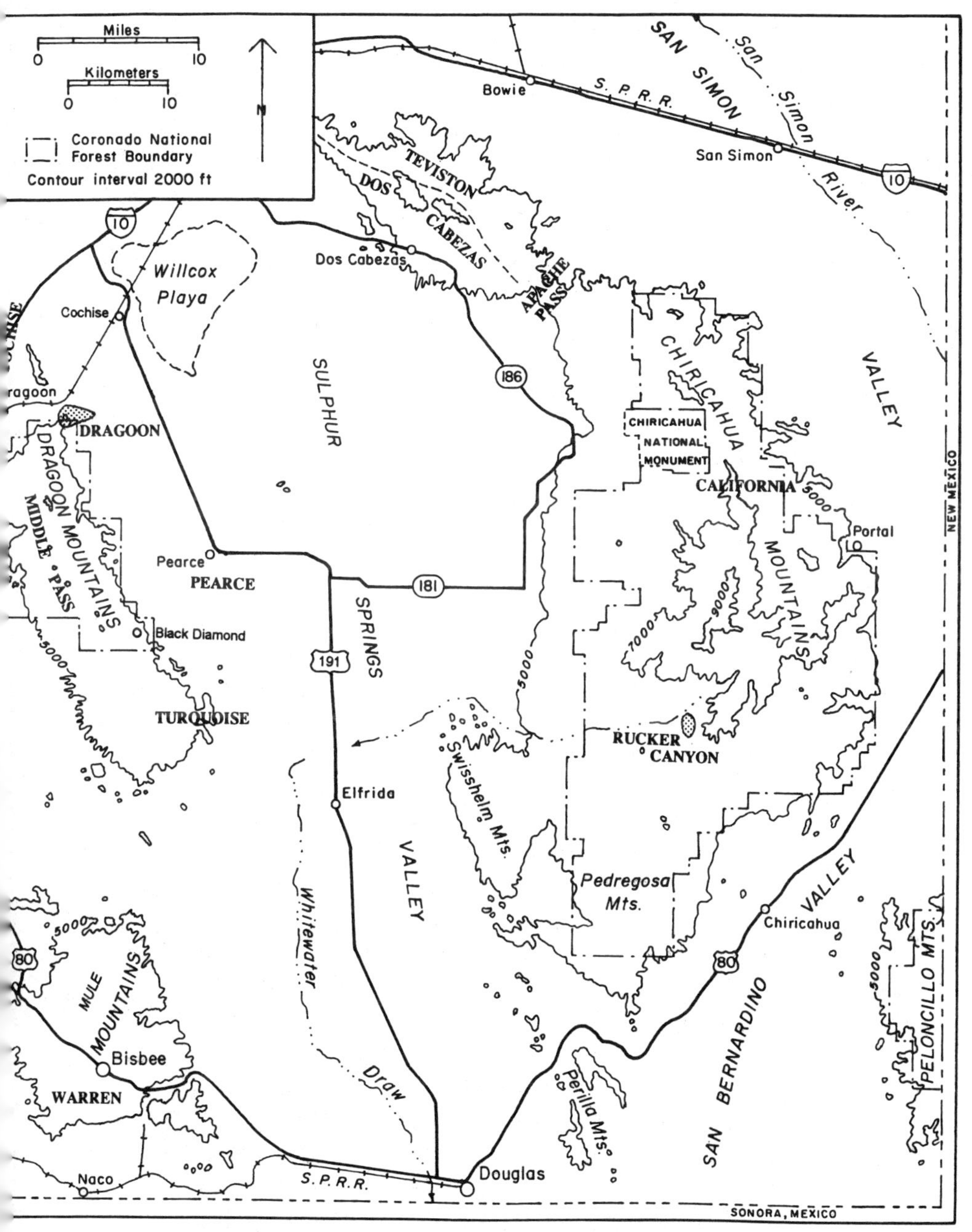

Map 19.
Mining districts in the Chiricahua, Dragoon, and other ranges east of the San Pedro River. (Map by Coronado National Forest.)

large excavations made by men previously engaged in mining; piles of metallic ore lay near the springs where they had been engaged in smelting."[6] Findings such as these quickly whetted interest. The boundary commissioner himself, Major W. H. Emory, grew effusive on southern Arizona's prospects for mineral wealth and added that "the country is now full of *prospectors* from California."[7]

The era of modern mining in Arizona dates from 1857, with the purchase of two Mexican land grants in the Santa Cruz Valley. Both grants, the Sopori and the Arivaca, were eventually rejected by the Court of Private Land Claims, but for a time they provided the legal basis for mining operations within their bounds. The Sopori silver mine or mines were the first to be reopened; work had started by the first months of 1857. The ores were not, as their promoter, Sylvester Mowry, confidently predicted, "destined to yield hundreds of millions." The Sopori Mine, evidently located in the northernmost reaches of the Tumacacori Mountains, soon dropped from sight amidst the maneuverings and conflicting title claims of several individuals and two Rhode Island–based mining companies.[8]

Three well-known early Arizonians and their Cincinnati-based company became the principals in another early landholding and mining venture. The individuals were an adventurer by the name of Charles D. Poston, an explorer and cartographer named Herman Ehrenberg, and an army officer, Samuel P. Heintzelman. The Sonora Exploring and Mining Co. was organized in March of 1856; two years later it spun off a subsidiary, the Santa Rita Silver Mining Co.[9]

Poston and Ehrenberg arrived in Arizona in August of 1856. Before the end of the year, they had established the Sonora Exploring and Mining Co. headquarters at the then-abandoned presidio of Tubac and had purchased the title to two *sitios* of land comprising the Arivaca Ranch. By early 1857 they reported the discovery of the Heintzelman Vein, on the southeastern side of the Cerro Colorado Mountains, and acquisition of the old Salero Mine in the Santa Rita Mountains.[10]

The prospects for this firm's mines were reported as fabulous. The reality was that during the first two years, they shipped limited quantities of ores to the East and to California, since the only facilities locally were two small smelting furnaces.[11] The first bar of silver from their works at Cerro Colorado was produced in March 1859. Sometime that year the company's engineers initiated use of the barrel amalgamation process for silver extraction, but the long-planned amalgamation works at Arivaca never quite reached completion. The business suffered from a host of labor and technical problems as well as a shortage of capital, and in 1861 Apache raids added to the

Heintzelman Mine on the Arivaca Ranch, from a sketch by Charles Schuchard, c. 1857. (Courtesy, Rio Grande Historical Collections, New Mexico State University Library.)

owners' woes. The result was an estimated production of only $75,000 in silver from 1858 through 1861.[12] Operations ended in late July of 1861, when Mexican bandits murdered Charles Poston's brother and two other men at the Cerro Colorado Mine.[13]

The Cerro Colorado district underwent a brief revival in the early 1880s, when the Consolidated Arizona Mine and Milling Co. built a stamp mill and amalgamation plant at Arivaca; sporadic operations continued into the 1930s. The total value of production since 1856 is estimated at $362,000.[14] The Arivaca district experienced intermittent, small-scale mining through 1941, for a total value of base and precious metal output of about $369,000. In both districts the economic values, mainly in gold and silver, were confined to spotty, near-surface exposures, where weathering and oxidation had enriched the vein deposits.[15]

Pajarito Mining District

In the rugged hills west of Nogales are a half-dozen small mines, reportedly worked since the middle 1800s for high-grade silver pockets. Perhaps these were the "New Silver Mine" announced in the April 28, 1859 *Weekly Arizonian* (p. 2):

> Capt. Donaldson, U.S. collector at Calabasas, has lately, after considerable search, discovered what he considers to be the old Tomocacari [*sic*] silver mine, located about eighteen miles from the Mission, in the range of mountains which lies west of the Santa Cruz valley. There are six openings at this mine, with a trench, the remains of furnaces, &c, which proves that extensive operations were once carried on.

In more recent years, the Sunset and the Morning and Evening mine groups plus the St. Patrick, White Oaks, and Big Steve mines operated sporadically. The primary values came from 1,000 tons of ore, mainly lead and silver, worth about $68,000.[16]

Oro Blanco Mining District

From six to a dozen miles southeast of Arivaca, in the hills to either side of Oro Blanco Wash and California Gulch, lie the mines and camps of the Oro Blanco district. The gold placers and lode deposits were first worked in the Spanish and Mexican periods. Of these we are told that "[t]he fact of gold mines having been worked by the Mexicans in that section years ago has been long known, . . . The ruins of arrastras, mining camps and cabins being scattered around, the basin wherein they are situated is now known as Old Oro Blanco, the present settlement of Oro Blanco being situated about seven miles more northerly."[17]

The first American location was made in 1873, on the Oro Blanco Vein. The Ostrich, Yellow Jacket, and other lode mines were located soon afterwards, about the same time that the placers were rediscovered. While placer deposits occurred throughout the Oro Blanco mountains, lode mining operations were concentrated in three principal areas. Within two miles or so of Oro Blanco and to the west lay the Oro Blanco, Ostrich, Yellow Jacket, and a number of smaller mines, while the Austerlitz Mine was south of the town. Many other mines, including the Margarita, Warsaw, Smuggler Gulch, and Rubiana mine groups, were about seven miles to the south along Warsaw Gulch, near Old Oro Blanco. Finally there was the Montana mine group, adjacent to the twentieth-century mining camp of Ruby.[18]

New discoveries made in 1880 included the Montana Ledge. Several small mills built during the early 1880s operated when water was available; at the Ostrich mill a roasting furnace for treating sulfide ores was attached. Miners lived at the Oro Blanco Camp, which one writer described after "a careful visit":

> Oro Blanco is a quiet little town, inhabited by a superior class of miners and workmen, and all are opposed to sharps, tramps and jumpers. They are an intelligent class generally, and are determined to keep a model mining camp, free from loafers, rowdies and reckless characters. The mining claims are numerous, and show prospects that will soon bring capital among them.[19]

By 1887 the better ore had largely been exhausted from the oxidized zones near the surface and mining had all but ceased. The gold output to the end of 1886 probably did not exceed $700,000.[20]

The principal mineral values during the earlier decades were in gold. The district received its name from the placer gold largely being alloyed with silver, so that the yellow color was lost. In lode mining the most successful ventures were the Montana, Austerlitz, Yellow Jacket, and Old Glory mines, all of which contained low-grade gold ores. At several of the larger veins the mineralization changed at shallow depths to zinc-lead-silver sulphides, which were not worked successfully until the 1920s.[21]

After its initial boom, the Oro Blanco district saw intermittent production for another forty years; much of the time the mines were inactive. When the silver mines closed in 1893, attention again turned to gold. Several of the old gold mines reopened and new mills were erected, only to lapse within a decade. Activity revived again in 1903, when eastern companies organized to operate the mines and build mills for both the amalgamation and cyaniding processes. However, all work had ceased by the end of 1904.[22] With respect to this history of sporadic activity at Oro Blanco, one mining engineer a few years later commented that ". . . most of the money was spent on reduction works rather than on underground development. As is usual, this kind of mining met with financial disaster in nearly every case."[23] There were other brief revivals, but by 1914 mining had virtually stopped. The Oro Blanco post office was discontinued in 1915.

Base-metal production (of lead and zinc) in the Oro Blanco district dates only from 1912 and first became significant in 1917–18. The Goldfield Consolidated Mines Co. leased the Montana Mine then, but only for a year. The first really large-scale operation in the district came when the Eagle Pitcher Lead Co. reopened the Montana Mine in 1927 and built a new mill to concentrate the lead-zinc ores. This mill closed in 1930, resuming in late 1934 with an increased capacity. The Montana Mine produced lead-zinc minerals, with gold and silver as important byproducts, until May of 1940, by which time the company had mined about 870,000 tons of ore. Since 1942 the district has seen only minor, sporadic activity. The estimated total value of both base- and precious-metal production through 1972 is $12,900,000.[24]

Ruby

The mining camp known originally as Montana Camp grew into the principal mining town in the Oro Blanco district. The camp was named for Montana Peak, just to the south of it. Its origin and early years are obscure, but the beginning probably does not predate the discovery of the Montana Ledge in 1880. Through the long years of intermittent mining, a small community persisted. During a brief revival of the Austerlitz and Oro mines in 1912, application for a post office was honored, and the old Montana camp became the mining town of Ruby.

Prior to his death in 1903, George Cheyney of Tucson had started a general store at Montana Camp. This passed through a series of owners until 1913, when Philip Clarke bought the business and erected a new adobe-frame building. This new store and post office became the setting for two episodes of murder that brought Ruby briefly into the headlines. The first, in February 1920, involved two brothers, John and Alex Frasier, who were running the store when two Mexican bandits shot and killed both men during a daring daylight robbery; John Frasier lived long enough to identify the murderers. Both robbers disappeared into Mexico, but one returned to a mining camp near Tucson. The sheriff sent two deputies to arrest him; the outlaw drew first and killed one of the deputies, but he was quickly gunned down by the other.[25]

A year and half later, Frank and Myrtle Pearson owned the Ruby store. Frank's half-sister Irene and his sister-in-law were visiting at the time of a bloody episode on August 26, 1921. Seven armed Mexicans broke in, shot Frank Pearson, and then murdered his wife, after forcing her to open the safe. The sister-in-law, an eyewitness, related what happened in an interview years later: "I saw a pistol lying on a table and picked it up. I don't know why I did so, for I didn't know how to use it. I pointed the gun at the bandits, and one of them fired at me! It was a near miss; the bullet came so close that it seared my face . . . " In the confusion, Irene grabbed the Pearsons' four-year-old daughter and dived out the door. "Although mortally wounded, Frank managed to get his gun and fire it, but he died as he pulled the trigger and his shots went wild, the last one ricocheting across the floor as he fell. I fainted."[26]

The robbers took their loot and fled across the border. Subsequently two of them, Plácido Silvas and Manuel Martínez, were captured and brought to trial. Silvas received life imprisonment, while the hangman carried out the sentence against Martínez.[27]

The depression years coincided with Ruby's heyday. The population rose to more than 1000 in the 1930s, with about 350 miners at work. The Montana mine and mill made Ruby the largest producer of lead and zinc in Arizona from 1935 to 1939. When the ore gave out in 1940, the mine closed, and the mill was moved to Sahuarita. Ruby itself became a ghost town, one of the best preserved in southern Arizona.[28]

The Santa Rita Mountains

At the time of their developments in the Cerro Colorado and Arivaca districts, the same early entrepreneurs began mining in the Santa Rita Mountains. By the 1880s the Santa Ritas had been extensively prospected, and many mines had been established. In all but two of the six mining districts, mineralization was found to be spotty and sparse, with most of the economic returns coming from oxidized deposits near the surface.

The Tyndall district is in Santa Cruz County, where it extends south from the border with Pima County along the western flank of the Santa Rita range as far as Sonoita Creek. At one time the southern part of the Tyndall district, so named in 1876, was called the Aztec district. To the east lies the Wrightson mining district, on the southeastern slope of the Santa Ritas and south of the divide that extends east from Mt. Wrightson ("Old Baldy") toward Sonoita Creek.[29]

North of the Wrightson district, the Greaterville district takes in most of the north-central Santa Rita Mountains in Pima County as far as Box Canyon. In the 1870s this was first known as the Santa Rita placers, then as the Smith district, and finally (since 1880) as the Greaterville district. Just to the west of it is the Old Baldy mining district, a small area that includes the mountainous slopes to either side of Madera Canyon and a prominent west-side spur of the Santa Ritas. At the northern end of this range are the Helvetia and Rosemont districts, the former covering the north and northwestern slope of the mountains. The Rosemont district comprises the eastern slope, east and southeast of the main Helvetia mining area.[30]

Tyndall Mining District

In 1858 the Santa Rita Silver Mining Company began reopening the Salero, Ojero, Asugarero, Bustillo, and other old mines in the southern Santa Ritas, seeking the argentiferous galena ore exposed in oxidized, near-surface deposits. The company managers accomplished little more than the construction of a mining camp, the Hacienda de Santa Rita, situated 1.5 miles from the Salero Mine in the southern part of the district.

The Salero Mine had been worked in the Spanish or Mexican periods. The new hacienda lay about 300 yards from what Charles Poston pointed out as "the old Hacienda of the Santa Rita mines, (which were destroyed some 35 years since by the Apaches who also massacred every soul belonging to the mines, not one escaping). Here were discovered the remains of old furnaces and other evidences of mining operations."[31] By 1861 the company's improvements at the new hacienda included several houses, the beginnings of a mill, and one furnace.[32]

There are good accounts of the Santa Rita Silver Mining Company's operations.[33] The experiences of Raphael Pumpelly, a mining engineer and the last manager before the Civil War, are especially apt, because he became familiar with the local geology. Pumpelly said that the veins were thin, their work was mere prospecting, and they did not have enough ore to meet expenses. The company, never well financed, ran out of money. Work was dangerous because the mine superintendents were as likely to be murdered by their Mexican workmen as by roving Apaches. Pumpelly ended up as "the only one of at least five successive managers of the Santa Rita who was not killed by Mexicans or Indians."[34]

The furnace at Santa Rita eventually made a single run, which required six weeks and was done using ore mostly from the Heintzelman (Cerro Colorado) mine. Harassed now by the Apaches and threatened by their own laborers, the surviving Americans packed up and headed for Tubac before the silver had even cooled. This was on June 15, 1861. Three years later the place still stood abandoned. In 1865 the Apaches murdered William Wrightson, sent out to reopen the mines, and work stopped again.[35]

The property was relocated and some $10,000 worth of ore shipped in the 1870s. About 1900 the Salero Mines Co. bought the claims; two years later they began development and operated intermittently until 1911. Total production from the Salero Mine is estimated at only 500 tons of lead-silver ore.[36]

Most of the other mines—the Alto (also known as the Gold Tree and El Plomo), Wandering Jew, Bland, Baca Float and Toluachi or Josiah Bond mines, Trenton, Arizona-Pittsburg, and Eureka (Old Mexican)—in the Salero-Alto area are a few miles north of the Salero property. These holdings were worked sporadically and produced small amounts of ore. The Alto Mine, another alleged Spanish discovery, saw occasional mining activity during the late nineteenth century and again through the 1920s. Estimated and recorded production of lead-copper-silver ore here totaled 3,500 tons.[37]

The Salero and Alto mines are historically the most significant in the Tyndall district. Nearby ghost towns are the remains of camps associated with the early twentieth-century workings. At Salero Camp the adobe buildings were still roofed and described as beautifully preserved as of 1980. The town of Alto had seven hundred people as of 1905, with the usual stores, bars, and a school. The post office remained in service there until 1933, and its ruins are the principal remaining structure today.[38]

In 1909 the entire Tyndall district contained forty or more mines and prospects. Most claims lay on or near major drainages that issued westward, toward the Santa Cruz Valley. Mines that were worked to some extent after 1900 included the Elephant Head group along Chino Canyon, the Devil's Cash Box and other prospects along Agua Caliente Canyon, and the Montosa mine, some 1.5 miles farther south. A smelter at the latter operated for four and one-half days in 1901. In Josephine Canyon the mineral deposits were in the upper parts of the canyon. These saw considerable development but little production, the ore being mostly low-grade. South of the Salero property lay the Montezuma Mine, a low-grade ore claim allegedly worked in the Mexican period but very little since then.[39]

The only modern production has come from the Glove group of mines along Cottonwood Canyon. These properties produced nearly 30,000 tons of argentiferous galena ore in the years between 1952 and 1972. Intermittent operations at the Jefferson Mine in the Alto area saw some 6,500 tons of lead-silver ore extracted between the early 1900s and 1950. The total estimated and recorded production of all metals from the Tyndall district through 1972 is about $3,600,000.[40]

Wrightson Mining District

Economic mineralization in the Wrightson district is spotty and sparse. The ores include argentiferous galena veins that are oxidized and enriched near the surface. The area was first prospected in the late 1870s and mined as recently as the late 1950s, much of the activity taking place from about 1906 through 1911. The total value of the lead, silver, copper, and gold recovered through 1972 is placed at $138,000.[41]

Greaterville Mining District

This district has both lode and placer deposits, but the history of mining essentially concerns the placer activity around Greaterville. Gold placers there occupied an area of about eight square miles, known initially as the Smith diggings or district, at the eastern foot of the Santa Rita Mountains. The first discoveries were made in 1874, and a rush developed the next summer. The Tucson *Arizona Citizen* of July 3, 1875, reported that:

> Wednesday of this week this town was again surprised at the products of placer-gold in Smith district. David Burroughs brought in from there 9 1/2 ounces of nice placer-gold, the product of three days' work of himself alone, and he carried the dirt three-fourths of a mile in a sack on his back to water, where he washed it under unfavorable circumstances. The gold averages coarse. One piece is worth about $50, another near $35, and others from $1 to $5. His claim is in a gulch making into the main placer-ravine from the Santa Rita Mountain side.
>
> We learn that Horace Arden has regularly made an ounce a day in the Smith district, and that he is not noted for working imprudently hard, but goes along cleverly, making his $16 to $20 per day; the gold being worth these figures per ounce.
>
> Since the above was written, Jack Ralston came in from Smith district with $150 more placer-gold—nuggets we should say. The largest piece is worth just $90.50, and the balance in bits from $1 to $10. This gold was washed, and by packing the dirt a long distance to water. The hills and gulches all about have gold in them, and with plenty of water, millions could soon be taken out.[42]

With news like this, the wonder is that Tucson did not become a ghost town.

The placer gold occurred in gravels exposed by a series of steep-sided gulches that drained toward the east. The productive gulches were spread over a distance of just 1.5 miles, from Boston on the south to Empire on the north. This proved to be the largest and richest placer ground in southern Arizona, and a number of mining camps sprang up.[43] One description from October 1875 said that Sucker Gulch was becoming quite thickly settled, with eight or nine different camps on it.[44] A correspondent in February 1876 regretted that space would not permit a description of the different camps, but noted that there were about six, with some 350 miners, and a reservoir at every camp.[45] Greater Creek (or Gulch) was presumably the original name for Ophir Gulch. A post office established there on January 3, 1879, was called Greaterville.

Placer mining requires water, and water was scarce here. The nearest permanent source was Gardner Canyon, four miles to the south. When the gulches were not flowing with runoff, the miners bought water that had been packed in on burros. To work the gravels they either used rockers, which were abbreviated riffleboxes mounted on traverse rockers, or long toms—long wooden troughs with baffles on the bottom.[46] Notwithstanding the difficulties the output amounted to $10 or more a day for each man. By February 1876 a prominent merchant, Herman Welisch, estimated that the placers had already yielded between $60,000 and $80,000 in gold.[47]

The Greaterville placers remained active for several years, but by 1881 the richer gravels had been worked over and the miners began to drift away; by 1886 the paying gravels were considered worked out. From then until 1900, Greaterville Camp was practically dead. For several months that year and again in 1904, two firms tried to work the ground of Kentucky Gulch by hydraulic methods. The returns were reportedly too low to warrant further work, and the operations ceased.[48]

Since 1905 several companies have tried various methods to work parts of the placer area; all failed because of insufficient water and poor selection of ground. Individuals meanwhile continued intermittent, small-scale placer mining, obtaining several hundred to several thousand dollars worth of gold a year by their efforts. Estimates of the total production of Greaterville's placers between 1873 and 1948 vary widely, from a minimum figure of $210,000 to an upper one in the millions of dollars.[49]

Lode deposits in this district were small and weak, with enriched, oxidized outcrops furnishing economic returns estimated at $30,000 through 1929. The principal lode mining took place at the Conglomerate, or Anderson, mine, worked sporadically from the early 1900s until 1955. It produced a small tonnage of lead-silver ore.[50]

Greaterville continued as a post office until 1946, long after its prosperity had fled. All that remains today are three small adobe homes, a collapsed wood-and-tin structure, and a small cemetery.[51] Kentucky Camp, scarcely a mile to the south, was bought up sometime before 1911 by a Tucson lawyer, Louis G. Hummel. His daughter and her husband later took up residence there and turned it into a cattle ranch, called the Fenter place. The last cattle were shipped about 1965, and the land was sold again, to a mining company.[52]

Old Baldy Mining District

This small area lies on the northwest side of the Santa Rita Mountains in both Pima and Santa Cruz counties, just west of the Greaterville district. Prospecting and superficial development began in the 1880s, but only one mine (the Jackson mine in Jackson Canyon) produced more than token amounts of ore. Stone Cabin and Jackson canyons held most of the other prospects, the values of which were principally in copper. The total estimated and recorded production of ore is valued at about $8,000. In addition to these lode deposits, there are molybdenite prospects about half a mile south of White House in Madera Canyon and the Old Baldy gold placers below the mouth of the canyon.[53]

Helvetia and Rosemont Mining Districts

These two districts at the northern end of the Santa Ritas have been the source of most base- and precious-metal production from this mountain range. The estimated and recorded values, primarily of copper and silver, totaled $7,780,000 through 1972.[54] The histories of these copper-production centers are closely linked, and they are treated here as a single district.

Rosemont was a classic example of boom and bust in copper mining. Mining claims had been located as early as 1879, but virtually no work was done until L. J. Rose organized the Rosemont Smelting and Mining Company. In 1894, with copper at rock-bottom prices, this firm commenced to develop its properties and erected a sixty-ton copper-smelting furnace. A copper smelter required a continuous air blast to increase the heat and reduce metallic copper from its chemical partners. When such a furnace began operation it was said to have been blown in, or put in blast; the one at Rosemont was blown in and operated sporadically until June 1896. At that time the claims and other possessions of this undercapitalized business passed into the possession of the Lewisohn Brothers, copper brokers, of New York City.[55]

The fortunes of Rosemont Camp rose and fell with the market price of copper. The new owners bought other nearby properties and began to develop these as well. A two-story frame hotel, the principal building in the camp, was erected around 1897. In 1899–1901 copper prices reached their highest level since 1883. The Lewisohns took out 3,000 tons of ore from their chief producer, the Mohawk mine in the adjoining Helvetia district, and packed 500 tons of it over the mountain crest to the Rosemont smelter. This smelter ran intermittently through 1901, then ceased operation.[56] The post office at Rosemont opened in 1894 and closed on May 14, 1910, after mining became inactive. The Lewisohns held onto the townsite and fifty-nine claims.[57]

When copper prices rose again with the beginning of World War I, mining resumed in the Helvetia-Rosemont districts. The Rosemont group of claims, located about 1.5 miles east of Helvetia, yielded large amounts of copper and zinc in 1917–18. After 1920 these claims saw only small, intermittent shipments of ore by lessees. Much more significant was the Narragansett claim, near the crest of the mountains on the Rosemont side. This property had been owned and developed by the same man, J. K. Brown since 1879. Brown sold his claim in July 1915, and the buyers, Narragansett Mines Co., began production in September. This mine became the largest single producer in the Helvetia-Rosemont districts, with a reported output of more than 34,000 tons of ore in the 1915–18 period, yielding a smelter return of $835,860.[58]

A mining camp referred to as New Rosemont, a short distance east of the Narragansett mine, came to life in 1915. Within two years this community had a population of about two hundred, with thirty to forty men employed on each mine shift. Here as elsewhere the usual dwelling was a tent or a pole-frame building covered with beargrass. Other buildings included the mineowner's house, a pool hall, an assayer's residence, a deputy's house, a boarding house and diner, a dance hall and saloon, and of course the company store. Operations ceased when copper prices plummeted in 1921.[59]

Since 1920 the mines on the Rosemont side of the Santa Ritas have been idle most of the time. During the 1944–47 period, when the Helvetia district saw levels of production exceeding 1,000,000 pounds of copper a year, most of the ore came from the Rosemont group, the Copper World, Mohawk, and probably the Narragansett mines. These were worked under lease from the Lewisohn Estate, with production renewed again (by the Lewisohn Copper Co.) in 1957–59. The last owner-operator, C. D. Wilson, continued until the end of February 1961.[60]

The Helvetia district, on the north and northwestern slope of the Santa Ritas, had quite a different history. There were approximately thirty-five mines, with the first locations established in the late 1870s. In 1881 a Tucson group organized the Omega Copper Co. and enlisted working capital from Philadelphia. They developed a considerable tonnage of high-grade oxidized ore and erected a small blast furnace, which was blown in in April of 1883. Six months later all work stopped. Meanwhile a second venture, the Columbia Copper Co., built a small furnace just east of the later Tiptop Camp, but closed it early in 1883 because of a drop in the price of copper.[61]

An 1899 report noted that the Helvetia district had been shipping copper ore for years, under circumstances that are rarely glimpsed: "These ores have been taken from the most superficial openings and pits here and there in a multitude of places, and without the aid of capital. The work has been done by poor prospectors who have been maintained by the proceeds of shipments of ores taken from the croppings."[62]

This prospecting soon changed to mining. The Helvetia Copper Co. of New Jersey acquired many claims in 1891 and commenced development work. Helvetia Camp reportedly began to form at this time. The company completed its assessments by March of 1899 and had a 200-ton blast furnace ready in September of that year. Helvetia was already a boomtown; by May 1898 it had permanent company buildings, several stores, a line of tents to house the laborers, four saloons, and an eating house. The work force grew from less than 55 men to 350 between March and December 1899, as expanded operations got underway. The total population of Helvetia reached nearly 550 people in December 1899, the same month the town received a post office. For several years this was Pima County's largest mining camp.[63]

The citizens enjoyed baseball games, dances, baptisms, weddings, and perhaps even the knife fights, but they did without established law and order until 1901. The consequence was "the somewhat uproarious nature of life at Helvetia," as one writer expressed it.[64] Mining and smelting of copper ore continued through 1900, hampered only by periodic shortages of water or of coke for the smelter. In December 1900, after a production of more than 2,00,000 pounds of copper, the smelter caught fire and burned to the ground. Layoffs followed and although reconstruction began, production did not resume, copper prices then being in decline. The Helvetia Copper Company shut down all operations by the end of 1902.

In 1903 the business was reorganized as the Helvetia Copper Company of Arizona. A year of development work followed and after that, construction of a 150-ton copper-matte smelter. This smelter did not prove a success and closed early in 1907. Thereafter the company shipped its ore, until 1911. By July of 1911 the mines had closed.[65] Other small mining enterprises in the Helvetia area included the Tip Top Copper Co., which started operations in September 1904 and sent its ore to El Paso. The company closed down in the 1907 financial panic and reopened only briefly in 1912.[66]

Helvetia lost both its importance and most of its population after 1911. A few dozen people continued to live there, buoyed by a hope that the mines would reopen, but this never happened. In 1921 the post office was discontinued; two years later the school closed. A large, abandoned store building emphasized the now-forlorn appearance of the town, where a weekly dance was still held in the old dining room of the abandoned, half-tumbled-down hotel. As for everything else, "the old buildings, most of them crumbling adobes long exposed to the weather, had been patched with whatever material was available at little cost. There were five fairly well preserved frame houses from which most of the paint had faded. The gaunt old pioneer schoolhouse with its tall steep roof was also of lumber, apparently never painted."[67]

Lessees of the mines continued small-scale, irregular production and carried output to another peak in 1944–47. Since the 1950s activity has been slight and the town itself was reduced to one roofless adobe ruin as of 1980.[68] There is still copper here and interest may revive again; ASARCO has applied for a mineral patent covering claims near the divide in the Helvetia-Rosemont district.

The Patagonia Mountains

Prospectors covered these hills in the late 1850s, when they still bore the name Santa Cruz Mountains. Two of the five mining districts in the Patagonia Mountains became major producers, while the Patagonia Mine, renamed the Mowry Mine in 1860, is one of the most famous in Arizona.

The Harshaw mining district, at the northeastern end of the Patagonias, is bounded on the north by Sonoita Creek, on the east by Harshaw Creek and Meadow Valley Flat, to the south by an east-west line through American Peak, and by the general crest of the mountain range on the west. Immediately to the east and northeast lies the Red Rock district, which extends east to the approximate axis of the Canelo Hills. This district's northern and southern limits are Sonoita Creek and Meadow Valley Flat, respectively. The Palmetto Mining District adjoins the Harshaw district on the west and takes in the northwestern flank of the Patagonias, from Sonoita Creek south to Paloma Canyon. It continues west to the eastern boundary of Baca Float no. 3. South of the Palmetto and Harshaw districts, to the Mexican border, is the Patagonia Mining District. Its eastern line is the west edge of the Santa Cruz Valley plain, while the western boundary is an extension of the Palmetto district west line, southward to the Santa Cruz River. West of the Palmetto and Patagonia districts, as far as Nogales Wash, lies the Nogales mining district.[69]

The predominant metalliferous mineralization in the Patagonias has been argentiferous lead, zinc, and some copper minerals. The oxidized zone near the surface gives way to sulfides at depth. The Harshaw and Patagonia districts are well mineralized, while mineral values in the Nogales, Red Rock, and Palmetto districts are spotty and weak, except for a large copper deposit at one mine in the Palmetto Mining District.

Harshaw Mining District

Mineral locations at the northern end of the Patagonias were rediscovered before the Civil War. Two of the earliest claims there, the Flux and the Trench, subsequently produced almost 85 percent of the estimated 1.3 million tons of ore yielded by mines of the Harshaw district through 1964.

The Flux Mine, four miles south of the present town of Patagonia, had allegedly been an old Spanish or Mexican working. After it was relocated in 1858, the owners smelted the richer ore in an adobe furnace near the mouth of Alum Gulch.[70] Then in late 1858, "Colonel" Henry Titus and George Mercer found two mines, the Trench and the Compadre, that exhibited more impressive evidence of earlier labors:

> Cols. Titus and Mercer discovered two of the best [mines] in this country about a month ago; they are situated on the Santa Cruz mountains, four miles from Ewell's.
>
> They are undoubtedly the best mines in the country, and were long and ardently sought after. They have been worked on the most extensive scale by the Spaniards, who abandoned them years ago on account of the Apaches, but before doing so, they covered them and they have been lost for years, until the recent discovery. The amount of labor done, exceeds that on the Sierra [*sic*] Colorado mine. They are the mines known in mineral works and in the traditions of the Mexicans as the Compadre mines. The one is argentiferous galena, of the richest kind, and can be reduced by the blast furnace in the cheapest manner. Thirteen old furnaces were found upon the ground, which had been extensively used by the miners who constructed them.[71]

Titus's Union Exploring and Mining Co. explored these claims for awhile, then sold them in 1859 to the New York and Compadre Mining Co. This company apparently did a little work, before abandoning the mines upon the outbreak of the Civil War.[72] About 1872 the Trench Mine was relocated and worked for the rich surface deposits, which yielded 87 ounces of silver per ton.[73]

The Herst estate bought the Trench Mine in 1880. A series of lessees then developed the property extensively, before the price of silver dropped and production ceased in 1894. Ore shipments resumed in 1918 and continued through 1925, after which lessees carried on sporadic operations. By 1939 American Smelting and Refining Co. (ASARCO) controlled the property and greatly increased the output of lead and zinc ores with high silver values. Twenty years later the major deposits were becoming depleted, to the point where production came to a virtual standstill in the mid-1960s.[74]

The Flux Mine, worked from the 1850s to 1963, accounted for more than half of the ore tonnage from the Harshaw district. This mine was relocated in 1882 and through 1884 supplied perhaps several thousand tons of ore to the Benson smelter. Everything then remained quiet until 1897, when lessees began sporadic operations that extended over the next sixty years, extracting lead and zinc, with copper and silver as important byproducts. An estimated 850,000 tons of ore were taken out before the deposits became uneconomical to mine.[75]

Within this same four-mile-long mineralized belt are the Alta, American, Blue Nose, Hardshell, Hermosa, January, Josephine, and World's Fair mines, all principal producing properties discovered in the late nineteenth century and worked in some instances into the 1960s. Between 1930 and 1970, the Harshaw district reached its peak as a major metal producer, with the total estimated and recorded production of base and precious metals through 1972 valued at about $41,500,000.[76]

David T. Harshaw, a Civil War veteran and member of the California Column, tarried briefly at the Greaterville placers before moving south into the Patagonias. He staked some silver claims there, and about 1879 the Hermosa Mining Co. acquired one of his properties, the Hermosa Mine. They promptly began development, constructed a 100-ton stamp amalgamation mill, and had this mine in production by October of 1880. The Hermosa mine and mill became the nucleus for the town of Harshaw.

Harshaw boomed overnight; the 1880 census reported six hundred people there. The businesses and professions represented at Harshaw (miners, laborers, merchants, blacksmiths; restaurants, lodging houses, saloons, and livery stables) made it a typical mining camp. In other ways Harshaw was not typical; it escaped most frontier violence, and many of the buildings were constructed of permanent materials.

Prosperity unfortunately was short-lived. The mine and mill closed in the latter part of 1881, after the better ore had been exhausted. This was a severe blow, although other mining activity in the surrounding mountains kept hopes alive. In 1890 James Finley of Tucson reopened the Hermosa mine and carried on operations until the price of silver dropped in 1893. Finley died in 1899, and lessees took over until 1903, when all work stopped. The only remaining building at Harshaw is the Finley house, built of bricks allegedly taken from the old smelter stack at the Mowry mine.[77]

After 1883 Patagonia became the principal settlement and mining center in the Harshaw district. It started as a railroad camp during construction of the New Mexico and Arizona Railroad, then served as a shipping point for the mines in the Patagonia Mountains. The town even had its own smelter for a brief time, blown in in August of 1897 and operated for three months.[78] This community still flourishes as a retirement and vacation center and as a supply point for ranches in the area. Memories of the half-dozen lesser mining camps scattered through this district have long since faded.[79]

Patagonia Mining District

This is one of the most historic mining districts in Arizona, primarily because of one mine, the Mowry, and one man, Sylvester Mowry. The two largest areas of mineralization are at the Mowry mine and about four miles to the south, at what is called the Duquesne-Washington group of mines. Both the Mowry Mine, originally known as the Patagonia, and the Montezuma and Empire claims in the Washington area were located in 1858.[80]

A metallurgist writing in 1860 said that the first loads of ore from the Mowry mine came "from shafts which had been sunk many years and which had been abandoned."[81] According to one correspondent, ". . . the whole country abounds with mines of silver, copper and other valuable ores." As for this particular discovery,

> In the mountains of Santa Cruz Valley, about thirteen miles from the Mexican line, a new mine has been opened. The company has not yet been organized. . . . A shaft has been sunk thirty feet deep, with drifts seven feet each way, from which thirty or forty tons of ore have been dug up. Capt. Newell [*sic;* Ewell] and Lieut. Moore are interested in this new undertaking. The vein is very broad, as the driftings have not yet discovered its margin.[82]

Captain Richard Ewell, then stationed at Fort Buchanan, visited the mine and apparently had mixed feelings about it. In a letter to his niece, he wrote that

> The Patagonia Mine (so they call the one in which I am interested) is fast sinking towards the centre of the earth. It is the darkest, gloomiest-looking cavern you can imagine, about 50 feet deep, with prospects looking quite bright. I have been offered $1,000 for my interest, having at that time expended about $100; so if we fail, the croakers can't say it was an absurd speculation.[83]

Until 1860 the property was known by its original name, although it had already changed ownership several times. Then on April 9, 1860, Sylvester Mowry bought the holdings for either $22,000 or $25,000 and changed the name to the Mowry Mine. His older brother Charles came west to superintend the operations, while Sylvester occupied himself elsewhere until the summer of 1861. With the outbreak of the Civil War, it became necessary to fortify the mining camp against assaults by Apache Indians and Mexican outlaws. Mowry by this time was employing a work force of up to three hundred men and handling the mine as if he had sole ownership, although this was evidently not so. He had twelve ordinary Mexican blast furnaces in operation and continued to work right through the period of Confederate occupation.[84]

Then on June 13, 1862, a detachment of California Volunteers arrived to arrest Sylvester Mowry and all other men on the premises as suspected Confederate sympathizers. Mowry was taken to Fort Yuma on the Colorado River and jailed for five months before being released. The mine continued under a receiver for a time, shut down, and then resumed a curious on-again, off-again pattern of operation with brother Charles returning again as superintendent until early in 1866, when the last period of operation by the Mowrys ended.[85]

During its entire early history, the production of the Mowry Mine went unrecorded. Sylvester claimed that he shipped about $1.5 million worth of ore, but more reasonable estimates place the value of silver and lead mined from 1858 to 1864 at between $100,000 and $485,000.[86] Whatever the truth, the Mowry Mine was the most valuable producing property in Arizona during these early years. It was relocated in the 1870s, but very little happened until Silverberg and Steinfeld of Tucson acquired the property in 1890. During three years of development work, they took out several hundred tons of ore. In 1904 the Mowry Mines Co. purchased the property and did extensive development work, but their venture failed with the business recession of 1907. The mine has been worked sporadically since, as recently as 1952. The total estimated and reported production of lead-silver ore is approximately 200,000 tons.[87]

The second large center of mineralization is the Duquesne-Washington camp area. About the time the Mowry Mine was discovered, two men named Thomas Gardner and Hopkins relocated two or three old mines about four miles south of Mowry, near what became Washington Camp. The Montezuma, Empire, and Belmont claims lay within a few hundred yards of one another and had allegedly been mined for silver during the Spanish and/or Mexican periods. Little work was done prior to the Civil War, and the district was abandoned.[88] Later in the nineteenth century, the Pocahontas, Washington (later called Pride of the West), Bonanza, Annie, Belmont, Empire, Holland, and a dozen or so other mines were worked for the high-grade lead-silver ores in their upper levels. The deposits change into massive copper-lead-zinc sulphides at shallow depths.

George Westinghouse of the Westinghouse Electric Co. acquired a number of claims in the area beginning in 1889. The Westinghouse interests, organized as the Duquesne Mining and Reduction Co., invested heavily in development and in equipping their property for large-scale production. Under the reduction methods of that time, the complex base-metal sulphides could not be treated economically, and attempts to unlock the values led to a long period of experimentation and sporadic operations. Major production finally began in 1912 and continued until about the end of 1918. The mill at Washington closed down then, and mining was turned over to lessees. Various deposits have since been worked intermittently, continuing into the mid-

1960s. The total production of the Duquesne-Washington group of mines came to more than 450,000 tons of ore, with zinc, lead, and copper the principal values and silver as an important byproduct.[89]

Farther west in the Patagonia district lay a series of small copper producers, exploited sporadically in the twentieth century. The Santo Niño, located in 1908 and operated through 1955, was the most important of these. For the entire Patagonia district, the value of base- and precious-metal production through 1972 is placed at $17.9 million, primarily from zinc, lead, copper, silver, and gold. Three-quarters of this total was recovered in the present century.[90]

The principal mining camps of the district were Mowry, Washington, and Duquesne. Mowry probably started in 1858; its heyday came between 1905 and 1907, when the Mowry Mines Co. had two hundred or more men engaged in development and operations. Only an extensive series of stone and adobe ruins remained in 1980. Washington Camp had been settled by the 1870s; the Duquesne Company added an elaborate concentrating plant and smelter, also building offices, bunkhouses, a boardinghouse, and a number of dwellings. Duquesne itself, one mile to the south, originated with the Westinghouse involvement and served as the mining-company headquarters. Today it retains many well-preserved frame buildings and residences.[91]

Red Rock Mining District

The Red Rock mining district, on the northeastern flank of the Patagonia Mountains, has small, shallow occurrences of oxidized copper, lead, and zinc. The first miners arrived in 1881, in search of oxidized silver ores. They located the La Plata, New York (Jensen) and Meadow Valley mines, all in the southeastern part of the district, and extracted small amounts of ore. Twentieth-century discoveries include the Blue Bird Mine, a manganese claim in the Canelo Hills in the far southeastern corner of this district, and the Frisco Fair mine group and Durham Copper claim. Sporadic workings in various of these operations continued as recently as the early 1950s. The value of base and precious metals is given as $15,000. Patagonia was the principal mining town for this region.[92]

Palmetto Mining District

The exposed mineralization on the northwestern side of the Patagonias consists of narrow veins of argentiferous lead plus an unusual and local deposit of disseminated copper minerals. The Domino, Jarilla, Palmetto (Tres de Mayo), and Sonoita mine groups were all located between 1879 and 1881 and worked during that period. Old shafts at the Palmetto mine may be much earlier. Sporadic operations at these mine groups recovered only from 100 to 500 tons of lead-silver ore at each.

Mining activity at both the older argentiferous galena claims and at the more recently discovered copper deposits continued into the 1960s. The largest single mine and the most important copper producer was the Three-R property, located in 1897 and situated well up on the western slope of the Patagonias. This body of high-grade copper ore was worked from 1908 through 1956 by a series of owners and lessees, who recovered some 130,000 tons of ore in all. The last recorded production from the Palmetto district dates from 1969, at which time the value of base- and precious-metal output was given as $2.1 million.[93]

Nogales Mining District

This broad region, lying to either side of the Santa Cruz River above Calabasas, has only two localities with reported lode deposits. One is the slopes of Mount Benedict, once called Gold Hill, an isolated peak north of the town of Nogales. This hill was reportedly prospected for its narrow, oxidized veins of lead-silver-gold ore as early as the middle 1800s. Several small mining properties there yielded a total of about 1,100 tons of ore, valued at $54,000. Work continued to 1967.

The other locality is the Reagan Camp, three miles north-northwest of Mount Benedict. Wolframite, a tungsten mineral, was found here in 1906. Between 1906 and the late 1930s, an estimated 1,500 tons of 50-percent WO_3 concentrates were produced. Limited commercial production of wolframite was achieved elsewhere in southern Arizona at the Edna mine group in the Patagonia district and from the Las Guijas and Hartford (Huachuca Mountains) districts.[94]

Gold placers, reputed to be "the oldest and largest placer mines in this part of the country," occur in the Quaternary gravels along Guebabi Canyon, east of the Santa Cruz River. Perhaps these placers were part of the gold mines reported near Guevavi in the Spanish and Mexican periods. They were worked as recently as the 1930s, the output always remaining small. Other gold placers in the Patagonias include the Palmetto placers, about 2.5 miles northwest of the Three-R mine; Quaternary gravels approximately two miles southwest of Patagonia; and the piedmont portion of Mowry Wash and its tributaries. At least $1,500 in gold has been recovered in the twentieth century. Miners returned to these when lode mining was suspended and in times of economic depression.[95]

CHAPTER SEVEN

Huachuca Mountains

Hartford Mining District

Sporadic mining of base-metal sulfides at scattered locations sums up recent mining history in the Huachucas. The total value of the ores extracted (lead, zinc, copper, tungsten, silver, and gold) is placed at between $140,000 and $154,000 in the twentieth century. There have been no consistent large operations, and a single mining district now takes in the entire mountain range.[96]

Nicolás de Lafora wrote in his diary entry for December 6, 1766, that the Huachuca sierra had "many silver mines producing very good ore."[97] As we saw earlier, this must refer to the silver-bearing deposits called the Cave Creek Mines on the south side of the range, rediscovered in late 1879. In April of that same year, a short-lived Evans district had been organized along Sycamore Creek (now Lyle Canyon), about eight miles west of Camp Huachuca. This appears to have been a small silver camp, where the prospectors did a limited amount of development and then waited for buyers, who in this case never came.[98]

Serious prospecting in the Huachucas dates from the summer of 1879, when a group of miners left Charleston, Arizona, and worked their way to the head of Ramsey Canyon. There they discovered silver chloride and galena, and located the Hartford mine. Other people swarmed in, and on September 10, 1879, they organized the Hartford mining district. By the following summer, at least two dozen mines had been located, but despite the usual glowing tributes, very little ore ever came from these prospects. A townsite named Turnerville, just within the entrance to Ramsey Canyon, was laid out in May of 1880 and seems to have folded within the year.[99]

Around 1880 there were also silver discoveries or relocations in Montezuma Canyon, just north of modern Coronado National Memorial. Assays at the time claimed values of from $12 to $400 per ton, undoubtedly from the richer surface "float." The State of Texas Mine was eventually developed here as a zinc-lead working and achieved moderate production during World War II.[100]

Small amounts of ore from this district were sent to the smelters at Charleston and Benson in the early 1880s, but when the smelters closed in 1885, work at the mines also ceased. Two years later a fundamentalist preacher named Samuel Donnelly and two partners located the Copper Glance Mine, high on the south side of the Huachucas. Initially the ore was rich (a single carload being worth up to $3,000), and their camp grew to about eighty

Baumkirscher Mine, Huachuca Mountains, was worked intermittently from 1925 through 1937; photographed in 1969. (Courtesy, U.S. Forest Service, Coronado National Forest.)

people. Donnelly ran the Copper Glance Mine as a communal enterprise and had the satisfaction of seeing most of his workmen and their families become converts to his fundamentalist beliefs. When the returns from mining grew lean, Donnelly established a sawmill at Sunnyside, several miles down the canyon, to supplement incomes. The mine finally shut down, and by Christmas of 1898 the last family at the mining camp had moved to Sunnyside. Records of production for the Copper Glance are not available.[101]

Some two dozen other mines in the Huachucas were worked occasionally between the early 1900s and the 1950s, yielding between ten and several hundred tons of base-metal ores per property. The Tungsten Reef, Exposed Reef, Lucky Strike, and Pomona mines were exploited for scheelite (a tungsten mineral) during World War I and intermittently in later years. The 25,000 short-ton units produced, nearly all from the Tungsten Reef Mine, were nearly 5 percent of Arizona's tungsten production to 1965. Since 1950 the Hartford district has seen little activity.[102]

At various times in the twentieth century, the Huachucas have supported two mining camps. Hamburg, a company town associated with the Hamburg mine and the Hartford-Arizona Copper Mining Co., flourished for a few years after 1906. It was situated in upper Ramsey Canyon and at one time boasted 150 people, a hotel, general store, boardinghouses, and the usual saloons; only the site remains today.[103] Garces, known in its early years as Reef and then as Palmerlee, was associated with the Reef Mines when these were operated as gold-silver properties. The camp had a post office from 1901 until May of 1926.[104]

Gold-bearing veins were once reported in Tanner Canyon, on the Fort Huachuca Military Reservation, but the more important source of gold in the Huachucas has been placer deposits. As of 1898 good placer ground was said to exist near the Harper mine, several miles southeast of Sunnyside.[105] Late in the winter of 1911, Ash Canyon in the southeastern part of the Huachucas experienced a minor gold rush. The placer gravels there extended for about three miles along the canyon bottom. Nuggets worth $50, $75, and even $450 turned up in the first year. Sluicing continued through the Depression era, with the reported yield from 1934 to 1944 amounting to $2,085.[106]

Whetstone Mountains

The Whetstone Mining District is coextensive with the Whetstone Mountains. The area has a diversity if not an abundance of metallic mineral resources. Considerable prospecting took place there in the late 1800s, with the earliest workings on record, the Two Peaks Mine at the southern end of the range, producing about 25 tons of copper-lead ore in 1915. During the 1950s the Nevada and Mascot mines, in Mine Canyon, and the Copper Plate Mine, on the southwestern slope, reached outputs of over 4,000 tons of low-grade copper ore. Reported values for the modest amounts of base (copper) and precious (silver) metal ores totaled $26,000. Tungsten ore was mined during the late 1930s to early 1940s, while the Star No. 1 (Bluestone) prospect and the Old Windmill No. 1 Mine both yielded small amounts of uranium ore. Quartz and fluorspar were produced in quantity between 1946 and 1967. The mines in this district have not been active since the late 1960s.[107]

Rincon Mountains

These mountains comprise the Rincon Mining District. Mountain ranges referred to as metamorphic core complexes, such as the Rincons, are not known to have large metallic-ore deposits. When this range was prospected at an early date, nothing more than prospect pits and a few adits resulted. Spotty pockets of mineralization with low values of copper, silver, and other metals occur around the flanks and foothill areas. Known mineral locations include the prospects between Colossal Cave and Hidden Spring; north of Happy Valley in the Bear Creek–Fresno Spring–Barney Ranch area; in the Roble Spring–Cañada Atravesada locale; and some "scratching" southwest of Italian Trap. Production through 1972 is estimated at 200 tons of ore valued at $8,000, chiefly in copper, lead, and silver. The Roble Spring–Cañada Atravesada claims are now chiefly valued for their low-grade uranium deposits. Fifty-eight tons of ore were shipped from there in 1956, while another 102 tons went to a uranium mill late in 1977.[108]

Santa Catalina Mountains

The Oracle Mining District, also known as the Control, Old Hat, or Santa Catalina district, lies immediately south of Oracle, on the northern slope of the Santa Catalina Mountains. The district spans parts of both Pima and Pinal counties, with lode mines as well as gold placers.

The most noted placer deposits were the gravels along Cañada del Oro Creek, from four to ten miles south of Oracle. Numerous old pits, trenchs, and tunnels showed that the gravels there had been worked in years past. J. Ross Browne in his 1868 report mentioned evidence of earlier work,[109] while *The Weekly Arizonian* added a few more details:

> Cañon del Oro is situated about thirty miles to the Northeast of Tucson, and is noted as having been the locality of gold washing operations, about a year since. It is a fact that gold exists there, and several experienced California miners believe it would pay a small company to "sluice" the little valley at the upper end of the Cañon, as there is an abundance of good water at most seasons of the year. The party who once attempted to work the Cañon, being annoyed by the Indians, withdrew, and since that time few white men have visited the spot . . .[110]

These placers were visited occasionally through the Depression years of the twentieth century and continued to yield small amounts of gold. For the period 1904–49, production was valued at $18,393.[111] Small operations in Alder Canyon, on the other side of the Santa Catalinas, recovered about 100 ounces of placer gold there.[112]

Mineralization in the Catalina Mountains is associated with geologic faults, and it is along the faults that mines have been developed. The south base of the mountains exhibits scattered prospects and one productive mine, the Pontotoc, which yielded about 5,000 tons of low-grade copper ore between 1907 and 1917; it has not been worked since. Most mining activity has been north of Mount Lemmon and particularly along Oracle Ridge. At the northern end, east and northeast of Apache Peak, lie a series of gold or gold and silver claims known as the American Flag group of mines. Isaac Lorraine made the first locations around 1878; by 1881 the main properties included his American Flag Mine, in addition to the Pioneer, Wedge, Good Luck, Black Bar, Bullion, and Commonwealth mines. Another holding, the Southern Belle, is said to have yielded large amounts of gold. The small mining camp gained a post office, under the name of American Flag. After 1884 the group declined and became virtually inactive. Lorraine, who had sold his interests in 1881, established his American Flag cattle ranch scarcely a mile away.[113]

In the early 1900s this same area became known as Campo Bonito, a name originally applied to a chicken ranch in Bonito Canyon. Around 1909 a Tucson mining promoter persuaded Colonel William F. "Buffalo Bill" Cody that a fortune was waiting to be made here in the Catalinas. Cody bought and leased several mines, including the Campo Bonito and Southern Belle, and hired men to work them for gold, silver, and tungsten. Unfortunately his properties had probably been worked out. Cody's Campo Bonito Mining and Milling Co. failed soon after the colonel's death in 1917.[114]

About five miles to the south in Pima County is the Marble Peak area. Emerson O. Stratton settled there in 1880 and was one of several who located mining claims. A firm from Boston, the Santa Catalina Copper Company, bought four of the copper claims known as the Apache Mine. By 1882 this company had built a smelter, sawmill, hotel, and other buildings and had erected a tramway between the mine and the smelter. The mine apparently produced little or no ore, and the business closed down after six months.

Difficult terrain and the high cost of transportation discouraged mining in the Marble Peak area, although in 1910 the Phelps Dodge company bought another group of early claims (the Leatherwood and Geesman mine groups) and revived the mining camp called Apache Camp. They did a considerable amount of development work, then had to shut down without achieving production. There were other small camps (Stratton Camp, Daily Camp, Cogdon's Camp), but until the Mt. Lemmon Control Road from Oracle via

Road camp, Stratton Copper Company, Santa Catalina Mountains, 1915. (Courtesy, U.S. Forest Service, Coronado National Forest.)

Apache Camp to Summerhaven was completed in the summer of 1920, this country remained largely inaccessible.

Even with the new road to Mt. Lemmon, there was no mineral production until 1937. In that year mining began on the Geesman and Daily claim groups. Sporadic mining continued as recently as 1968, with some 136,000 tons of ore produced. Most of this output was in copper values with lesser amounts of lead, zinc, and silver, and about 100 tons of tungsten ore. During times of high metal prices, mining for tungsten minerals also revived several of the old Campo Bonito mines.[115]

The Dragoon Mountains and Nearby Ranges

The Dragoon Mountains were little known prior to 1876, because they lay within the part of Arizona dominated by the Chiricahua Apaches. When the Indians were moved to San Carlos and their former reservation thrown

Apache Camp mining claim in the Santa Catalina Mountains, Bob Leatherwood owner, September 1915. (Courtesy, U.S. Forest Service, Coronado National Forest.)

open, prospectors moved in to explore the hitherto inaccessible ranges. Their hopes of mineral wealth were soon realized.

The lesser ranges and hills that surround the Dragoon Mountains contain the richest mining districts in southeastern Arizona. For example, north of Dragoon Pass and the Southern Pacific Railroad lie the Cochise Mining District and the Little Dragoon Mountains, where the mines at Johnson Camp and other locations produced over $32 million worth of copper, zinc, and silver, mainly between 1945 and 1957.[116] To the south is the famous Tombstone district, the setting of the San Pedro or Brunckow Mine before the Civil War. Development ended there in July 1860, when workmen murdered three of the supervisors.[117] Ed. Schieffelen rediscovered the Tombstone deposits in 1877 and within a year the rush was underway. This silver camp boomed through the early 1880s, then slowed due to progressive flooding of the underground workings and decreasing prices for silver. Through 1901 the camp yielded $25 million in silver. Operations continued as recently as 1951, the value of production in the twentieth century adding an estimated $13.8 million to the earlier total.[118] Popular interest in Tombstone and its gunfighters has led to the creation of a vast literature about this colorful frontier mining town.

East of Tombstone and southeast of the Dragoons lies the Turquoise district, known originally for its prehistoric workings of turquoise deposits. Silver-lead ores were mined here until 1893, then in the late 1890s this became a copper-mining district, built around the twin camps of Gleeson and Courtland. Mining continued in most years until 1958, with values reaching over $14 million, mostly from copper, silver, and gold.[119] North of Courtland is the Pearce Mining District, with its principal property, the Commonwealth Mine. This was worked almost continuously from 1895 into the early 1940s, producing ores with valuations in excess of $10.6 million, mainly in silver and gold. Since 1971 fluorite has been mined there.[120]

The first mention of mining in the Dragoon Mountains came early in 1879, as a spectacular story about some fifty to a hundred human skeletons being found in and around an old tunnel, "which has every indication of being an old mine."[121] Unfortunately nothing more was said about this. By the end of 1879, the Silver Cloud Mine had been located and a cut started, with the trails from Tombstone said to be "filled with prospectors bound on a prospecting trip through the Dragoons." Indeed a townsite (Dragoon City) had been chosen, and a brisk traffic in buying and selling prospective bonanzas was underway.[122] The boom was a brief one and probably centered around Black Diamond Peak. People drifted back to Tombstone when the first mills came into service and serious production got underway there.

Within a few years prospectors had found the Dragoon Mountains mineralized at their northern and southern ends, to a point where modest productions of base-metal ores, gold, and silver could eventually be achieved. The southern part, from Cochise Stronghold south to the Black Diamond Camp, is the Middle Pass Mining District. The Dragoon district at the north end includes the mines and quarries south and east of the community of Dragoon. Neither of these districts is a particularly rich one. Mining continued into the 1960s, but it is quiet at present.

The town of Dragoon began not as a stagecoach station or a railroad siding, but as a mining camp. In 1908 one J. P. Richardson, formerly with the Copper Queen Consolidated Mining Co. at Bisbee, began developing a modest copper discovery, the Centurion Mine. By 1911 operations were well established, and the newspapers started to take notice:

> Things are happening about Dragoon. Everybody for miles about has wakened up. An eighty acre town has been platted. Lots are selling. Two new stores have been completed. A new post office is under construction. A well finished school building twenty-four by

> thirty-six [feet] is now occupied. Lands are being homesteaded and all about the mining properties are getting busy. Plans for the erection of a union club house for mine visitors are under way and pretty soon Douglas and Bisbee will be infants in arms compared to our neighbor, Dragoon. . . .
>
> There is being developed within a mile of Dragoon station the Centurion mine which bids fair to rival the best copper properties of the territory.[123]

Dragoon never quite managed to eclipse Douglas or Bisbee, although the mine achieved a moderate production of more than 1,400 tons of ore between 1911 and 1944. Several miles to the northeast, the Texas-Arizona Mining Co. began operation of their lead-silver-gold mine at virtually the same time (1910). This property was turned over to lessees after 1917 and was worked intermittently until 1928.[124]

Dragoon (Golden Rule) Mining District

The Golden Rule or Old Terrible Mine, about four miles east of Dragoon, was the only major operation in the Dragoon district. This property had been located in the late 1870s and was first credited with an output ($125,000) in 1883. The ores yielded mainly gold and lead, but never again so much as in the first year. Operations continued intermittently through 1902, were suspended for three years, resumed with a new mill from 1905 to 1908, then suspended again. Mining continued sporadically from 1916 to 1957, largely under lessees. Other mines showed mostly lead-zinc mineralization and shipped a few hundred tons of ore each. The total value of base and precious metals extracted through 1970 amounted to $340,000.[125]

The Dragoon district also had a series of marble quarries. These reportedly began with claims staked by one Leon Ligier in 1909. The early history of these quarries is unclear and appears to involve promotion with very little development. One company proposed to install equipment and begin quarrying right after World War I, but nothing came of this. About 1922 the Painted Desert Marble Company of San Francisco solicited investments in a venture that was supposed to see marble from their Dragoon leases superseding the marbles of Egypt, Greece, and Italy. Investors stayed away.

Finally in the fall of 1931, the Arizona Marble Company of Tucson set to work. Their twelve-man crew began quarrying a mound near the south end of the Gunnison Hills, between Dragoon and Cochise. They expected to ship huge slabs of marble to eastern markets, but their plans ran afoul of the Depression. In 1946 Bud Ligier, son of the original claimant, started the Ligier marble quarries. Initially this business produced various types of colored dimension stone, adding marble granules and chips for roofing and for a type of flooring called terrazzo during the 1950s. By the time work ceased, about 1966, at least eight quarries were active, most of them to the north or west of Dragoon Peak. For the period 1953–59, marble production from the Ligier quarries was valued at $151,424.[126]

Middle Pass Mining District

This district had a number of scattered mines and prospects, none of them large producers nor any of them worked for more than a few years at a time. The outputs consisted mostly of base-metal sulfides, with a little tungsten and barite ore. Principal values were in zinc and copper, with lesser amounts of lead, silver, and gold, amounting to about $1.725 million through 1970.[127]

The largest single operation, the Abril Mine north of China Peak, produced nearly 30,000 tons of zinc-copper ore, mainly in the period from 1945 to 1952. Two miles to the south, the owners and lessees at the San Juan or Gordon group of claims recovered over 17,000 tons of zinc ore, primarily from 1947 to 1951. The smaller Cobre Loma Mine at the head of Middlemarch Canyon yielded about 5,000 tons of copper ore between 1915 and 1920.

In 1897 Chinese merchants of Tombstone and San Francisco financed the original work at the Middlemarch Mine, along the canyon of the same name. They sold out a year later, and until 1916 little was done. The mine reopened that year, and a substantial amount of low-grade sulfide ore was blocked out below the oxidized zone. Operation continued until the drop in metal prices at the end of 1920, a concentrator having been added in 1919. The value of production through 1920 was about $85,000.[128] Work continued intermittently until the 1950s.

The Black Diamond Mine and Camp

At the lower end of this district, about 1.5 miles south of Middlemarch Pass, was the Black Diamond Copper Mining Co., a venture that is exceptionally well known, thanks to preservation of the company records and a recent comprehensive study.[129] The first mining claims were filed in 1891. In 1898 some West Virginia capitalists organized the Black Diamond Copper Mining Co., bought out existing claims, and hired the first in a series of five superintendents. Little happened until a 200-ton smelter and an aerial tramway to the mine were ready in 1902. By this time the Black Diamond Camp sported a hotel, company offices, a saloon, a store, a jail, a schoolhouse, employees' bungalows, and miners' cabins, but copper prices had dropped substantially. Mining probably got underway in 1902, and the smelter was finally blown in in April 1903.

The management had sufficient water, piped in from the Commonwealth Mine at Pearce, but otherwise experienced nearly everything that could go wrong with a new mining venture. The business was undercapitalized and attempted to operate during a period of low copper prices. It fell behind in paying the men. In 1904 the workers went on strike. The ore itself was refractory and could not be smelted economically. There were accidental deaths and robberies, followed by the murder of a deputy sheriff. Even the principal stockholders could not get along with one another! Yet the people at Black Diamond maintained a positive attitude, and the fourth of July 1903 saw a grand celebration, topped by a race between the company president, E. D. Kennedy, and a greased pig:

> The most exciting number on the program was a race between Mr. E. D. Kennedy, of Warren, Ohio, and a sleek Berkshire from the San Simone pork farm. The latter had been shaved and greased for the occasion and the former, by reason of having in primary, state and national handicaps, entered the contest with the avidity that would have placed Mark Hanna on the tailboard of Teddy Roosevelt's chariot race for the White House. . . . The porker kept in the lead and Mr. Kennedy remained a close second in the race for supremacy.
>
> The judges, men good and true, gave the event to Mr. Kennedy, not withstanding the fact that the pig crossed the line and no doubt now adds to the aroma of some pisano's [*sic*] frijole feast. Meantime Mr. Kennedy wears his honors very becomingly.[130]

The day ended with dinner at the Black Diamond Hotel and dancing to the strains of the Black Diamond Band.

Faced with all of its difficulties, the company applied for bankruptcy on November 28, 1904. The mine and smelter shut down, reopened briefly, and closed again by the end of 1907. The operations had yielded about 7,000 tons of ore, from which 1 million pounds of copper, valued at $150,000, were extracted. In 1912 the mine was sold for taxes and brought just $1,381.95. After a few years the only resident was a watchman. The old hotel was dismantled in the late 1930s, and the heavy mining equipment was shipped to Japan as scrap metal.[131]

The story of Black Diamond epitomizes the experiences of hundreds of small mines in Arizona. Distant management, insufficient capital, ores unsuitable for economical smelting, and labor troubles were all typical problems. The Black Diamond Mining Co. might have overcome these, but there was no remedy for their misjudgment in beginning operations at a time of low copper prices. The revival in 1906–7, when copper prices were high once again, may have failed because of the business recession in the latter year or from technical problems with the ore.

Winchester Mountains

The Winchester Mining District centers in Severin Canyon, in the southern reaches of this low desert range. Sometime in the 1890s underground workings were opened at a property known as the Hearst Mine, and some silver ore was reportedly shipped. In 1924 about 266 tons of "siliceous silver ore" were obtained, probably from the old dumps, for use as smelter flux. The only other activity took place in the mid-1930s and in 1941 and 1949, when 268 ounces of silver and several hundred pounds of copper and lead were recovered. Prospects for significant economic mineralization are poor.[132]

Galiuro Mountains

The Galiuro Mountains are mostly Tertiary-age volcanic rocks, with little mineralization. Ore bodies were found and exploited to some extent at the older exposed strata, but in this part of Arizona, the principal developments lay just to the west, across the San Pedro River. The mines at Mammoth were major gold producers until World War II, when gold mining ceased and attention shifted to the base-metal ores found at deeper levels. By the time these ore shoots ran out in the early 1950s, values from this camp approached $37 million. The San Manuel Mine, a few miles to the south, is one of Arizona's major copper sources, with nearly 5 billion pounds of the metal extracted as of 1981, twenty-five years after the operation began.[133] In 1991 this mine still ranked as one of the world's largest underground copper producers.

With respect to the Galiuros themselves, we have good, recent information about mineral potential and past mining activities. This range contains two mining districts, besides several mines and mine groups unassigned to any district. On the northwestern slope, north of Sombrero Butte and centered around the mines along Copper Creek, is the Copper Creek or Bunker Hill district. The Rattlesnake district includes several mines along Rattlesnake and Kielberg creeks, in the approximate geographic center of the Galiuro range.[134]

Copper Creek Mining District

The workings in this district were the most significant and probably the oldest of any in the Galiuros. There is an apocryphal story that high-grade lead-silver ore was mined from the Bluebird Vein as early as 1863.[135] This is unlikely, however, because of the remoteness of the area and the ongoing war with the Apaches. Nearly all of the mineral exploration at that time was concentrated in the western part of Arizona.[136]

In 1883 the Copper Creek area was organized as the Bunker Hill Mining District. Little work was done until 1903, when the Copper Creek Mining Co. acquired the existing claims. The first producing mine was probably the Old Reliable, which yielded most of the 30,000 tons of ore concentrated from the district between 1908 and 1919. The American Eagle and Bluebird mines both began production in 1914 and were worked intermittently, the Bluebird (a lead-silver prospect) being the only active mine in this district between 1917 and 1933. Other properties had value mainly for their copper, with the Childs-Aldwinkle Mine, opened in 1933, being a major source of molybdenite as well. Copper output peaked in 1936–38, at more than 1 million pounds of metal each year. After 1938 production tapered off, and only one or two mines remained active. Metal values from the Copper Creek district through 1958 totaled $4,759,129, the last recorded activity there being in 1959. In 1972 Ranchers Exploration and Development Corp. shattered the Old Reliable Mine, detonating 4 million pounds of explosives within it, to facilitate leaching of the remaining copper ore.[137]

The principal mining camp, Copper Creek, straggled along the steep banks of the stream with the same name. A post office opened there in 1907; three years later the town boasted fifty buildings, with two hundred miners and their families. Now the townsite has only building foundations and scattered lumber; reputedly the wooden buildings were torn down in 1958 and the materials used for corrals, sheds, tack rooms, and outbuildings at nearby ranches. The U.S. Geological Survey 15' topo map for this area suggests that another, smaller camp may have lain along Scanlon Creek below Sombrero Butte, near the Magna and Bunker Hill mines.[138]

Rattlesnake Mining District

The Rattlesnake district consists of three low-grade gold mines, all of them along mineralized sections of a single fault zone in upper Rattlesnake and Kielberg Canyons. The Powers Mine, discovered around 1908, gained notoriety ten years later from its association with three members of the

Powers's Cabin in the Galiuro Mountains, before restoration. (Courtesy, U.S. Forest Service, Coronado National Forest.)

Power family, who shot it out with a sheriff's posse at their cabin in the Galiuros. The Powers had worked the mine on a small scale until the gunfight left three lawmen and Jeff Power killed, and Jeff's two sons the objects of a huge manhunt. In 1932–33 the Consolidated Galiuro Gold Mines Inc. shipped small lots of gold ore from this property, but recent sampling has found high gold and silver values only in small, erratic ore pods.[139]

One mile south of the Power property is the Knothe or Long Tom Mine, with two mine shafts about 700 feet apart. This claim was originally worked at about the same time as the Powers Mine and yielded a few small shipments of sorted, high-grade gold ore.[140] About two miles north of the Powers tunnel are the Gold Mountain claims in Rattlesnake Canyon. In 1902 this was called a recent discovery, owned or controlled by the Consolidated Gold Mountain Mining Co. of Tucson. The prospects yielded only a small amount of gold ore and have been idle for many years. For the Rattlesnake district as a whole, recorded production is only 163 ounces of gold.[141]

Forest Service pickup truck (1921 Dodge) at Powers Garden Ranger Station, Galiuro Mountains, 1960. From viewer's left: Jack McCombs, U.S. Forest Service; Bob Thomas, Arizona Republic; Dan Williams, Arizona Daily Star. (Courtesy, U.S. Forest Service, Coronado National Forest.)

Other Mines in the Galiuros

In the northern part of the Galiuros, on the west side of Virgus Canyon, are the Table Mountain copper claims. The first known locations date from 1882, with little beyond construction of a toll road accomplished in the next fifteen years. Then in 1897, with copper prices rising, the newly reorganized Table Mountain Copper Co. purchased the claims. By early 1898 the company had seventy-five men employed, mining and erecting a smelter. The prospects were very optimistic:

> The company now has fifty or sixty tents pitched, and these constitute the present living and business apartments. Lumber and material are being hauled into the camp, and more comfortable and commodious quarters will soon be erected. . . . The ore contains silver and gold in addition to the copper. The copper values average from 12 to 13 per cent. On the dumps and in plain sight are many

> thousands of tons of ore which are supposed to possess good smelting value.

With respect to the smelter,

> The heavy stone and timbers are already in place, and much of the machinery which has been purchased has been delivered at Willcox and is being removed to the scene of operations as rapidly as possible. . . .

As for amenities,

> . . . there has sprung up quite a lively camp at Table Mountain. There are general merchandise stores, restaurants, butcher shops, saloons, of course, and lodging houses, and business in all departments is reported as very brisk.[142]

Within a year the Table Mountain Copper Company had ground to a halt, probably because the ore, described as a black oxide and carbonate of copper (instead of the more usual sulfides) was unsuited for smelting. Estimated production prior to 1928 totaled 400 to 600 tons of ore, which carried minor gold and silver values as well. Foundations and the remains of boilers and smelting equipment may yet be seen at the old camp.[143]

South of the mines in the Rattlesnake district, along the same fault zone, lies the Jackson Mine. The actual production features comprise four shafts, two adits, and six pits and cuts; these plus additional shafts and exploration prospects are not dated. Mineral sampling has revealed variable but generally low values of silver and negligible percentages of gold and copper.[144] Lastly there is the Sixteen-to-One Mine in a deep tributary of Kielberg Canyon, about 2.5 miles west of the Long Tom shafts. The main workings at the Sixteen-to-One consist of two crosscut adits. Neither this property nor the Jackson Mine appear to have records of production.[145]

Santa Teresa Mountains

The Santa Teresas are a remote corner of Arizona where the mineral prospects are split between two mining districts. At the northern end, north and east of Old Deer Creek, is the Stanley Mining District. The workings here returned small amounts of copper and lead ores during the late nineteenth and early twentieth centuries. These properties lie within the San Carlos mineral strip, a tract that was joined to the San Carlos Indian Reservation in the 1960s. The western parts of the Santa Teresas fall within the Aravaipa Mining District, an irregular area bounded by Old Deer Creek on the north,

Aravaipa Creek on the west, and the divide between streams tributary to Aravaipa Creek and those flowing into the Gila River on the east.[146]

Aravaipa Mining District

The Aravaipa district is traditionally divided into two groups. Most of the Aravaipa group of mines and prospects are within 2.5 miles of the old mining camp of Aravaipa. At one time this town had as many as sixty people, but in 1960 only a caretaker lived there. At Klondyke, a one-time distribution point about ten miles to the south, the Grand Reef group of mines extends along an arc from four miles north to three miles east of that tiny community. As of 1960 Klondyke consisted of a store and a gas pump, schoolhouse, and teacher's house. More recently these buildings have been restored.[147]

A Colonel W. C. Bridwell reportedly built a small smelter at Aravaipa as early as the late 1870s, but production figures are lacking. In 1890–95 the Aravaipa Mining Co. shipped two cars of what proved to be lead-silver and lead-zinc ores from their Arizona, Orejana, and No. 1 claims, all near Aravaipa, for a mill test. The company also constructed about eight buildings at the Aravaipa townsite, including a stone residence still standing in 1990. Their only subsequent work consisted of $90,000 worth of lead-carbonate ore shipped from the No. 1 claim in 1916.

The Copper Bar and Sam Jones prospects along the north side of Copper Canyon, about two miles east of Aravaipa, were worked in 1902. One carload of ore transported to the El Paso smelter yielded 29.7 percent copper. In 1906–7 the Royal Tinto Mining and Smelting Co. developed these holdings, but made no new shipments. Another copper property was the Cobre Grande Mine, about 0.7 miles north of Cobre Grande Mountain. The deposits there were first located in 1905, and one carload of ore was sent to the smelter at Globe. These workings had been abandoned by 1922.

The more significant mines of the Aravaipa group lie within a few thousand feet of one another, about two miles northeast of Aravaipa. Here between 1926 and 1928 the Grand Central Mining Co. recovered 3.5 million pounds of lead, more than 1 million pounds of zinc, and $20,000 in silver from their Grand Central Mine and other properties. In 1942 the Athletic Mining Co. acquired the principal holdings; two years later production was underway at the Head Center and Iron Cap mines, with a small amount from the Sinn Fein working. Between 1947 and 1957, these mines yielded between 1 and 5 million pounds of base metals, mostly lead and zinc, each year. At the end of 1957, all of the Athletic Mining Co. properties were shut down.[148]

The mines and prospects of the Grand Reef group lie mostly along or near the Grand Reef Fault, between Imperial Mountain (about one and three-quarters miles south of Aravaipa) and Klondyke Wash, east of Klondyke. These were lead-silver mines that also yielded small amounts of copper. Those farthest to the north (the Windsor Mine on Imperial Mountain and the Tenstrike Mine) had seen work as early as the 1890s, but achieved little production. The Grand Reef Mine in Laurel Canyon, the largest working in this area, underwent a long period of development in the 1890s, until 1915. It then yielded about 30,000 tons of ore from 1915 to 1920, became inactive, and then produced another 10,000 tons in 1929–31 and 1939–41. Ore from smaller mines along branches of Laurel Canyon generally required concentration before shipping.

Still farther south on branches of Klondyke Wash east of Klondyke were the La Clede and Silver Coin mines, low-grade copper-silver(?) and lead-silver properties. Only small amounts of ore were ever shipped, including an unknown tonnage from the Silver Coin Mine in 1947 plus a few tons from the Tenstrike Mine in 1952.[149]

In addition to the developed mines, the Aravaipa district contained a large number of undeveloped claims and prospect pits. Northernmost of these was the Princess Pat group. The holdings on the slopes southwest of Cobre Grande Mountain were called the Landsman group. Other claims lay mostly in the same areas as the developed mines.[150] The total value of production from the Aravaipa district, 1915 to 1958, is placed at $8,355,870.[151]

Pinaleño Mountains

The Precambrian granite and gneiss in the Pinaleños are virtually unmineralized. There are nonetheless five small metallic mineral districts, none of them very old or the scene of significant ore production; indeed only two have yielded any ore at all.

The Clark district, in the broad pass between the Santa Teresa and Pinaleño mountains, has witnessed sporadic mining since 1900 or before. A few hundred tons of gold-bearing quartz were shipped in 1933 and a small tonnage of lead-copper-silver ore was shipped at a more recent date. Veins of barite and fluorite are reported as well.[152] At the north end of the Pinaleños a total of 220 tons of manganese concentrates and ten tons of manganese ore are reported from vein deposits in the Black Hawk district. The dates of production are not known.[153]

The Black Beauty district on the western slope of the Pinaleño Mountains, evidently in the upper reaches of Van Valer Canyon, consists of tungsten claims. Near the south end of this range, in upper Willow Spring Canyon, is the Golandrina district, a series of low-grade uranium claims. More uranium claims and also manganese in vein deposits are reported for the Fisher Hills district, northwest of Bowie, Arizona.[154]

Chiricahua Mountains

Mining in the Chiricahuas began in the late 1860s, lapsed during the period of the Chiricahua Reservation, then resumed in the late 1870s, with a series of short-term, sporadic ventures. All of these failed. The first really successful mineral development got underway in the mid-1920s. Most of the mining activity took place in the California district, which covered the eastern slopes south of Apache Pass. The Rucker Canyon district, a much smaller mining area, lay in Rucker Canyon, on the southwestern side of this range.

Apache Pass Mining District

Apache Pass was a district in its own right and the setting for the earliest claims, which were principally for gold. An 1868 report said that soldiers and others had located a number of lodes south of the pass.[155] John Finkle Stone, president of the Apache Pass Mining Co., bought a half-interest in two of these claims and installed a stamp mill in Siphon Canyon. His plans to start mining went awry early in October of 1869; the Apaches caught Stone and five others on a stage several miles east of Dragoon Springs and massacred the entire party.[156]

Stone's company failed, but some mining did take place during the 1880s and again in the twentieth century. As of 1910 this district boasted a number of properties, most of them inactive, plus the ruins of two stamp mills and a lingering prospector.[157] The total production for the Apache Pass district amounted to 600 tons of ore, valuable mainly for gold, silver, and lead.[158]

California Mining District

In the late 1870s a number of locations (claims) were filed at copper and lead-silver outcrops on the eastern side of the Chiricahuas, especially along Turkey Creek. Former Apache Agent Tom Jeffords had three claims himself, in Pinery Canyon. By October of 1880 the mines and prospects on the eastern slope had been organized as the California Mining District.[159]

A rush was underway, and the Tombstone and Tucson newspapers did an exceptionally good job of documenting this boom. In November activity centered at "the new town of Chiricahua City." According to "Spicer," writing to the Tucson *Citizen,*

> I will say that a new camp with a boom is springing up here and a town is being laid off. The people in camp commenced to take and improve the lots as fast as marked off. It is located on a beautiful mesa or plateau of land, with at least 200 acres without a break, and slightly undulating toward San Simon valley. The rush for lots became a stampede. Tents went up every fifteen minutes; fence poles, wickyups, hockells and all kinds of cheap improvements were in order. From Turkey Creek, near by, poles and brush and posts and rails and house logs were being brought on wagons and carts, on horseback and on foot.

The prospects were impressive. "Spicer" continued:

> The new town of Chiricahua City looks more and more like New York city every day; and then it looks some like Rio Janeiro, having a large plaza 300 feet square in the center of the town, with an avenue eighty feet wide on each side. And around this plaza the racket commences. A. C. Rynerson & Co. are going to move their store on to the northeast corner; the Dickson House will adorn the southeast corner, as Mrs. E. A. Dickson is now putting up temporary houses so as to be ready to accommodate with restaurant and lodging house in a few days; Douglass Gray will have his assay office at the southwest corner, and other business houses will soon fill up the rest of the space.
>
> There are from 30 to 40 people coming into the camp every day, most of them from the eastward. . . .[160]

Within a month, however, Chiricahua City's prospects dimmed and then disappeared.

John H. Galey, an oil man from Pennsylvania, and his partners bought two of the richest silver claims, known later as the Dunn and the Texas mines. Galey organized the Texas Consolidated Mining and Smelting Co. with himself as president and began developing the Texas claim. He ordered a smelting furnace and by early December 1880 had platted a new town of Galeyville.[161]

Galeyville became the company town, while Chiricahua City, half a mile below, was forgotten. Galey erected his smelter on the flat below the Texas mine; just above the smelter lay the main portion of Galeyville. When the smelter was blown in in 1881, it was found that the ore from the mine was not self-fluxing and could not be treated. A suitable flux was found at the Granite Gap mine, just over the New Mexico line. Galey's company bonded the new property, mixed the ore with that from the Texas Mine, and the smelting process was a success.[162]

The first ten-day smelter run late in 1881 reportedly produced 80,000 pounds of lead from ore that assayed 45 percent lead and 60 ounces of silver to the ton. The smelter operated for several weeks using Granite Gap ore, then suspended early in 1882, when shipments were delayed. About this time the Texas company went broke, and all work shut down. The miners themselves tried to continue but failed when they could not obtain the Granite Gap ores. The smelter was dismantled and reputedly moved to Benson; Galeyville itself was soon abandoned. The output for 1881–82, including 13,717 ounces of silver, was valued at only $19,420.[163]

Galeyville's anecdotes are more impressive than the c. fifty tons of ore credited to the Texas Mine.[164] People reminisced that it was a lively camp, employing upwards of a hundred men. In January 1881 a Tombstone newspaper described Galeyville as ". . . a flourishing town, containing a Post Office, fourteen stores, seven saloons, six boarding houses, four meat markets, three blacksmith shops, two corrals, one assay office, one doctor's office, and about forty houses and tents."[165] That same year another 'growth' industry took root, namely the running of livestock across the Arizona-Sonora border and the subsequent sale of same, without the owners' consent. A gang known as the "cow-boys" kept busy at this, and as one Galeyville correspondent wrote,

> The cow-boys frequently visit our town and often salute us with an indiscriminate discharge of fire arms, and after indulging in a few drinks at the saloons, practice shooting at the lamps, bottles, glasses &c., sometimes going to the length of shooting the cigar out of ones mouth; this of course produces a nervous feeling, among visitors especially.[166]

As of 1911 a local newspaper could find only a slag dump from the smelter and a number of the old building foundations at Galeyville and Chiricahua City.[167]

Galeyville's short life coincided with early activity at the Dunn Mine, about four miles to the northwest. Jack Dunn located this claim, near Hands Pass, in 1881. He evidently sold it to some Chicago capitalists, who erected a smelter (in 1884?) a mile west of the mine. After some years the smelter was taken down, and about 1899 the Dunn workings were renamed the Hilltop Mine. This property subsequently yielded 68 percent of the total mineral output from the California Mining District.[168]

Twenty years after Galeyville's boom and bust, a copper-mining camp grew up about 1.5 miles to the south. A couple of prospectors are said to

Eastern slope of the Chiricahua Mountains, c. 1915. (Courtesy, U.S. Forest Service, Coronado National Forest.)

have staked out a small lead-silver claim there in 1900, making their camp at a spring where several madrone trees, called trees of paradise by the prospectors, were growing. By the late fall of 1901, the camp warranted a post office and had received the name Paradise.

The boom here started in 1904, over a rich copper find. Soon the ground was said to have been located for twenty miles around. Several major companies were formed to gain control of the best holdings, among which were the Chiricahua Mine, King Ainsworth mine group, Scanlon Mine, and Sullivan mine group. At the same time, some of the lead-silver lodes formerly worked by the Texas company were relocated and mined intermittently.[169]

The copper-mining activity mostly went into development. Two of the mines had insufficient ore, while all of the claims exhibited base-metal carbonates and sulfides that complicated the reduction process. The boom broke in 1907, due to financial and transportation problems, as well as a 30-percent drop in the value of copper.[170] Production through 1907 had come mostly from the Leadville mine group, a lead-silver proposition that reputedly yielded more than $25,000 in ore.[171]

The development and intermittent production of copper and lead continued near Paradise until 1918. Sporadic mining as recently as 1952 resulted in small lots of ore. At its peak in 1904, Paradise claimed a population of around three hundred, along with several stores, a hotel, a butcher shop, a schoolhouse, a jail, thirteen saloons, and the usual array of miners' cabins. Although most of the people left after 1907, Paradise still has a few residents today.[172] Like Galeyville, Paradise is more notable for its anecdotes than for its ore production.

Most of the mineral wealth in the California district came from the Hilltop Mine. This property revived in 1916, when two men from Kansas City acquired the claims and incorporated the Hilltop Metals Mining Co. They then spent eight years developing their holdings, which extended to either side of the mountain crest. Production at the Hilltop and Hilltop Extension mines commenced in 1924 and continued to 1926–27. During that short period, the ground gave up more than $480,000 in lead and silver, this being almost one-third of the metal values mined in the Chiricahuas. The Hilltop Mine reopened in 1952–53, and another quarter of a million dollars worth of ore, mostly lead and silver, was extracted then.[173]

Miners worked intermittently at the King of Lead, Savage, Willie Rose, Homestake, Humboldt, Harris group, Morning Star group, and other claims in the northern Chiricahuas. The Silver Prince and the Pine-Zinc properties, on the north fork of Pinery Canyon, and El Tigre, in Pinery Canyon itself, were all mined in the 1940s, while recovery work at the King of Lead continued as recently as 1970. Altogether between 1881 and 1970, the California Mining District gave up at least 38,000 tons of ore and concentrates, valued at about $1.75 million.[174]

Marble in the Chiricahuas

The northern end of the Chiricahuas once held a marble quarry. Denver capitalists formed the Arizona Marble Co. in 1909 and set about developing some eleven claims. They installed what was then a highly mechanized operation and began active work in the summer of 1910. The marble itself was described as "white, with pronounced dark veinings, and a predominating flesh tint."[175]

Marble from the original quarry was utilized for building construction. Early projects included the First National Bank Building in Denver, Colorado, as well as bank buildings in Champaign, Illinois, and Missoula, Montana. By late August of 1910, the company also had other quarries, several miles distant, in production. A news item at the end of October said that the company's Whitetail [Creek] property was expected to commence work soon.[176]

In 1910 "the first year in which any marble has been reported," total production by the Arizona Marble Co. amounted to 5,043 cubic feet, valued at $10,086.[177] Unfortunately the venture lasted only a few years before shutting down.[178] In addition to these quarries and those in the Dragoons, marble has been mined in the Tucson Mountains, the Santa Catalinas near Marble Peak, and the northern end of the Santa Rita range. As of 1966 a successor to the Santa Rita Granite, Marble and Mining Co. was the only firm still quarrying marble in southern Arizona.[179]

Rucker Canyon Mining District

A mineralized occurrence west of Rucker Lake in the southern Chiricahuas yielded a small tonnage of precious-metal ore in 1935–36. One source placed the production at 15 tons of ore from open-cut and shaft workings in some weakly mineralized fault zones.[180]

The Mining Frontier: A Perspective

In constructing a mining history, it is important to look beyond the anecdotes, the folklore, and embellishments, and instead learn what actually happened. Perhaps then we can explain why mining was so often a sporadic activity and why so many ventures failed. Precious metals have always had a sentimental or romantic value that pushed districts producing these to the forefront in public awareness, although the principal values lay with the vastly larger amounts of base metals extracted. Most important of all, we come to realize that the driving force in mining was market prices. Miners expected to get rich, although profits generally came from pursuing systematic development, not by chasing bonanzas. Southeastern Arizona has an extremely long mining tradition, one that exemplifies almost every aspect of the industry.

Mineral explorations after the Gadsden Purchase focused upon silver, for the excellent reason that silver in the period between 1858 and 1861 brought $1.35 an ounce, a price not seen again for more than a century.[181] With such rich rewards waiting, any silver mine became a valuable property. Companies were organized in the East to exploit and promote this treasure-house in the Southwest. The managers sent out to reopen the old Spanish mines soon encountered problems with the local labor and Indians, banditry, lack of machinery, a continuing shortage of capital, and eventually the Civil War. The difficulties that defeated these first ventures were primarily technical ones, as with ore veins that proved to be thin, ores that were not always reducible by smelting, and older mines that had already been exhausted of their more easily reduced surface deposits. The few technicians at hand were possibly the best of their day, but overall expertise remained in short supply. Local superintendents were reluctant to admit that problems existed, especially to distant employers and shareholders. Variations on these circumstances were played out through the remainder of the century.

Gold mines of course were always valuable. Gold discoveries in central Arizona began in 1863. The fair and consistent price for gold offered by the government meant that it was always attractive, especially when economic downturns and depressed prices put other types of metal mining out of business. The southeastern part of the territory had few important gold properties; most of the gold there derived from surface deposits that soon became depleted or came as a by-product of base-metal processing.

When serious mineral exploration resumed in the 1870s, southern Arizona fell into a pattern that endured for another quarter-century. This was an era of individual prospectors and small-scale developments. From about 1877 people poured over the hills and one discovery followed another, many of the booms dying out as quickly as they began. In all of this activity, there were a few important developments, such as Tombstone and Bisbee, but many miners learned that it was far easier to make money buying and selling claims than by trying to develop them. The peculiar and infectious optimism that surrounds mining encouraged this attitude, particularly in the newer districts. The hope of selling out at a profit was the best prospect a claimant had, since the costs of bringing a mine into production were prohibitive for most individuals. Many prospects had relatively low-grade ore beneath the richer surface "float," making the poorer deposits unworkable without extensive development. If no buyers for claims showed up, then a booming district could deflate almost overnight.

Outside investment during this period was often misguided. One common mistake was to put money into production facilities, such as mills and concentrators, at the expense of underground development. This typically led to financial disaster. A related problem (and probably not an uncommon one) was to hire agents and managers who had little knowledge of their business. Then too, the understanding of ore chemistry was very imperfect, and the grading or alteration of ores from one type to another with increasing depths was not yet generally recognized. Such a change might require a radical difference in smelting equipment, and a misjudgment could result in reduction works that were useless. Galeyville, Paradise, Black Diamond, Table Mountain, and the earlier years at Oro Blanco provide examples where poor judgment and unskilled operation resulted in capital investments that were largely wasted. This situation changed gradually, after the appearance of gold cyanization in 1887 and the selective flotation process in 1905.[182] The latter made possible the commercial production of zinc, one of the principal metals recovered in southeastern Arizona. Still, even the best-managed ventures had to measure success and failure by the rise and fall of metal prices.

There were outstanding successes, chief among them the Warren Mining District, better known as Bisbee. Through almost a century of production, until the mines closed in 1975, Bisbee recorded an output of nearly 8 billion pounds of copper, more than 300 million pounds each of lead and zinc, and more gold and silver than any other district in Arizona.[183] The silver output from Bisbee was triple that of its famous neighbor, Tombstone. Much more modest but still on a multi-million dollar scale were Harshaw, Patagonia, the Cochise (Johnson Camp) and Oro Blanco districts, Helvetia and Rosemont, Turquoise, Pearce, the Aravaipa district, and Copper Creek.

These successes, nearly all of them in the twentieth century, have certain features in common. They were well-financed, professionally managed corporate ventures, headquartered outside of Arizona. The mining, except at the silver camps of Tombstone and Pearce, was principally for base metals (lead, copper, zinc), with precious-metal values an important but secondary interest. The driving force was always market prices, which for lead and zinc tended to be stable over long periods, in the range of 4 to 6 cents per pound. A lead-zinc mine, once started, might therefore remain in operation until the ores had been exhausted. Copper was subject to wide price swings, and values of less than 18 to 20 cents per pound (in this century) meant that copper mines closed. The figures for ore volumes and dollar values in the twentieth century dwarf those from the nineteenth. By a similar comparison, the great copper-mining districts at Miami-Inspiration, Copper Mountain (Morenci), and Pima, all elsewhere in southern Arizona, individually yielded (through 1981) about the same amounts of metal as the Warren and San Manuel districts.[184] Southeastern Arizona has been and continues to be a substantial metal contributor.

The keys to success in mining lay with access to capital, cheap long-distance transportation, and beneficial market prices. Without these factors development was scarcely possible, while with them success might be attainable. The rare exceptions were the Copper Glance Mine in the Huachucas, run for ten years by Sam Donnelly practically as a religious commune, and the

World's Fair Mine in the Harshaw district, developed with almost no original capital.[185]

Today mining is virtually limited to the copper and other minerals at San Manuel. This compression of activity reflects the exhaustion of some ore bodies and the fact that currently the smaller lodes and lower-grade ores cannot be recovered economically. In the absence of substantially higher prices, mineral mining in southeastern Arizona is, with the important exception of copper, almost surely a matter of history.

8
CATTLE, GOATS, AND DUDES

Ranching, together with mining and farming, has provided a livelihood for many southern Arizonians. Writers have given us numerous accounts of the stock-raising industry, but as with any good subject, there are always new perspectives and other aspects to explore.

Livestock raising started with Father Kino's efforts to establish herds at the missions. In the eighteenth century, settlers at Sopori and Arivaca, and in the San Luis section of the upper Santa Cruz Valley, achieved some success with ranching, until the Pima Revolt drove them out in 1751. Stock growing flourished once again during the time of the Apache peace establishments, and it was then that petitioners began to ask for cattle-ranching grants, *sitios de ganado mayor.*

All of the sitios lay along river valleys or in lowland areas with good water supplies. These grants saw fairly brief periods of occupation; for example the San Bernardino Ranch began in 1821 with the purchase of four thousand head of cattle from the Tumacácori mission, yet by 1851 boundary commissioner John R. Bartlett estimated that San Bernardino had been abandoned for about twenty years. The large ranching grants along the upper San Pedro River and Babocomari Creek were petitioned for in 1827 and the titles received between 1827 and 1833. Yet when the Ortiz family abandoned their Arivaca ranch by 1835, Apache attacks were forcing other grantees to leave their lands as well. In the San Rafael Valley the "partners" (as they were called) held onto their lands until 1843. Ranch buildings at the San Bernardino Ranch and at Babocomari were substantial affairs, walled and fortified, although none of the southern Arizona establishments would have qualified as *haciendas.* [1]

Commissioner Bartlett claimed that not less than forty thousand head of cattle roamed the Babocomari Ranch at the time the Apaches drove the owners away.[2] When the Mormon Battalion marched by the springs at Agua Prieta in 1846, Lieutenant Colonel Philip St. George Cooke said it was thought that as many as five thousand cattle watered there. The forty-niner Benjamin Harris passed a herd that he judged numbered between five and fifteen thousand head.[3] These were feral animals from the abandoned ranches in the upper San Pedro and San Bernardino valleys. Other early travelers commented on the ruined ranch buildings and the wild cattle roaming the countryside, yet by 1854 these herds had all disappeared, probably to provide dinners for Apaches and forty-niners.[4]

During the 1850s cattle drovers from farther east took many herds of cattle and sheep west in the path of the forty-niners, to sell in California. These speculative drives brought great profits at first. By 1855 the California market was becoming glutted, but the flocks (one numbered forty-six thousand sheep) and droves continued nonetheless.[5] A later writer characterized this period.

> The passage of immense drives of both sheep and cattle from New Mexico and Texas, to meet the demand of mining camps in California, occasioned between 1849 and 1870 the temporary use of grass lands in Arizona. These movements have little direct connection with the permanent stock of the country; for although the Mexicans of the Santa Cruz valley often secured foot-sore animals from drivers en route west no amount of vigilance enabled them to grow many cattle, owing to the Indians. Aside from the half dozen sparcely populated towns the only demand for beef and mutton up to 1870 was at the military posts. These distant garrisons were supplied from California and New Mexico for many years, . . .[6]

Until 1861 the southern Apaches let these drives pass unmolested. When herds were trailed to California after the Civil War, the Apaches attempted to stampede and run off the stock.[7]

Cattle

Some General Considerations

There is a huge literature on the history of the range-cattle industry, including that portion of it in Arizona.[8] In the days of open ranges, nearly all cattle ranchers shared the same problems, whether these were of markets, prices, range resources, water, or even rustlers. The history of cattle ranching mirrors the history of each ranch, and what happened to the industry came to affect each part of it. With occasional exceptions, such as the Sierra Bonita Ranch, the individual ranches blend into the history of the business as a whole.

Southern Arizona ranching in the post–Civil War years developed along certain lines. Large corporate ranches were present, but they did not dominate the ranges. These corporations were locally owned and not financed by foreign capital, unlike those elsewhere in the West. Eventually they proved to be less successful than the smaller, family-size operations. The ranges themselves were primarily semidesert grasslands, grazed the year around. Overgrazing and droughts reduced the original vegetation to brush in many places. Ranches in this part of Arizona require as much investment in water development as in the rangelands, and with careful management they can be moderately productive.[9]

Outside of the Santa Cruz Valley, with its permanent water and good pasture lands, ranchers located in the valleys and along the permanent streams and ciénegas (low-lying swampy areas) near the base of the mountains. Water controlled the range, and by 1883–84 every running stream and permanent spring had been preempted. The ranges were stocked with cattle brought from Mexico and Texas. In the Sulphur Springs Valley, ranches lay about ten to fifteen miles apart, supplied with water piped from the mountains or from dug wells. At Henry Hooker's Sierra Bonita Ranch, the five springs, two wells, and several ciénegas allowed Hooker to claim use of a territory up to twenty-five miles square as securely as if he had fenced it. His "fences" were the Galiuro and Pinaleño mountain ranges.

Since the mountains generally lacked accessible watering places, the ranchers did not locate there, nor did they move their stock seasonally to highland pastures. The herds instead occupied the ciénega areas in hot weather. Cattle would penetrate the mountains at times during the spring and fall, when ephemeral streams and wet-weather springs made these ranges available.[10]

The Rise of an Industry

The big, rangy Texas and Mexican longhorns driven through Arizona in the 1850s and 1860s had little connection with the development of a local livestock industry. These transients made only temporary use of the territory's grasslands, and they had serious shortcomings as beef animals. William S. Oury is credited with being the first to introduce improved stock—a herd of 4 shorthorn bulls and 102 heifers that he drove from Illinois in 1868. Depredations and other problems combined to keep his herd small, but in 1873–76 Henry C. Hooker introduced high-grade shorthorn and Devon bulls to his newly established Sierra Bonita Ranch in the northern Sulphur Springs Valley.

These animals did not adapt well, so in 1876 Hooker brought the first Herefords to the Sierra Bonita. In 1883 Colin Cameron imported a carload of pedigreed Herefords to his San Rafael de la Zanja ranch, where they not only survived but thrived. Meanwhile the Murphey brothers, from California, located a large herd of graded shorthorn and Devon cattle on the lower

San Pedro in 1877. Of all the breeds, it was the rustling ability, early maturing qualities, and prolific reproduction of the Herefords that made them the favorite on Arizona's ranges.[11]

Until the early 1870s, no one in Arizona had large livestock holdings; the 1870 census reported only 5,132 cattle of all descriptions. Among these would have been Oury's shorthorns and the herds of 20 to 75 head of Mexican stock held by a dozen or so Hispanic cattle owners in the Santa Cruz Valley. The stockmen's situation began to change in 1872, when all of the Apaches were finally placed on reservations and issued rations of corn and beef. This combination of a newfound security for life and property with the creation of a big, local market at the Indian reservatons led to the rapid development of a livestock industry. Parts of southern Arizona soon became a giant holding pen for the beef herds of Henry Hooker, until 1871 part of the firm of Hinds and Hooker, and for John S. Chisum, from New Mexico. Both contractors supplied cattle for army needs as well as for the Indian reservations.[12]

In February 1873 Hooker located his Sierra Bonita Ranch in the Sulphur Springs Valley and held 10,000 head of Texas cattle there, to meet contract demands. That year the *Tucson Citizen* proclaimed that "There never has been such activity in securing eligible stock ranches in this part of Arizona as at present."[13] By the end of 1873, the new ranches included Sanford's near Pantano, Steel and McKenzie's in the Sulphur Springs Valley, and the firm of Marsh and Driscoll at the Canoa Ranch on the Santa Cruz above Tucson. Chisum's claim lay along the San Pedro, from St. David north to a few miles above Benson; a few years later he started the Eureka Springs Stock Ranch in the Aravaipa Valley. As of 1995, the Sierra Bonita is the oldest continuously operated cattle ranch in Arizona and is still owned by a Hooker descendant.[14]

Many other settlers in the Sulphur Springs Valley began their operations between 1873 and 1878. The Riggs family, headed by Brannick Riggs, arrived in this period and laid the foundation for their cattle holdings. In the middle 1880s, White, Vickers, Pursley and others combined their herds and holdings to form another big outfit, the Chiricahua Cattle Company. Their headquarters ranch lay along West Turkey Creek on the western slope of the Chiricahua Mountains, while their stock ranged over an area seventy-five by thirty-five miles in Cochise and Graham counties. In the meantime, in 1876 Walter Vail and H. R. Hislop bought a small ranch east of the Santa Ritas. They were later joined by John Harvey and Edward Vail, and their operation grew into one of the largest cattle companies in the Southwest—the Empire Land and Cattle Co.[15] On the upper Santa Cruz, however, there were still only three herds as recently as 1877.

Open-Range Ranching and the Range-Cattle Industry

The first half of the 1880s was the golden age of the range-cattle industry everywhere in the West; a time of high prices, when the open ranges carried as many head of stock as the owners could buy. The demands for beef came from the army posts and Indian reservations, from booming mining camps that were spreading across southern Arizona, and from people in the new towns springing up along the Southern Pacific Railroad. Not until 1883 and 1884 did large cattle ranches extend into the San Simon Valley. This absence had created a bright spot of opportunity that rustlers were not slow to appreciate. For a time they had a thriving business supplying the mining camp at Galeyville with beef out of Mexico.[16] During the early 1880s, rustling in fact seems to have focused upon the Galeyville and Tombstone markets.

The livestock industry soon expanded so that, in 1885, production exceeded demand within Arizona for the first time.[17] That year ranchers were confronted with the necessity for developing markets in the East. The following year was the last time mature, range-fattened cattle were sold in any numbers. The next decade witnessed massive changes in the Arizona livestock business as the result of market forces, and it came out of this period operating on a very different basis.[18]

Until 1892 ranchers kept their cows and sold range-grown steers, generally three-year-olds, to farmers in the Midwest or in Arizona. The farmers in turn fattened these animals in pastures or feedlots and sent them on to market. Arizona ranges in 1892 were stocked to capacity, with an estimated 1.5 million head of cattle, but less than one-half of the usual amount of moisture fell during the rainy season that year. Ranchers held their cattle through the next summer, when another drought occurred, and many animals died. Ranchmen then had to sell or move their cattle out of the territory, a situation that continued into the summer of 1893. By this time northern buyers were refusing to take three-year-old steers, unless they could buy two-year-olds as well. The average age of range cattle at marketing moved downward, from 2.18 years in 1890 to 1.63 years in 1900. Cattle growers began to view the traditional tradeoff of range resources and marketing age differently, when they realized that they received bigger returns from selling younger animals. The result was that by 1896, all stockmen in southern Arizona were supplying buyers with yearlings; their herds had become breeding herds.[19]

By 1897 the rangelands returned to normal, and cattlemen grew prosperous again. No longer did they try to fatten cattle on the open range or market full-grown steers, however. Most stock from Arizona was sold as feeders and stockers, a practice that continues today. These terms, often used synonymously and in combination, both refer to young animals—large calves and yearlings. Stockers are cattle capable of additional growth and finish on pasturage, while feeders are used for rapid growth by intensive feeding. For many years California markets have taken practically all of the range cattle exported from Arizona. As early as the late 1880s, some cattle were being fattened on alfalfa in Maricopa County and then marketed, but the fattening of cattle in Arizona feedlots first became important around 1950.[20]

The return of good cattle prices in 1896, plus abundant forage brought by copious rains in 1897–98, marked the start of a long period of prosperity for the livestock industry. Some outsiders sought to share in this good fortune; indeed, around 1900 rustling became so bad that a special force, the Arizona Rangers, was created to stop cattle thefts. Prices remained stable even through the panic of 1907 and then began a rapid advance that culminated in wartime peaks of $10 to $11.25 per hundredweight for good to choice feeders and $9.25 to $10.75 for comparable stockers. As 1917 opened, the *Southwestern Stockman-Farmer* accurately predicted that "the cattle feeders are going to make a killing." In general as the prices for livestock moved up, the numbers of animals increased as well.[21]

The open-range period—the time when cattlemen operated with virtually no restrictions, fees, or fences—continued to about 1905. By then many of the large corporate outfits were quitting business or had already done so, to be succeeded by smaller, family-based stock ranches.

Did the Range Cattle Business Really Pay?

Actually, when the romance is cleared away, there is a legitimate question as to whether open-range ranching did pay. Ranch schoolteacher Eulalia Bourne, writing at a later date, explained the business philosophy of the old-time cattleman in this way: "Old-time cowmen were out to get rich, and they did. The way they accumulated money was not to spend any. Whatever their steers brought went into the bank, not into living expenses such as food and housing."[22] Will C. Barnes, an Arizona pioneer who had seen every side of the cattle business, remarked shrewdly that "for a few years millions were made, principally in speculation, promotion, and on paper."[23]

Three recent scholars have considered this question and given it a more qualified answer:

> The range cattle industry . . . in the more tangible matter of dollars and cents it probably was also profitable—at least in instances where good management prevailed, and in the period when the land could be used with little or no cost, when taxes were insignificant and such

controls as existed were more honored in the breach than in the observance.[24]

Another student of the range offered a more negative assessment, asking first "[f]or the Eastern financier, had the cattle industry been a profitable investment? Regarding the majority of investors, the answer is a qualified no."[25]

Conclusions such as these mean that the claims about profits and loses or success and failure need to be weighed carefully, since they may be difficult to prove. More studies of surviving business records and correspondence are needed, and the results may be truly surprising. For example, two prominent cattle companies founded in Lincoln County, New Mexico, in 1885 were seen by people in that territory as pillars of strength and financial success. In reality both firms were kept on their feet by huge infusions of capital from a New York businessman. He finally stopped supporting his spendthrift local partners after eight years, having seen just two years of dividends on his investments.[26] In Arizona a Hooker descendant observed that the production of fine carriage horses on the Sierra Bonita Ranch was responsible for a large part of the ranch income in the early 1880s.[27]

The Cattle Industry Faces Changes

In the first decade of the twentieth century, prices continued to be good to excellent. The industry faced far-reaching changes nonetheless, with the breakup of open-range cattle operations. Abundant rainfall in 1905 doubled the normal amount in Sulphur Springs Valley; while this benefited the forage, it also encouraged the first large movement of homesteaders into the Sulphur Springs and San Simon valleys. A Forest Homestead Act of 1906 made tracts in the mountains available as well.

More years of good rains brought settlers by the thousands, some to the former open ranges, others to the mountain parks and valleys. The new people were dry farmers, who soon found that it was necessary to develop artesian and pump wells to ensure good crops. Many persisted only until they 'proved up' and received a title to their claim, then sold out and moved on. The land as often as not reverted to range. By the mid-1920s dry farming had been discredited, and ranchers were buying up the patented homestead claims.[28]

Another change ushered in at the turn of the century was regulation of grazing on public lands. After 1897 the Interior Department, which controlled the newly created forest reserves, required grazing permits, although it charged no fees. In 1905 administration of the forest reserves shifted to the Forest Service within the Department of Agriculture, and in less than a year this new agency adopted a schedule of grazing fees. Complementing these fees was a system of allotments, whereby each rancher had a specific tract assigned for his livestock. Only in 1936 did the Interior Department begin charging a fee for grazing stock on public-domain lands.[29] Initially stock raisers mounted strong opposition to these new rules and regulations.[30]

One goal of the allotment and fee system was to provide a fair means for reducing livestock numbers on overgrazed rangelands. At the turn of the century, overgrazing in southern Arizona was largely confined to the broad valley areas and adjacent foothills, the National Forest grasslands being mostly unavailable, due to a lack of water supplies for domestic herds. This underutilization disappeared between 1908 and 1917, with a virtual doubling of the numbers of cattle on forest allotments. After rising to a wartime peak, these numbers declined to between forty-one and thirty-seven thousand on Coronado National Forest lands. Ranchers were slow to adjust to the diminished need for livestock products. As one student put it, "when soldiers returned home to the farms and raised more cattle, the animals stacked up on the ranges. In hopes that the markets would improve, forest grazing restrictions were eased; and by the 1920's the carrying capacity was greatly exceeded."[31]

In 1920–21 southern Arizona was struck by drought and cattle prices tumbled. In the words of one rancher who survived that period, "[d]uring the prolonged drouth in 1921, like so many of his counterparts, [Wiley M.] Morgan went broke, but hung on to the ranch. In those days when there was no feed or water, the cattle just died."[32] Prices made a gradual recovery, and markets were very good in the late 1920s. Values declined steadily as the Depression set in, and in 1933–34 another drought added to the ranchmen's woes. Government programs helped for a time, but the major benefit was a dramatic price improvement, beginning in 1935 and continuing into World War II.[33]

The long-term trend since the 1920s has been toward stability in land-tenure, production, and management practices. The economics of range-cattle operations in the low-capacity, semidesert lands of southeastern Arizona do not permit much investment, and the ranches there continue to be marginal propositions.[34] One recent assessment noted quite accurately that in the use of western rangelands, there are really no new issues.[35]

The Sierra Bonita Ranch—An Enduring Success

With all that has happened, it may be useful to ask why Henry Hooker's Sierra Bonita Ranch has survived and prospered for more than a century. Superior management seems to have been its competitive edge, more than any benefits realized through improved breeding, range improvements, or restricting livestock numbers. For one thing Hooker practiced cattle feeding almost from the beginning, instead of depending strictly upon the open range.[36] A visitor in 1880 described the operation this way:

> This vast stretch of land is nearly level. Running through its entire length, with branches to the foothills on either side, is a strip of meadow land varying in width—averaging, probably, nearly a mile. This meadow land is almost invaluable to the stock-raiser. Despite the fact that it is the favorite grazing ground of the large bands of cattle, Mr. Hooker annually sends his mowing machines over its level surface and cuts all the hay, of splendid quality, necessary for his large stables and corrals.

Another factor was strategic placement of three main, permanent water sources within his range. Complementing these were more ephemeral supplies in tanks, as well as runoff that allowed other parts of the range to be grazed.[37]

Hooker's provisions grew more sophisticated through time. One knowledgeable writer (a dean of agriculture) described these refinements:

> Mr. Hooker availed himself of the flood waters in his vicinity for the growing of corn, sorghum, and Johnson grass, and for the betterment of his range. By means of diversion ditches so placed as to spread the run-off from the adjacent slopes over the grass country in the vicinity, he improved thousands of acres of grass lands. Following flood-water distribution of this character new areas of perennial sacaton grass, of great value in time of drought, were established, and aided him greatly in maintaining his herds at certain seasons of the year. In the bottom of the valley he impounded water by means of traverse embankments. From the storm-water reservoirs thus created he irrigated fields of sorghum and corn, and when such reservoirs were emptied of their store of water he planted sorghum in the wet soil remaining in their bottoms. In this way considerable quantities of forage were produced which were preserved and utilized in times of scarcity. In time of extreme need he would plow his Johnson grass fields, turning up the succulent roots and stolons that were then eagerly consumed by famishing cattle, which were thus carried over a period of scarcity.[38]

Such improvements imply not only foresight and technical knowledge, but also managerial talent and the availability of adequate capital. After Colonel Hooker's death in 1907, these irrigated pastures and provisions for raising forage were discontinued, but in 1935 his grandson started to revive and improve upon them, drilling both shallow and deep wells. This developed into a self-contained feeding and finishing operation that produced upwards of twelve hundred head of finished cattle each year. These steers were then marketed locally or shipped to California.[39]

Sheep

Cattle were the most numerous class of livestock in southern Arizona, but not the only one. Large herds of sheep had been driven west to California before the Civil War, at a time when southern Arizona residents owned only a few hundred head. By 1880 more than six hundred thousand sheep grazed in Arizona, primarily in the northern counties, although the Cienega Ranch (probably the Ciénega de los Pimos, east of Tucson) had the largest single herd, twenty-three thousand sheep. Never again did the southern part of the territory see such a concentration. Indeed, the same census report noted that "[t]he stock-owners as a whole think the extensive country better adapted to cattle than to sheep, and only Mexican breeds of sheep thrive on the juiceless grasses of this region [that is, the Pima County ranges]."[40]

Two large flocks grazed in the San Pedro Valley, while the entire Sulphur Spring Valley had only two herds of mutton sheep.[41] Perhaps these local animals were the descendants of California sheep driven to Arizona in the 1870s.[42] By the late 1890s, when the sheep industry had become well established in northern Arizona, Pima County reported only between two and three thousand head. In Cochise County sheep tallied approximately one-tenth the number of cattle.[43] In later years allotees on Crook and Coronado National Forest land ran few if any sheep. These at times were more profitable than cattle, but southern Arizona ranchers preferred to raise cows.[44]

Goats

Another type of stock raising flourished around the turn of the century and for some years afterward. Goat ranching carried low prestige, and many ranchers resisted being identified with it, even though the economics of raising goats were sometimes very attractive. As one stockman said, "This was a lucrative business and at one time mohair was selling for 60 cents a pound while steers were bringing $3.00 a head."[45]

Goats were raised primarily for their hair, which on Angoras is called mohair. The clip from an Arizona-raised Angora goat during that period might weigh between 2.5 and 4 pounds.[46] Normally the animals would have been shorn twice a year. The milk and meat were marketable as well.

Goat ranching in southern Arizona had a slow beginning. Yavapai County

Angora goats feeding on alligator junipers in the Datil National Forest, early twentieth century. (Courtesy, The National Archives.)

in 1880 had a herd of 2,000 graded Angoras, the only ones reported in the territory at that time. During the 1890s the business expanded, perhaps in response to depressed cattle prices early in that decade, later following the boosterism for mohair. In 1900 the U.S. Census enumerated goats for the first time and tabulated only 765 fleeces from Graham and Pima counties in southeastern Arizona, a small portion of the 13,874 fleeces shorn in the territory, or of the 16,619 goats the governor had just reported in Graham, Pima, and Cochise counties.[47]

In 1901 the Angora industry was stated to be "in a thriving condition."[48] The market for mohair remained good and even improved, the price doubling by 1918. Not surprisingly the number of goats in Arizona increased two and one-half times between 1900 and 1910, from 98,403 to 246,617 animals, and the fleeces multiplied by a factor of eight (from 13,874 to 103,226).[49]

Goat ranching suffered from a poor image, despite its favorable economics. Ranchers typically thought of themselves as *cattle* men and had little incentive to shift to another type of livestock when good returns could be made from cattle and sheep.[50] On the other hand, goats required much less capital investment than did cattle, and mohair brought consistently good prices. Goats did take the constant attention of a herder, and the Forest Service viewed these animals as a major cause of range deterioration, which they tried to ameliorate by eliminating goats from forest lands. Opinions about the impact of goats on the landscape were divided, and there is some evidence that the deterioration of goat ranges may have been due to close herding practices. Forest Service studies and a recent, excellent review of goat ranching in the region of Aravaipa Canyon, one of Arizona's principal goat ranges, are our best sources of information about this type of stock raising in the Southwest.[51]

Within Arizona the raising of Angoras may have peaked around 1909. The 170,588 animals assessed as property that year, although less than the number listed by the 1910 Census, far exceeded the numbers assessed in any prior or subsequent year. There were also shifts in distribution, more than 25 percent of the goats in Arizona in 1910 being in Cochise, Graham and Pinal counties, while in 1925 this proportion was less than 15 percent, with the number of animals in these three counties having dropped as well, by one-third.[52] In 1908 when the Forest Service first reported numbers of livestock on allotments by type of animal, there were 31,704 goats pastured on Arizona forest lands, with 3,669 of these in the Coronado National Forest. The numbers thereafter decreased for about eight years, increased in 1918–20, then declined again. On Coronado Forest lands, the last goat permittees quit in 1920–21, due to animals being crippled by loose rocks on steep hillsides, as well as because of the owners' failure to make a success in the business.[53]

Across southeastern Arizona the number of actual goat ranches was few, and these were concentrated in two areas. Down in the southern Peloncillos, a Mr. Moon lived on Bercham Draw from 1907 to 1918 and herded goats there for his stepfather, Bill Bercham. He recalled two other goat ranchers in that part of the Peloncillos and estimated the size of each herd at between 600 and 1,900 animals.[54]

The principal area given over to goat ranges was the brush-covered mountains and canyons east of Winkelman; between Aravaipa Creek on the south and the Gila River on the north; and east through the Santa Teresa Mountains. Between 1900 and the 1930s, the goat ranches there included some that maintained herds of both cattle and goats. The industry may have peaked in this area during the 1920s, and one estimate placed the number of goats as high as 40,000. Several ranchers in the Aravaipa–Stanley Butte country and along the Gila River ran as many as 25,000 animals at times, while others had between 1,000 and 10,000 head.[55] One ranch in upper Hawk Canyon raised as many as 7,000 Angoras in good years.[56] Two operators kept goats as recently as the 1940s and the Weathersby Angoras, the largest herds in the eastern part of the Aravaipa section, ranged the Santa Teresas until 1951.[57]

The drought that struck southern Arizona in 1920 and the first half of 1921 caused heavy livestock losses. Many cattle, including cows and calves, were shipped out or moved to other ranges. Then another calamity virtually killed sales. On June 14, 1921, newspapers announced a proposed credit-relief measure whereby bankers would raise $50 million to aid financially strapped cattlemen. This never came to be, but the immediate impact of the announcement was a decline by one-third in the prices offered for stockers and feeders at midwestern cattle markets. Prices stayed down, and in August they drifted as low as $3.00 per 100 lbs. on the Denver market, before recovering somewhat. What was worse, the ranchers in Arizona complained that no market existed for their stock at any price.[58] Federal loans to cattlemen and high tariffs on imported animals failed to bring much relief.[59] It was the summer of 1925 before prices finally began to recover.[60]

During this four-year interim when the cattle industry was floundering, sheep and wool were bringing good money, and the prices for mohair more than doubled nationally between 1921 and 1922, rising through 1928. Stockmen elsewhere turned to raising sheep or goats, as did many in the Aravaipa country in southern Arizona, but at least two dozen cattlemen found another way to keep their ranches and to make money as well. They began to accept paying guests, introducing dude ranching to Arizona.

Dudes

Dude Ranching's Beginnings

In the Dakota Badlands and the northern Rocky Mountains, periodic downturns in livestock prices had spurred a number of family-owned cattle ranches into accepting paying guests. This tradition dated from the late nineteenth century, when the vacationers (that is, the dudes) made their reservations and then arrived to stay two weeks or more at these ranches. Dude ranching became well established there prior to World War I.

Dude ranches had the appearance and substance of cattle ranches, which indeed they were. They usually featured a large ranch house or lodge, which did double duty as a social center and place where meals were served. There were corrals and other facilities, running streams or reservoirs, and individual cabins for the visitors. Guests could enjoy horseback riding, roundups, rodeos, hiking, mountain climbing, cookouts, pack trips, and even polo. In time the more successful ranches added swimming pools, golf courses, and tennis courts, becoming indistinguishable from resorts.[61]

In southern Arizona there was already a winter-resort tradition, based upon the bright sunshine and warm winter weather. Eastern visitors began arriving in October and stayed at the Congress or the Santa Rita hotels in Tucson.[62] The lodges, resorts, and other attractions there had no association with ranching until sometime after 1920.

Dude Ranches in Southern Arizona

This prior existence of a resort tradition probably helped dude ranching become established in Arizona. Two miles west of Oracle, George Stone Wilson already had a large cattle ranch where he began taking guests in 1924, calling his place the Linda Vista Ranch. As he put it, "the guests really roughed it and took part in the work."[63] Even before this, rancher Neil Erickson's daughter Lillian expanded the old Erickson homestead on the western side of the Chiricahuas into the Faraway Ranch, a combination cattle and dude ranch; it owed its success to the establishment of Chiricahua National Monument in 1924. The Faraway Ranch operated from about 1917 into the 1960s.[64]

Southern Arizona blossomed into a center of dude ranching. In 1925 a popular writer visited half a dozen of these new establishments. He found the Triangle L Ranch at Oracle and George Wilson's Linda Vista Ranch just west of town. Donee's Dude Ranch also had its main ranch building in Oracle. Farther to the east, in the Little Dragoon Mountains, lay the impressive new facilities at the Seven Dash Ranch. South of there, only twelve miles from Tombstone on the old Pearce-to-Tombstone road through South Pass in the Dragoon Mountains, stood the Bar O Ranch. The dudes at this working cattle outfit were encouraged to ride the range with the cowboys.

Even farther south Frank Moson had his YW Guest Ranch, later known as the Y-Lightning Ranch, about seven miles west of Hereford, Arizona. Described in 1925 as "fairly new," the accommodations for guests were "strictly first class" and had all modern conveniences. The proprietor had installed a billiard room, tennis court, and even leveled a polo field.[65] The writer did not mention it, but the Zinsmeister Brothers' Circle Z Ranch, on Sonoita Creek southwest of Patagonia, must also have been in operation by this time. In 1927 this ranch advertised "[m]odern, comfortable buildings with electric light, hot and cold water, baths, swimming pool."[66] The Circle Z blended dude ranching into its cattle operations and continues as a guest ranch today.[67]

By the late 1920s, guest ranching had become important enough for the proprietors to form an association. Some establishments were open the year around; others closed for the summer. A few, such as the Hacienda de la Osa and El Mirador Ranch, were a bit remote, but many clustered around Tucson or the mountain ranges farther east, convenient to National Forest lands. A Coronado National Forest recreation plan compiled in 1930 included fourteen dude ranches situated outside of the forest and five similar resorts on private lands within the forest.[68]

As of 1930 the Tanque Verde Ranch was still the only guest ranch listed in the immediate area of Tucson; it had been a cattle ranch. Beginning in 1928 it offered visitors horseback and pack trips into the mountains and hunting parties in the National Forest. The Flying V Ranch, at the foot of the Santa Catalinas, was another old stock ranch, revived in 1927 but catering largely to transient guests as of 1930.[69] Two to three years later, the guest ranches within twenty miles of Tucson included the Flying V, Tanque Verde, Las Moras, Harding, Hales, Glovers, Silverbell, and Desert Willows ranches.[70] At the beginning of World War II, the Tucson area boasted ten guest ranches, a number that ballooned to seventy-five by 1960! These were mostly resorts, rather than ranch-type operations. Twenty years later urban growth had reduced the number back to ten.[71]

Up at Oracle the three dude ranches in 1925 dwindled to the Rancho Linda Vista a few years later. The 1927 resort directory extolled it as "[a] typical cattle ranch, . . . in live oaks of the Catalina Mountains, . . . Ranch house and cottages with running water and bath rooms. Tennis, riding, trap shooting, and all cattle ranch activities. Stage from Tucson daily. Telephone at the ranch. Saddle horses and guides available for trips." Rates were moderate: $35 a week or $130 per month.[72] The Rancho Linda Vista proved to be an enduring success. After he discontinued the dude operations around 1950, George Wilson continued his cattle ranch there. Today it is an artist's colony.[73]

South of Tucson the old town of Tubac included a Prince Ranch in 1933 and a Rancho Santa Cruz in a 1936 listing. Both evidently lasted for only a short time.[74] At the Zinsmeisters' Circle Z Ranch on Sonoita Creek, guests could use the adjacent foothill and mountain country for horseback, pack, and hunting trips. Three miles south of the Circle Z lay the Los Fresnos Ranch, another old, established cattle ranch that welcomed guests among the oak groves of the Patagonia foothills.[75] The oak parks on the eastern side of the Santa Ritas sheltered a small resort called the Oakland Ranch.

Scarcely a mile south of Sonoita lay the Hacienda Los Encinos, a cattle ranch converted to a dude ranch that specialized in the care of school-age children. In that same area as of 1932 was an Eagle Nest Ranch.[76] South of

Elgin, in the Canelo Hills, were other, little-known dude ranches. An Outlook Ranch was listed in 1932 and 1936, while from the same period a Mrs. C. Moson managed the Diamond C Ranch. The 1940 USDA Forest Service map showed a J. Parker Guest Ranch eight miles southwest of Elgin, on Forest Service lands.[77]

About 1911 Frank Moson, stepson of the southern Arizona copper magnate, Colonel William C. Greene, began putting together his own cattle company. This grew into the 25,000-acre YW Ranch. By 1927 Moson had changed its name to the Y-Lightning Guest Ranch, a dude as well as a cattle ranch, which continued until 1940 or later.[78] As of 1940 there was also a Carr Canyon Guest Ranch, on Forest Service lands west of the Y-Lightning, and a Border Guest Ranch, on private lands just outside the entrance to what became Coronado National Memorial. A Major Healey occupied the Carr Canyon ranch by the late 1940s and used it for breeding horses.[79]

In the western foothills of the Pinaleños, northwest of old Fort Grant, Mr. and Mrs. Webb welcomed guests at the Seventy-Six Ranch. They claimed that the ranch dated from 1876 and hosted guests there throughout the year.[80] The Seventy-Six still exists, as a working ranch. Dropping farther south, two sisters named McEwen ran the Seven Dash Ranch, in the northern part of the Little Dragoon Mountains.[81] The Dragoons harbored several guest ranches, including the Triangle T Ranch, called "The Pioneer Dude Ranch" by one former owner. It was evidently started by Miss Katherine Tutt before 1930 and managed after her death by her mother. Early in 1937 Paul Van Cleve Jr., owner of a large guest ranch near Melville, Montana, purchased the Triangle T. Although it has since changed hands at least twice, it continues as a dude ranch; guests may now bring their travel trailers.[82] A listing in 1933 placed the Bar C (or C Bar) Ranch, another old cattle spread developed as a dude ranch, four miles from Dragoon.[83] Three years later there was an Apache Guest Ranch in the Dragoon area.[84] As of 1930 a dude ranch called the Two Bar Ranch lay at "a very attractive location" in the lower part of East Stronghold Canyon.[85] In recent years a new guest ranch, the Grapevine Ranch, has started up in this same general area.

Still farther south, west of Courtland, Harry Kendall's Bar O Ranch nestled by the Dragoon Mountains at the foot of some cliffs. The Bar O's attractions included the "[m]ain building, community hall, individual cabins for guests, in live oak grove. Hot and cold shower baths. Riding, camping, hunting in season, cattle ranch life."[86] At $50 a week, his rates were among the highest. Perhaps the compensation was the "Million Dollar View," with eleven different mountain ranges in sight from the front porch of the main ranch house. For one visitor,

> That evening on the Bar O Ranch will be long remembered. Beginning with the cigars on the broad front porch, while we watched the sun drop below the Catalinas in a glorious mass of vari-hued clouds, and later with the dying embers in the great stone fireplace, listening to the tales of old Tombstone, the storming of the Cochise Stronghold, not many miles from the ranch, . . . it fittingly ended when we blew out the romantic little oil lamp from our comfortable cot and relinquished the bunk house to darkness with lots of fresh air as tonic for a long night's sleep.[87]

The Bar O Ranch continued in business at least as recently as 1936.[88]

East across Sulphur Springs Valley, the Chiricahua Mountains provided another setting for dude ranching. In West Turkey Creek Canyon lay El Coronado Ranch, built as a dude ranch or a resort hotel. It became an exclusive boys' school instead, opening in 1930; the University of Arizona currently operates it as an educational retreat.[89] About ten miles farther north, in lower Bonita Canyon, Mrs. Lillian Riggs ran the Faraway Ranch. Attractions there included a central lodge with a dining room, guest cottages, outdoor swimming pool, saddle horses, pack trips into Chiricahua National Monument, and hunting excursions in the higher mountains.[90] In 1945 a group from Buffalo, New York, bought eighty acres east of the Faraway and converted old Civilian Conservation Corps buildings there into the Silver Spur Guest Ranch. This facility closed around 1954 and was later torn down.[91]

On the eastern side of the Chiricahua Mountains, Mr. and Mrs. C. B. Conrad operated the Sierra Linda Ranch, at the mouth of Cave Creek Canyon. They advertised hunting and fishing in season and also lion hunts. Their business started some time before 1930 as a small resort with a lodge and two cabins.[92] East of Douglas, the old San Bernardino Ranch, developed by pioneer ranchman John Slaughter, became a ranch resort at one time. A description in 1930 characterized it as "[a] resort located at an old cattle ranch where fishing and hunting in Mexico is easily reached. Shade trees, lakes and artesian wells add to the features of the ranch itself."[93] More recently the Nature Conservancy purchased this property. The Johnson Historical Museum of the Southwest subsequently acquired it and now has the restored Slaughter Ranch open to visitors.[94]

Requiem for an Industry

Dude ranches in southern Arizona flourished after 1924, literally as a means of saving family ranches. Their success depended upon access to nearby National Forest lands, to provide the guests with trail rides, pack trips, hunting expeditions, and other outdoor recreation. The new industry thrived and expanded during its first decade and came through the Depression years handsomely. It provided a welcome means for the owners to cushion a drop in cattle prices after 1929 and ultimately to keep their ranches. After World War II the Tucson area saw a boom in new 'ranches' that were resorts in all but name. Today the old Tanque Verde, Flying V, Triangle T, Circle Z, and Rancho de la Osa guest ranches still continue the business, while several others have gone back to being cattle ranches. The majority, however, are only memories.

9
LUMBERING AND TIMBER RESOURCES

Soon after 1900 many of southeastern Arizona's desert islands became forest reserves and then national forests, primarily to safeguard their value as watersheds. Saw timber stands were not extensive, although the piñon-oak-juniper woodlands on the mountain flanks supplied timbers used in nearby corrals and mines, as well as a large fuelwood industry.[1] The forest lands have also provided grazing for approximately 35,000 head of livestock and extended many opportunities for recreation.

In the early territorial years, timber resources attracted scarcely more than a passing mention.[2] One railroad survey included only a very general account of forest trees.[3] In 1878, army officers who responded to a questionnaire about forest conditions in the West failed to record any lumbering around the posts in southeastern Arizona.[4] In 1891 the Phelps Dodge company invited Gifford Pinchot to visit southern Arizona to survey lands suitable for planting trees, on a trip that became mostly an adventure for this future head of the Forest Service.[5]

The beginning of large-scale timber cutting coincided with the mining boom of the late 1870s. Railroad building soon followed, and new towns sprang up along the rail lines; then in the 1880s came the range-cattle industry. All of these developments required sawn timber of one kind or another and cordwood as well. By the time the first forest reserves were declared, the accessible timber in southern Arizona had largely been cut out.[6]

The Early Years

William Kirkland, one of the first American settlers in southern Arizona, came to Tucson in January 1856.[7] In September, after hearing that the army might soon build a military post along the Santa Cruz or in Tucson, he established the first pinery in Arizona; *pinery* was the name then used for a lumber camp and sawmill. Kirkland's mill lay in a dense grove of ponderosa pines in Madera Canyon, on the northwestern side of the Santa Rita Mountains. He paid for the grading of a road into the canyon and then employed a half-dozen lumberjacks to fell trees.[8] One eyewitness described his pinery as follows:

> The Kirkland Pinery was located on the side of the Santa Rita Mountains about two thousand feet above the level of the plain at the foot of the mountain; the entrance to the Pinery was through a rocky cañon or pass, and in order to reach the pine timber with wagons and teams, it was necessary to build roads, construct bridges, &c., at a very heavy expense, in consequence of the broken and rocky surface over which they had to be built. . . .
>
> The lumber was manufactured in saw-pits, with whip-saws. The saw-pits were located near the foot of the mountain. A great many of the logs that were obtained beyond where the roads reached in the mountains, had to be slid down to the roads. Tackle and falls were sent into the Pinery for the purpose of aiding in getting the logs down to the roads and saw-pits, but I never saw them used. I have been in these Pineries after the roads were constructed, and have a personal knowledge of them.[9]

A sawpit was a rectangular excavation about six feet deep. A whipsaw was a long, tapered saw with a handle on either end, operated by two men, with somewhat finer teeth than a crosscut or felling saw. To produce boards, a log was maneuvered over the pit, squared, and then sliced lengthwise into boards of the desired thickness by one sawyer who pulled the saw from above and a second man pulling from below. Whipsawing was strictly a manual operation, and the resultant lumber cost $250 per thousand board feet.[10]

Kirkland supplied the lumber needed at Camp Moore, the short-lived army post near Calabasas. In the spring or summer of 1857, he began marketing to the new silver mines and to townsfolk in Tucson. Then in the late spring of 1860, Kirkland sold his pinery claims and sawmill site to William S. Grant, a newly arrived contractor who soon enjoyed the special favor of the War Department.[11]

Grant anticipated being awarded government contracts to furnish all commissary and quartermaster supplies to the army posts in southern New Mexico and Arizona. In September 1860 he did receive these contracts and set up offices in Tucson, where he carried on a variety of businesses and built a new gristmill. He also bought the Canoa Ranch, about ten miles north of Tubac, and fitted it up as the Canoa Hotel. He expanded and improved Kirkland's old pinery "at a very heavy expense" and put to work a number of lumbermen from Grant's home state of Maine. These men stayed at the Canoa Hotel.[12]

Grant had need for a pinery, if only to furnish materials for his flouring mill, corrals, and other buildings in Tucson. He also contracted to supply lumber for Forts Buchanan and Breckenridge and the army posts in southern New Mexico, charging only $132 per thousand board feet.[13] When the army requisitioned 150,000 board feet of pine lumber for the construction of Fort Breckenridge, a new post on the lower San Pedro, he put thirty men to work and delivered over 100,000 feet on this order.[14]

Grant either purchased or set up a second pinery on the eastern side of the Santa Ritas, possibly in what was later called Sawmill Canyon. He employed fifteen men there, sawing timbers for Fort Buchanan. On or about July 15, 1861, his pineries in the Santa Ritas were abandoned and most of Grant's other property in Arizona destroyed or abandoned, as the army made ready to pull out of the territory at the onset of the Civil War.[15]

There were other early lumbering operations, including Thomas Gardner's mill in Sawmill Canyon. Gardner had arrived in Arizona in 1859; later he and a fellow worker, J. Lander Young, purchased this sawmill. As of 1901 the site was reported as "all grown up with trees and brush."[16] Another pioneering family, the Penningtons, came to southern Arizona in 1857; sometime later they began cutting timber in Madera Canyon and hauling it to a sawmill at Tubac. In the 1860s Elias Pennington operated a sawpit in Tucson in a street called the Calle del Arroyo, since renamed Pennington Street.[17]

The Post–Civil War Years: Lumbering in the Santa Ritas

The California Volunteers made efforts to get out timber in the Santa Ritas in 1865.[18] Several years later Thomas Gardner apparently reentered the lumber business with a new partner, Edward Fish. They erected a sawmill in Gardner Canyon and hoped (in vain) for a contract to supply lumber for newly designated Camp Crittenden. Later they may have operated their sawmill in Fish Canyon. In 1873 they were delivering lumber in Tucson at $125 per thousand board feet. When mining camps opened at Greaterville and other places, the partners supplied them, until Gardner sold his lumber interests in 1878.[19]

These early ventures did little to satisfy the demand for lumber. In 1869 *The Weekly Arizonan* editorialized that "Almost all the timber thus far employed in building up the town of Tucson has been imported from New Mexico, and set down here, at what cost we know not, but sold to consumers at the rate of twenty cents per foot.[20]

A turning point came in the fall of 1869, when A. Lazard, popularly known as "Frenchy," had a steam sawmill transported to Arizona. Lazard and his partner, Thomas Yerkes, organized the Santa Rita Saw Mill Co. and evidently located their mill in Sawmill Canyon, on the eastern side of the Santa

Ritas. This pair started off with a contract to furnish lumber for the Army Quartermaster's Depot at Tucson, at 9.98¢ per board foot. As *The Weekly Arizonan* commented, "[t]his is the greatest fall from ruling prices which we have yet witnessed in any article supplied the government by contract here."[21] Lazard and Yerkes's steam sawmill began its operation in February 1870. In little more than a month, they flooded the local market with "a large stock of the very best grade of pine lumber," at ten cents a board foot.[22]

There are no known descriptions of Lazard's sawmill or of most other early sawmills in southern Arizona. One type developed before 1850 made use of a vertical, reciprocating saw plate; this was called a "muley sawmill." Whether any were ever used is not known. Circular sawmills had come into widespread use even earlier and had the advantage of requiring only a few men to produce from fifteen to twenty thousand board feet daily. They were also inexpensive; the Lane Manufacturing Company's #1 mill cost $450, and their #0 was priced at only $350 in 1876. In the years after the Civil War, portable, steam-powered circular sawmills were in great demand, and the mills in southern Arizona's canyons were probably of this type.[23]

Timber and Sawmills in the Santa Catalinas

Two Tucson entrepreneurs, James Lee and William Scott, already had a mine in the Tucson Mountains when they built a large flouring mill at Tucson. In 1873 they looked over the timber resources of the Santa Catalinas, then hired twenty men to open a wagon road and dig sawpits. In May they hauled their first timber to town; the *Tucson Citizen* described this as "the longest and straightest we have ever seen here." Lee built a saw- and planing mill next to his flour mill and began delivering lumber for the construction of Fort Lowell. Soon he expanded these operations by installing a steam-powered sawmill in the Santa Ritas. By late March of 1875, this mill was producing lumber for Tucsonians as well as for the army.[24]

Mines provided a big local market for timber products. The Santa Catalina Copper Company installed a sawmill in the Marble Peak area of the Catalina Mountains in 1882, in connection with their Apache Mine. This may have been the mill described later as below Sawmill Hill, on Oracle Ridge. The superintendent at the Apache Mine reported that he received five thousand board feet of lumber per day, but the company closed down after only six months of operation.[25]

Also in the Catalinas, at the head of Alder Canyon, lay Louis Ziegles's sawmill. By 1905 it had been abandoned "some years ago," and the remains consisted of ". . . all of the machinery generally used in a one-horse mill, about 200 feet of 3-inch pipe and several small frame buildings."[26] The new owners in 1905 proposed to move the old mill equipment, but it evidently remained in place until 1921 or later, near what became known as the Control Road.[27]

In 1916 a Forest Service ranger named Jim Westfall moved "a new saw mill" to the site of the future Summerhaven summer colony, high in the Catalinas near Mt. Lemmon.

> This is a saw mill of small capacity, Mr. Johnson [supervisor of Coronado National Forest] stated yesterday, and is being erected by Westfall entirely as a private proposition. It is for the purpose of cutting timber for the erection of bungalows and houses for residents on the Webber homestead, which has been taken over by the Summerhaven company, composed of Tucson capitalists. Timber from trees on the Webber homestead will be cut, starting September 1.[28]

The heaviest parts of the equipment had to be winched up the mountainside, over tracks laid on the slopes; the rest of the mill was packed up on burros.[29]

The Mt. Lemmon Lumber Company owned and operated this sawmill and by 1920 was contracting to build summer cabins using its own lumber. The mill had already become something of a focal point for the new mountaintop community:

> At ten minutes to 5 o'clock on July 26 the continued blowing of the sawmill whistle startled the inhabitants of Summerhaven and vicinity. Many people ran to the spot, fearing that a fire had broken out, but found that amid clouds of steam the whistle was blowing for the last time this summer. That act officially closed the sawmill of the Mt. Lemmon Lumber company for the season. Neat piles of lumber filling the lumber yard show for the season's work. Some of this lumber has already been sold, but as yet has not been removed from the yard.[30]

As recently as 1968, the Mt. Lemmon sawmill operated six to eight months out of the year, providing both finished lumber and firewood.[31]

Sawmills in the Huachuca Montains

Three other mountain ranges in southeastern Arizona (the Huachucas, Chiricahuas, and Pinaleños) had commercial lumbering operations. The garrison from Camp Wallen, a new post on the Babocomari River, maintained a wood camp in the Huachuca Mountains in 1866–67 but had no sawmill.[32] In the spring of 1879, Captain Samuel Whitside began construction of Fort

Huachuca and set up a portable sawmill at the mouth of Huachuca Canyon. Soldiers performed the work of cutting trees, snaking the logs down the mountainsides, and sawing them into boards.[33] The men who volunteered for such duty received 20¢ a day extra for their labors.[34]

One year following the silver rush at Tombstone, miners filed numerous copper and silver claims at the head of Ramsey Canyon, in the Huachucas. At Turnerville, near the entrance to Ramsey Canyon, the Mountain View Hotel catered to the miners. All of this activity created a big new demand for lumber in this part of Arizona, and the Huachuca Mountains soon had three civilian sawmills.

Wm. K. Gird and John McCloskey set up the first mill in December 1878, probably in Carr Canyon; their plant passed into the possession of James Carr in April 1880. The rig itself was a steam-powered circular sawmill with a 24-horsepower engine driving a 60-inch saw, capable of turning out 8,000 to 10,000 board feet of lumber per day. The work force consisted of six mill hands, with twenty-five other men engaged in felling and snaking timber and acting as teamsters. By early June of 1880, Carr's Huachuca Saw Mill had produced 1.75 million board feet of lumber for the Tombstone-area markets, specializing in mining timbers. The owner estimated that accessible timber reserves would furnish another 3.5 million board feet of lumber or more.[35]

Just over the mountain crest from Ramsey Canyon, probably at the head of present-day Sawmill Canyon or in upper Tanner Canyon, lay Francis Tanner's sawmill. Thirty men worked there as of June 1880, shipping from 5,000 to 7,000 feet of lumber daily to Harshaw, a booming miners' camp in the Patagonias. One mile above Turnerville, Turner and Campbell's sawmill commenced cutting lumber on May 10, 1880. The 90,000 board feet produced in the first month were all hauled to Tombstone. J. H. Turner employed fifty men and estimated the timber in Ramsey Canyon at 4 million board feet, 400,000 of which would be supplied to the mill at its initial site. The sawmill would then be relocated, two miles up the canyon. Meanwhile woodcutters in Ramsey Canyon were getting out cordwood for the Charleston mills.[36]

This frenetic timber cutting lasted for less than a decade, as the mining boom tapered off and the demand for lumber slowed. Timber resources in the Huachucas were becoming depleted, in any case. In December 1894 another sawmill began operation at Sunnyside, on the south side of the mountains, and continued there for about twenty-five years. Eventually this mill lost its principal market, at Washington Camp.[37] As of 1902 a Bureau of Forestry examiner found that all of the good timber had been cut out of the Huachucas years ago, although natural reforestation was well underway.[38]

Riggs's sawmill on the west side of Barfoot Park, Chiricahua Mountains. (Courtesy, U.S. Forest Service, Southwestern Region. A. F. Potter, photographer, April 26, 1902.)

Lumbering in the Chiricahuas

The report from Captain Tidball's reconnaissance through the Chiricahua Mountains in 1864 praised the timber resources of that range.[39] As of January 1865 Fort Bowie's post commander, under orders to construct a new post, set up a lumber camp about twenty miles distant, probably at Pine or Pinery Canyon in the Chiricahuas. A company of New Mexico Volunteers set to work there digging sawpits and then whipsawing logs into lumber, completing their work by March.[40] That summer a large detachment from the same company marched to the Ojo del Carriso, approximately twenty miles from Bowie, to spent the summer and fall there getting out more lumber.[41]

Sweeney's sawmill in Barfoot Park, Chiricahua Mountains: mill to the viewer's left; yard to the right; sawdust piled in the hollow this side of the mill. (Courtesy, U.S. Forest Service, Southwestern Region. J. S. Holmes, Photographer, June 4, 1906.)

Commercial lumbering in the Chiricahuas began in 1879, when Philip Morse ordered a 40-horsepower portable steam sawmill from San Francisco. This plant passed through Tucson in June; by mid-July it had been set up in a tributary of West Turkey Creek Canyon once known as Morse Canyon, but now called Turkey Pen Canyon. Morse's installation included a shingle mill for producing wooden shingles and a planing mill that turned out tongue-and-groove flooring. He gradually increased lumber production to 20,000 board feet per day.[42]

The new mining camps at Bisbee, Tombstone, and Dos Cabezas, all started in 1878, created a strong demand for mining timbers. Toward the end of 1880, miners invaded the Chiricahuas and established the California district, with the short-lived boom town of Galeyville. At that time Downing's sawmill began turning out timbers in Pinery Canyon for the mines on the eastern slopes.[43]

Although lumber from both mills found willing buyers, people already recognized that the pine forests were limited in extent.[44] How long these two operations continued at their original locations is not known, but changes in both location and ownership became quite frequent. After Downing had cut the timber out of Pinery Canyon, he moved his sawmill to Pine Canyon and occupied several locations there. A pioneering ranch family, the Riggses, bought Downing's mill and subsequently moved it twice, until it was situated in Barfoot Park. As of 1902 Brannick Riggs estimated that the forest in the vicinity would yield 4 million board feet of lumber. Two other owners subsequently operated the Riggs sawmill. Another rig in the Chiricahuas, the Ross sawmill, was active in 1887 and prior to 1906; by the latter date it had occupied three sites in Rock Creek Canyon.[45]

A Forestry Bureau examiner in 1902 estimated that 50,000 acres in the Chiricahua Mountains were capable of sustained forest growth, with an average stand of 5,000 board feet per acre.[46] As recently as 1941 proprietors of the Davies-Mason sawmill in this range bid successfully on 1.1 million board feet of timber in Pine and Rattlesnake canyons, in what was expected to be the last block of timber advertised for sale in the Chiricahuas. Later that year the Coronado National Forest newsletter commented that "[i]n the past few years a small sawmill operator [the Davies-Mason mill] on the Chiricahua division has cut 7,190,190 board feet of timber and 161,300 linear feet of smelter poles, all this material going to local markets."[47]

Lumbering Operations in the Pinaleño Mountains

In 1873 the army initiated timber cutting in the Pinaleño Mountains, when it began construction of the new Camp Grant, situated near the western base of this range. The earliest sawmill here was an army one, located at the post and used to cut all of the lumber for the construction of the buildings.[48]

Commercial lumbering started when Hyrum Weech, Ebenezer Bryce, and John Moody, of Pima, Arizona, purchased a second-hand sawmill in the Chiricahuas and transported it to the Pinaleños. Their plant, the so-called Mormon sawmill, consisted of a 50-horsepower steam engine and boiler, a circular saw, an edging saw, and a shingle mill. As of September 1882, the new owners had found a suitable location on the west fork of Nuttall Canyon, on the north slope of the Pinaleños, and had built a road to move the mill to their site. Weech soon became sole owner of the business, but he found the transportation of logs so difficult that after running the mill for a few years, he sold it to John H. Nuttall.[49] About this time a Frys sawmill was also operating, atop Mt. Graham.[50]

Later in that decade the Cluff family, pioneers in Ash Canyon, decided to put a sawmill at the head of Ash Creek. Their business, known as the Mt. Graham Lumber Co., was finally ready to saw timber by October of 1895. To solve the problem of getting the lumber out of the mountains, they built a nine-mile flume down Ash Canyon to the planing mill at the eastern base of the mountains. They then hauled the lumber to market, mostly to local buyers in the Gila Valley.[51]

By 1916 the flume had broken down, but the son of one of the new owners helped to rebuild it. He recalled many years later that "[i]n those days the principals of hydraulics were not as well known as they are today, for if they were, the flume would never have been built, . . ." The main problem was three steep hills, which gave the flume an uneven grade and caused the water to flow unevenly:

> The water flowed in surges or slugs about 6 to 12 inches deep, then tapering back to 1 to 2 inches deep, then to another slug. This made the transportation of lumber very difficult for the steep hills would cause the lumber to travel faster than the water, creating a large fan six feet high in front and leaving a practically dry flume behind. Lumber following would hit the dry flume and gain such speed that it would become airborne and leave the flume and even lodge in some of the trees.[52]

Their business literally soared. The partners, Martini, Freeman and Fisher, ceased operating this sawmill in the fall of 1920. Several years later another set of associates acquired the mill and built a tram with overhead cables, using equipment from abandoned mining trams in southern Arizona. This cable conveyor system began hauling lumber by the summer of 1925 but closed down within a year.[53]

Back in the spring of 1902, the Bureau of Forestry examined the Pinaleño Mountains and Mt. Graham; two months later President Theodore Roosevelt declared the range a forest reserve. The examiner's report noted that illegal sawmills had at one time operated in every accessible canyon. At Jacobson's sawmill, the General Land Office confiscated 100,000 board feet of lumber; ". . . the lumber is of average quality and contains many knots, as usual."[54] Nine years later four sawmills (the Sherwood, Chlarson, Lee, and the Cluffs' Mt. Graham Lumber Co.) were back in business, now regulated by the Forest Service and sawing timber purchased from the government. These mills all lay on the north slope. The Mt. Graham Lumber Co. had an average daily capacity of 25,000 board feet; the other mills each produced about one-fifth of that amount. Timber sales in the fiscal year ending June 30, 1911, had totaled 1,517,000 board feet, with the remaining timber resources estimated at 134 million board feet. Sometime around 1911–15, the Mt. Graham Lumber Co. reportedly purchased the rights to 50 million board feet at a single timber sale.[55] The best oak and juniper stands were in Jacobson Canyon and Stockton Pass, but in the latter nearly everything had been cut out for sale as firewood at Fort Grant.[56]

By 1924 several small sawmills still produced slightly more than 1 million board feet of lumber each year. Reserves of sawtimber then stood at an estimated 376 million board feet, much of this in rugged mountains. It was the difficulties of access that eventually brought an end to lumbering in the Pinaleños.[57]

Retrospect

The lumbering industry in southern Arizona was never a very large one and is almost nonexistent now. This lack of growth as compared with mining and ranching was a result of limited resources. In 1963 Coronado National Forest contained an estimated 85 million board feet of timber; earlier figures for some of the individual ranges and the amounts cut from them have been given above. Numbers such as 5,000 board feet per acre in the Chiricahuas and timber sales that totaled more than 1 million board feet are actually quite small in comparison with the Pacific Northwest, for instance, where the Forest Service once disallowed a series of homestead claims that contained from 2 million to 5 million board feet of merchantable timber on individual, 160-acre entries, within prime forest lands.[58]

Mining and related building construction created the first large market for lumber in Arizona, beginning in the late 1870s. Sawmills were started in several mountain ranges, but almost at the same time (1880), the railroad arrived, bringing large shipments of West Coast lumber of superior grade and at a lower price. Lumber from the Pacific states and the sawmills around Prescott, Arizona, then dominated the southern Arizona markets.[59]

Local sawmills could not produce the quality or quantities of wood products needed, but neither were they driven out of business. The Arizona mills survived and in some cases continued for many years, probably because they met the needs for rougher lumber at the mines, ranches, and small agricultural communities. By finding their own outlets, southern Arizona's sawmills continued to operate until they had either cut out the accessible timber resources, run into Forest Service restrictions, or met with production costs too high to continue.

Related to the lumber industry was fuelwood cutting, which expanded in response to the growth of mining. Cordwood to feed the boilers that powered the mines and reduction works, plus smaller timbers for mining props, corrals, and domestic purposes, were cut from extensive stands of mesquite, oak, juniper, and piñon. Tremendous quantities of fuelwood were removed, much of it in the late nineteenth century; by the mid-1880s the Dragoon, Mule, eastern slopes of the Huachucas, and southeastern slopes of the Whetstone mountains had been heavily cut over. One study estimated that between 729,000 and 909,000 cords of fuelwood were consumed for domestic purposes in Cochise County from 1890 to 1940, while Tombstone and Charleston in their bonanza years used between 396,000 and 486,000 cords. Although large trees are now scarce, regrowth in the oak-juniper woodlands has produced a volume of standing fuelwood probably greater than at any time during the past century.[60] As with lumbering, woodcutting left the landscape heavily altered, a situation that in time will largely be restored through natural regrowth.

10
HOMESTEADS ON FOREST LANDS

President Abraham Lincoln's approval of the original Homestead Act in 1862 provided settlers with a way to become landowners. If they met the conditions of the act by living on a claim and cultivating it for five years, they could receive a title (patent) to up to 160 acres of land in the public domain. In time Congress modified provisions of the original act, liberalizing the requirements and creating new types of land-entry systems. By the early twentieth century, a knowledgeable person could select from many alternative provisions in satisfying conditions for 'proving up' a homestead claim. Case files from the period c. 1909 through 1922, when homesteading was at its peak both in Arizona and throughout the Far West, show that successful claimants met the terms in many different ways, all quite legally.[1]

One new entry system was the Forest Homestead Act of June 11, 1906. This provided for the homesteading of certain lands within already declared forest reserves. Until these reserves were proclaimed, they had been part of the public domain and their lands subject to entry under the existing systems administered by the General Land Office. With the establishment of a forest reserve, any new filings under these laws became invalid.[2] The 1906 act (34 Stat. 233) applied specifically to National Forests.

This act was conventional in some respects, but it had other features that made it quite unique among public-land laws. It basically provided that settlers could make entry upon lands within forest reserves chiefly valuable for agricultural purposes, in tracts not exceeding 160 acres and not more than one mile in length. They had five years to qualify for a patent. Requirements included residence upon the land and its cultivation, together with an accurate survey of the boundaries.

The unique features of the act were that it did not provide for commutation, that is, for purchase of the land by the claimant, and it authorized metes-and-bounds surveys. The claim could therefore be quite irregular in shape, so long as it was less than a mile in length. The erratic boundaries of many forest homesteads conformed with sections of valleys. Lands could also be entered before a public lands survey had been done. The five-year proving-up period continued in effect after the qualifying time for other types of homesteads was cut to three years in 1912. Finally the U.S. Forest Service had responsibility for listing the lands available for entry as well as for ac-

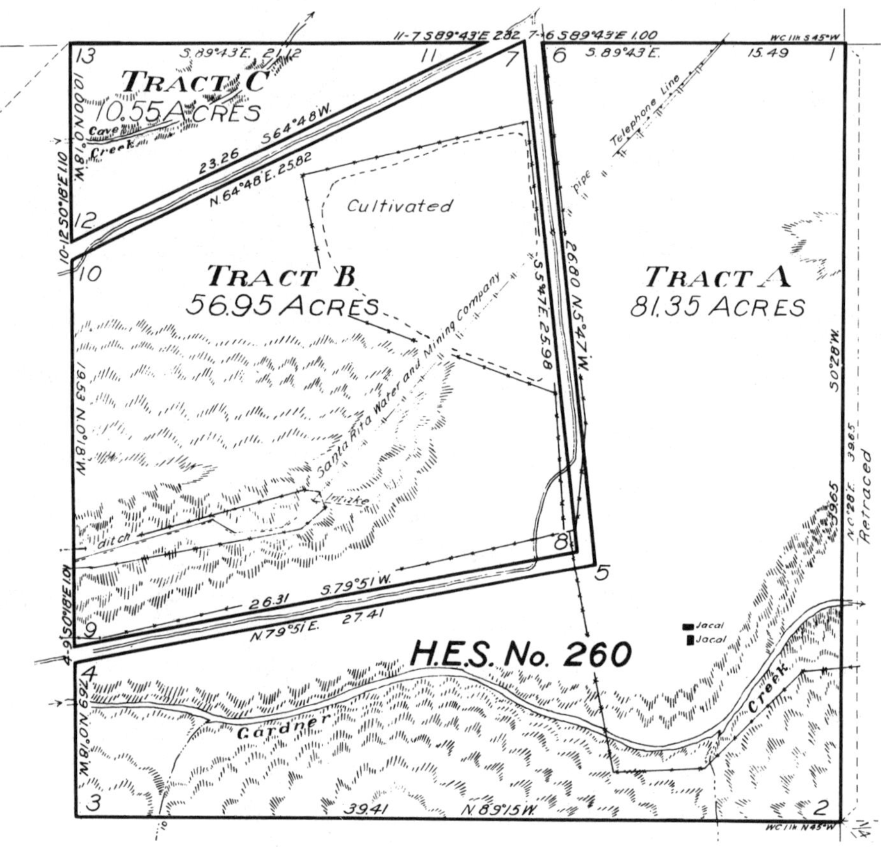

J. Sande Young's forest homestead on the eastern side of the Santa Rita Mountains. (Courtesy, U.S. Forest Service, Coronado National Forest.)

cepting or rejecting applications. The Forest Service also carried out inspections, although authority for approval remained with the General Land Office.

The Forest Service welcomed the 1906 act and issued regulations for implementing it.[3] The claims themselves were usually called "June 11 homesteads." The agency's policy was to encourage settlement of those areas within the forests that would be better suited for agriculture, putting these lands to their highest economic use. The settlers would be available to assist with locating and fighting forest fires as well and to work on forest-improvement projects.[4]

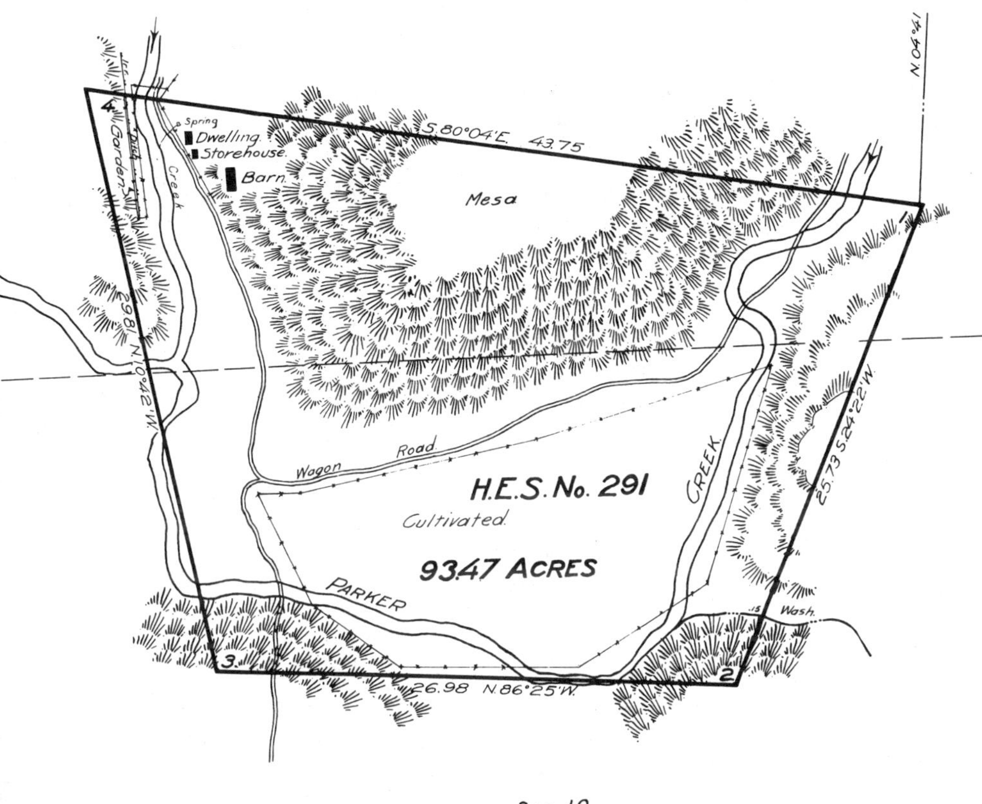

R. Lee Parker's forest homestead at Parker Canyon in the Canelo Hills. (Courtesy, U.S. Forest Service, Coronado National Forest.)

The requirement for the Forest Service to list the lands opened to entry with the Secretary of the Interior was handled in two ways. For several years following passage of the act, the Forest Service responded only to specific applications. This became awkward since it meant two separate land surveys; one by the Forest Service as part of the listing process, and one by the General Land Office when the patent was applied for. By the latter part of 1911, this had been reduced to a single survey. Settlers at the same time were relieved from having to pay for the survey. The next year Congress funded a land-classification study of all lands within National Forests. This speeded up the listing process, but by 1919 reclassification had seen more than 12 million acres eliminated from the forests. The excluded areas contained most of the potential agricultural lands. A total of about 1.8 million acres did go to patent under the Forest Homestead Act.[5]

At the time this act became law, the Forest Service clearly had a concern about potential abuse, that is, of fraudulent claims. Such problems had already developed under existing land-entry systems.[6] In one annual report, the forester gave a fascinating litany of the types of frauds worked upon the Forest Service.[7] By 1906 the agency was alerted to most of these and, since the schemes generally involved attempts to claim timberlands, the 1906 act was worded so that fraud with respect to timberlands was virtually excluded. In Coronado National Forest, all of the land entries appear to have been in good faith.

Homesteading under the 1906 act enjoyed only a few years of popularity. Claims declined rapidly after 1915, and by 1924 they amounted to almost nothing, although the law remained on the books until 1962 (76 Stat. 1157). The official explanation was that arable areas had been excluded from the forests and no additional lands were available for agricultural settlements. Yet when the percentages of lands patented vs. lands listed are compared, it seems clear that some eligible tracts were not taken up.[8]

In the Southwest it was the decline in dry farming, a type of cultivation inexorably linked with homesteading, and the drop in cattle prices in 1921 that account for much of this loss of interest. A lessening enthusiasm by the Forest Service for forest homesteads shows up as well in the annual reports of the forester, after the potential management problems posed by multiple small inholdings and by metes-and-bounds surveys began to sink in. Technically, the homesteader still had a lengthy five-year period of proving up to go through, although in practice this was sometimes cut to three years. By 1924 the 1906 act had become an anachronism when viewed against its original purpose.

Forest Service records for Coronado National Forest allow us a detailed look at forest homesteads. Coronado National Forest, established in 1908, included individual reserves proclaimed up to six years earlier. It grew by incorporating Garces and Chiricahua National Forests in 1911 and 1917, respectively, and later by the addition of the Mt. Graham, Santa Teresa, Galiuro, and Winchester units of the former Crook National Forest. As of 1914 there were 294 tracts opened for entry on Coronado and Chiricahua National Forests lands, with 23,926.64 acres of potential agricultural land. Eighty-eight parcels with almost 45 percent of the lands offered eventually went to patent, and in 1924 it was announced that no additional lands were available for settlement in Coronado National Forest. Claims work accordingly dropped to almost nothing.[9] Altogether within New Mexico and Arizona, slightly more than 152,000 acres were patented under the Forest Homestead Act, of the 354,155 acres listed and entered.[10]

A Homestead Entry Survey Plat Book in the Coronado National Forest Supervisor's office lists ninety-one forest homesteads, with a total of 10,653.38 acres. The approval dates for the surveys fell between 1910 and 1924. Three claims, for 319.95 acres, lay in the Pinaleño Mountains, at that time part of Crook National Forest. Approximately 16 percent of all forest homesteads within the Southwestern Region, containing about 7 percent of the patented acreage, lay in Coronado National Forest.

The plat book shows the following gross distribution for patented claims:[11]

Santa Catalina Mountains	(1 claim)	16.48	acres
Dragoon Mountains	(1 claim)	159.87	
Walker Cànyon and Tres Bellotes (= west of the Santa Cruz River)	(2 claims)	295.09	
Pinaleño Mountains	(3 claims)	319.95	
Santa Rita Mountains	(6 claims)	791.15	
Patagonia Mountains	(10 claims)	995.36	
Chiricahua Mountains	(27 claims)	3188.45	
Huachuca Mountains and Canelo Hills	(41 claims)	4887.03	
		10,653.38	

One of these claims, that of Wm. F. Ratliff on the southeastern slope ofthe Huachuca range, has recently been reported as an archaeological site. Ratliff made his original entry on July 13, 1912; the survey of his tract was approved on August 8, 1917.[12]

For the old Chiricahua National Forest (which included the Dragoon, Chiricahua and Peloncillo mountain ranges), the forest supervisor in 1913 compiled a comprehensive "Record of Settlement, Improvement and Cultivation of Forest Homesteads." Out of forty-three claims then active, only twenty-one showed evidence of cultivation. Many of the others had not yet been settled, while on some of them crop raising had not been attempted or was unsuccessful. On the twenty-one homesteads then being farmed, the amount of land under the plow ranged from 0.25 to a maximum of 42 acres per homestead, with a grand total of 239.75 acres cultivated in 1913 and an average of 11.4 acres per active farm.

The crops raised on these farms consisted almost entirely of "garden truck," various fodder crops (cane, sorghum, kafir corn), milo, and corn. The produce from J. H. Barton's 42-acre farm was valued at $1400; Gabe Choate cultivated 21 acres, but most of his $1445 in crop returns derived from a fruit orchard. Only three of the remaining sixteen claims where crops were actively being raised had produce valued at $200 or more. Out of forty-three forest homesteads in and around the Chiricahua Mountains in 1913, two or three of these could have been called serious farms.[13] It appears that twenty of these claims went to patent. There is no reason to think that these statistics were untypical. The more interesting question raised by these figures is, if so few of the forest homestead claimants on Coronado National Forest lands were serious farmers, and evidence of fraud is absent, what was it that these people were trying to accomplish?

The answer is that they were trying to become small ranchers, something that others in the Southwest were trying to achieve as well.[14] As early as 1913, the Forest Service recognized that economic interests under the Forest Homestead Act lay with livestock raising rather than in farming, and the agency did not object to claimants combining the two activities.[15] The land-classification studies done for Coronado National Forest in 1915 and 1924 were quite explicit as to what was happening. On the Santa Catalina unit, there were five unpatented forest homesteads as of 1915: "Three are used primarily for stock headquarters and only small amounts of garden truck are raised, on one some sorghum and fodder is raised and the fifth has just recently been occupied and improving has just begun."[16]

Three out of five patented homesteads in the Catalinas were used solely for stock headquarters. On the Whetstone, Santa Rita, Huachuca, and Tumacacori divisions, the same forest examiner found that most of the tracts taken up before the National Forest was created were used for grazing or stock headquarters, while the majority of the June 11 claims were being farmed to some degree.[17]

By 1924 this trend had developed fully. The Huachuca Division had the best agricultural lands and forty-one of the ninety-one patented forest homesteads, which were distributed principally in the northern Canelo Hills and on the slopes south of Sunnyside, extending to the Mexican border. The grazing examiners found that

> A large number of Forest homestead listings on the Lyle, Vaughn, Parker Canyon, Red Rock and Harshaw ranges have resulted in a goodly number of dry farmers, most of whom raise a limited number of cattle in connection with other agricultural operations. In fact, the crops raised on these farm units in an average year will not support the settler without some supplemental means of livelihood, either by grazing livestock or outside employment.[18]

This "supplemental means of livelihood" was implemented in the following way:

> With the coming of semi-agricultural settlements and the small dry farmer, the largest holdings [grazing permits] have been reduced and many smaller preferences, varying from a few head to several hundred, have been built up. Intensity of range demand is keen for the majority of the grazing allotments, both by increases from present permittees and from new applicants. . .
>
> The Huachuca Division has the largest number of agricultural claims of any division of the Forest, a large majority of the claimants being grazing permittees, and the protective limit is therefore 130 head which number, while in excess of the average permit, is considered to be the least number with which a fair living can be made. There are enough farm units on the particular allotments just mentioned to seriously disrupt the stock industry should they all be used as base for future grazing preferences. Under existing regulations, should the farm owners qualify and apply for permits it would result in the reduction of all Class B preferences to the protective limit, which latter would probably have to be reduced to a number considerably less than the present 130.[19]

Implicit here was the grazing examiner's understanding that these farms, so-called, were less important for raising crops than as a basis of claiming grazing permits. On the Chiricahua Division this process had been taken even further:

> Forest homesteads have already practically all passed into the hands of the larger outfits on whose range they exist, or are now being used as base for grazing permits. . . . Regulations requiring the recognition of Class A applicants have placed several Class B permittees on this unit to more or less expense. This situation probably exists to a certain extent over practically all divisions of this Forest but was not called to the Examiner's attention until the field work on this particular work was in progress. J. N. Hunsaker on the Big Bend Range paid $3500.00 for two Forest listings after they had passed to patent in order to protect his permit from reduction for applications using these lands as base. Charles L. Rak on the Rucker Community Allotment purchased the Doane holdings for the same purpose, price unknown. C. C. Kimble purchased the unperfected homestead of Robert Caldwell who had qualified as a new Class A applicant and was holding a small permit with the homestead entry as base. The lands themselves are of but little or no value to the purchasers except through the elimination of a probable reduction in their permits in consequence of their ownership.[20]

The value of forest homesteads actually derived from their being the basis for patentees to claim Forest Service grazing permits. A homesteader who owned property adjacent to the forest would receive a Class A permit, while Class B permits went to individuals who owned nonadjacent ranch property and traditionally used public-forest ranges.[21] The large cattle outfits, holding Class B permits, protected their ranges by buying out forest homesteads at good prices, thereby eliminating the base for new permits.

This process of homesteads becoming ranches rather than farms in part reflects Forest Service grazing regulations of the time. A legitimate homesteader could claim and receive grazing privileges on forest lands (that is, a Class A permit), even where ranges were fully stocked. In such cases the numbers of animals permitted for existing stock owners were decreased, with the largest owners being reduced the most.[22]

Intentionally or otherwise, the homesteaders with grazing permits were in a position to squeeze the surviving large cattle operations during a period when livestock prices were disastrous. Homestead claims had considerable value, because they could be used to command grazing permits. As just seen in the Chiricahuas, this value could be very high. The alternative for the larger rancher was to risk a homestead becoming the source of a new ranch, rather than a farm.

The use of forest homesteads in the Coronado National Forest as a means of gaining grazing rights was not unique. A similar development occurred in an area of public domain in eastern New Mexico, where the claimants had little hope for succeeding by dry farming. Instead they ran small-scale feeding operations, until such time as their patents were issued. Then they sold out and moved elsewhere.[23] Most of the southern Arizona homesteaders evidently did likewise.

Congress did pass a Stock-Raising Homestead Act and in so doing recognized that certain lands were valuable chiefly for grazing, but this 1916 act did not apply to forest lands. In 1921 Congress also extended the provisions of the 1909 Enlarged Homestead Act to the National Forests.[24] The highest economic use of agricultural lands within the forests turned out to be ranching, not farming, and it is doubtful whether any homesteaders attempted to continue farming once they received their patent.

In perspective the act of June 11, 1906, was promoted in the early years after its passage but less so as time went on. The idea was well-intentioned but had not been thought through. Small farmers in remote areas, even where rainfall was adequate for crops, were left with no way to market their produce. In semiarid southern Arizona, such farm units were not economically viable without supplemental income; they became valuable instead for claiming grazing permits on national forest lands. Within the first decade after passage of the 1906 act, there came a realization that these multiple small inholdings complicated long-term management for the Forest Service. In time some of the homesteaded areas would be put to yet another productive use, as the settings for recreational developments.

SOMEBODY CERTAINLY OUGHT TO PROTECT THOSE CITIZENS DOWN IN DOUGLAS, ARIZONA.

BOUNDARY LINE

McCutcheon

—Courtesy Chicago Tribune

Douglas, Arizona, during the battle in Agua Prieta, Sonora, April 17, 1911. (From the Arizona Daily Star, May 6, 1911.)

11
THE U.S. ARMY AND THE MEXICAN REVOLUTION, 1910–1933

The Mexican General Porfirio Díaz seized the presidency of his country in 1876 and ruled as a sometimes beneficent dictator for the next third of a century. During this time Mexico's mines and ranches poured forth a stream of profits to foreign investors and to a very small number of wealthy Mexicans. By contrast most of the citizenry became landless peasants and sank ever deeper into poverty. The Díaz regime suppressed opposition while keeping the country generally peaceful. Mexico and the United States enjoyed excellent relations.

In the summer of 1910, Díaz maneuvered his reelection to another six-year term. An opposition candidate, Francisco Madero, had been clapped into jail during the campaign, but he managed to escape on October 5, the day following Díaz's inauguration. Madero became the voice of opposition to the old dictator and, once safely inside the United States, he called upon all Mexicans to rise against Díaz. By mid-November guerrilla bands had started to form; these *insurrectos,* as they were generally called, then began skirmishing with Mexican federal troops.[1]

The U.S. Army quickly took precautions. Soldiers moved to the border in Texas on November 3. Three days later fifty men from Company B, 18th U.S. Infantry, arrived at Naco, Arizona, and about the same number moved into Douglas. They immediately began patrolling the border, to enforce America's neutrality laws and to stop the smuggling of arms and ammunition into Mexico. Another detachment from the same company garrisoned Nogales, Arizona, beginning on November 26.[2]

Early in 1911 the number of infantry at Douglas doubled, to one hundred men, which allowed a systematic patrolling of the border to begin. Twenty miles to the east, a detachment established an outpost near John Slaughter's San Bernardino Ranch buildings.[3] Troop B of the 1st U.S. Cavalry arrived at Nogales the first week in February; detachments from it were sent to the Santa Cruz River crossing and twenty-five miles east to Duquesne, Arizona. An officer and ten men patrolled to the west for about twenty-five miles.[4] On March 12, Troop M, 3d U.S. Cavalry, found itself on patrol from five miles west to fifteen miles east of Douglas, "opposite a place where the Mexican soldiers and the Insurgents were having an engagement."[5]

The Mexican revolution spread rapidly within the country, the major opening actions being fought in the north. The numerous rebel factions all recognized the international boundary as a focal point, for it was from the north that they sought contraband arms and ammunition as well as recruits, and they hoped to take refuge there if things went badly. By controlling the Mexican customs houses, they gained a source of money to pay for needed supplies. Agua Prieta, just across the line from Douglas, was the setting for a major battle on April 17, 1911, when a Mexican federal army sought to wrest control of the town from insurrectos led, when he was sober, by the colorful Arturo "Red" Lopez. Agua Prieta changed hands four times that spring.

The *federales* abandoned both Agua Prieta and Naco, Sonora, after the fall of Ciudad Juárez, Chihuahua, on May 9, 1911. Two Chihuahuan rebel leaders, Pascual Orozco and Pancho Villa, had taken that city by storm and handed Díaz his first major setback. With this insurgent success, President Díaz recognized that there could be no peace so long as he held office. He resigned his office on May 25, 1911, and paved the way for Francisco Madero to assume the presidency.[6]

Madero proved to be weak and unstable. In February 1913 Victoriano Huerta, one of a number of ambitious generals, assumed the presidency himself, after arranging the murders of Madero and his vice-president. Opposition formed swiftly and for a time centered in Sonora, where General Alvaro Obregón and Governor José Maytorena led Sonoran state forces in warring against *huertista* garrisons. By July of 1914 Obregón's army, with that of Pancho Villa in Chihuahua, had chased Huerta out of Mexico. Obregón took control of Mexico City and installed Venustiano Carranza, a governor of the state of Coahuila, as the new "first chief" of Mexico. Carranza held power from August 1914 until May of 1920, when he was forced to flee, only to be assassinated.

Americans saw this whole period in Mexico's history as a kaleidoscope of rebel armies and irregular bands contending with one another as well as fighting whatever federal authority existed at the moment. Respect for life and property disappeared, and insurrectos became indistinguishable from bandits in a continuing struggle for power. Major battles in the Mexican border towns brought Americans crowding to the boundary line as eager spectators. Stray bullets killed and wounded a number of U.S. citizens, both civilians and soldiers.

By the spring of 1913, Mexican federal troops controlled the border communities of Agua Prieta, Naco, and Nogales, as well as the interior towns in Sonora, while at least four varieties of rebels dominated the countryside. One group of revolutionists, led by General Obregón, besieged Nogales,

Sonora, on March 12, while the 5th U.S. Cavalry kept watch from Nogales, Arizona. The federales defending Nogales were led by a former Díaz stalwart, Colonel Emilio Kosterlitzky. His forces survived a series of assaults, the first one launched at 1:30 A.M. the following morning. By late afternoon Kosterlitzky's men evacuated Nogales, retreating into the United States and surrendering to the U.S. Army.

Little more than a week later, the victorious Obregón laid siege to Naco, Sonora, while six troops of the 9th U.S. Cavalry looked on from the Arizona side. The contest for Naco really came to life on April 8, when the rebels sent a railroad car loaded with dynamite hurtling down the tracks towards the town! There was a tremendous explosion, but the car blew up short of the settled area and caused little damage. Obregón launched a series of attacks, until most of the remaining federal soldiers crossed into the United States and surrendered on April 13.[7] The federales had been virtually expelled from Sonora; for a few months fighting swung away from the border area.

With the ascension of Venustiano Carranza as "first chief" in Mexico City, new fighting broke out in the north. The battered town of Naco, now held by government supporters *(carranzistas)*, withstood a three-month siege in the last months of 1914. Stray bullets wounded eight cavalrymen in the 9th and 10th U.S. Cavalry. The soldiers had great difficulty in holding back crowds of sightseers who flocked to Naco, Arizona, to watch the battles in Mexico from the U.S. side.[8]

Pancho Villa's fortunes peaked in 1914 and then declined rapidly during 1915, as Carranza's forces drove him northward. Villa needed a victory as well as supplies to restore his lost stature. He sought both by striking at Agua Prieta. The United States anticipated this move and shifted one field artillery regiment, three infantry regiments, and units of mounted troops (more than sixty-five hundred men in all) to Douglas, where they entrenched near the border. Villa meanwhile approached Agua Prieta with an army estimated to number between eight to ten thousand men. General Plutarco Elías Calles led the carranzista defenders.

The first afternoon, November 1, 1915, the opposing sides skirmished and traded artillery fire. After dark everything grew quiet. Then at 1:30 A.M. Villa launched one of his night assaults, throwing waves of infantry and cavalry against the entrenched defenders. The *villistas* were met by machine-gun fire from guns positioned to give interlocking fields of fire, supported by barbed-wire entanglements, artillery fire, and strategically placed mines that Calles's men detonated electrically. The attackers also ran into a tactical first in Mexican history: three powerful carbon-arc searchlights that revealed the assaulting troops and blinded them as well, until these lights were finally shot out. Villa sent his soldiers against General Calles' defenders three times and was beaten back each time. By 6:30 A.M. the Battle of Agua Prieta was over; Pancho Villa had lost an estimated four hundred killed and five hundred wounded, while many more deserted his ranks.

Stray bullets fell on the Arizona side during much of the battle, wounding five civilians and four soldiers. Two people were killed, including Private Harry J. Jones of Company C, 11th U.S. Infantry. The name for the army garrison at Douglas was changed from Camp Douglas to Camp Harry J. Jones a short time later.[9]

The villistas moved on and attacked Hermosillo, Sonora, where they received another mauling. Then in late November the remnants of this army, now reduced to scattered groups of bandits, occupied Nogales, Sonora. On November 26 their taunts and insults of U.S. troops across the border turned to sniping. The American soldiers responded vigorously, and some forty villista snipers died in this exchange, but a bullet also mortally wounded Private Stephen D. Little of Company L, 12th U.S. Infantry. Within a month the army formally renamed the post at Nogales, Arizona, Camp Stephen D. Little.[10]

In other incidents that same year, Carranza troops and Mexican raiders fired across the border or made brief forays into Arizona. During one short action near Lochiel, Arizona, some Mexican soldiers attempted to run off cattle and fired on an American patrol. The Americans from Troop K, 10th Cavalry, shot back and a long-range fire fight developed; it ended with no casualties.[11]

Brigadier General Frederick Funston commanded the U.S. Army's Southern Department, which included Arizona. He had arrived at Douglas, Arizona, on the morning of November 2, 1915, before the Battle of Agua Prieta ended. Funston saw the Mexican revolution at first hand here and witnessed a scaled-down version of a state-of-the-art World War I battle right across the U.S. border in Agua Prieta. This must have made a deep impression, since his own troops would have been well equipped for the Indian fighting of thirty years earlier, but not for a modern war. Funston reinforced the garrisons at Naco and Nogales and immediately began erecting substantial buildings at Douglas. A brigade amusement pavilion opened on the north side of the "10th Street road" on December 15, 1915, opposite Camp Harry J. Jones. An enlisted men's club went up at the same time, directly in the center of the camp. The army was going to stay in Douglas for a long time, in fact until 1933.[12]

Over the years the United States stationed troops at a number of border locations. Camp Douglas lay one mile east of the city post office at Douglas. Post returns mentioned patrolling the boundary as far east as Slaughter's ranch.[13] In 1914 troops from the 10th U.S. Cavalry, headquartered at Fort Huachuca, Arizona, rotated between Naco, Nogales, and two places in between called Forrest and Osborne. The next year they alternated in tours of Naco, Nogales, and Lochiel. A few years later the regimental historian recalled that "[t]he border stations were not at all attractive. The poor little shacks and 'dobes were eagerly sought for by officers and their wives. Naco was about as it is now, only more so. The usual border patrols were made along the line, enforcing neutrality, and keeping down gunrunning. Every troop, during 1914, had a tour at Naco . . ."[14]

Four troops of this regiment had ringside seats at Douglas during the Battle of Agua Prieta. Detachments also manned substations at Harrison's Ranch, in the Patagonias, and much farther west at Arivaca, Sasabe, La Osa, and San Fernando. During 1916 most of the regiment marched into Mexico with General Pershing's punitive expedition, and on their return in 1917 relieved reserve or National Guard units patrolling the border. One troop generally took station at Naco, one each at Lochiel and Arivaca, and two troops at Nogales. The Battle of Ambos Nogales on August 27, 1918, drew in three troops from the 10th Cavalry, along with almost six hundred officers and men of the 35th U.S. Infantry on the American side.[15]

A U.S. Army map compiled some years later sought to show the positions of many outposts in the Arizona District, Mexican border patrol, during the World War I period. In 1917–19 a total of thirty-four patrol stations, plus the main post at Fort Huachuca, were active, with headquarters at Camp Harry J. Jones, in Douglas. Small garrisons were scattered from Yuma to Roosevelt Dam to Hudspeth's Ranch. East of Nogales lay Lochiel and Naco, while to the west there were no stations directly on the border. The postings between Naco and Douglas were, in order, Osborne, Crooks Tunnel, Christianson Ranch, Forrest Station, and Cooks Ranch. The two stations east of Douglas to the New Mexico line were San Bernardino Ranch and Hudspeth's Ranch. North and west from Nogales, troops had been placed at Calabasas, Crittenden, Arivaca, and Arivaca Junction. Fairbanks, Benson, and Bowie also had detachments, probably because they were railroad junctions.[16]

The border conflicts reached a critical point with Pancho Villa's raid on Columbus, New Mexico, the night of March 8–9, 1916. Within a week Brigadier General John Pershing, ordered in pursuit of Villa, had crossed into Mexico at the head of a large expeditionary force. By May the entire U.S. Regular Army stationed in the United States, except for one cavalry regiment and some Coast Artillery, was either distributed along the border or accompanying Pershing's expedition. On May 9, following threats by Mexican leaders to attack Pershing and possibly even invade Texas, President Wilson ordered out the militias of Texas, New Mexico, and Arizona. In Arizona the nine hundred-odd men, constituting a single infantry regiment, were sent to Douglas.[17]

By mid-June Mexican resentment against the United States and the punitive expedition had mounted to a level where open war was threatened between the two countries. The only military reserves available in the United States were the Organized Militia and the National Guard of the several states. Upon taking a federal oath, officers and men in the militia changed their status to that of the National Guard. On June 18, the president sent telegrams to the governors of all the states, ordering specific units to assemble at state mobilization camps in preparation for federal service. By the end of June 36,000 men, few of whom possessed military experience, were already en route to the border. As of July 31 almost 111,000 of these untrained troops had been transported thence, while another 40,000 waited in their state mobilization camps.

Despite the complaints raised at the time and the U.S. Army's near-lack of experience with large-scale troop movements, this operation went rather smoothly. In Arizona, Douglas and Nogales were made the major assembly areas. At Douglas the troop ranks swelled by 5,000 men in July, with the arrival of the New Jersey National Guard and an infantry regiment of the Montana National Guard. Nogales received a total of six infantry regiments, four squadrons of cavalry, three field artillery batteries, and additional service companies, almost 9500 men in all, from California, Connecticut, Idaho, and Utah. As tensions lessened with Mexico, the guardsmen assumed the duties of patrolling the border. They continued to do so until the punitive expedition returned to United States soil, as of February 5, 1917. Mid-March saw the National Guard units all on their way home to be mustered out.[18]

It has been stated that no National Guard troops crossed into Mexico or had a fight with raiders.[19] Actually there was an incident on January 26–27, 1917 at Casa Piedra or Stonehouse, in Warsaw Gulch about five miles south of Ruby, Arizona. Carranza troops had apparently been stationed at the Stonehouse, which lay about 1000 yards north of the border. As of late January, they occupied some adobe houses right on the international boundary, with outposts on two hillocks to the east and west. On the morning of January 26, a number of cowboys from the Arivaca Land and Cattle Company, accompanied by four Utah cavalrymen, discovered Mexicans driving cattle south across the border. The Mexicans opened fire and the Americans replied, whereupon firing continued by both sides. Early that afternoon Lieutenant Stark with six men from Ruby joined in the fight. When he ran low on ammunition and sent for help, First Lieutenant Carl Arns responded with nineteen men of Troop E, Utah cavalry. They rode out of Arivaca and reached the border just before midnight.

The Utah cavalrymen had been posted at the Stonehouse. During the

Bear Valley allotment, Atascosa Ridge and oak savannah, c. 1958–66. (Courtesy, U.S. Forest Service, Coronado National Forest.)

night Arns shifted to some rocks about halfway between there and the border fence, then moved closer to the line, until he occupied an adobe about twenty feet from the boundary. By 7:30 the next morning, twenty or twenty-five Mexicans positioned south of the border opened fire on the Americans in the adobe. Late in the morning Lieutenant Arns led fourteen troopers west of the Mexican position and crossed the border to take the carranzistas in the rear. He was spotted, however, and the Mexicans pulled back. Arns followed for a mile and a half into Mexico, but the fighting was over, with no casualties reported on either side. The Utah men wrecked and burned the buildings the Mexicans had been using.

This affair, the so-called "Battle of Ruby," made headlines in the Tucson newspapers for two days, then dropped from sight. The army's own reports agreed with newspaper accounts that shooting took place across the border and that the Mexicans were Carranza soldiers, some not in uniform. When things quieted again, Troops E and F of the Utah cavalry divided into detachments and took stations at Arivaca, Ruby, Stonehouse, and also Tres Bellotas, eight miles farther to the west. This was almost at the end of the National

Guard period, and a troop of the 10th U.S. Cavalry soon replaced the Utah cavalrymen.[20]

Almost a year later another incident just a few miles to the east harked back to the Indian wars. On January 9, 1918, Troop E of the 10th Cavalry was on outpost duty in Atascosa Canyon, in an area called Bear Valley. A sentinel on a high ridge to the east spotted a column of Indians moving along a lower ridge one-quarter mile or more west of the cavalry camp. The troopers mounted and rode to the crest of the low ridge, then pushed forward on foot through the brush. The Indians, who were Yaquis from Mexico, opened fire from behind boulders and gradually fell back, dodging from rock to rock while the cavalrymen advanced.

Soon the Indians signaled that they had surrendered. The troopers came up, surrounded them, and found ten Yaquis, who had fought a rear-guard action to give another twenty or so of their people time to escape. One Indian, shot in the stomach, died the next morning. Some of the Yaquis said later that they fired on the patrol because they mistook the black men of the 10th Cavalry for Mexican soldiers.[21]

There were other brief actions. In August 1918 the Battle of Ambos Nogales started when a Mexican customs guard shot and killed a U.S. infantrymen. By the time firing stopped later that same day, the 35th U.S. Infantry and the 10th Cavalry had occupied part of Nogales, Sonora. On the American side, 5 soldiers and several civilians were killed, with 31 wounded. Intelligence reports placed Mexican losses at 129 killed and 300 wounded. Claims that two Germans had been shot while directing the Mexican troops were later discounted, although German agents did have grandiose plans for fomenting violence along the U.S.-Mexico boundary.[22]

Years of internal strife left Mexico exhausted, so that periodic rebellions grew weaker and broke out at less frequent intervals. No longer was the border threatened. During the summer of 1923, the 10th Cavalry dismantled its old camp at Lochiel. Earlier that year they had salvaged the frame buildings at Camp Harry J. Jones, while in the fall Troop B closed out the camp at Naco. The troopers came back to Naco in April 1929, during the Escobar rebellion, but after the attack on Naco (when both Sonoran and Mexican federal troops used airplanes for bombing), the era of military *caudillos* became a thing of the past. The last border posts, Camp Stephen D. Little at Nogales and Camp Harry J. Jones at Douglas, were both abandoned in 1933.[23]

12
SUMMER COLONIES IN THE MOUNTAINS

In the early territorial years, people looked to the mountains for mineral wealth and timber resources but seldom thought of them as a setting for relaxation or recreation. Yet by 1868 the army had a camp somewhere near present-day Oracle, Arizona, where malaria victims could recuperate. Names such as Soldier Camp and Hospital Flat, in the Santa Catalina and Pinaleño ranges, imply a convalescent role. May Stacey, the wife of an officer stationed at Camp Thomas, turned a timber-cutting detail to the Pinaleños into a camping trip, relieving the monotony of post life.[1]

The Beginnings of a Tradition

By the early 1900s, many well-to-do Tucson residents sought relief from Arizona's summer heat by heading for the Pacific Coast. Other members of the social set chose the summer for extended visits to working ranches owned by friends, relatives, and business associates. Oracle, at the foot of the Santa Catalinas, made the transition from mining camp to resort town when the Mountain View Hotel there began playing host to Tucsonians seeking cooler temperatures.[2] People came to realize that relief from the heat of the desert and a change of scenery were available right in Tucson's backyard.

The hardier types began to camp out or to build summer cabins in the canyons and parks of the Santa Catalina, Santa Rita, Huachuca, and Chiricahua mountains. In 1905 the supervisor of the Santa Catalina Forest Reserve wrote that his reserve was known locally as Tucson's summer resort; residents took to the mountains during the summer months and remained there for from thirty to sixty days.[3] The year 1908 saw Joel Huntsman, the Overland automobile dealer in Tucson, building the first modern cabin in the Catalinas, at what is now the Marshall Gulch picnic area, on Mt. Lemmon.[4]

The Pinaleños held a similar attraction for people in the nearby Gila River Valley. In the 1890s settlers from Pima camped out and then built log cabins on Mt. Graham, at a spot they called Columbine. Their cabins were summer homes, where families could escape the heat of the valley below. The colony on Mt. Graham became very popular, with the celebration on July 4, 1896,

Weber's Camp—a hunting party in the tall cool pine forest of the Santa Catalinas, c. 1900. (Courtesy, U.S. Forest Service, Southwestern Region.)

attracting some 250 people to join in ball games, sack races, horseshoe pitching, and other games, winding up with a dance that night.[5] When a forest examiner arrived in 1902, he found that "[q]uite a popular summer resort for the residents of the Gila Valley has been established at an elevation of 9,000 feet in the head of Ash Canyon. Another summer camp was formerly maintained at 6,300 feet in Jacobson Canyon. This was called Arcadia, but has recently been neglected and does not deserve its name."[6]

The examiner went on to describe the Graham Mountains (the Pinaleños) as "the most beautiful and picturesque that we have examined." More cabins were built at places such as Riggs Flat and Hospital Flat, and people even raised potatoes at five of the largest flats and coves. Getting to the top as of 1915 meant a six-hour horseback trip.[7] Construction of a good road to the crest of the Pinaleños lay twenty years in the future.

Camping in the cool mountains was a favorite summer pastime. Probably shown is Weber's Camp in the Santa Catalinas in 1900. (Courtesy, U.S. Forest Service, Southwestern Region.)

The Santa Catalinas and Summerhaven

In 1915 Congress authorized the Forest Service to lease forest land to private persons or associations for the construction of summer homes, hotels, stores, or other recreation-related facilities.[8] In the Santa Catalinas this official recognition of recreation in the national forests had already been outpaced by events. As of 1910 a number of prominent Tucsonians were spending their summers at two recognized campgrounds, Soldier Camp and Mount Lemmon, where several planned to build cabins.[9] Late in the fall of that year, Frank Weber of Oracle received his patent to a 152-acre homestead on Mt. Lemmon, under authority of the 1862 Homestead Act. His quarter-section, surrounded by National Forest lands, became the basis for the summer resort colony known as Summerhaven.

Access to the top of the Catalinas was by a trail from the bottom of Sabino Canyon up Box Camp Canyon into Soldier Camp. In 1911–12 the Forest

Washing by the spring while camping in the Santa Catalina Mountains, c. 1900. (Courtesy, U.S. Forest Service, Southwestern Region.)

Service, together with Pima County, the Tucson Chamber of Commerce, and a local power company, raised money to construct an easier route, known as the Palisades or the Pine Ridge Trail. A pack train operated by the Knagge family kept the summer residents at Soldier Camp and thereabouts supplied. From bottom to top the pack trip up the mountains required eight hours.[10]

A few new cabins went up; then in 1916 the Forest Service announced plans to survey plats for two hundred or more summer cottages at Soldier Camp.[11] This survey apparently was not carried out, because development had to wait for better access, which meant a road up the mountains.[12] That same summer the Forest Service, together with a copper-mining company, summer colonists, and the Summerhaven Land and Improvement Co., lent

Huntsman (Breazeale) cabin in Marshall Gulch is the oldest (1908) summer home in the Santa Catalina Mountains. (Courtesy, U.S. Forest Service, Coronado National Forest, 1957 photo.)

enthusiastic support to a proposal for a Mount Lemmon road.[13]

Enthusiasm quickly translated into action, and a route was surveyed up the north side of the Santa Catalinas early in 1917. This led from Oracle via Apache Camp to Summerhaven. World War I intervened and delayed the beginning of road construction until June 1919. The work then went ahead rapidly, and just one year later the twenty-two mile route up to Summerhaven had been completed. Another month and a half saw the last two miles into Soldier Camp opened.[14]

A Tucson automobile dealer, eager to show what his cars could do, drove an air-cooled Franklin from Tucson to Soldier Camp in an elapsed time of seven hours and one minute deliberately driving in low gear all the way. The following summer a Willys-Knight car, stripped of its fan, made the run

Pack train packing supplies to Mt. Lemmon, Santa Catalina Mountains, 1922. (Courtesy, U.S. Forest Service, Coronado National Forest.)

Lower end of the Control Road near Apache Camp, Santa Catalina Mountains, 1922. (Courtesy, U.S. Forest Service, Coronado National Forest.)

Control Road under construction, Santa Catalina Mountains, June 1920. (Courtesy, The National Archives. F. E. Bonner, photographer.)

from Tucson to Summerhaven in only three hours and thirty minutes—without boiling or overheating! Motorists generally made the drive from Tucson in less than five hours.[15]

At a later time, people began to use the name Control Road for this new route. The last seven miles were too narrow at places for cars to pass one another, and in consequence all vehicles waited until a scheduled time to start up the grade, followed in 1.5 hours by a string of vehicles descending from the top. This alternating use of the road was repeated four times a day.[16]

Completion of the Control Road launched a building spree on Mount Lemmon. At Soldier Camp lessees built cabins on land leased from the Forest Service. At Summerhaven some individuals constructed their own cab-

Sporleder Residence at Soldier Camp, Santa Catalina Mountains, 1921. (Courtesy, U.S. Forest Service, Coronado National Forest.)

Ryland summer homesite at Soldier Camp, Santa Catalina Mountains, c. 1920. (Courtesy, U.S. Forest Service, Coronado National Forest.)

ins, while the development company erected others and rented them out. Jim Westfall, a former forest ranger, had opened La Mariposa Lodge at Summerhaven by 1920. His hotel featured sixteen large, airy bedrooms for guests, plus a dance hall and reception room "at least forty feet square" that provided ample room for everyone to have a good time.[17] The facilities included hot and cold showers and "fine home cooking"; attractions consisted of fishing, riding, tennis, dancing, and hiking. The rates, as of 1927, were $4 a day or $25 per week, with meals extra.[18] That same year 2060 hotel and resort guests logged into Coronado National Forest, among 29,246 forest visitors of all kinds.[19]

Tucson newspapers in the early 1920s carried columns of news about the summer colonies. The papers estimated that half of the socialites were at Mt. Lemmon and the remainder at White House Canyon, in the Santa Ritas. In these settings the McNeals, the Sporleders, the Kitts, and other prominent Tucsonians rusticated, as the newspapers put it, for anywhere from several weeks to an entire summer. On weekends as many as a hundred cars would drive up to Sumerhaven for the parties. Soldier Camp remained the principal camp, with additional leased sites in Upper and Middle Sabino Canyon, Bear Canyon, Carter Canyon, and eventually at other locations.[20]

Summering in the Mountains, 1920

Every few days the newspapers chronicled the comings and goings between Tucson and Mt. Lemmon, detailing for their readers the social season of 1920. The Control Road had been completed as far as Summerhaven by around June 2, just in time for the season opening, and the remaining two miles into Soldier Camp were open by July 20. The summer exodus to the mountains began promptly:

> The Mount Lemmon social season will be both an early and a full one, according to plans being made at the present time for the opening of camps and cottages by many Tucsonans who have been, for several years, accustomed to spend the hot months at this lofty resort. Many new summer homes are in process of construction at Summerhaven and Soldiers Camp. . . . Handsome lodges are now being built for Mr. and Mrs. S. L. Kingan and Mr. and Mrs. Stanley J. Kitt, of this city. The cottage of Mr. and Mrs. F. E. Adams at Soldiers Camp has been completed . . . The first of the summer colonists to make the ascent will be Mr. and Mrs. A. M. Franklin and family, with their houseguest, Miss Hattie Morford of San Francisco, who will go up on Monday. The family of S. J. Kitt will follow shortly. E. W. Childs and family will open the Childs place about the middle of June. Mr. and Mrs. John Mets will occupy their camp about the first of July.[21]

By the third week of June, most of the summer colonists appear to have arrived, to stay for anywhere between several weeks and the rest of the summer.

In that pretelevision era, with a total of two telephones at the camps, no electricity, and the only water for recreation a couple of trout streams, what did people do after they settled in? The vacationers came as families, and they were quite adept at providing their own entertainment. Some of the men supervised the construction of their cabins. With two population cen-

Foot bridge at Soldier Camp, Santa Catalina Mountains, 1921. (Courtesy, U.S. Forest Service, Coronado National Forest.)

ters (Summerhaven and Soldier Camp) plus outlying camps, there were plenty of opportunities for visiting. Hiking, picnics, horseback rides, luncheons and dinner parties, card parties, candy pulls, and skits at evening campfires were all mentioned. On the Fourth of July, Jim Westfall hosted a barbeque at Summerhaven. In mid-July the cottage of Mr. and Mrs. A. M. Franklin was the setting for a party, with a campfire in a circle of trees and

> . . . logs to serve as benches . . . pulled close to the flames for greater comfort. The house was cleared for dancing and the porch was dimly lighted by a single lantern, making it ideal for moonlight waltzes. The younger people spent the earlier part of the evening dancing but later joined the rest of the crowd around the campfire.

Popcorn and cookies appeared then, accompanied by ghost stories, songs, and stunts.[22] One week later the occasion was a farewell dance, where the younger set came attired as a Villa soldier, a ghost, a rag doll, an Alpine guide, a cowgirl, and a gypsy. And as before, "[t]he house and porch, dimly lighted, were used for dancing. A Victrola supplied music and delicious punch and cookies were served for refreshments."[23]

Eventually September came, and it was time to think of leaving. This prompted a new round of social affairs:

> One of the largest of these was the housewarming presided over last week by Mr. and Mrs. Stanley J. Kitt of Kamp Kitt, signalizing the completion of their new cabin on the mountain. A feature of the affair was a volunteer orchestra which was composed of Messrs. Sporleder, Lopez, and Walker and which furnished music for dancing throughout the evening. A huge bonfire built close to the cabin supplemented Japanese lanterns by way of illumination. Guests of the festivity included Mr. and Mrs. E. G. Sporleder, Mr. and Mrs. James Westfall, Mr. and Mrs. John Mets, Dr. and Mrs. E. H. Stiles, Mr. and Mrs. Carlos Jacome . . . Misses Harriet Morford, Dorothy Heighton, Edith Failor, Elizabeth Franklin, Irene Childs, . . . Messrs. Elmer Staggs, Glenn Harrison, Orville Shook, Herbert Morrison . . . and Jack Ryland.[24]

Gradually, through the remainder of September, people closed their summer cabins and left the mountains, to return to Tucson or elsewhere around southern Arizona. Most would return in 1921.

Despite the ballyhoo given to the Summerhaven development, this was not an early success. By 1930 the resort consisted of only about fifteen cabins plus a lodge, "not up to a very high standard; the buildings being unpainted."[25] No one estimated the size of its summer population. As for facilities on nearby Forest Service lands, Soldier Camp

Summer cabin, Madera Canyon recreation area in the Santa Rita Mountains, c. 1921–23. (Courtesy, U.S. Forest Service, Coronado National Forest.)

> . . . was one of the first to be developed on any Forest in this Region. Thirty-one lots of a total of 45 laid out have been placed under permit and structures erected. Construction has been limited to summer homes with a fairly high standard prevailing. Most of the summer homes are well maintained and have been built in good taste.[26]

In the 1970s some 248 people were still leasing cabin sites in the Santa Catalinas from the Forest Service.[27]

Summer Camps in the Santa Ritas

Thirty-eight miles south of Tucson, another summer colony grew up at Madera or White House Canyon on the western slope of the Santa Rita Mountains. The original "White House" was a little adobe, at one time whitewashed, that stood near the mouth of the canyon.[28] By 1910 the Franklin, Hofmeister, Heighton, and other Tucson families already had a summer camp, the Mountain Retreat resort, in White House Canyon. Campers commuted

from Tucson by auto or by taking the railroad as far as Canoa station. That same year a group of Tucson promoters announced plans to build "a great resort" in the same canyon with a large hotel, an auditorium, log cabins, swimming pools, and other attractions.[29] These plans dropped from sight, but by the following summer three Tucson families had built cottages ("most convenient and well fitted up") in the canyon.[30]

More new cabins went up, and by 1920 White House Canyon was attracting as many as eighty city residents on a weekend.[31] Completion of an improved road the next year placed the canyon less than two hours from Tucson. This easy access plus a new, cemented swimming pool, helped the

Manning Camp in the Rincon Mountains, c. late 1920s. (Courtesy, U.S. Forest Service, Coronado National Forest.)

resort grow to the point that at least twenty families had summer homes there.[32]

White House Canyon became the most popular recreation area in the mountains around Tucson. By the summer of 1927, the Santa Rita Trails Resort offered cottages, cabins, riding, and mountain climbing, with a small central store and dining room. An estimated two thousand persons used its accommodations in 1930, and the next few years saw the number of cabins in the canyon increase to more than fifty. As with Mt. Lemmon, White House Canyon (or Madera Canyon, as it is now generally called) is still a summer resort area today.[33]

Summer Colonies in Other Ranges

Summer camps grew up in several other mountain ranges in southeastern Arizona. In the Rincon Mountains, the Manning Camp had been built around 1904 by former Arizona surveyor-general and Tucson mayor Levi H. Manning. He used it as a summer home at least as recently as 1910. In later years the Manning cabin became a Forest Service ranger station and then a fire-fighting camp, maintained by Saguaro National Monument.[34]

Ramsey Canyon, in the Huachuca Mountains, was another favorite summer setting for a time.[35] In the late 1920s the Hood-Berner resort there advertised itself modestly as ". . . doubtless . . . the most popular summer resort of this section of the country. . . ." The twenty-five or thirty cabins were "equipped with cots and bedding, and separate kitchenettes with stoves and cooking utensils. A store is in operation during the summer when supplies can be purchased. A large open air dance pavilion is also in operation during the summer, which gives the visitor excellent diversion."[36]

As for natural attractions, the resort lay in the heart of big pine and spruce trees, with a profusion of wild flowers and a rose garden as well, the cabins lying to either side of a cold mountain creek. Farther upstream were a large box canyon, forests, and an old mine, all accessible to the hiker.

In spite of the natural and constructed wonders, this area failed to develop. A few years later Ramsey Canyon's resorts still consisted of rental cabins on private lands. Farther east, in the Chiricahuas, summer homesites were staked out and leased along Cave Creek and West Turkey Creek.[37]

People in the nearby Gila Valley continue to use the Pinaleño Mountains as their resort area. Here too was another successful summer colony, beginning in 1929 with the first leases for summer homesites. The Forest Service made thirty-nine lots available at the Turkey Flat Recreational Area, at the head of Swift Trail, the auto road to the Pinaleño high country. Cabin construction on the leases began almost immediately. Soon a store was added. The early 1930s saw the Cluff Dairy established nearby, to sell milk and cream to the summer residents. The Forest Service continued to survey new cabin sites, and by 1937 Turkey Flat had sixty summer homes. Eventually that area held seventy-seven lots plus a lodge, tennis court, and public campground. It remains a summer resort today.

The Civilian Conservation Corps extended Swift Trail along the crest of the Pinaleños in the mid-1930s to the Old Columbine special-use area at the head of Ash Canyon. A plat from 1936 showed a camp ground and ten cabin sites there, which has been about the number of leases in effect in more recent years.[38] Arcadia, just below Turkey Flat, was a summer camp in the 1890s and today is a picnic area.

Summer Homes, Yesterday and Today

Summer homes in the mountains flourished during the 1920s and even into the Depression years, as welcome alternatives to enduring the heat of southern Arizona's valleys. In the Santa Catalinas, the top of the mountains became even more accessible with construction of the General Hitchcock Forest Highway up the south slope, directly from Tucson. It took thirteen years to build this highway with prison labor, from its beginning in 1933 until the roadway was graded out at Soldier Camp in the late fall of 1946.[39] Frank Harris Hitchcock, namesake and chief early proponent of this route, was a former postmaster general and editor of the *Tucson Citizen*. Completion of this road made summer cabins attractive once again, especially to those of modest means.[40]

The most recent round of summer-homesite leasing on Coronado National Forest lands began in 1946 and continued into the early 1950s. The Willow Canyon and Loma Linda summer-home areas and their extensions added some 170 new lots at this time. Another building boom followed, which included hundreds of new cabins at Summerhaven as well. With the 1960s and the widescale appearance of home air conditioning, summer comfort was only a switch away, and the principal appeal a summer cabin held for city dwellers diminished. Today with the mountaintop still a prime recreational area, problems exist with erosion, sewage disposal, and water supplies, while Forest Service policies now favor the restoration of developed areas to a more natural environment, dooming summer cabins on leased sites to eventual elimination. Madera Canyon in the Santa Ritas is also being restored to natural conditions. Elsewhere summer home areas will continue as they are, into the future.[41]

In their peak period of popularity before World War II, southern Arizona enjoyed the distinction of two strong resort traditions: dude ranches, in the valleys and foothills and summer colonies in the higher mountains. These coexisted in the same areas, although they shared very little in common. Dude ranching originated outside the state and took root as a means whereby ranchers could hold onto their property during economic downturns. Their guests were from out of state, primarily in the winter season.

Summer camps on the other hand began as a way for southern Arizona's valley dwellers to escape the summer heat. In the Pinaleño range the early campers were farmers from the Gila Valley, and their cabins were unpretentious. In contrast it was Tucson's upper middle class who discovered the Santa Catalinas and began to summer there rather than travel to the California coast. Their colonies became a resort, mostly on lands leased from the Forest

Service. From 1929 the Forest Service leased cabin sites in the Pinaleños as well, and a summer colony even larger than those in the Catalinas developed at Turkey Flat.

Despite their differences in clientele and seasonality and their independent origins, the two resort traditions did have recreation as a common theme. Even more importantly it was their location near to or even within Arizona's desert islands that allowed both dude ranching and summer homes to flourish as they did. Without the mountains the ranches would have lost much of their appeal, and summer colonies would have been nonexistent.

13
ISLANDS IN THE DESERT: RETROSPECT AND PROSPECT

Even as the names of southeastern Arizona's mountains have changed with time, so have their roles. When first seen by nonnatives, these ranges were the homes and place of refuge for the Jano, Jocome, and Suma Indians. Later the Apaches dwelt here and fought many times with the military forces of Spain, Mexico, and the United States.

Spanish missionaries and settlers gave little attention to the mountain ranges, some of which may not even have borne names. Native Americans farmed the intervening valleys and harvested acorns and agave from the foot-hill country. The mid-1730s brought a silver rush to the ranges that border the present U.S.-Mexico boundary, and sporadic mining continued into the 1840s, interrupted by occasional Piman revolts and harassed later by hostile Apaches.

The early American occupation witnessed another boom, as newcomers from the East tried to bring the old Spanish silver mines back into production and discover new veins. Their work was not extensive, and these ventures collapsed with the onset of the Civil War. At the same time, other developers were trying to exploit Arizona's timber resources to meet both army and civilian needs. Sawpits appeared at several locations around the Santa Ritas.

The desert ranges continued to shelter the Apaches until, by 1872, most of them had gone onto reservations. The Chiricahua leader Cochise kept the Chiricahua and Dragoon mountains for a few more years as the anchors of his short-lived (1872–76) reservation. After this reservation was terminated, miners began to scour the country for gold, silver, and copper. They found all of these and extracted substantial amounts of wealth from the mountains in the ensuing century, although the largest mineral discoveries lay outside of the principal ranges. The new mines, mills, and smelters also provided a big market for timber products—fuelwood, charcoal, and lumber. The lower slopes were soon cut over for cordwood, while steam-powered sawmills in the Huachucas, Chiricahuas, and other ranges cut the sawtimber there into lumber for the towns, ranches, and army posts, as well as for the mines.

This combination of military campaigns, mineral discoveries, timber cutting, and sawmill operations, together with ranching, brought more activity to the mountains of southeastern Arizona during the 1880s than at any time before or since. Later in that decade, the mining boom tapered off, while the more accessible timber resources were cut out, even as the new railroad brought in West Coast lumber that undersold the local sawmills. By the time the first forest reserves were set aside in 1902, commercial lumbering had been underway for more than twenty years in southern Arizona.

The twentieth century brought new controls as well as new interests. The Bureau of Forestry and later the Forest Service extended authority over forest reserves that had been established mainly for watershed protection. This came as part of a newly emerging conservation ethic; runoff from the desert ranges contributed significantly to the water supplies downstream. One of the new controls was use of the forest by livestock, and eventually grazing fees became the single largest revenue source for Coronado National Forest. One new interest was forest homesteads, the June 11 claims. By 1924 when the patenting of such claims had effectively been completed, 294 individuals had received deeds to 40,290 acres within Coronado National Forest.[1] At the same time, sweltering Tucsonians began camping or building summer cabins in the nearby mountains, to have a place to cool off during the hottest months. These summer visitors were the first large group of recreational users in the southern desert mountains. The dude ranches that sprang up in the 1920s added another large block of vacationers to the more accessible ranges.

In the foregoing pages it has been necessary to keep only a loose focus on the forest uplands and to weave the narrative around the Native Americans, soldiers, miners, recreational users, and others who had their day in southern Arizona's mountains. These ranges attracted little attention until the late nineteenth century. Each group who came made its own impress, with none leaving the landscape unaltered. For many the mountains were almost incidental, a means to an end such as protection, minerals, or lumber. Now all but the ranchers and recreation seekers have departed. The natural resources that could be removed economically are largely gone, and the renewable ones (forage, watershed protection, recreation) are actively managed to enhance their value.

The topics examined have scarcely been exhausted; for example the role of the Forest Service itself has rarely been mentioned, while the coming of the railroads, the growth of towns and cities, and the development of farming all merit their own studies. The Civilian Conservation Corps and its legacy is another important facet, especially from the standpoints of watershed management and recreation.[2] Our ability to perceive such interests is limited only by our horizons; as interests change, even the existing studies will be subject to new scrutiny and more searching interpretations.

NOTES

Chapter 1

1. This geologic background is drawn primarily from the following sources: Nevin M. Fenneman, *Physiography of Western United States* (New York: McGraw-Hill, 1931); James Gilluly, *General Geology of Central Cochise County, Arizona,* U.S. Geological Survey Professional Paper 281 (Washington, D.C.: U.S. Government Printing Office, 1956); John R. Cooper and Leon T. Silver, *Geology and Ore Deposits of the Dragoon Quadrangle, Cochise County, Arizona,* U.S. Geological Survey Professional Paper 416 (Washington, D.C.: U.S. Government Printing Office, 1964); U.S. Geological Survey, Arizona Bureau of Mines, and U.S. Bureau of Reclamation, *Mineral and Water Resources of Arizona,* Bulletin 180 (Tucson: Arizona Bureau of Mines, 1969); Eldred D. Wilson, *A Résumé of the Geology of Arizona,* Arizona Bureau of Mines Bulletin 171 (Tucson: University of Arizona, 1962); J. F. Callender, Jan C. Wilt, and R. E. Clemons, eds., *Land of Cochise: Southeastern Arizona,* New Mexico Geological Society (in cooperation with the Arizona Geological Society), 29th Field Conference (Socorro: New Mexico Geological Society, 1978); S. P. Marsh, S. J. Kropschot, and R. G. Dickinson, eds., *Wilderness Mineral Potential: Assessment of the Mineral-Resource Potential in U.S. Forest Service Lands Studied 1964–1984,* U.S. Geological Survey Professional Paper 1300, vols. 1 and 2 (Washington, D.C.: U.S. Government Printing Office, 1984).

2. W. P. Martin and Joel E. Fletcher, *Vertical Zonation of Great Soil Groups on Mt. Graham, Arizona, as Correlated with Climate, Vegetation, and Profile Characteristics,* University of Arizona Agricultural Experimental Station Technical Bulletin no. 99 (Tucson: University of Arizona, 1943); Charles O. Wallmo, "Vegetation of the Huachuca Mountains, Arizona," *American Midland Naturalist* 54:466–80; R. H. Whittaker and W. A. Niering, "Vegetation of the Santa Catalina Mountains, Arizona, I. Ecological Classification and Distribution of Species," *Journal of the Arizona Academy of Science* 3(1): (1964):9–34; David E. Brown, ed., "Biotic Communities of the American Southwest—United States and Mexico," *Desert Plants* 4(1–4):37–39, 43–48, 59–65, 70–71; David E. Brown and Charles H. Lowe, *Biotic Communities of the Southwest,* General Technical Report RM-78 (Fort Collins, CO: Rocky Mountain Forest and Range Experiment Station, 1983).

3. Conrad J. Bahre, *Land-Use History of the Research Ranch, Elgin, Arizona, Journal of the Arizona Academy of Science* 12 (supplement 2), August 1977; Brown, "Biotic Communities," 115–21, 123–31; Brown and Lowe, *Biotic Communities.*

4. Brown, "Biotic Communities," 169–79, 181–221; Brown and Lowe, *Biotic Communities.*

Chapter 2

1. Lawrence Kinnaird, *The Frontiers of New Spain: Nicolás de Lafora's Description, 1766–1768* (Berkeley: Quivira Society, 1958), 108.

2. Ernest J. Burrus, *Kino and Manje: Explorers of Sonora and Arizona* (Rome: Jesuit Historical Institute, 1971), 315. Charles W. Polzer, "Long Before the Blue Dragoons: Spanish Military Operations in Northern Sonora and Pimería Alta" In: *Views on the Military History of the Indian-Spanish-American Southwest: 1598–1886,* Bruno J. Rolak, ed. (Fort Huachuca, Ariz: 1976) p. 13. Thomas H. Naylor and Charles W. Polzer, eds., *The Presidio and Militia on the Northern Frontier of New Spain* (Tucson: University of Arizona Press, 1986) 1:575.

3. Naylor and Polzer, 1986:492.

4. Charles W. Polzer, *Kino's Biography of Francisco Javier Saeta, S.J.* (Rome: Jesuit Historical Institute, 1971), 166–67, 267.

5. Juan Nentvig, *Rudo Ensayo: A Description of Sonora and Arizona in 1764* (Tucson: University of Arizona Press, 1980), 21, 125.

6. Luis Navarro García, *Sonora y Sinaloa en el siglo XVII* (Sevilla: Escuela de Estudios Hispano-Americanos, 1967), 278.

7. Naylor and Polzer, 1986:585–718. For an excellent summary of this expedition, see Polzer, 1971:258–330.

8. General Juan Fernández de la Fuente, "Journal of the Pima Campaign of 1695," entry for September 12, 1695 (f. 167v). Archivo de Hidalgo del Parral, microfilm 1695, ff. 5–208. Copy courtesy of Dr. Thomas H. Naylor, Documentary Relations of the Southwest, Tucson, Arizona.

9. Kinnaird, 1958:106; Naylor and Polzer, 1986:646 ff.; Alfred B. Thomas, ed., *Forgotten Frontiers* (Norman: University of Oklahoma Press, 1932), 208; George P. Hammond and Edward H. Howes, eds., *Overland to California on the Southwest Trail, 1849* (Berkeley: University of California Press, 1950), 184.

10. Byrd H. Granger, *Will C. Barnes' Arizona Place Names* (Tucson; University of Arizona Press, 1960), 130; Luis Navarro García, *Don José de Gálvez y la comandancia general de las provincias internas del norte de Nueva España* (Sevilla: Escuela de Estudios Hispano-Americanos, 1964), maps 113 and 123.

11. Burrus 1971:369; Naylor and Polzer 1986:644 ff.

12. Ross Calvin, ed., *Lieutenant Emory Reports* (Albuquerque: University of New Mexico Press, 1951), 110, 112, 116, 118, 202.

13. A. W. Whipple, "Itinerary," in *Reports of Explorations and Surveys to Ascertain the Most Practicable and Economical Route from the Mississippi River to the Pacific Ocean,* vol. 3, pt. 1 (Washington, D.C.: Beverley Tucker, Printer, 1854), 93. A. W. Whipple, Thomas Ewbank, and Wm. W. Turner, "Report upon the Indian Tribes," Ibid., vol. 3 pt. 3 (Washington, D.C.: Beverley Tucker, Printer, 1855), 14.

14. De la Fuente, "Journals," f. 171v.

15. Charles H. Lange and Carroll L. Riley, eds., *The Southwestern Journals of Adolph F. Bandelier, 1883–1884* (Albuquerque: University of New Mexico Press, 1970), 218.

16. Henry F. Dobyns, *From Fire to Flood: Historic Human Destruction of Sonoran*

Riverine Oases (Socorro, N.M.: Ballena Press, 1981), 21.

17. Francisco Salas Bohorques, "Diario de las Novedades ocurridas en la campaña ... don Roque de Medina," Archivo General de la Nación, Provincias Internas, tomo 193 (copy courtesy of the Bancroft Library, Berkeley, California). "Territory and Military Department of New Mexico . . . 1859," map located at National Archives and Records Administration, Washington, D.C. (hereafter NARA), Record Group (RG) 77, Sheet W55(1); Carl Sauer, "A Spanish Expedition into the Arizona Apachería," *Arizona Historical Review* 6(1) (1935):3–13; Alfred B. Thomas, *Teodoro de Croix and the Northern Frontier of New Spain, 1776–1783* (Norman: University of Oklahoma Press, 1941), 177, 186, 193–94, 209; Albert H. Campbell, *Report upon the Pacific Wagon Roads* (Fairfield, Wash.: Ye Galleon Press, 1969; reprint of 1859 ed.), 79; Albert H. Schroeder, "A Study of the Apache Indians. Part V-A, 'Tonto' and Western Apaches," in *Apache Indians IV*, David A. Horr, ed. (New York: Garland Publishing, 1974), 357–58.

18. Bohorques 1789; Thomas 1932, map opposite p. 252; Navarro García 1964, maps 113 and 123.

19. "Affairs in Department of New Mexico," in *Report of the Secretary of War* (1859), 36th Cong. 1st Sess. Senate Executive Document 2, vol. 2, pt. 2 (serial no. 1024) (Washington, D.C.: George W. Bowman, Printer, 1860), 301–2; Navarro García 1964, maps 113 and 123.

20. Granger 1960, 57; Campbell 1969, maps in pocket; "Territory and Military Department of New Mexico . . . 1859," map, NARA, RG 77, Sheet W55(1); "Parts of South-Eastern Arizona, Atlas Sheet No. 10," 1878, NARA, RG 77, Sheet W275-10; "Outline Map of the Field of Operations against Hostile Chiricahua Indians . . . 1886," map, photocopy in author's possession; Hammond and Howes 1950, vii, 191.

21. Burrus 1971, 376–77; John L. Kessell, *Mission of Sorrows: Jesuit Guevavi and the Pimas, 1691–1767* (Tucson: University of Arizona Press, 1970), 141; Henry F. Dobyns, *Spanish Colonial Tucson* (Tucson: University of Arizona Press, 1976), 17–18, 68, 186.

22. See maps in n. 20, above; Thomas 1941, 193; Granger 1960, 278; Navarro García 1964, maps 113 and 123; "Official Map of the Territory of Arizona . . . 1880," map, photoreproduction by Tucson Blueprint Co.; Kieran McCarty, *A Spanish Frontier in the Enlightened Age: Franciscan Beginnings in Sonora and Arizona, 1767–1770* (Washington, D.C.: Academy of American Franciscan History, 1981), 86–87.

23. William H. Emory, *Report on the United States and Mexican Boundary Survey, Made under the Direction of the Secretary of the Interior*, 34th Cong. 1st Sess., Senate Exec. Doc. No. 108, vol. 1, pt. 1 (Serial no. 832) (Washington, D.C.: A. O. P. Nicholson, Printer, 1857), 118–20; Ignaz Pfefferkorn, *Sonora, a Description of the Province* (Albuquerque: University of New Mexico Press, 1949), 238.

24. See maps in n. 20, above; Thomas 1941, 192; Kinnaird 1958, 108; Navarro García 1964, maps 113 and 123; "Map of Part of Arizona Showing the Chiricahua Reserve," map located at NARA, RG 75, Bureau of Indian Affairs, Map 392; Samuel W. Cozzens, *The Marvellous Country* (Minneapolis: Ross and Haines, 1967; reprint of 1874 ed.), 166; John L. Kessell, *Friars, Soldiers, and Reformers: Hispanic Arizona*

and the Sonora Mission Frontier 1767–1856 (Tucson: University of Arizona Press, 1976), 169; Kieran McCarty, *Desert Documentary* (Tucson: Arizona Historical Society, Historical Monograph No. 4, 1976), 84.

25. Granger 1960, 322; John C. Reid, *Reid's Tramp* (Austin: Steck Company, 1935; reprint of 1858 ed., 192–93; Constance Wynn Altshuler, "The Case of Sylvester Mowry: The Mowry Mine," *Arizona and the West* 15(2) (1973):161–63.

Chapter 3

1. Fanny Bandelier, trans., *The Narrative of Alvar Núñez Cabeza de Vaca* (Barre, Mass: Imprint Society, 1972).

2. Percy M. Baldwin, ed., *Discovery of the Seven Cities of Cibola by the Father Fray Marcos de Niza,* Historical Society of New Mexico Publications in History, vol. 1 (Albuquerque: El Palacio Press, 1926); Adolph F. Bandelier, "The Discovery of New Mexico by Fray Marcos of Nizza," *New Mexico Historical Review* 4(1) (1929):28–44; Henry R. Wagner, "Fr. Marcos de Niza," *New Mexico Historical Review* 9(2) (1934):202–11; George P. Hammond and Agapito Rey, *Narratives of the Coronado Expedition 1540–1542* (Albuquerque: University of New Mexico Press, 1940), 58–82.

3. George Parker Winship, "The Coronado Expedition, 1540–1542," *Fourteenth Annual Report of the Bureau of Ethnology . . . 1892–93,* part 1 (Washington, D.C.: U.S. Government Printing Office, 1896), 363–67; Wagner 1934, 222–25.

4. Winship 1896; Hammond and Rey 1940.

5. The most important modern studies on the probable route(s) of Fray Marcos and Coronado include the following: Adolph F. Bandelier, *Final Report of Investigations among the Indians of the Southwestern United States, Carried on Mainly in the Years from 1880 to 1885,* parts 1, 2 (Cambridge, Mass.: John Wilson and Son, 1890, 1892), pt. 1 106–78, pt. 2, 398, 409, 476; Wagner 1934; Carl O. Sauer, *The Road to Cibola,* Ibero-Americana 3 (Berkeley: University of California Press, 1932); Carl O. Sauer, "The Discovery of New Mexico Reconsidered", *New Mexico Historical Review* 12(3) (1937):270–87; Lansing R. Bloom, "Who Discovered New Mexico?" *New Mexico Historical Review* 15(2) (1940):101–32; George J. Undreiner, "Fray Marcos de Niza and His Journey to Cibola," *The Americas* 3(4) (1947):415–86; Albert H. Schroeder, "Fray Marcos de Niza, Coronado and the Yavapai," *New Mexico Historical Review* 30(4) (1955):265–96, 31(1) (1956):24–37; Adolph F. Bandelier, *A History of the Southwest,* supplement to volume 1 (Rome: Jesuit Historical Institute, 1969), map 33; Basil C. Hedrick, "The Location of Corazones," in *Across the Chichimec Sea,* Carroll L. Riley and Basil C. Hedrick, eds. (Carbondale: Southern Illinois University Press, 1978); Daniel T. Reff, "The Location of Corazones and Señora: Archaeological Evidence from the Rio Sonora Valley, Mexico," in *The Protohistoric Period in the North American Southwest, AD 1450–1700;* David R. Wilcox and W. Bruce Masse, eds. (Tempe: Arizona State University Anthropological Research Papers no. 24, 1981); Charles C. DiPeso, John B. Rinaldo, and Gloria J. Fenner, *Casas Grandes: A Fallen Trading Center of the Gran Chichimeca,* vol. 4

(Dragoon, Ariz.: Amerind Foundation, 1974), 75–103; Carroll L. Riley, "The Location of Chichilticale," in *Southwestern Culture History: Collected Papers in Honor of Albert H. Schroeder,* Charles H. Lange, ed. (Santa Fe: Papers of the Archaeological Society of New Mexico 10, 1985); Stewart L. Udall, "In Coronado's Footsteps," *Arizona Highways* 60(4) (1984):3–11, 20–33.

6. L. R. Bailey, ed., *The A.B. Gray Report* (Los Angeles: Westernlore Press, 1963; republication of 1856 ed.), pp. 75–77; John Russell Bartlett, *Personal Narrative of Explorations and Incidents, . . .* vol. 1 (Chicago: Rio Grande Press, 1965; reprint of 1854 ed.), 379; Douglas Preston, "Following—Painfully—the Route of Coronado after 450 Years," *Smithsonian* 20(10) (1990):40–53.

7. Winship 1896, 516.

8. Winship 1896, 484, 515–16, 533, 572.

9. Bandelier 1892, 407–9; Winship 1896, 387, 482, 516–17, 554–55, 584–86; Hammond and Rey 1940, 165–66, 207–8, 297–98; Carl O. Sauer and Donald Brand, *Pueblo Sites in Southeastern Arizona,* University of California Publications in Geography, vol. 3(7) (Berkeley: University of California Press, 1930), 419, 422–23; Herbert E. Bolton, *Coronado, Knight of Pueblos and Plains* (Albuquerque: University of New Mexico Press, 1964), 105–9; Emil W. Haury, "The Search for Chichilticale," *Arizona Highways* 60(4) (1984):14–19.

10. Winship 1896, 555, 564; Bandelier, in Madeleine Turrell Rodack, ed., *Adolph F. Bandelier's The Discovery of New Mexico by the Franciscan Monk, Friar Marcos de Niza, in 1539* (Tucson: University of Arizona Press, 1981), 90, said that on horseback he had ridden from Zuni to the Gila River near San Carlos in eight days, averaging twenty-six miles per day. When Coronado's army marched east from Pecos Pueblo in New Mexico to find Quivira, the troops averaged 6 or 7 leagues a day (Winship 1896, 507–8). This appears to be the only contemporary statement on the length of a day's march by Coronado's men.

11. Hammond and Rey 1940, 71–73, 250–51; Schroeder (1955, 282) and Hodge, in Frederick W. Hodge and Theodore H. Lewis, eds., *Spanish Explorers in the Southern United States, 1528–1543* (New York: Barnes and Noble, 1971; reprint of 1907 ed.), 326, 371, also recognized the Valley of Suya as Sobaipuri country.

12. Baldwin 1926, 30; Ernest J. Burrus, *Kino and Manje: Explorers of Sonora and Arizona* (Rome: Jesuit Historical Institute, 1971), 198–99, 358–59.

13. Hammond and Rey 1940, 232–33, 250, 268–70, 277–78, 293.

14. Hammond and Rey 1940, 233, 250; Burrus 1971, 358–59.

15. France V. Scholes, "Church and State in New Mexico, 1610–1650", *New Mexico Historical Review* 11(4) (1936):301–2; Albert H. Schroeder, "Southwestern Chronicle: The Cipias and Ypotlapiguas," *Arizona Quarterly* 12(2) (1956):106.

16. Schroeder 1956; Juan Mateo Manje, *Unknown Arizona and Sonora, 1693–1721,* Harry J. Karns and Associates, trans. (Tucson: Arizona Silhouettes, 1954), 280–82; John Francis Bannon, *The Mission Frontier in Sonora, 1629–1687* (New York: United States Catholic Historical Society, 1955), 86–87, 104; Jack D. Forbes, *Apache, Navaho and Spaniard* (Norman: University of Oklahoma Press, 1960), 140–42; Charles W. Polzer, "The Franciscan Entrada into Sonora, 1645–1652: A Jesuit Chronicle," *Arizona and the West* 14(3) (1972):253–77.

17. Herbert Eugene Bolton, *Spanish Exploration in the Southwest, 1542–1706* (New York: Barnes and Noble, 1967; reprint of 1908 ed.), 453.

18. Bannon 1955, 87, 103–5; Forbes 1960, 141–42, 159, 162; William B. Griffen, *Indian Assimilation in the Franciscan Area of Nueva Vizcaya,* Anthropological Papers of the University of Arizona, no. 33 (Tucson; University of Arizona Press, 1979), 35; Juan Nentvig, *Rudo Ensayo: A Description of Sonora and Arizona in 1764* (Tucson; University of Arizona Press, 1980), 103–4.

19. Hammond and Rey 1940, 252.

20. Rex E. Gerald, "The Suma Indians of Northern Chihuahua and Western Texas," in *Apache Indians III,* David A. Horr, ed. (New York: Garland Publishing, 1974), 69–114; Thomas H. Naylor and Charles W. Polzer, eds., *The Presidio and Militia on the Northern Frontier of New Spain,* vol. 1 (Tucson: University of Arizona Press, 1986), 594.

21. Luis Navarro García, *Sonora y Sinaloa en el siglo XVII* (Sevilla: Escuela de Estudios Hispano-Americanos, 1967), 265–71, 278.

22. Forbes 1960, 190–94; France V. Scholes and H. P. Mera, *Some Aspects of the Jumano Problem,* Contributions to American Anthropology and History, no. 34 (Washington, D.C.: Carnegie Institution of Washington, 1940), 288–89; Jack D. Forbes, "The Appearance of the Mounted Indian in Northern Mexico and the Southwest, to 1680," *Southwestern Journal of Anthropology* 15(2) (1959):202.

23. Manje 1954, 285–86.

24. Albert H. Schroeder, "Documentary Evidence Pertaining to the Early Historic Period of Southern Arizona," *New Mexico Historical Review* 27(2) (1952):141–44; Morris E. Opler, "The Apachean Culture Pattern and Its Origins," in *Handbook of North American Indians,* vol. 10, *Southwest,* Alfonso Ortiz, ed. (Washington, D.C.: Smithsonian Institution, 1983), 385.

25. Albert H. Schroeder, "A Study of the Apache Indians, Parts IV and V," in *Apache Indians IV,* David A. Horr, ed. (New York: Garland Publishing, 1974), 181–84; Kieran McCarty, *A Spanish Frontier in the Enlightened Age: Franciscan Beginnings in Sonora and Arizona, 1767–1770* (Washington, D.C.: Academy of American Franciscan History, 1981), 94–95.

26. Schroeder 1974, 37.

27. Charles W. Polzer, "Long Before the Blue Dragoons: Spanish Military Operations in Northern Sonora and Pimería Alta," in *Views on the Military History of the Indian-Spanish-American Southwest: 1598–1886,* Bruno J. Rolak, ed. (Fort Huachuca, Ariz.: 1976); Manje 1954, 1, 35, 46–47, 74; Forbes 1960, 207–11, 217–20; Griffen 1979, 20ff; Nentvig 1980, 124–25; Naylor and Polzer 1986, 575. Manje's repeated references (see also Burrus 1971) to the massacre of Pimas at Mototicachi were an evident confusion of that incident in 1688 with a similar one perpetrated by Lieutenant Antonio de Solís at the Ciénega del Tupo in June of 1695. See Manje 1954, 62–63; Nentvig 1980, 127; Naylor and Polzer 1986, 584, 622–23; Herbert Eugene Bolton, ed., *Kino's Historical Memoir of Pimería Alta,* vol. 1 (Cleveland: Arthur H. Clark, 1919), 142.

28. Governor Vargas sent the campaign records to Mexico City in January 1692, but these have apparently not survived. The following are published references to

this campaign: Forbes 1960, 230–31; Polzer 1976, 14–15; J. Manuel Espinosa, *Crusaders of the Rio Grande* (Chicago: Institute of Jesuit History, 1942), 37–40; Guillermo Porras Muñoz, *La frontera con los indios de Nueva Vizcaya en el siglo XVII* (Mexico City: Fomento Cultural Banamex, 1980), 328–29.

29. Manje 1954, 79, 247; Forbes 1960, 244–45; Polzer 1976, 15.

30. Manje 1954, 6, 35, 47–50, 63–71, 96–98; 174–175, 247; Forbes 1960, 231ff; Bolton 1967, 451; Schroeder 1974, 30–35; Griffen 1979, 20ff; Charles Wilson Hackett, *Historical Documents Relating to New Mexico, Nueva Vizcaya, and Approaches thereto, to 1773,* vol. 2 (Washington, D.C.: Carnegie Institution of Washington, 1926), 291–97, 315–17, 353–55, 377–81, 419–25; Jack D. Forbes, "The Janos, Jocomes, Mansos and Sumas Indians," *New Mexico Historical Review* 32(4) (1957):319–34.

31. Manje 1954, 47, 247, 285; Burrus 1971, 315, 351, 654; Naylor and Polzer 1986, 492, 585.

32. Schroeder 1952, 142–43; Forbes 1957; Gerald 1974, 70–71; Griffen 1979, 22, 29, 33–35; Naylor and Polzer 1986, 610.

33. Bolton 1919, 1:145–46; Griffen 1979, 22; Naylor and Polzer 1986, 583–96.

34. Manje 1954, 66–67; Naylor and Polzer 1986, 640–56.

35. Bolton 1919, 1:119–20, map; Fay Jackson Smith, John L. Kessell, and Francis J. Fox, *Father Kino in Arizona* (Phoenix: Arizona Historical Foundation, 1966), 58–63.

36. Bolton 1919, 1:119–23, 127; Manje 1954, 47; Smith et al. 1966, 57–64.

37. Bolton 1919, 1:164–71; Manje 1954, 74–83; Smith et al. 1966; Burrus 1971.

38. Father Kino said that the enemies were Jocomes and Janos; Manje claimed they were Apaches (Burrus 1971, 336) or Jocomes (Burrus 1971, 361), while Lieutenant Martín called them Jocomes and Sumas. In any event the Lieutenant and some of his soldiers joined in the Sobaipuris' scalp dance! Bolton 1919, 1:164–69; Smith et al. 1966, 35; Burrus 1971, 336–37, 361.

39. Bolton 1919, 1:178–83; Manje 1954, 97–98; Smith et al. 1966, 47–50.

40. Bolton 1919, 1:204–5, 207, 210–211, 233, 236, 2:27, 182; Smith et al. 1966, 13–14, 79–80, 83, 91.

41. Bolton 1919, 1:235–36; Smith et al. 1966, 90–95; George P. Hammond, "Pimería Alta after Kino's Time," *New Mexico Historical Review 4(3) (1929):221–22;* Ignaz Pfefferkorn, *Sonora, a Description of the Province* (Albuquerque: University of New Mexico Press, 1949), 256–57; Bernard L. Fontana, *Biography of a Desert Church: The Story of Mission San Xavier del Bac, The Smoke Signal,* no. 3 (Tucson: The Westerners, Tucson Corral, 1963); John Augustine Donohue, *After Kino: Jesuit Missions in Northwestern New Spain, 1711–1767* (Rome: Jesuit Historical Institute, 1969), 256–57.

42. Hammond 1929, 223–35; Nentvig 1980, 125; Hubert Howe Bancroft, *North Mexican States,* vol. 1, 1531–1800 (vol. 10 of his *History of The Pacific States of North America*) (San Francisco: A. L. Bancroft and Company, 1883), 523–25; Alfred B. Thomas, *Forgotten Frontiers* (Norman: University of Oklahoma Press, 1932), 204; Alfred B. Thomas, *Teodoro de Croix and the Northern Frontier of New Spain, 1776–1783* (Norman: University of Oklahoma Press, 1941), 203; Henry F. Dobyns, *From Fire to Flood: Historic Human Destruction of Sonoran Riverine Oases* (Socorro, N.M.: Ballena Press, 1981), 68.

43. John L. Kessell, *Mission of Sorrows: Jesuit Guevavi and the Pimas, 1691–1767* (Tucson: University of Arizona Press), 1970, 145–46.

44. Donohue 1969, 154; Kessell 1970, 161–62; Nentvig 1980, 73; Henry F. Dobyns, *Pioneering Christians among the Perishing Indians of Tucson* (Lima, Peru: Editorial Estudios Andinos, 1962), 12–14; John L. Kessell, ed., "San José de Tumacácori—1773," *Arizona and the West* 6(4) (1964):303–12; Henry F. Dobyns, *Spanish Colonial Tucson* (Tucson: University of Arizona Press, 1976), 19–21; John L. Kessell, *Friars, Soldiers, and Reformers: Hispanic Arizona and the Sonora Mission Frontier 1767–1856* (Tucson: University of Arizona Press, 1976), 88.

45. Donohue 1969, 156.

46. Kessell 1970, 51–52, 60, 74; Nentvig 1980, 81–82; Donald Rowland, "The Sonora Frontier of New Spain, 1735–1745," in *New Spain and the Anglo-American West* (New York: Kraus Reprint, 1969; reprint of 1932 ed.), 159–60; Theodore E. Treutlein, trans., "Document: The Relation of Philipp Segesser," *Mid-America* 27(3) (1945):153; Daniel S. Matson and Albert H. Schroeder, ed., "Cordero's Description of the Apache—1796," *New Mexico Historical Review* 32(4) (1957):350–52; Lawrence Kinnaird, *The Frontiers of New Spain: Nicolás de Lafora's Description, 1766–1768* (Berkeley: Quivira Society, 1958), 106, 127–28; Kieran McCarty, *Desert Documentary* (Tucson: Arizona Historical Society, Historical Monograph no. 4, 1976), 33, 86.

47. Thomas 1932, 5; Rowland 1969; Kessell 1970, 51; Nentvig 1980, 82, 106, 123–28.

48. Treutlein 1945, 149, 164; Kessell 1970, 57, 110; McCarty 1976, 13–14.

49. Manje 1954, 93; Nentvig 180; Rufus Kay Wyllys, ed., "Padre Luis Velarde's *Relación* of Pimería Alta, 1716," *New Mexico Historical Review* 6(2) (1931):127; Peter Masten Dunne, *Jacobo Sedelmayr: Missionary, Frontiersman, Explorer in Arizona and Sonora; Four Original Manuscript Narratives, 1744–1751* (Tucson: Arizona Pioneers' Historical Society, 1955), 37; Alan Probert, "Bartolomé de Medina: The Patio Process and the Sixteenth Century Silver Crisis," *Journal of the West* 8(1) (1969):90–124.

50. Dunne 1955, 37.

51. Treutlein 1945, 184.

52. Pfefferkorn 1949, 241–42.

53. Nentvig 1980, 55–56, 118.

54. Donohue 1969, 83.

55. Winship 1896, 533.

56. McCarty 1976, 32–33; Eldred D. Wilson, *Gold Placers and Placering in Arizona*, Bulletin 168 (Tucson: Bureau of Geology and Mineral Technology, Geological Survey Branch, 1981; reprint of 1961 ed.), 78–82.

57. Pfefferkorn 1949, 90.

58. Bancroft 1883, 525–28; Hammond 1929, 237–38; Treutlein 1945, 183–84; Pfefferkorn 1949, 89–90; Dunne 1955, 37–38; Donohue 1969, 69–70, 80–83; Nentvig 1980, 100. See especially Patricia Roche Herring, "The Silver of El Real de Arizonac," *Arizona and the West* 20(3) (1978):245–58, and Charles W. Polzer, *Legends of Lost Missions and Mines, The Smoke Signal*, no. 18 (Tucson: Tucson Corral of the Westerners, 1968), 177–80.

59. Dunne 1955, 38; Polzer 1968; Carol Clarke, "The Longoreña", *Arizoniana* 2(2) (1961):31–34; Duane Kendall Hale, "Mineral Exploration in the Spanish Borderlands, 1513–1846," in *Mining in the West,* Alan Probert, ed. (Manhattan, Kans.: Sunflower University Press, 1981), 12–13. The reader should be aware that Hale's references do not always support his assertions.

60. Nentvig 1980, 99.

61. Nentvig 1980, 107, 126.

62. McCarty 1976, 33.

63. Kinnaird 1958, 107.

64. *Arizona Daily Star,* October 21, 1879, p. 3, December 2, 1879, p. 3.

65. Clarke 1961; Kessell 1970, 74, 106; Nentvig 1980, 99, 107, 126; Herbert Eugene Bolton, *Anza's California Expeditions,* vol. 2 (Berkeley: University of California Press, 1930), 4–5, 138–39.

66. Bolton 1930, 138.

67. Bolton 1930, 5.

68. Thomas 1941, 172, 207; Kinnaird 1958, 109–10.

69. Bolton 1930, 4–5, 138–39; Kinnaird 1958, 110; McCarty 1976, 32.

70. Clarke 1961, 33.

71. Thomas 1941, 172; Kinnaird 1958, 109–10, 128; Clarke 1961; J. Ross Browne, *Adventures in the Apache Country* (Tucson: University of Arizona Press, 1974; reprint of 1950 ed.), 271; William A. Duffen, ed., "Overland Via 'Jackass Mail' in 1858: The Diary of Phocion R. Way," *Arizona and the West* 2(3) (1960):284–85; Diane M. T. North, *Samuel Peter Heintzelman and the Sonora Exploring and Mining Company* (Tucson: University of Arizona Press, 1980), 125, 147–48, 154, 157.

72. Otis E. Young, Jr., *How They Dug the Gold* (Tucson: Arizona Pioneers' Historical Society, 1967), 26–28; Paige W. Christiansen, *The Story of Mining in New Mexico, Scenic Trips to the Geologic Past,* no. 12 (Socorro: New Mexico Bureau of Mines and Mineral Resources, 1974), 91–93.

73. Bolton 1930, 141.

74. William P. Blake, "Sketch of Pima Co., Ariz., Mining Districts, Minerals, Climate and Agriculture", *Arizona Daily Star,* June 26, 1910, 1st section, p. 6. This long article was serialized in the *Star* beginning June 12, 1910, and continuing each Sunday into July of that year.

75. North 1980, 103–28. The best all-around account of eighteenth-century hardrock mining in Sonora was by Father Joseph Och, S.J.; see Theodore E. Treutlein, *Missionary in Sonora: The Travel Reports of Joseph Och, S.J., 1755–1767* (San Francisco: California Historical Society, 1965), 143–51. Father Pfefferkorn (1949, 91–93) described the placer workings. See also Young 1967, 35–38; and Christiansen 1974, 95.

76. Dunne 1955, 38; Kessell 1976, 195; North 1980, 101, 147–48, 157.

77. *Arizona Daily Star,* April 23, 1910, p. 7.

78. Raphael Pumpelly, *My Reminiscences,* vol. 1 (New York: Henry Holt and Company, 1918), 197–99.

79. Robert H. Jackson, "The Last Jesuit Censuses of the Pimería Alta Missions, 1761 and 1766," *The Kiva* 46(4) (1981):246–47.

80. Young 1967, 36–38.

81. North 1980, 57–58, 74, 134, 140–41, 157.

82. Browne 1974, 208; Frank C. Schrader, *Mineral Deposits of the Santa Rita and Patagonia Mountains, Arizona,* U.S. Geological Survey, Bulletin 582 (Washington, D.C.: U.S. Government Printing Office, 1915), 22–23.

83. Treutlein 1945, 142, 164; Kessell 1970, 51, 53, 57–58, 60.

84. Treutlein 1945, 165ff; Donohue 1969, 84–86.

85. Kessell 1970, 102–6, 115–17; Nentvig 1980, 100–101; Russell Charles Ewing, "The Pima Uprising of 1751: A Study of Spanish-Indian Relations on the Frontier of New Spain," in *Greater America: Essays in Honor of Herbert Eugene Bolton* (Berkeley: University of California Press, 1945); Peter Masten Dunne, *Juan Antonio Balthasar: Padre Visitador to the Sonora Frontier, 1744–1745* (Tucson: Arizona Pioneers' Historical Society, 1957), 46–48.

86. Ewing 1945, 264; Kessell 1970, 106; Nentvig 1980, 73, 99, 107.

87. Kessell 1970, 106–8, 136–37, 144.

88. Ewing 1945, 271.

89. Bolton 1930, 5; Ewing 1945; Donohue 1969, 132; Kessell 1970, 107–9; Nentvig 1980, 73.

90. Ewing 1945, 277–79; Donohue 1969, 133–35; Kessell 1970, 110–23, 134–36.

91. Kessell 1970, 135–36, 140–47; Dobyns 1976, 16–17, 186–87.

92. Kessell 1970, 141–42; Arthur D. Gardiner, "Letter of Father Middendorff, S.J., Dated from Tucson 3 March 1757," *The Kiva* 22(4) (1957):5–7.

93. Kessell 1970, 142–47, 154–56.

94. Kessell 1976, 160–63.

95. Rowland 1932; Kinnaird 1958, 14; Forbes 1960, 208; Smith et al. 1966, 86; Donohue 1969, 24–30, 50–52, 56; Kessell 1970, 33, 38; Polzer 1976, Nentvig 1980, 81, 124–25; Max L. Moorhead, *The Presidio: Bastion of the Spanish Borderlands* (Norman: University of Oklahoma Press, 1975), 21–23.

96. Thomas 1941, 197–99; Rex E. Gerald, *Spanish Presidios of the Late Eighteenth Century in Northern New Spain,* Museum of New Mexico Research Records, no. 7 (Santa Fe: Museum of New Mexico Press, 1968), 21.

97. Rowland 1932; Donohue 1969, 75–76, 108–9; Kessell 1970, 76–78, 90; Moorhead 1975, 51; Nentvig 1980, 81, 126; John L. Kessell, "The Puzzling Presidio: San Phelipe de Guevavi, Alias Terrenate," *New Mexico Historical Review* 41(1) (1966):21–46.

98. Nentvig 1980, 126.

99. Kinnaird 1958, 106–7.

100. Kessell 1976, 21; McCarty 1981, 86.

101. Thomas 1941, 31–32, 151, 201, 204; Sidney B. Brinckerhoff and Odie B. Faulk, *Lancers for the King* (Phoenix: Arizona Historical Foundation, 1965), 93.

102. Thomas 1941, 144, 153–54, 204–5; McCarty 1976, 77–78; Jack Williams, "The Presidio of Santa Cruz de Terrenate: A Forgotten Fortress of Southern Arizona," *The Smoke Signal,* nos. 47–48 (Tucson: Tucson Corral of the Westerners, 1986), 129–48.

103. Thomas 1932, 209–10.

104. Thomas 1941, 150; Kessell 1966, 38–39; Deni J. Seymour, "The Dynamics of Sobaipuri Settlement in the Eastern Pimería Alta," *Journal of the Southwest* 31(2) (1989):205–21.

105. Donohue 1969, 133; Kessell 1970, 125–27, 1976, 38.

106. Kessell 1970, 51, 60, 74, 165–70.

107. Kessell 1976, 48–50; McCarty 1976, 12–14, 1981, 86–95. One of the soldiers captured at Redington Pass escaped five months later.

108. John L. Kessell, "Father Eixarch and the Visitation at Tumacácori, May 12, 1775," *The Kiva* 30(3) (1965):79; Kessell 1976, 56–57, 88.

109. Kessell 1976, 63, 78, 98–99, 110–11; McCarty 1976, 26; Henry F. Dobyns, *Lance, Ho! Containment of the Western Apaches by the Royal Spanish Garrison at Tucson* (Lima, Peru: Editorial Estudios Andinos, 1964), 5.

110. Kessell 1976, 137.

111. Kinnaird 1958, 127.

112. McCarty 1981, 85, 88; Hugo de O'Conor, *Informe de Hugo de O'Conor sobre el estado de las provincias internas del norte* (Mexico City: Editorial Cultura, 1952), 77; William B. Griffen, *Apaches at War and Peace: The Janos Presidio, 1750–1858* (Albuquerque: University of New Mexico, 1988), 29.

113. McCarty 1976, 6.

114. Kessell 1976, 50, 56, 61–62, 160, 162; Dobyns 1964, 1981, 15–26; Francisco Salas Bohorques, "Diario de las Novedades occurridas en la campaña . . . don Roque de Medina," Archivo General de la Nación, Provincias Internas, tomo 193, copy courtesy of the Bancroft Library, Berkeley, California; Carl Sauer, "A Spanish Expedition into the Arizona Apachería," *Arizona Historical Review* 6(1) (1935):3–13; John L. Kessell, ed., "Anza, Indian Fighter: The Spring Campaign of 1766," *The Journal of Arizona History* 9(3) (1968):155–63.

115. Dobyns 1964, 6–39, 1976, 63–91; McCarty 1976, 41–46; Kessell 1976, 162; Griffen 1988, 46–48.

116. Dobyns 1964, 39–42, 1976, 92–96.

117. Moorhead 1975, 260–61; Dobyns 1976, 97–98, 101; McCarty 1976, 61–63; William B. Griffen, "Apache Indians and the Northern Mexican Peace Establishments," in *Southwestern Culture History: Collected Papers in Honor of Albert H. Schroeder*, Charles H. Lange, ed. (Santa Fe: Papers of the Archaeological Society of New Mexico, 10, 1985), 183–95.

118. Moorhead 1975, 261–65; Dobyns 1976, 42–45, 99–104; Kessell 1976, 200–201, 203, 261; Griffen 1985a, 1988.

119. Brinckerhoff and Faulk 1965, 116–17; Dobyns 1976, 104; Griffen 1985a.

120. Kessell 1976, 300, 307–8, 315; U.S. War Department, Surgeon General's Office, *A Report on Barracks and Hospitals, with Descriptions of Military Posts* (Washington, D.C.: U.S. Government Printing Office, 1870), 464–65; Bernard L. Fontana, *Calabazas of the Rio Rico, The Smoke Signal*, no. 24 (Tucson: Tucson Corral of the Westerners, 1971), 79; James E. Officer, *Hispanic Arizona, 1536–1856* (Tucson: University of Arizona Press, 1987), 309–10, 328. See also L. R. Bailey, ed., *The A. B. Gray Report* (Los Angeles: Westernlore Press, 1963; republication of 1856 ed., 209–13.

121. Kessell 1976, 39.

122. Kessell 1976, 245–46; Dobyns 1962, 1976; Jackson 1981; Henry F. Dobyns, "Indian Extinction in the Middle Santa Cruz River Valley, Arizona," *New Mexico Historical Review* 38(2) (1963):161–81.

123. Kessell 1976, 245–46; James Rodney Hastings, "People of Reason and Others: The Colonization of Sonora to 1767," *Arizona and the West* 3(4) (1961):321–40.

Chapter 4

1. Sidney B. Brinckerhoff, "The Last Years of Spanish Arizona, 1786–1821," *Arizona and the West* 9(1) (1967):5–20; Kieran McCarty, *Desert Documentary* (Tucson: Arizona Historical Society, Historical Monograph no. 4, 1976), 32–33, 84, 87; John L. Kessell, *Friars, Soldiers, and Reformers: Hispanic Arizona and the Sonora Mission Frontier 1767–1856* (Tucson: University of Arizona Press, 1976), 247, 282, 294; Eldred D. Wilson, *Gold Placers and Placering in Arizona,* Bulletin 168 (Tucson: Bureau of Geology and Mineral Technology, Geological Survey Branch, 1981; reprint of 1961 ed.), 77.

2. Kessell 1976, 239, 284, 305–6; John L. Kessell, *Mission of Sorrows: Jesuit Guevavi and the Pimas, 1691–1767* (Tucson: University of Arizona Press, 1970), 106.

3. Kessell 1976, 306.

4. Rossiter W. Raymond, *Statistics of Mines and Mining in the States and Territories West of the Rocky Mountains; . . . Eighth Annual Report,* 44th Congress, 1st Session, House Exec. Doc. No. 159 (Washington, D.C.: U.S. Government Printing Office, 1877), 343.

5. Kessell 1976, 159, 174, 202; Bernard L. Fontana, *Biography of a Desert Church: The Story of Mission San Xavier del Bac, The Smoke Signal,* no. 3 (Tucson: Tucson Corral of the Westerners, 1963); Henry F. Dobyns, *Spanish Colonial Tucson* (Tucson: University of Arizona Press, 1976), 136–37.

6. Brinckerhoff 1967, 15–17; Dobyns 1976, 42, 47, 193–94. Jack Williams, *San Agustín del Tucson. The Smoke Signal,* nos. 47–48 (Tucson: Tucson Corral of the Westerners, 1986), 113–28.

7. Kessell 1976, 220, 222, 225, 232; Bernard L. Fontana, "Santa Ana de Cuiquiburitac: Pimería Alta's Northernmost Mission," *Journal of the Southwest* 29(2) (1987):133–59.

8. Kessell 1976, 202–3, 245–54, 269–71, 308; John L. Kessell, "Father Ramón and the Big Debt, Tumacácori, 1821–1823," *New Mexico Historical Review* 44(1) (1969):53–72.

9. Brinckerhoff 1967, 15; McCarty 1976, 85, 90.

10. Ignaz Pfefferkorn, *Sonora, a Description of the Province* (Albuquerque: University of New Mexico Press, 1949), 98–102; Sandra L. Myres, *The Ranch in Spanish Texas, 1691–1800,* Social Science Series no. 2 (El Paso: Texas Western Press, 1969).

11. Ray H. Mattison, "Early Spanish and Mexican Settlements in Arizona," *New*

Mexico Historical Review 21(4) (1946):286–88; Jay J. Wagoner, *Early Arizona: Prehistory to Civil War* (Tucson: University of Arizona Press, 1975), 159–67.

12. Brinckerhoff 1967, 16; Wagoner 1975, 161, 197–98.

13. Mattison 1946, 306–9; Wagoner 1975, 210–14.

14. Wagoner 1975, 177–84; James E. Officer, *Hispanic Arizona, 1536–1856* (Tucson: University of Arizona Press, 1987), 108, 171.

15. Wagoner 1975, 200–208.

16. Mattison 1946, 298–300; Kessell 1970, 144; Wagoner 1975, 185–88.

17. William B. Griffen, "Apache Indians and the Northern Mexican Peace Establishments," in *Southwestern Culture History: Collected Papers in Honor of Albert H. Schroeder*, Charles H. Lange, ed. (Santa Fe: Papers of the Archaeological Society of New Mexico, 10, 1985a), 189.

18. Wagoner 1975, 217–18; John Russell Bartlett, *Personal Narrative of Explorations and Incidents, . . .* vol. 1 (Chicago: Rio Grande Press, 1965; reprint of 1854 ed., 393, 396–97; L. R. Bailey, ed., *The A. B. Gray Report* (Los Angeles: Westernlore Press, 1963; republication of 1856 ed., 77; Ralph P. Bieber, ed., *Exploring Southwestern Trails, 1846–1854* (Philadelphia: Porcupine Press, 1974; reprint of 1938 ed., 129, 132–33, 143–44; Frank Cullen Brophy, "San Ignacio del Babacomari," *Arizona Highways* 42(9) (1966):2–17.

19. Mattison 1946, 285, 289; Wagoner 1975, 159–61; Hubert Howe Bancroft, *History of Arizona and New Mexico, 1530–1888* (vol. 15 of his *Works*) (San Francisco: History Company, 1889), 750–51; "Report of the Governor of Arizona [1896]," *Report of the Secretary of the Interior* . . . vol. 3, 54th Congress, 2nd Session, House Doc. no. 5 (Washington, D.C.: U.S. Government Printing Office, 1896), 223.

20. "Report of the Governor of Arizona [1896]," 222–23.

21. Mattison 1946, 315–17; Wagoner 1975, 229–32; Officer 1987, 15, 89, 148, 366–67.

22. "Journal of Captain A. R. Johnston, First Dragoons," in W. H. Emory, *Notes of a Military Reconnoissance, from Fort Leavenworth, in Missouri, to San Diego, in California*, 30th Cong., 1st Sess., House Exec. Doc. no. 41 (Washington, D.C.: Wendell and Van Benthuysen, Printers, 1848), 586.

23. Lawrence Kinnaird, *The Frontiers of New Spain: Nicolás de Lafora's Description, 1766–1768* (Berkeley: Quivira Society, 1958), 127; Ralph A. Smith, "Apache Plunder Trails Southward, 1831–1840," *New Mexico Historical Review* 37(1) (1962a):20–42; Ralph A. Smith, "The Scalp Hunter in the Borderlands, 1835–1850," *Arizona and the West* 6(1) (1964):5–22; Dwight L. Clarke, ed., *The Original Journals of Henry Smith Turner: With Stephen Watts Kearny to New Mexico and California 1846–1847* (Norman: University of Oklahoma Press, 1966), 95–102.

24. Smith 1964; Bartlett 1965, 266; Kessell 1976, 282–88, 297–303, 308–14; Griffen 1985a, 191–92; Samuel E. Chamberlain, *My Confession* (Tucson: Arizona Silhouettes, 1956), 259–90; Ray Brandes and Ralph A. Smith, *The Scalp Business on the Border, 1837–1850, The Smoke Signal*, no. 6 (Tucson: Tucson Corral of the Westerners, 1962); Bernard L. Fontana, *Calabazas of the Rio Rico, The Smoke Signal*, no. 24 (Tucson: Tucson Corral of the Westerners, 1971).

25. Bailey 1963, 211; Kessell 1976, 284–86, 313; Officer 1987, 124–25, 169–71,

190–91, 206–7. Officer gives details on many campaigns in the 1830s and 1840s.

26. Kessell 1976, 305; Officer 1987, 209.

Chapter 5

1. James O. Pattie, *The Personal Narrative of James O. Pattie* (Lincoln: University of Nebraska Press, 1984; republication of 1831 ed.; Thomas Maitland Marshall, "St. Vrain's Expedition to the Gila in 1826," *The Southwestern Historical Quarterly* 19(3) (1916):251–60; David J. Weber, *The Taos Trappers: The Fur Trade in the Far Southwest, 1540–1846* (Norman: University of Oklahoma Press, 1971), 112–33; John L. Kessell, *Friars, Soldiers, and Reformers: Hispanic Arizona and the Sonora Mission Frontier 1767–1856* (Tucson: University of Arizona Press, 1976), 268–304.

2. W. H. Emory, *Notes of a Military Reconnoissance, from Fort Leavenworth, in Missouri, to San Diego, in California,* 30th Cong., 1st Sess., House Exec. Doc. no. 41 (Washington, D.C.: Wendell and Van Benthuysen, Printers, 1848); "Journal of Captain A. R. Johnston, First Dragoons," in Emory 1848; George Walcott Ames, Jr., ed., "A Doctor Comes to California," *California Historical Society Quarterly* 21(3) (1942):193–224; Dwight L. Clarke, ed., *The Original Journals of Henry Smith Turner: With Stephen Watts Kearny to New Mexico and California 1846–1847* (Norman: University of Oklahoma Press, 1966); Jay J. Wagoner, *Early Arizona: Prehistory to Civil War* (Tucson: University of Arizona Press, 1975), 260–67.

3. Ralph P. Bieber, ed., *Exploring Southwestern Trails, 1846–1854* (Philadelphia: Porcupine Press, 1974; reprint of 1938 ed.); Charles S. Peterson et al., *Mormon Battalion Trail Guide,* Western Trail Guide Series no. 1 (Salt Lake City: Utah State Historical Society, 1972); James E. Officer, *Hispanic Arizona, 1536–1856* (Tucson: University of Arizona Press, 1987), 194–202.

4. Wagoner 1975, 273–76; Officer 1987, 210–14; Samuel E. Chamberlain, *My Confession* (Tucson: Arizona Silhouettes, 1956), 257–60; Henry F. Dobyns, ed., *Hepah, California! The Journal of Cave Johnson Couts from Monterey, Nuevo Leon, Mexico to Los Angeles, California During the Years 1848–1849* (Tucson: Arizona Pioneers' Historical Society, 1961).

5. John Russell Bartlett, *Personal Narrative of Explorations and Incidents, . . .* (Chicago: Rio Grande Press, 1965; reprint of 1854 ed.) 2:309.

6. Kenneth Hufford, "Travelers on the Gila Trail, 1824–1850, Part 2: An Annotated Bibliography," *Journal of Arizona History* 8(1) (1967):30–44.

7. George P. Hammond and Edward H. Howes, eds., *Overland to California on the Southwestern Trail, 1849* (Berkeley: University of California Press, 1950); Officer (1987, 122) says that an American party came this way as early as 1831, however.

8. Wagoner 1975, 281–88; Bartlett 1965; Edward S. Wallace, *The Great Reconnaissance* (Boston: Little, Brown and Company, 1955), 23–92; William H. Goetzmann, *Army Exploration in the American West, 1803–1863* (New Haven: Yale University Press, 1959), 153–86; Robert V. Hine, *Bartlett's West: Drawing the Mexican Boundary* (New Haven: Yale University Press, 1968).

9. Wallace 1955, 93–100; Goetzmann 1959, 195–206; Wagoner 1975, 288–97; Bernard L. Fontana, *Calabazas of the Rio Rico, The Smoke Signal,* no. 24 (Tucson: Tucson Corral of the Westerners, 1971), 80; Charles R. Ames, "Along the Mexican Border—Then and Now," *Journal of Arizona History* 18(4) (1977):431–46.

10. Goetzmann 1959, 289–91; Wagoner 1975, 323–25; John G. Parke, "Report of Explorations . . . in *Reports of Explorations and Surveys,* . . . vol. 2, 33d Cong., 2d Sess., Senate Exec. Doc. No. 78 (Washington, D.C.: Beverley Tucker, Printer, 1855), 1–15; "Report of Explorations from Pimas Villages to Rio Grande," in *Reports of Explorations and Surveys,* . . . vol. 7, part I, no. 2, 33d Cong., 2d Sess., Senate Exec. Doc. No. 78 (Washington, D.C.: Beverley Tucker, Printer, 1857), 19–28.

11. Wagoner 1975, 325–28; L. R. Bailey, ed., *The A. B. Gray Report* (Los Angeles: Westernlore Press, 1963; republication of 1856 ed.).

12. William A. Bell, *New Tracks in North America* (Albuquerque: Horn and Wallace, 1965; reprint of 1870 ed., 277–341. A map accompanying the report of surveys of the Kansas Pacific Railway Co. is reproduced in *Arizoniana* 3(4) 1962: between pp. 27 and 28.

13. *Daily Alta California,* November 4, 1858, p. 1; Albert H. Campbell, *Report upon the Pacific Wagon Roads* (Fairfield, Wash. Ye Galleon Press, 1969; reprint of 1859 ed.); W. Turrentine Jackson, *Wagon Roads West* (New Haven: Yale University Press, 1965), 218–32. Wayne R. Austerman, *Sharps Rifles and Spanish Mules* (College Station: Texas A&M University Press, 1985), 127–31.

14. William A. Duffen, ed., "Overland Via 'Jackass Mail' in 1858: The Diary of Phocion R. Way," parts 1–4, *Arizona and the West* 2(1–4) (1960).

15. "Overland Mail Route between San Antonio, Texas, and San Diego, California," *Texas Almanac for 1859* (Galveston, TX: 1859). Captain William Banning and George Hugh Banning, *Six Horses* (New York: Century, 1930); Roscoe P. Conkling and Margaret B. Conkling, *The Butterfield Overland Mail, 1857–1869,* (Glendale, Cal.: Arthur H. Clark, 1947) 2:373.

16. Duffen 1960, 159, 161.

17. Banning and Banning 1930; Conkling and Conkling 1947, 2:373, 3:92–97; Austerman 1985; *The Washington Union,* October 17, 1857, p. 3; Yndia Moore, comp., *The Butterfield Overland Mail across Arizona* (Tucson: Arizona Pioneers' Historical Society, 1958?); Dorman H. Winfrey, "The Butterfield Overland Mail Trail," in *Along the Early Trails of the Southwest,* Wayne Gard et al., contrib. (Austin: Pemberton Press, 1969); Constance Wynn Altshuler, ed., *Latest from Arizona!* (Tucson: Arizona Pioneers' Historical Society, 1969), 211; Robert H. Thonhoff, *San Antonio Stage Lines, 1847–1881,* Southwestern Studies, monograph no. 29 (El Paso: Texas Western Press, 1971).

18. The Butterfield Overland Mail is the subject of a vast literature. For general accounts and travelers' narratives, see the following: Conkling and Conkling 1947, vols. 1–3; Winfrey 1969; Walter B. Lang, ed., *The First Overland Mail—Butterfield Trail* (N.p.: privately printed, 1940); Lyle H. Wright and Josephine M. Bynum, eds., *The Butterfield Overland Mail* (San Marino, Cal.: Huntington Library, 1962).

19. *The Mesilla Times,* October 18, 1860, p. 2; October 25, 1860, p. 3; November 1, 1860, p.4.

20. San Francisco *Daily Evening Bulletin,* November 27, 1858.

21. Moore 1958, 30–31. For additional details see the following: Banning and Banning 1930, 138–143; Conkling and Conkling 1947, 2:140–48; Wright and Bynum 1962, 40–41, 84.

22. Conkling and Conkling 1947, 1:131–37. Winfrey 1969.

23. Lang 1940, 119; Altshuler 1969, 28, 212.

24. Altshuler 1969, 213; Winfrey 1969, 40–41; *The Mesilla Times,* June 8. 1861, p. 2.

25. *The Mesilla Times,* May 11, 1861, p. 2.

26. Winfrey 1969, 41; Austerman 1985, 168–71; *The Mesilla Times,* May 17, 1861, p. 2, June 8, 1861, p. 2; *Los Angeles Star,* June 15, 1862, p. 2; *Arizona Weekly Star,* July 24, 1879, p. 4; U.S. Geological Survey, *San Simon, Ariz.–N. Mex.* 15' topo map (1950).

27. Altshuler 1969, 212; San Francisco *Daily Evening Bulletin,* November 19, 1858.

28. *Los Angeles Star,* May 21, 1859, p. 2.

29. Robert H. Forbes, *The Penningtons, Pioneers of Early Arizona* (Tucson: Arizona Archaeological and Historical Society, 1919), 23.

30. Fontana 1971; Ray Brandes, *Frontier Military Posts of Arizona* (Globe, Ariz.: Dale Stuart King, 1960), 21–22; James E. Serven, *The Military Posts on Sonoita Creek, The Smoke Signal,* no. 12 (Tucson: Tucson Corral of the Westerners, 1965), 27; B. Sacks, "The Origins of Fort Buchanan, Myth and Fact," *Arizona and the West* 7(3) (1965):207–26; Constance Wynn Altshuler, *Starting With Defiance* (Tucson: Arizona Historical Society, 1983), 47–48.

31. *Los Angeles Star,* September 4, 1858, p. 2.

32. Richard H. Coolidge, *Statistical Report on the Sickness and Mortality in the Army of the United States* (Washington, D.C.: George W. Bowman, Printer, 1860), 211.

33. Coolidge 1860, 210–11, 219; Brandes 1960, 22; Sacks 1965; "Affairs in Department of New Mexico," in *Report of the Secretary of War* (1859), 36th Cong., 1st Sess., Senate Exec. Doc. No. 2, vol. 2, pt. 2 (serial no. 1024) (Washington, D.C.: George W. Bowman, Printer, 1860), 299–310.

34. *Report of the Secretary of War* (1857), 35th Cong., 1st Sess., Senate Exec. Doc. No. 11, vol. 2 (serial no. 920) (Washington, D.C.: William A. Harris, 1858), 136–41; Percy Gatling Hamlin, ed., *The Making of a Soldier: Letters of General R. S. Ewell* (Richmond, Va.: Whittet and Shepperson, 1935), 82–83; George P. Hammond, ed., *Campaigns in the West, 1856–1861* (Tucson: Arizona Pioneers' Historical Society, 1949), 28–31; Robert M. Utley, *Frontiersmen in Blue* (New York: Macmillan, 1967), 155–57.

35. George W. Webb, *Chronological List of Engagements . . .* (St. Joseph, Mo.: Wing Printing and Publishing, 1939), 17.

36. Capt. R. S. Ewell, Chiricahua Mts., to A. A. A. G. Santa Fe, January 26, 1859, National Archives (NA), Microcopy M1120, Roll 9, File No. [NM-1859] E4; Ibid, Fort Buchanan, to A. A. A. G. Santa Fe, February 2, 1859, NA, Microcopy M1120, Roll 9, File No. [NM-1859] E5; M. Steck, Apache Pass, to Supt. Ind. Affairs, January

25, 1859, NA, Microcopy T-21, Roll 4; St. Louis *Daily Missouri Republican,* February 22, 1859, p. 2, March 10, 1859, p. 2; *The Weekly Arizonian,* March 3, 1859, p. 3.

37. Webb 1939, 20; Utley 1967, 159–60; *Daily Alta California,* January 11, 1860, p. 1.

38. Forbes 1919; Altshuler 1969, 64–67; *Daily Alta California,* April 6, 1860, p. 1; Capt. R. S. Ewell, Fort Buchanan, to A. A. A. G. Santa Fe, April 10, 1860, NA, Microcopy M1120, Roll 11, File No. E-14. Mrs. Page's own contemporary account, in a letter from "Hesperian," appeared in the St. Louis *Missouri Republican,* May 8, 1860, and the *Oquawka* (Ill.) *Spectator,* May 17, 1860; see also Virginia Culin Roberts, *With Their Own Blood* (Fort Worth: Texas Christian University Press, 1992).

39. *The San Francisco Herald,* December 27, 1860, p. 3, January 1, 1861, p. 3, January 28, 1861, p. 3, February 25, 1861, p. 1; Albert H.Schroeder, "A Study of the Apache Indians, Parts IV and V," in *Apache Indians IV,* David A. Horr, ed. (New York: Garland Publishing, 1974), 472, 479; Dan L. Thrapp, *Victorio and the Mimbres Apaches* (Norman: University of Oklahoma Press, 1974), 65–74.

40. Utley 1962, 10–17; Altshuler 1969, 171–78, 220–27; Raymond A. Mulligan, "Sixteen Days in Apache Pass," *The Kiva* 24(2) (1958):1–13; Benjamin H. Sacks, ed., "New Evidence on the Bascom Affair," *Arizona and the West* 4(3) (1962):261–78.

41. Brandes 1960, 23; Constance Wynn Altshuler, "Arizona in 1861: A Contemporary Account by Samuel Robinson," *Journal of Arizona History* 25(1) (1984):52; Edwin R. Sweeney, *Cochise, Chiricahua Apache Chief* (Norman: University of Oklahoma Press, 1991), 176; *Los Angeles Star,* July 20, 1861, p. 2; *San Francisco Herald,* September 21, 1861, p. 2.

42. Serven 1965, 37–38; *War of the Rebellion: A Compilation of the Official Records of the Union and Confederate Armies* (hereafter cited as *War of the Rebellion*), Series I, vol. 4 (Washington, D.C.: U.S. Government Printing Office, 1882), 49; John P. Wilson, "Retreat to the Rio Grande: The Report of Captain Isaiah N. Moore," *Rio Grande History* 2(3–4) (1975): 4–8.

43. Altshuler 1984, 55–57; Raphael Pumpelly, *My Reminiscences,* vol. 1 (New York: Henry Holt and Company, 1918), 239–42; Joseph F. Park, "The Apaches in Mexican-American Relations, 1848–1861," *Arizona and the West* (3(2) (1961):144; Richard R. Willey, *La Canoa: A Spanish Land Grant Lost and Found, The Smoke Signal,* no. 38 (Tucson: Tucson Corral of the Westerners, 1979), 165–66. For a definitive account see *San Francisco Herald,* September 21, 1861, p. 2.

44. Altshuler 1984, 64–65.

45. *Daily Alta California,* September 2, 1861, p. 1.

46. (Los Angeles) *Semi-Weekly Southern News,* August 30, 1861, p. 2, September 6, 1861, p. 2; *Daily Alta California,* September 2, 1861, p. 1; *Los Angeles Star,* September 7, 1861, p. 2.

47. Austerman 1985, 181–82, 188; *Daily Alta California,* September 29, 1861, p. 1, December 17, 1861, p. 1; Boyd Finch, "Sherod Hunter and the Confederates in Arizona," *Journal of Arizona History* 10(3) (1969):154–55.

48. Finch 1969, 141, 160–63.

49. Finch 1969, 166–69, 202–3; Martin Hardwick Hall, *Sibley's New Mexico Campaign* (Austin: University of Texas Press, 1960), 53.

50. Finch 1969, 173–78.

51. Finch 1969; *Daily Alta California,* July 10, 1862, p. 1; Ray C. Colton, *The Civil War in the Western Territories* (Norman: University of Oklahoma Press, 1959), 100–106.

52. Finch 1969, 190; (Los Angeles) *Semi-Weekly Southern News,* June 4, 1862, p. 3; *Daily Alta California,* June 11, 1862, p. 1.

53. *Daily Alta California,* August 10, 1862, p. 1.

54. *Daily Alta California,* August 10, 1862, p. 1, August 16, 1862, p. 1; *War of the Rebellion,* Series I, vol. 9 (Washington, D.C.: U.S. Government Printing Office, 1883), 586–87.

55. Colton 1959, 114–15; *Daily Alta California,* August 16, 1862, p. 1; *War of the Rebellion,* Series I, vol. 50, pt. 1 (Washington, D.C.: U.S. Government Printing Office, 1897), 128–32.

56. Colton 1959, 108–10; Wagoner 1975, 456–60, 464–68; Constance Wynn Altshuler, "The Case of Sylvester Mowry: The Charge of Treason," *Arizona and the West* 15(1) (1973a):63–82; Altshuler, "The Case of Sylvester Mowry: The Mowry Mine", *Arizona and the West* 15(2) (1973b):149–74.

57. J. Ross Browne, *Adventures in the Apache Country* (Tucson: University of Arizona Press, 1974; reprint of 1950 ed.), 203–10.

58. *Washington Union,* September 16, 1857, p. 3; (San Francisco) *Daily Evening Bulletin,* November 19, 1858.

59. (Corpus Christi, Texas) *Ranchero* , November 3, 1860, p. 2.

60. Wagoner 1975, 446, 470, 479.

61. Jay J. Wagoner, *Arizona Territory 1863–1912: A Political History* (Tucson: University of Arizona Press, 1970), 33–38.

62. Wagoner 1970, x.

63. Utley 1967, 20–21; Robert W. Frazer, *Forts and Supplies* (Albuquerque: University of New Mexico Press, 1983), 190–91; and Darlis A. Miller, *Soldiers and Settlers* (Albuquerque: University of New Mexico Press, 1989), 352–55, both document the financial importance of the army to the economies of Arizona and New Mexico in the nineteenth century. Federal money is no less important today.

Chapter 6

1. *War of the Rebellion: A Compilation of the Official Records of the Union and Confederate Armies,* Series I, vol. 9 (Washington, D.C.: U.S. Government Printing Office, 1883), 565; Robert M. Utley, *A Clash of Cultures: Fort Bowie and the Chiricahua Apaches* (Washington, D.C.: National Park Service, 1977), 27.

2. Asst. Inspector-General N. H. Davis, Fort Bowie, to Brig. Gen. James H. Carleton, Santa Fe, February 20, 1864, National Archives (NA), Record Group (RG) 393, Department of New Mexico 1849–66, Headquarters Records, Records of Staff Officers, Inspector, Letters Sent Dec. 1863–May 1865 (RG 393, vol. 1, Entry 3192); *War of the Rebellion,* Series 1, vol. 50, pt. 2:1134–35.

3. Ray Brandes, *Frontier Military Posts of Arizona* (Globe, Ariz.: Dale Stuart

King, 1960), 49–51; Thomas H. Peterson, Jr., *Fort Lowell, A. T., Army Post During the Apache Campaigns, The Smoke Signal,* no. 8 (Tucson: Tucson Corral of the Westerners, 1963); Constance Wynn Altshuler, *Starting with Defiance* (Tucson: Arizona Historical Society, 1983), 33–37.

4. *War of the Rebellion,* Series 1, vol. 50, pt. 1:401–3; James. E. Serven, *The Military Posts on Sonoita Creek, The Smoke Signal,* no. 12 (Tucson: Tucson Corral of the Westerners, 1965), 40.

5. *War of the Rebellion,* Series 1, vol. 50, pt. 2:422–23, 431–32; William A. Bell, *New Tracks in North America* (Albuquerque: Horn and Wallace, 1965; Reprint of 1870 ed.), 303–4. "Appended Compilation," in *Indian Battles and Skirmishes on the American Frontier 1790–1898,* Joseph P. Peters, comp. (New York: Argonaut Press, 1966), 39; Don Schellie, *Vast Domain of Blood* (Los Angeles: Westernlore Press, 1968), 21; Jay J. Wagoner, *Arizona Territory 1863–1912: A Political History* (Tucson: University of Arizona Press, 1970), 22–23.

6. *War of the Rebellion,* Series 1, vol. 50, pt. 1:213, 232–34.

7. *War of the Rebellion,* Series 1, vol. 50, pt. 2:827–29.

8. *War of the Rebellion,* Series 1, vol. 34, pt. 3:200–210.

9. Charles and Jacqueline Meketa, *One Blanket and Ten Days Rations* (Globe, Ariz., Southwest Parks and Monuments Association, 1980), 46–47.

10. Meketa 1980, 47–60; *War of the Rebellion,* Series 1, vol. 50, pt. 1:360–77, Series 1, vol. 34, pt. 1:917–20, Series 1, vol. 41, pt. 1:45–48, 81–86.

11. *War of the Rebellion,* Series 1, vol. 50, pt. 1:362.

12. *Santa Fe Weekly Gazette,* October 15, 1864, p. 2.

13. *War of the Rebellion,* Series 1, vol. 50, pt. 1:376, Series 1, vol. 34, pt. 1:123.

14. *War of the Rebellion,* Series 1, vol. 50, pt. 2:1180; Meketa 1980, 64–65.

15. Meketa 1980, 60–61.

16. Ralph H. Ogle, *Federal Control of the Western Apaches, 1848–1886* (Albuquerque: University of New Mexico Press, 1970; reprint of 1940 ed., 51–75; Robert M. Utley, *Frontier Regulars* (New York: Macmillan, 1973), 173.

17. S. H. Drachman, "Pioneer History of Arizona—Arizona Pioneers and Apaches," *Arizona Graphic* 1(10) (1899):4, 7.

18. A. M. Gustafson, ed., *John Spring's Arizona* (Tucson: University of Arizona Press, 1966), 60.

19. Gustafson 1966, 149–50.

20. Capt. R. F. Bernard, n.p., to Bvt. Lt. Col. Thos. S. Dunn, Camp Bowie, A. T., January 30, 1870, NA, RG 393, Post Records, Fort Bowie, Ariz. Letters Sent., vol. 18 (June 11, 1869–February 8, 1871), 81.

21. Gustafson 1966, 101–2.

22. "Journal of Captain A. R. Johnston, First Dragoons," in W. H. Emory, *Notes of a Military Reconnoissance, from Fort Leavenworth, in Missouri, to San Diego, in California,* 30th Cong., 1st Sess., House Exec. Doc. no. 41 (Washington, D.C.: Wendell and Van Benthuysen, Printers, 1848), 589.

23. *War of the Rebellion,* Series 1, vol. 41, pt. 1:84.

24. See n. 2, above, N. H. Davis entry.

25. *Annual Report of the Commissioner of Indian Affairs . . . for the Year 1868*

(Washington, D.C.: U.S. Government Printing Office, 1868), 141.

26. Capt. R. F. Bernard, Camp Bowie, A. T., to A. A. A. G., Prescott, August 31, 1870, NA, RG 393, Post Records, Fort Bowie, Ariz., Letters Sent, 18:131–33.

27. Peters 1966, 21; Anonymous, "Col. John Finkle Stone and the Apache Pass Mining Company," *Arizona Historical Review* 6(3) (1935):74–80; Marian E. Valputic and Harold H. Longfellow, "The Fight at Chiricahua Pass in 1869, As Described by L. L. Dorr, M.D.," *Arizona and the West* 13(4) (1971):369, 375; Mardith K. Schuetz, *Archaeology of Tom Jeffords' Chiricahua Indian Agency,* COAS Monograph no. 6 (Las Cruces, N.M.: COAS Publishing and Research, 1986), 5–8.

28. 1st Lt. W. H. Winters, Camp Bowie, A.T., to Bvt. Brig. Gen. T. C. Devin, Tucson Depot, October 10, 1869, NA, RG 393, Post Records, Fort Bowie, Ariz., Letters Sent, 18:43–46; Edwin R. Sweeney, *Cochise, Chiricahua Apache Chief* (Norman: University of Oklahoma Press, 1991), 268–72.

29. Sweeney 1991, 273–75; Capt. R. F. Bernard, Camp Bowie, A.T., to Bvt. Brig. Gen. Thomas C. Devin, Comdg. Sub. Dist. Sou. Arizona, October 22, 1869, NA, RG 393, Post Records,Fort Bowie, Az., Letters Sent, 18:47–52. U.S. Army, *The Medal of Honor of the United States Army* (Washington, D.C.: U.S. Government Printing Office, 1948).

30. Enclosure in File No. 925-P-1869, Letters Received by the Office of the Adjutant General (Main Series) 1861-1870; NA, Microcopy M619 Roll 737.

31. Capt. R. F. Bernard, Camp Bowie, A.T., to Bvt. Brig. Gen. T.C. Devin, Comdg. Sub. Dist. of Southern Arizona, November 2, 1869, NA, RG 393, Post Records, Fort Bowie, Ariz., Letters Sent, 18:56.

32. Ibid., 53–58; Valputic and Longfellow 1971; Don Russell, *One Hundred and Three Fights and Scrimmages* (Washington, D.C.: United States Cavalry Association, 1936), 72–78; Thomas Edwin Farish, *History of Arizona* (Cleveland: Arthur H. Clark, 1918) 8:27–30.

33. Capt. R. F. Bernard, Camp Bowie, A.T., to Bvt. Brig. Gen. Thomas C. Devin, Comdg. Sub. Dist. Sou. Arizona, November 14, 1869, NA, RG 393, Post Records, Fort Bowie, Az., Letters Sent, 18:63–67. See also reference n. 32.

34. Lansing B. Bloom, ed., "Bourke on the Southwest, II," *New Mexico Historical Review* 9(1) (1934):66–67.

35. See n. 29 above, Bernard entry, p. 50.

36. Capt. R. F. Bernard, Camp Bowie, A.T., to Bvt. Lt. Col. Thos. S. Dunn, Comdg. Post, February 1, 1870, NA, RG 393, Post Records, Fort Bowie, Ariz., Letters Sent, 18:82–85.

37. Altshuler 1983, 1–4.

38. Russell 1936, 79; Peters 1966, 25–27; George W. Webb, *Chronological List of Engagements . . .* (St. Joseph, Mo.: Wing Printing and Publishing, 1939), 52, 57–59. For testimonies on raiding in the 1869–71 period, see J. T. Alsop, T. J. Bidwell, and F. H. Goodwin [Indian Committee], *Memorial and Affidavits Showing Outrages Perpetrated by the Apache Indians, in the Territory of Arizona, for the Years 1869 and 1870* (Tucson: Territorial Press, 1964; reprint of 1871 ed.).

39. Schellie 1968; Ogle 1970, 92–93, 105, 109; Vincent Colyer, *Peace with the Apaches of New Mexico and Arizona* (Washington, D.C.: U.S. Government Print-

ing Office, 1872); *Annual Report of the Commissioner of Indian Affairs . . . for the Year 1872* (Washington, D.C.: U.S. Government Printing Office, 1872), 172–73.

40. Schellie 1968, 106.

41. Gustafson 1966, 237–38.

42. Farish 1918, 114–15; Webb 1939, 56–57; Peters 1966, 24–25.

43. *Arizona Citizen,* May 20, 1871, p. 3; Dan L. Thrapp, *The Conquest of Apacheria* (Norman: University of Oklahoma Press, 1967), 63–78; Donald N. Bentz, "Sword of Revenge," *Golden West* 1(6) (1965):22–26, 58–59. Bentz's article, an excellent account of the affair, was reprinted in the January 1972 issue of *Golden West.*

44. Eve Ball, *Indeh, an Apache Odyssey* (Provo: Brigham Young University Press, 1980), 27.

45. Bentz 1965; Personal communication, Conrad R. McCormick, Sierra Vista, Ariz., September 3, 1986.

46. Bloom 1934, 67–68; Sweeney 1991, 326–27; James M. Barney, *Tales of Apache Warfare* (n.p.: publ. by author, 1933), 22–24.

47. Ogle 1970, 82–90; *Annual Report of the Commissioner of Indian Affairs . . . for the Year 1871* (Washington, D.C.: U.S. Government Printing Office, 1872), 369–71, 399–400; *Annual Report of the Commissioner of Indian Affairs . . . for the Year 1872* (Washington, D.C.: U.S. Government Printing Office, 1872), 176, 306–7. The fascinating history of the Southern Apache Agency at Cañada Alamosa, New Mexico, is yet to be written.

48. Ogle 1970, 53–54.

49. Colyer 1872, 45–46; *Report of the Commissioner of Indian Affairs . . . for the Year 1869* (Washington, D.C.: U.S. Government Printing Office, 1870), 102–3; *Annual Report of the Commissioner of Indian Affairs . . . for the Year 1870* (Washington, D.C.: U.S. Government Printing Office, 1870), 136–37, 139–40.

50. Colyer 1872, 45–46; Ogle 1970, 86–93.

51. *Annual Report of the Commissioner of Indian Affairs . . . for the Year 1871* (Washington, D.C.: U.S. Government Printing Office, 1872), 369–70; *Annual Report of the Commissioner of Indian Affairs . . . for the Year 1872* (Washington, D.C.: U.S. Government Printing Office, 1872), 148–49, 306–7.

52. *Annual Report of the Commissioner of Indian Affairs . . . for the Year 1872* (Washington, D.C.: U.S. Government Printing Office, 1872), 155–56, 175.

53. Utley 1973, 194–96; Albert H. Schroeder, "A Study of the Apache Indians, Parts IV and V," in *Apache Indians IV,* David A. Horr, ed. (New York: Garland Publishing, 1974), 259–60.

54. Sweeney 1991, 262–64, 283–85, 297–99, 315–54; Appointment of Thos. J. Jeffords, Cañada Alamosa, N.M., September 16, 1872, Brig. Gen. O.O. Howard, Rio Cuchillo, N.M., to Comdg. Officer, Fort Craig & McRae, September 19, 1872, NA, RG 75, Records of the Bureau of Indian Affairs, Entry 310, I.S.P., Letters of General O. O. Howard, 1872.

55. Sweeney 1991, 355–65; (Washington, D.C.) *Daily Morning Chronicle,* November 10, 1872, pp. 1, 4. Captain J. A. Sladen, "Making Peace with Cochise, Chief of Chiricahua Indians, 1872," U.S. Army Military History Institute, Carlisle Barracks, Pennsylvania, copy courtesy of Coronado National Forest, Tucson, Arizona.

56. "Order Setting Apart Chiricahua Reservation," October 12, 1872, in NA, Microcopy T21, Roll #30; Brig. Gen. O. O. Howard, San Pedro Crossing A.T., to Mr. Thos. J. Jeffords, October 13, 1872, in NA, RG 75, Entry 310, I.S.P., Letters of General O. O. Howard, 1872.

57. Wagoner 1970, 139–41; Utley 1973, 196–98.

58. Brig. Gen. O. O. Howard, Dragoon Mts., to Genl. Geo. Crook, Comdg. Dept. of Arizona, October 11, 1872, and Brig. Gen. O. O. Howard, San Pedro Crossing, A.T., to Genl. Geo. Crook, Comdg. Dept. of Arizona, October 13, 1872, NA, RG 75, Entry 310, I.S.P., Letters of General O. O. Howard, 1872. See also Sweeney 1991, 363–65, 371; and *Annual Report of the Commissioner of Indian Affairs . . . for the Year 1872* (Washington, D.C.: U.S. Government Printing Office, 1872), 178.

59. Schuetz 1986; Harry G. Cramer III, "Tom Jeffords—Indian Agent," *Journal of Arizona History* 17(3) (1976):265–300; *Annual Report of the Commissioner of Indian Affairs . . . for the Year 1874* (Washington, D.C.: U.S. Government Printing office, 1874), 287; *Annual Report of the Commissioner of Indian Affairs . . . for the Year 1875* (Washington, D.C.: U.S. Government Printing Office, 1875), 209. Lieut. John G. Bourke visited the reservation in 1873 and later wrote that "[a]ll the troubles of the Chiricahuas can be traced to this sale of intoxicating fluids to them by worthless white men," John G. Bourke, *On the Border with Crook* (Glorieta, N.M.: Rio Grande Press, 1969; reprint of 1891 ed.), 236.

60. Ogle 1970, 132–36, 162–65; Utley 1977, 40.

61. John A. Rockfellow, *Log of an Arizona Trail Blazer* (Tucson: Arizona Silhouettes, 1955; republication of 1933 ed.), 85.

62. Ralph H. Ogle, "The Apache and the Government—1870's," *New Mexico Historical Review* 33(2) (1958):83.

63. Ogle 1970, 132, 165.

64. Peters 1966, 38. Thrapp 1967, 169–70; Cramer 1976, 288–90; *Annual Report of the Commissioner of Indian Affairs . . . for the Year 1876* (Washington, D.C.: U.S. Government Printing Office, 1876), 3–4.

65. Bvt. Maj. Gen. August V. Kautz, Prescott, A.T., to A.A.G. San Francisco, Ca., October 23, 1876, NA, Microcopy M666, Roll 265, File no. 5456-AGO-1876 (with eight enclosures, F/W 2576-AGO-1876).

66. Ibid.

67. 19 Stat. 53 (Act of May 9, 1876); Wagoner 1970, 146; Acting Comm. of Ind. Affairs to Hon. Sec. of the Interior, and Sec. of the Interior to Hon. Sec. of War, Washington, D.C., both May 8, 1876, NA, Microcopy M666, Roll 265, File No. 2654-AGO-1876 w/enclosure, F/W 2576-AGO-1876; Robert M. Utley, *Historical Report on Fort Bowie, Arizona,* 2d ed. (Santa Fe: USDI National Park Service, Region Three, 1962), 31–33.

68. Wagoner 1970, 146; Bvt. Maj. Gen. August V. Kautz, Prescott, A.T., to A.A.G. San Francisco, Ca., June 30, 1876, and October 23, 1876, both in NA, Microcopy M666, Roll 265, File Nos. 4396(AGO) 1876, 5456-AGO-1876, F/W 2576-AGO-1876.

69. See n. 65; *Annual Report of the Commissioner of Indian Affairs . . . for the Year 1876* (Washington, D.C.: U.S. Government Printing Office, 1876), 4.

70. Webb 1939, 77; Peters 1966, 40; (Silver City, N.M.) *Herald,* September 23, 1876, p. 2.

71. See n. 65.

72. *Annual Report of the Commissioner of Indian Affairs . . . for the Year 1874* (Washington, D.C.: U.S. Government Printing Office, 1874), 296–98; *Annual Report of the Commissioner of Indian Affairs . . . for the Year 1875* (Washington, D.C.: U.S. Government Printing Office, 1875), 215–20; John P. Clum, "Geronimo," *New Mexico Historical Review* 3(1) (1928):7–8.

73. Clum 1928; Dan L. Thrapp, *Victorio and the Mimbres Apaches* (Norman: University of Oklahoma Press, 1974), 179, 188–90.

74. William L. Chapel, "Camp Rucker: Outpost in Apacheria," *Journal of Arizona History* 14(2) (1973):95–112; S. R. Albert, "History of Camp John A. Rucker," *Arizona Cattlelog* 30(10) (1974):18–27, 30(11) (1974):24–27; Jeanne L. Graham, "The Canyon Named for a Hero," *Cochise Quarterly* 9(2) (1979):3–17; E. R. Martin, "Old Camp Rucker: Its Place in History," *Periodical* 11(1) (1979):42–49; Buddy Noonan, "Camp Rucker, The Army's Forgotten Outpost," *Desert* 43(10) (1980):18–20.

75. Clum 1928, 18–19; Thrapp 1974, 178–80; Bvt. Maj. Gen. August V. Kautz, Prescott, A.T., to A.A.G. San Francisco, Ca., June 30, 1876, NA, Microcopy M666, Roll 265, File no. 4396(AGO)1876, F/W 2576-AGO-1876.

76. Thrapp 1974, 183–85; 2nd Lt. J. A. Rucker, Camp Bowie, to A.A. Camp Bowie, A.T., January 14, 1877, NA, Microcopy M666, Roll 265, File no. 1005-AGO-1877, F/W 2576-AGO-1876.

77. Thrapp 1967, 178–79, 1974, 195–99; Ogle 1970, 169, 185.

78. Camp Bowie, A.T., Order no. 43 (March 27, 1878) and Order no. 48 (April 4, 1878), NA, RG 393, Order Book—To & From Troops in the Field, Southeastern Arizona, July 1878—November 1880; Capt. D. Madden to A.A.G. Prescott A.T., April 4, 1878, NA, RG 393, Camp Supply [John A. Rucker] A.T., Letters Sent., no. 1, copies at Forest Supervisor's Office, Coronado National Forest, Tucson.

79. Ogle 1970, 186; Graham 1979, 4–5; Camp Supply, A.T., Post Orders no. 7 (April 26, 1878), also Capt. D. Madden to Maj. C. E. Compton, Camp Grant, A.T., April 28, 1878, Camp Supply [John A. Rucker] A.T., Letters Sent, no. 7, both in NA, RG 393, Camp Supply [John A. Rucker] A.T., Post Records, copies at Forest Supervisor's Office, Coronado National Forest, Tucson.

80. Post. Adjt, Camp Supply, A.T. to 1st Lt. Austin Henely, June 3, 1878; Camp Supply [John A. Rucker] A.T., Letters Sent, no. 16; Capt. D. Madden, Camp Supply, A.T. to A.A.G. Prescott A.T., June 5, 1878, Letters Sent, no. 19; 1st Lt. Austin Henely, White River, Az. to Adjt. Camp Supply Az., June 3, 1878, Letters Received, no. 46; 1st Lt. J. H. Sands, Camp Supply, A.T. to Post Adjt., June 3, 1878, Letters Received, no. 48; Maj. C. E. Compton, Camp Grant, A.T., to C.O. Camp Supply A.T., June 9, 1878, Letters Received, no. 64; Camp Supply, A.T., Endorsements Book, nos. 36, 40 for 1878. All in NA, RG 393, Camp Supply [John A. Rucker] A.T., Post Records, copies at Forest Supervisor's Office, Coronado National Forest, Tucson.

81. Graham 1979, 8–10; 1st Lt. H. T. Winchester, Camp Supply, A.T. to Adjt. Gen., Washington, D.C., July 12, 1878, Camp Supply [John A. Rucker] A.T., Letters

Sent, no. 43, and 1st Lt. H. T. Winchester, Camp Supply [John A. Rucker] to Genl. Sheridan, Chicago, Ill., July 12, 1878, Letters Sent, no. 44, both in NA, RG 393, Camp Supply [John A. Rucker] A.T., Post Records, copies at Forest Supervisor's Office, Coronado National Forest, Tucson.

82. Camp Supply, A.T., Post Orders no. 59(October 11, 1878) and no. 78 (December 9, 1878), NA, RG 393, Camp Supply [John A. Rucker] A.T., Post Records, copies at Forest Supervisor's Office, Coronado National Forest, Tucson.

83. Inspection Report, Camp John A. Rucker, A.T., January 17, 1879, NA, RG 159, Records of the Inspector General's Office, Entry 15: Letters Received #253-1879, copy at Forest Supervisor's Office, Coronado National Forest, Tucson; Monthly Post Returns, Camp John A. Rucker, Az., January, February 1879, NA, Microcopy 617, Roll 556, Returns from U.S. Military Posts, 1800–1916, Camp John A. Rucker, Az., December 1878–October 1880.

84. Maj. Gen. Irvin McDowell, *Outline Descriptions of Military Posts in the Military Division of the Pacific* (San Francisco, Cal.: Presidio of San Francisco, 1879), 31–32.

85. 1st Lt. James Halloran, Camp J. A. Rucker A.T. to A.A.G. Dept. Az., February 19, 1880, Letters Sent, no. 19; 1st Lt. J.H. Hurst, Camp John A. Rucker A.T. to A.A.G. Dept. Az., April 4, 1880, Letters Sent, no. 43; 1st Lt. J. H. Hurst, Camp John A. Rucker, A.T. to A.A.G. Dept. Az., July 1, 1880, Letters Sent, no. 87; Capt. A. B. MacGowan, Camp John A. Rucker, A.T. to A.A.G. Dept. Az., October 1, 1880, Letters Sent no. 133 and November 10, 1880, Letters Sent, no. 147 (for 1880); Camp John A. Rucker, A.T., Post Orders no. 66 (November 22, 1880). All in NA, RG 393, Camp Supply [John A. Rucker] A.T., Post Records, copies at Forest Supervisor's Office, Coronado National Forest, Tucson. Monthly Post Returns, Camp John A. Rucker, Az., May, July 1880, NA, Microcopy 617, Roll 556, Returns from U.S. Military Posts, 1800–1916, Camp John A. Rucker, Az., December 1878–October 1880.

86. Chapel 1973, 104; Albert 1974, 26; Camp Supply, A.T., Post Orders no. 13 (May 10, 1878), Camp John A. Rucker, A.T., Post Orders no. 12 (February 10, 1879) and no. 15 (February 22, 1879), all in NA, RG 393, Camp Supply [John A. Rucker] A.T., Post Records, copies at Forest Supervisor's Office, Coronado National Forest, Tucson.

87. Capt. A. B. MacGowan, Camp John A. Rucker, A.T. to Messrs. Morton & Stewart, July 28, 1880, Letters Sent, no. 98, and July 28, 1880, Letters Sent, no. 99; Camp John A. Rucker, A.T., Endorsements Book, no. 39 for 1880. All in NA, RG 393, Camp Supply [John A. Rucker] A.T., Post Records, copies at Forest Supervisor's Office, Coronado National Forest, Tucson.

88. *Arizona Daily Star,* December 31, 1879, p. ?, January 7, 1880, p. 3, January 8, 1880, p. 4; (1st Lt. H. L.) Haskell, A.D.C., Whipple Barracks, A.T. to Adjt. Gen. San Francisco, Ca., December 16, 1879 (copy), NA, Microcopy M234, Roll 581, File No. 829H-AGO-1879; Ogle 1970, 198–99.

89. Camp John A. Rucker, A.T., Post Orders no. 66 (November 22, 1880), NA, RG 393, Camp Supply [John A. Rucker] A.T., Post Records, copy at Forest Supervisor's Office, Coronado National Forest, Tucson.

90. Albert 1974; NA, RG 393, Order Book—To & From Troops in the Field, South-

eastern Arizona, heliograph communications [1886], copy at Forest Supervisor's Office, Coronado National Forest, Tucson.

91. Thrapp 1967, 198–99, 206, 1974, 194ff; John P. Wilson, *Merchants, Guns and Money* (Santa Fe: Museum of New Mexico Press, 1987), 125.

92. Ogle 1970, 198–99; S. M. Barrett, ed., *Geronimo, His Own Story* (New York: Ballantine Books, 1971; republication of 1906 ed.).

93. Clum 1928, 129–37; Webb 1939, 92; Thrapp 1967, 233–34; Ogle 1970, 209–10; *Tombstone Daily Nugget,* October 4, 1881, p. 2, October 5, 1881, pp. 2, 3.

94. Peters 1966, 53; Thrapp 1967, 235–49; Ogle 1970, 213–14; George A. Forsyth, *Thrilling Days in Army Life* (New York: Harper and Brothers, 1900), 108–19; Neil Erickson, "Trailing the Apache," *Our Army* 3(11) (1931):6–7, 45–46.

95. Thrapp 1967, 267–71; Ogle 1970:218–19; Utley 1977, 48; Ball 1980, 50–51; William H. Mullane, ed., *This Is Silver City 1882–1883–1884,* volume 1 (reprints from the *Silver City Enterprise*) (Silver City, N.M.: Silver City Enterprise, 1963), 4–5 (1883 section).

96. Thrapp 1967, 274–78, 283–93; Ogle 1970, 216–21; Utley 1977, 50, 56.

97. Thrapp 1967, 293–94; Ogle 1970, 220; Britton Davis, *The Truth about Geronimo* (Lincoln: University of Nebraska Press, 1976; reprint of 1929 ed., 34–35, 83–101.

98. Ogle 1970, 231–32; Davis 1976, 137–54; William H. Mullane, ed., *Indian Raids As Reported in the Silver City Enterprise, 1882–1886* (Silver City, N.M.: Silver City Enterprise, 1968).

99. Thrapp 1967, 324–27.

100. Thrapp 1967, 334–39; Ogle 1970, 233–34.

101. Thrapp 1967, 342–49; Ogle 1970, 235–36; Davis 1976, 198–218.

102. *Arizona Daily Star,* April 28, 1886, p. 1, May 2, 1886, p. 4.

103. *Arizona Daily Star,* May 2, 1886, p. 4.

104. *Arizona Daily Star,* April 30, 1886, p. 4, May 4, 1886, p. 4, May 6, 1886, p. 4, May 11, 1886, p. 4, May 23, 1886, p. 4.

105. *Arizona Daily Star,* May 11, 1886, p. 4; William H. Leckie, *The Buffalo Soldiers* (Norman: University of Oklahoma Press, 1967), 243–44; Jack C. Gale, "Lebo in Pursuit," *Journal of Arizona History* 21(1) (1981):11–24.

106. *Arizona Daily Star,* May 26, 1886, p. 4; Thrapp 1967, 351–52; Davis 1976, 219–20; Jack C. Gale, "Hatfield under Fire, May 15, 1886," *Journal of Arizona History* 18(4) (1977):447–68; Allan Radbourne, "Captain Hatfield and the Chiricahuas," in "Ho, for the Great West!," Barry C. Johnson, ed. (London: English Westerners' Society, Special Publication no. 6B, 1980), 70–81.

107. Thrapp 1967, 352–66; Ogle 1970, 236–41; Davis 1976, 219–30; Utley 1977, 79; Jack C. Lane, ed., *Chasing Geronimo: The Journal of Leonard Wood, May-- September 1886* (Albuquerque: University of New Mexico Press, 1970); Lieutenant Charles B. Gatewood, "The Surrender of Geronimo," *Journal of Arizona History* 27(1) (1986):53–70.

108. Wagoner 1970, 300–303; Ball 1980, 256–260; (Wilcox, A.T.) *Southwestern Stockman* May 31, 1890, p. 5; *Tombstone Prospector,* August 4, 1890, p. 1; Neil Erickson, "Some Facts about (Bigfoot) Massai," located at Western Archeological

and Conservation Center, Tucson, Faraway Ranch Papers (MS1), Series 4, box 18, folder 7; Mertice Buck Knox, "The Escape of the Apache Kid," *Arizona Historical Review* 3(4) (1931):77–87; Dan R. Williamson, "Al Sieber, Famous Scout of the Southwest," *Arizona Historical Review* 3(4) (1931):67; Cornelius C. Smith, Jr., *Fort Huachuca, The Story of a Frontier Post* (Washington, D.C.: U.S. Government Printing Office, 1981), 263–65. Karl W. Laumbach, "Massai (New Mexico's Apache Kid)," paper presented to the Historical Society of New Mexico, April 23, 1993.

109. Webb 1939, 97; Peters 1966, 48; Smith 1981, 149; (Wilcox, A.T.) *Sulphur Valley News* , May 12, 1896, p. 3; *El Paso Daily Herald,* May 18, 1896, p. 4; Anonymous, "Campaigning in Arizona and New Mexico, 1895–6," *Journal of the United States Cavalry Association* 10(36):1897:25–28.

Chapter 7

1. (St. Louis) *Sunday Morning Republican* , June 26, 1859, p. 2.

2. J. Ross Browne, *Report of J. Ross Browne on the Mineral Resources of the States and Territories West of the Rocky Mountains* (Washington, D.C.: U.S. Government Printing Office, 1868), 481.

3. Stanley B. Keith, et al., *Metallic Mineral Districts and Production in Arizona,* Bulletin 194 (Tucson: University of Arizona, Bureau of Geology and Mineral Technology, Geological Survey Branch, 1983). For the historical background on the organization and management of Arizona mining districts, see John C. Lacy, "Early History of Mining in Arizona; Acquisition of Mineral Rights 1529–1866," in *History of Mining in Arizona,* J. Michael Canty and Michael N. Greeley, eds. (Tucson: Mining Club of the Southwest Foundation, 1987), 7–10.

4. Otis E. Young, Jr., *How They Dug the Gold* (Tucson: Arizona Pioneers' Historical Society, 1967), 125–26.

5. Stanton B. Keith, *Index of Mining Properties in Pima County, Arizona,* Bulletin 189 (Tucson: University of Arizona, Bureau of Geology and Mineral Technology, Geological Suvey Branch, 1974); Stanton B. Keith, *Index of Mining Properties in Santa Cruz County, Arizona,* Bulletin 191 (Tucson: University of Arizona, Arizona Bureau of Mines, 1975).

6. William H. Emory, *Report on the United States and Mexican Boundary Survey, Made under the Direction of the Secretary of the Interior,* 34th Cong., 1st Sess., Senate Exec. Doc. no. 108, vol. 1, pt. 1 (serial no. 832) (Washington, D.C.: A. O. P. Nicholson, Printer, 1857), 119.

7. Emory 1857, 94–95.

8. Sylvester Mowry, *Memoir of the Proposed Territory of Arizona* (Washington, D.C.: Henry Polkinhorn, Printer, 1857), 12; John C. Reid, *Reid's Tramp* (Austin: Steck Company, 1935; reprint of 1858 ed.), 192; J. Ross Browne, *Adventures in the Apache Country* (Tucson: University of Arizona Press, 1974; reprint of 1950 ed., 262; James Brand Tenney, *History of Mining in Arizona* (Tucson: Bureau of Geology and Mineral Technology, Geological Survey Branch, 1927–29), 242; Constance Wynn Altshuler, "The Case of Sylvester Mowry: The Charge of Treason," *Arizona*

and the West 15(1) (1973a):63–82; Altshuler, "The Case of Sylvester Mowry: The Mowry Mine," *Arizona and the West* 15(2) (1973b):162–63; Diane M. T. North, *Samuel Peter Heintzelman and the Sonora Exploring and Mining Company* (Tucson: University of Arizona Press, 1980), 32, 56, 198–99.

9. North 1980, 19–22, 39.

10. North 1980, 24–25, 28; Charles D. Poston, *Building a State in Apache Land* (Tempe: Aztec Press, 1963; republication of 1894 ed., 69–73.

11. North 1980, 30–40; *Los Angeles Star,* September 4, 1858, p. 2; *The Washington Union,* October 21, 1858, p. 2.

12. Tenney 1927–29, 270–73, 478; North 1980; "Silver and Copper Mining in Arizona, with a Map," and "Processes for the Extraction of Silver, Followed at the Reducing Establishments of the Heintzelman Mines, Arizona, and the Real del Monte Mines, Mexico," *The Mining Magazine and Journal of Geology,* Second Series 1(1):1–18 (hereafter cited as Anonymous 1859).

13. Constance Wynn Altshuler, ed., "Arizona in 1861: A Contemporary Account by Samuel Robinson," *Journal of Arizona History* 25(1) (1984):60–61.

14. Tenney 1927–29, 270–74, 478; Keith 1974, 19–21, 113–14.

15. Tenney 1927–29, 270–74, 478; Keith 1974, 12–14, 103–7.

16. Keith 1975, 18–19, 72.

17. *Daily Arizona Citizen,* September 16, 1880, p. 2.

18. Tenney 1927–29, 283; Keith 1975, 15–17, 61–69; James E. Sherman and Barbara H. Sherman, *Ghost Towns of Arizona* (Norman: University of Oklahoma Press, 1969), 113; Eldred D. Wilson, J. B. Cunningham, and G. M. Butler, *Arizona Lode Gold Mines and Gold Mining,* Bulletin 137 (Tucson: University of Arizona, Bureau of Geology and Mineral Technology, Geological Survey Branch, 1983), 188–91.

19. *Daily Arizona Citizen,* October 11, 1880, p. 2.

20. Tenney 1927–29, 284.

21. Tenney 1927–29, 287–88; Keith 1975, 16; Eldred D. Wilson, *Gold Placers and Placering in Arizona,* Bulletin 168 (Tucson: Bureau of Geology and Mineral Technology, Geological Survey Branch, 1981), 82–83.

22. Tenney 1927–29, 284, 287–88; Wilson et al. 1983, 188–89.

23. Maxwell C. Milton, "The Oro Blanco District of Arizona," *Engineering and Mining Journal* 96(22) (1913):1005.

24. Tenney 1927–29, 283–84, 287–88, 321–24, 488; Keith 1975, 65; "Report of the Governor of Arizona [1898]," *Annual Reports of the Department of the Interior . . .* 55th Cong., 3d Sess., House Doc. No. 5, Misc. Reports (Washington, D.C.: U.S. Government Printing Office, 1898), 258; Arizona Bureau of Mines, *Arizona Zinc and Lead Deposits, Part II,* Bulletin 158, University of Arizona Bulletin 22(3) (Tucson: University of Arizona, 1951), 41–49 (hereafter cited as Ariz. Bur. of Mines 1951).

25. Tenney 1927–29, 322–23; James A. Long, "Bloodstained Ghost Town," *Frontier Times* 39(2) (1965):24–25, 71–72; Carol Clarke Meyer, "The Rise and Fall of Ruby," *Journal of Arizona History* 15(1) (1974):22–23.

26. Long 1965, 25.

27. Long 1965.

28. Ariz. Bur. of Mines 1951, 41–49; Meyer 1974; Jerry Jenkins, "Ruby is All Alone," *Desert* 30(12) (1967):28–30; Philip Varney, *Arizona's Best Ghost Towns* (Flagstaff: Northland Press, 1980), 88–90.

29. Keith 1975, 25–28.

30. Keith 1974, 25–33; Frank C. Schrader, *Mineral Deposits of the Santa Rita and Patagonia Mountains, Arizona,* U.S. Geological Survey Bulletin 582 (Washington, D.C.: U.S. Government Printing Office, 1915), plate 1.

31. H. C. Grosvenor, "Letter From Arizona," *Railroad Record,* August 12, 1858, p. 293.

32. Browne 1974, 228; H. C. Grosvenor, "Early Efforts on the Santa Rita and Salero," *Arizona Cattlelog* 29(7) (1973):15.

33. Altshuler 1984, 21–76; Raphael Pumpelly, *My Reminiscences,* vol. 1 (New York: Henry Holt and Company, 1918); William A. Duffen, ed., "Overland Via 'Jackass Mail' in 1858: The Diary of Phocion R. Way," parts 1–4, *Arizona and the West* 2(1–4) (1964).

34. Pumpelly 1918, 199, 207, 224–26.

35. Tenney 1927–29, 244, 314–15; Browne 1974, 228–30; North 1980, 201; *War of the Rebellion: A Compilation of the Official Records of the Union and Confederate Armies* (hereafter cited as *War of the Rebellion,)* Series 1, vol. 50, pt. 1 (Washington, D.C.: U.S. Government Printing Office, 1897), 402.

36. Schrader 1915, 194–97; Tenney 1927–29, 315; Keith 1975, 87.

37. Schrader 1915, 197–214; Tenney 1927–29, 314–17; Keith 1975, 83.

38. Sherman 1969, 133; Varney 1980, 80–82.

39. Schrader 1915, 180–220; Tenney 1927–29, 314–21.

40. Keith 1975, 27, 85–86.

41. Schrader 1915, 220–39; Tenney 1927–29, 317–19; Keith 1975, 28–29, 88–90.

42. Rossiter W. Raymond, *Statistics of Mines and Mining in the States and Territories West of the Rocky Mountains; . . . Eighth Annual Report,* 44th Cong., 1st Sess., House Exec. Doc. no. 159 (Washington, D.C.: U.S. Government Printing Office, 1877), 342.

43. Schrader 1915, 158, 162–64; Wilson 1981, 74–76.

44. *Arizona Weekly Citizen,* October 9, 1875, p. 3.

45. *Arizona Citizen,* February 5, 1876, p. 2.

46. Schrader 1915, 158; Young 1967, 54–56.

47. Schrader 1915, 159; see n. 45.

48. Schrader 1915, 158–59; Tenney 1927–29, 277.

49. Schrader 1915, 159–60; Tenney 1927–29, 277–78; Wilson 1981, 72–73.

50. Schrader 1915, 152–58; Tenney 1927–29, 278; Keith 1974, 25–27, 120–21. Varney 1980, 79 refers to the Anderson mine as the "Snyder mine."

51. Sherman 1969, 70–71; Varney 1980, 78.

52. *Tucson Citizen,* September 4, 1979, Section C, pp. 1–2.

53. Schrader 1915, 166–80; Keith, 1974, 33, 1975, 15; Wilson 1981, 80.

54. Keith 1974, 31.

55. Tenney 1927–29, 252, 473–74; "Report of the Governor of Arizona [1895]," *Report of the Secretary of the Interior . . .* vol. 3, 54th Cong., 1st Sess., House Doc.

no. 5 (Washington, D.C.: U.S. Government Printing Office, 1895), 354, 426; "Report of the Governor of Arizona [1898]," 279; James E. Ayres, *Rosemont: The History and Archaeology of Post–1880 Sites in the Rosemont Area, Santa Rita Mountains, Arizona,* Archaeological Series no. 147, vol. 3 (Tucson: Cultural Resource Management Division, Arizona State Museum, 1984), 27–28.

56. Schrader 1915, 115; Tenney 1927–29, 252; Ayres 1984, 30; "Report of the Governor of Arizona [1899]," *Annual Reports of the Department of the Interior . . .* Misc. Reports, part 2, 56th Cong., 1st Sess., House Doc. no. 5 (serial no. 3918) (Washington, D.C.: U.S. Government Printing Office, 1899), 146–49.

57. Sherman 1969, 130; Ayres 1984, 30–38; William P. Blake, "Sketch of Pima Co., Ariz., Mining Districts, Minerals, Climate and Agriculture," *Arizona Daily Star,* June 19, 1910, 1st Section, p. 6.

58. Tenney 1927–29, 254–55, 473–74; Ayres 1984, 132–34.

59. Ayres 1984, 132–38, 523–30.

60. Ayres 1984, 136; S. C. Creasey and George L. Quick, *Copper Deposits of Part of Helvetia Mining District, Pima County, Arizona,* U.S. Geological Survey Bulletin 1027-F (Washington, D.C.: U.S. Government Printing Office, 1955), 304, 312–13, 318–19; Keith 1974, 31.

61. Schrader 1915, 96; Tenney 1927–29, 251–52; Lin B. Feil, "Helvetia: Boom Town of the Santa Ritas," *Journal of Arizona History* 9(2) (1968):77–95.

62. "Report of the Governor of Arizona [1899]," 149.

63. Feil 1968, 80–83; Sherman 1969, 78; Varney 1980, 77.

64. Feil 1968, 85–86.

65. Schrader 1915, 97; Feil 1968, 92–94.

66. Tenney 1927–29, 253–54.

67. Eulalia "Sister" Bourne, *Ranch Schoolteacher* (Tucson: University of Arizona Press, 1974), 68–70, 75, 84, 100.

68. Feil 1968, 94; Keith 1974, 31, 123–29; Varney 1980, 77.

69. Schrader 1915, 239, 245–46, 279, 292, 348; Keith 1975, 11, 14, 19–20, 24.

70. Schrader 1915, 259; Tenney 1927–29, 309.

71. (Marshall) *Texas Republican,* February 18, 1859, p. 2, extracting from a letter dated Fort Buchanan, December 16, 1858.

72. Anonymous 1859, 8; Schrader 1915, 253; Tenney 1927–29, 306; *Weekly Arizonian,* March 3, 1859, p. 2, April 28, 1859, p. 3, June 30, 1859, p. 3, July 7, 1859, p. 3.

73. Raymond 1877, 343–44; Tenney 1927–29, 303; Keith 1975, 58–59.

74. Schrader 1915, 253–54; Tenney 1927–29, 306–8; Keith 1975, 12–13, 59.

75. Schrader 1915, 258–63; Tenney 1927–29, 309–10; Keith 1975, 13, 58.

76. Schrader 1915, 245–79; Tenney 1927–29, 301–309, 312–13, 486; Keith 1975, 11–14, 55–60.

77. Schrader 1915, 246, 265–66, 272–73; Tenney 1927–29, 303–5; Sherman 1969, 76–77; Varney 1980, 97; *Daily Arizona Citizen,* July 15, 1880, p. 2; *Arizona Daily Star,* July 30, 1910, p. 3; Georgia Wehrman, "Harshaw: Mining Camp of the Patagonias," *Journal of Arizona History* 6(1) (1965):21–36.

78. Schrader 1915, 246, 266; Tenney 1927–29, 295, 305–6; *Arizona Daily Star,* October 2, 1910, pp. 6, 11.

79. Schrader 1915, 246.

80. Schrader 1915, 296. Tenney 1927–29, 239–40, 289, 293; Keith 1975, 4, 22. *Weekly Arizonian,* April 28, 1859, p. 3.

81. Tenney 1927–29, 239.

82. *Los Angeles Star,* September 4, 1858, p. 2.

83. Percy Gatling Hamlin, ed., *The Making of a Soldier: Letters of General R. S. Ewell* (Richmond, Va.: Whittet and Shepperson, 1935), 85–86.

84. Tenney 1927–29, 238–40, 289; Altshuler 1973, 67, 161–64; *Arizona Daily Star,* August 16, 1910, p. 6; Bernard L. Fontana, "The Mowry Mine: 1858–1958," *The Kiva* 23(3) (1958):14–16.

85. Altshuler 1973, 152–71; Browne 1974, 203–10.

86. Schrader 1915, 296; Tenney 1927–29, 243–44, 290–91.

87. Schrader 1915, 296–98; Tenney 1927–29, 291–93; Fontana 1958; Keith 1975, 81; *Arizona Daily Star,* October 2, 1910, p. 6.

88. Browne 1868, 448, 1974, 195; Schrader 1915, 322, 340–41; Tenney 1927–29, 293; Keith 1975, 4, 22.

89. Schrader 1915, 321–47; Tenney 1927–29, 293–300; Keith 1975, 5, 22–23, 76–81; *Arizona Daily Star,* August 16, 1910, p. 6.

90. Schrader 1915, 306–21; Tenney 1927–29, 299–300, 313; Keith 1975, 23, 75, 79–82.

91. Schrader 1915, 292–93, 308, 312, 317, 321; Sherman 1969, 103–5, 167–68; Varney 1980, 98–100.

92. Schrader 1915, 239–45; Keith 1975, 24, 82.

93. Schrader 1915, 279–92; Tenney 1927–29, 311–12; Keith 1975, 19–20, 73–74.

94. Schrader 1915, 348–55; Keith 1975, 14–15, 60–61, 76; U.S. Geological Survey, Arizona Bureau of Mines, and U.S. Bureau of Reclamation, *Mineral and Water Resources of Arizona,* Bulletin 180 (Tucson: Arizona Bureau of Mines, University of Arizona, 1969), 277–80 (hereafter cited as USGS 1969).

95. Schrader 1915, 279, 348, 355; Wilson 1981, 83–84.

96. Ariz. Bur. of Mines 1951, 36–40; Keith et al., 1983, 30–31; Stanton B. Keith, *Index of Mining Properties in Cochise County, Arizona,* Bulletin 187 (Tucson: Bureau of Geology and Mineral Technology, Geological Survey Branch, 1985), 9–10, 64–67.

97. Lawrence Kinnaird, *The Frontiers of New Spain: Nicolás de Lafora's Description, 1766–1768* (Berkeley: Quivira Society, 1958), 106.

98. *Arizona Daily Star,* September 5, 1879, p. 3, January 11, 1880, p. 4, January 14, 1880, p. 3, February 8, 1880, p. 4.

99. *Tombstone Epitaph,* June 12, 1880, p. 2.

100. Ariz. Bur. of Mines 1951, 37–39; Keith 1985, 9–10, 64–67. Also see n. 99.

101. "Report of the Governor of Arizona [1895]," 410; [1898], 287; [1899], 143–44; Tenney 1927–29, 148, 229–30; Sherman 1969, 148; Keith 1985, 65; John A. Rockfellow, *Log of an Arizona Trail Blazer* (Tucson: Arizona Silhouettes, 1955; republication of 1933 ed., 135–38; Roberta (Biff) Lamma, *A Place Called Sunnyside* (Tucson: A and W Limited Editions, 1982); Ervin Bond, *Cochise County, Arizona, Past and Present* (Douglas: published by the author, 1984), p. 118.

102. Ariz. Bur. of Mines 1951, 36–40; USGS 1969, 280; Keith 1985, 10.

103. Tenney 1927–29, 230; Sherman 1969, 73.

104. Sherman 1969, 59.

105. *Arizona Daily Star,* October 17, 1879, p. 4. "Report of the Governor of Arizona [1898]," 260.

106. Wilson 1981, 69–70; *Arizona Daily Star,* February 26, 1911, p. 7, March 18, 1911, p. 6, March 21, 1911, p. 9, April 4, 1911, p. 6.

107. USGS 1969, 348–51; Keith 1974, 47, 1985, 15, 50, 90–91; S. P. Marsh, S. J. Kropschot, and R. G. Dickinson, eds., *Wilderness Mineral Potential: Assessment of the Mineral-Resource Potential in U.S. Forest Service Lands Studied 1964–1984,* U.S. Geological Survey Professional Paper 1300, vols. 1 and 2 (Washington, D.C.: U.S. Government Printing Office, 1984), 126–29.

108. Keith 1974, 42, 141; Marsh et al. 1984, 103–5; H. C. Granger and R. B. Raup, *Reconnaissance Study of Uranium Deposits in Arizona,* U.S. Geological Survey Bulletin 1147-A (Washington, D.C.: U.S. Government Printing Office, 1962), A4–A5, A34–A37; Charles H. Thorman, Harald Drewes, and Michael E. Lane, *Mineral Resources of the Rincon Wilderness Study Area, Pima County, Arizona,* U.S. Geological Survey Bulletin 1500 (Washington, D.C.: U.S. Government Printing Office, 1981), 17–19, 40–55.

109. Browne 1868, 450; Wilson 1981, 61.

110. *Weekly Arizonian,* March 31, 1859, p. 2.

111. Wilson 1981, 61–62.

112. Keith 1974, 35.

113. "Report of the Governor of Arizona [1898]," 257, 267–68; Sherman 1969, 11; Keith 1974, 113; Marsh et al. 1984, 97–99; Anne E. Harrison, *The Santa Catalinas: A Description and History* (Tucson: Coronado National Forest, 1972), 70–76, 98.

114. *Arizona Daily Star,* June 19, 1910, p. 3; Harrison 1972, 76–79, 167; William P. Blake, "Sketch of Pima Co., Ariz., Mining Districts, Minerals, Climate and Agriculture," *Arizona Daily Star,* June 19, 1910, 1st section, p. 6; Charles Bowden, "Frog Mountain Blues," (Tucson) *City Magazine* 2(4) (1987):29–34; Juanita Daniel Zachry, "Mining Adventures of Buffalo Bill Cody," *True West* 37(4) (1990):37–41.

115. Tenney 1927–29, 250–51; USGS 1969, 195, 280; Harrison 1972, 79–84, 169, 178; Keith 1974, 33–35, 130–31.

116. Tenney 1927–29, 221–23; Keith 1985, 7–8, 55–60; Arizona Bureau of Mines, *Arizona Zinc and Lead Deposits, Part I,* Bulletin 156, University of Arizona Bulletin 21(2) (Tucson: University of Arizona, 1950), 30–39 (hereafter cited as Ariz. Bur. of Mines 1950); John R. Cooper and Leon T. Silver, *Geology and Ore Deposits of the Dragoon Quadrangle, Cochise County, Arizona,* U.S. Geological Survey, Professional Paper 416 (Washington, D.C.: U.S. Government Printing Office, 1964), 134–40, 159–89.

117. *The San Francisco Herald,* August 21, 1860, p. 3; Constance Wynn Altshuler, ed., *Latest from Arizona!* (Tucson: Arizona Pioneers' Historical Society, 1969), 56, 72–73, 107–8.

118. Tenney 1927–29, 136–79; Keith 1985, 12–13, 73–80.

119. Tenney 1927–29, 209–17; Sherman 1969, 44–47, 62–63; Keith 1985, 13–14,

80–85; F. L. Ransome, "The Turquoise Copper-Mining District, Arizona," in *Contributions to Economic Geology, 1911,* Part I, U.S. Geological Survey, Bulletin 530 (Washington, D.C.: U.S. Government Printing office, 1913), 125–27.

120. Tenney 1927–29, 214–16; Sherman 1969, 116–17; Keith 1985, 11, 69–70.

121. *Arizona Daily Star,* January 12, 1879, p. 2.

122. *Arizona Daily Star,* December 5, 1879, p. 2, January 16, 1880, p. 4, February 1, 1880, p. 4.

123. *Arizona Daily Star,* March 9, 1911, p. 6, March 12, 1911, third section, p. 5, March 21, 1911, p. 9.

124. Tenney 1927–29, 220; Keith 1985, 56–59.

125. Tenney 1927–29, 218; Ariz. Bur. of Mines 1951, 28–29; Keith 1985, 9, 63–64.

126. Cooper and Silver 1964, 138–40; USGS 1969, 396; Keith 1985, 9, 43, 65; Nell Murbarger, "They Mine Marble in Apacheland," *Desert* 18(5) (1955):11–15; "Mountains of Marble" brochure, n.d. (ca. 1922), located at Arizona Historical Society ephemera file, Mountains/Arizona/Dragoon. The same ephemera file contains five newspaper clippings dated 1919 (2), 1923, 1931 (2) on marble in the Dragoons.

127. Keith 1985, 10–11, 67–69.

128. Tenney 1927–29, 218–19; Ariz. Bur. of Mines 1951, 20–26; Sherman 1969, 98; Marsh et al. 1984, 60; Keith 1985, 10–11, 46, 67–69; W. J. "Jack" Way, *Ghosts and Ghost Towns* (n.p., published by the author, 1966), 17.

129. Ellen Predmore, "History of Black Diamond Historic Site, Black Diamond Smelter Historic Site," n.d., unpublished manuscript located at Forest Archeologist's Office, Coronado National Forest, Tucson.

130. Predmore n.d., 25.

131. Predmore n.d.; "Report of the Governor of Arizona [1898]," 285; Tenney 1927–29, 219–20; Keith 1985, 68.

132. Cooper and Silver 1964, 134, 161; Marsh et al. 1984, 130–32; Keith 1985, 15, 91.

133. USGS 1969, 133–34, 166; Keith et al. 1983, 34–35, 46–47; Charles H. Dunning, *Rocks to Riches* (Pasadena, Cal.: Hicks Publishing Corporation, 1966), 227–29, 233–39, 267–68; H. Wesley Peirce, *Geologic Guidebook 2—Highways of Arizona. Arizona Highways 77 and 177,* Bulletin 176 (Tucson: Arizona Bureau of Mines, 1967), 16.

134. Marsh et al. 1984, 65–68; S. C. Creasey et al., *Mineral Resources of the Galiuro Wilderness and Contiguous Further Planning Areas, Arizona,* U.S. Geological Survey, Bulletin 1490 (Washington, D.C.: U.S. Government Printing Office, 1981).

135. Ariz. Bur. of Mines 1951, 56; Frank S. Simons, *Geology of the Klondyke Quadrangle, Graham and Pinal Counties, Arizona,* U.S. Geological Survey, Professional Paper 461 (Washington, D.C.: U.S. Government Printing Office, 1964), 132, 167.

136. Michael N. Greeley, "The Early Influence of Mining in Arizona," in *History of Mining in Arizona,* J. Michael Canty and Michael N. Greeley, eds. (Tucson: Mining Club of the Southwest Foundation, 1987), 13–30.

137. Ariz. Bur. of Mines 1951, 56–65; Simons 1964, 132, 154–68; USGS 1969,

149; Creasey et al. 1981, 29–33, 87–92; Marsh et al. 1984, 65–68; David F. Myrick, *Railroads of Arizona* (San Diego: Howell-North Books, 1980) 2:737–46; Diana Hadley, Peter Warshall, and Don Bufkin, *Environmental Change in Aravaipa, 1870–1970, An Ethnoecological Survey,* Cultural Resources Series no. 7 (Phoenix: Arizona State Office of the Bureau of Land Management, 1991), 114–16.

138. Sherman 1969, 42; U.S.G.S. Galiuro Mts., Ariz. 15' topo map (1943); Bob Thomas, "Galiuros: Mountain Paradise Steeped in History," *Arizona Republic,* January 13, 1983.

139. Creasey et al. 1981, 72–73; Wilson et al. 1983, 193–94; Darvil McBride, *The Evaders* (Pasadena, Cal.: Pacific Book and Printing, 1984).

140. Creasey et al. 1981, 73–75; Wilson et al. 1983, 194.

141. Creasey et al. 1981, 33, 75–80; Wilson et al. 1983, 194; William P. Blake, "The Geology of the Galiuro Mountains, Arizona, and of the Gold-Bearing Ledge Known as Gold Mountain," *Engineering and Mining Journal* 73:546–47.

142. "Report of the Governor of Arizona [1898]," 286–87.

143. "Report of the Governor of Arizona [1899], 143; Simons 1964, 132, 150–54; Hadley et al. 1991, 112–13.

144. Creasey et al. 1981, 80–85.

145. Creasey et al. 1981, 86; Marsh et al. 1984, 67.

146. Keith et al. 1983, 48–49; Hadley et al. 1991, 109–11; Clyde P. Ross, *Geology and Ore Deposits of the Aravaipa and Stanley Mining Districts, Graham County, Arizona,* U.S. Geological Survey, Bulletin 763 (Washington, D.C.: U.S. Government Printing Office, 1925), 76–77; Henry P. Walker and Don Bufkin, *Historical Atlas of Arizona* (Norman: University of Oklahoma Press, 1979), 44.

147. Ross 1925, 76–77; Simons 1964, 2–4, 131; Eleanor Claridge, *Klondyke and the Aravaipa Canyon* (Safford, Ariz.: published by the author, 1989).

148. *Arizona Daily Star,* July 27, 1911, p. 6; Ross 1925, 92–103; Ariz. Bur. of Mines 1950, 51–60; Simons 1964, 131–44; Hadley et al. 1991, 103–6.

149. Ross 1925, 78–92; Ariz. Bur. of Mines 1950, 55–56, 60–63; Simons 1964, 131, 144–49; Hadley et al. 1991, 106–9.

150. Ross 1925, 98–102; Simons 1964, 138–46, 149.

151. Simons 1964, 132.

152. USGS 1969, 314, 352; Keith et al. 1983, 22–23; Wilson et al. 1983, 192–93; Lorraine Schnabel and John W. Welty, *Bibliography for Metallic Mineral Districts in Cochise, Graham, and Greenlee Counties, Arizona,* Circular 24 (Tucson: University of Arizona, Bureau of Geology and Mineral Technology, Geological Survey Branch, 1986), 27.

153. USGS 1969, 217; Keith et al. 1983, 18–19; Schnabel and Welty 1986, 26–27.

154. Granger and Raup 1962, A-15; Keith et al. 1983, map; Schnabel and Welty 1986, 26–28; *Reported Occurrences of Selected Minerals in Arizona,* U.S.G.S. Mineral Investigations Resource Map MR-46 (South Half) (Washington, D.C.: U.S. Geological Survey, 1967).

155. Browne 1868, 450.

156. Anonymous, "Col. John Finkle Stone and The Apache Pass Mining Company," *Arizona Historical Review* 6(3) (1935):74–80; Marian E. Valputic and Harold

H. Longfellow, "The Fight at Chiricahua Pass in 1869, As Described by L. L. Dorr, M.D.," *Arizona and the West* 13(4) (1971):369–78; Mardith K. Schuetz, *Archaeology of Tom Jeffords' Chiricahua Indian Agency,* COAS Monograph no. 6 (Las Cruces, N.M.: COAS Publishing and Research, 1986), 58.

157. *Arizona Daily Star,* August 26, 1910, p. 5; Tenney 1927–29, 224; Keith 1985, 71.

158. Keith et al. 1983, 16–17.

159. *Daily Arizona Citizen,* October 25, 1880, p. 1; Harry G. Cramer III, "Tom Jeffords—Indian Agent," *Journal of Arizona History* 17(3) (1976):288.

160. *Daily Arizona Citizen,* November 24, 1880, p. 2. See also (Tombstone) *Daily Nugget,* November 12, 1880, p. 2.

161. *Tombstone Epitaph,* December 6, 1880, p. 1; *Daily Nugget,* December 15, 1880, p. 2.

162. *Arizona Daily Star,* February 21, 1911, p. 6, quoting the *Paradise Record.*

163. Ibid.; Tenney 1927–29, 227–28, 459; Keith 1985, 6; Frank C. Lockwood, "Fifty Years in Paradise," *Progressive Arizona* 11(13) (1931):16.

164. Keith 1985, 54; Frank C. Lockwood, "Fifty Years in Paradise," *Progressive Arizona* 12(1) (1932):13–14, 18. James Cary published a series of anecdotes in his column "Galeyville Days," in *Arizona Days and Ways,* the Sunday magazine of the *Arizona Republic,* commencing February 14, 1954.

165. *Tombstone Epitaph,* January 10, 1881, p. 1.

166. Joseph Bowyer, Galeyville A.T., to Hon. John J. Gosper, Acting Governor, A.T., September 17, 1881, National Archives, Interior Department Territorial Papers, Arizona, 1868–1913, Microcopy M429 Roll 3.

167. See n. 162.

168. "Report of the Governor of Arizona [1898]," 269–70, [1899], 173; Keith 1985, 52; Harald Drewes and Frank E. Williams, *Mineral Resources of the Chiricahua Wilderness Area, Cochise County, Arizona,* U.S. Geological Survey, Bulletin 1385-A (Washington, D.C.: U.S. Government Printing office, 1973), A5–A6.

169. Tenney 1927–29, 228; Lockwood 1931, 18; Fayette Jones, *Old Mines and Ghost Camps of New Mexico* (Fort Davis, Tex.: Frontier Book Co., 1968; reprint of 1905 ed.), 68–69.

170. *Arizona Daily Star,* June 18, 1910, p. 3; Tenney 1927–29, 228; Keith 1985, 51–54.

171. *Arizona Daily Star,* July 1, 1910, p. 6.

172. Tenney 1927–29, 229; Lockwood 1931; Sherman 1969, 114–15; Keith 1985, 51–54; Nelle Merwin, "Tales of Paradise, Arizona," *The West* 6(6) (1967):36–41, 67–69.

173. Tenney 1927–29, 229; Sherman 1969, 79–80; Drewes and Williams 1973, A5–A6, A37–A38; Varney 1980, 119–21; Keith 1985, 52.

174. Keith 1985, 6–7, 42, 51–55.

175. Anonymous, "Marble Quarrying in Arizona," *Mine and Quarry,* October 1910, 440–43; *Arizona Daily Star,* October 30, 1910, p. 20.

176. Ibid.; *Arizona Daily Star,* August 26, 1910, p. 5, August 30, 1910, p. 6, February 7, 1911, p. 6.

177. "Report of the Governor of Arizona . . . for the Year Ended June 30, 1911," *Reports of the Department of the Interior for the Fiscal Year Ended June 30, 1911,* Administrative Reports (Washington, D.C.: U.S. Government Printing Office, 1912) 2:582–83.

178. USGS 1969, 396; Keith 1985, 72.

179. USGS 1969, 390; *Arizona Daily Star,* April 22, 1910, p. 4, September 6, 1911, p. 5; William P. Blake, "Sketch of Pima Co., Ariz., Mining Districts, Minerals, Climate and Agriculture," *Arizona Daily Star,* June 26, 1910, 1st section, p. 6.

180. Keith 1985, 12, 70. See also Keith et al. 1983, 46–47, for a much different estimate.

181. Tenney 1927–29, 291, 478.

182. USGS 1969, 159, 184.

183. Keith et al. 1983, 52–53; R. W. Graeme, "Bisbee, Arizona's Dowager Queen of Mining Camps; A Look at Her First 50 Years," in *History of Mining in Arizona,* J. Michael Canty and Michael N. Greeley, eds. (Tucson: Mining Club of the Southwest Foundation, 1987), 51.

184. Keith et al. 1983.

185. Tenney 1927–29, 301; Lamma 1982.

Chapter 8

1. John Russell Bartlett, *Personal Narrative of Explorations and Incidents, . . .* (Chicago: Rio Grande Press, 1965; reprint of 1854 ed., 1:255–56; Colin Cameron, "Report of Colin Cameron, Esq.," in "Report of the Governor of Arizona [1896]," *Report of the Secretary of the Interior . . .* 54th Cong., 2d sess., House Doc. no. 5 (Washington, D.C.: U.S. Government Printing Office, 1896) 3:223; John L. Kessell, "Father Ramón and the Big Debt, Tumacácori, 1821–1823," *New Mexico Historical Review* 44(1) (1969):53–72; Jay J. Wagoner, *Early Arizona: Prehistory to Civil War* (Tucson: University of Arizona Press, 1975), 159–241; James E. Officer, *Hispanic Arizona, 1536–1856* (Tucson: University of Arizona Press, 1987), 106–10, 148–49, 171.

2. Bartlett 1965, 396–97.

3. Benjamin Butler Harris, *The Gila Trail: The Texas Argonauts and the California Gold Rush* (Norman: University of Oklahoma Press, 1960), 72–73; L. R. Bailey, ed., *The A. B. Gray Report* (Los Angeles: Westernlore Press, 1963; republication of 1856 ed.), 77; Ralph P. Bieber, ed., *Exploring Southwestern Trails, 1846–1854* (Philadelphia: Porcupine Press, 1974; reprint of 1938 ed.), 135.

4. J. Evetts Haley, ed., "A Log of the Texas-California Cattle Trail, 1854," *Southwestern Historical Quarterly* 35(3–4) (1932):305.

5. Haley 1932; Bieber 1974, 377; Bert Haskett, "Early History of the Cattle Industry in Arizona," *Arizona Historical Review* 6(4) (1935):9–11; Milo Milton Quaife, ed., *Kit Carson's Autobiography* (Chicago: Lakeside Press, 1935), 146–47; J. J. Wagoner, *History of the Cattle Industry in Southern Arizona, 1540–1940,* Social Science Bulletin no. 20, University of Arizona Bulletin 23(2) (Tucson: University of

Arizona, 1952), 30; Robert W. Frazer, *Forts and Supplies: The Role of the Army in the Economy of the Southwest, 1846–1861* (Albuquerque: University of New Mexico Press, 1983), 52–53. The continuing drives are documented in the *Daily Alta California*, September 29, 1858, p. 4; *Los Angeles Star*, November 20, 1858, p. 2; *Weekly Arizonian*, October 27, 1859, p. 2; and other contemporary sources.

6. Clarence W. Gordon, "Arizona Territory," in "Report on Cattle, Sheep, and Swine," *Report on the Productions of Agriculture As Returned at the Tenth Census (June 1, 1880)* (Washington, D.C.: U.S. Government Printing Office, 1883), 93.

7. Haskett 1935, 14–15; Richard J. Morrisey, "The Early Range Cattle Industry in Arizona," *Agricultural History* 24(3) (1950):132.

8. Gordon 1883, 92–103; Cameron 1896, 222–31; Haskett 1935, 3–42; Morrisey 1950, 151–56; Wagoner 1952; Robert A. Darrow, *Arizona Range Resources and Their Utilization: I. Cochise County*, Arizona Agricultural Experiment Station, Technical Bulletin no. 103 (Tucson: University of Arizona, 1944), 312–15; Virgil V. Peterson, "Arizona Range Cattle," *American Cattle Producer* 28(3) (1946):9–10, 24–26; Earle R. Forrest, "The Fabulous Sierra Bonita," *Journal of Arizona History* 6(3) (1965):132–147; Noel M. Loomis, "Early Cattle Trails in Southern Arizona," *Arizoniana* 3(4) (1962):18–24; Frank Cullen Brophy, "San Ignacio del Babacomari," *Arizona Highways* 42(9) (1966):2–17; Yjinio F. Aguirre, "Echoes of the Conquistadores: Stock Raising in Spanish-Mexican Times," *Journal of Arizona History* 16(3) (1975):267–86.

9. Haskett 1935, 36–37; Peterson 1946, 24; Mont H. Saunderson, *Western Stock Ranching* (Minneapolis: University of Minnesota Press, 1950), 37–38.

10. Gordon 1883, 95–97; Cameron 1896, 224; *Daily Arizona Citizen*, October 11, 1880, p. 1.

11. Gordon 1883, 93, 97; Cameron 1896, 223, 227; Haskett 1935, 37–39. Peterson 1946; Morrisey 1950, 153–54; Cornelius C. Smith, Jr., *William Sanders Oury, History-Maker of the Southwest* (Tucson: University of Arizona Press, 1967), 185.

12. Gordon 1883, 93; Cameron 1896, 223; Harwood P. Hinton, Jr., "John Simpson Chisum, 1877–84," *New Mexico Historical Review* 31(3–4) (1956):190, 201, 310; Lily Klasner, *My Girlhood among Outlaws* (Tucson: University of Arizona Press, 1972), 253, 290; Mary Whatley Clarke, *John Simpson Chisum* (Austin: Eakin Press, 1984), 42–45, 133; Darlis A. Miller, *Soldiers and Settlers: Military Supply in the Southwest, 1861–1885* (Albuquerque: University of New Mexico Press, 1989), 199–206.

13. Morrisey 1950, 152; Miller 1989, 206.

14. *Daily Arizona Citizen*, October 11, 1880, p. 1; Gordon 1883, 93, 103; Forrest 1965; Mrs. Harry Hooker, "Five Generations of Hookers on the Sierra Bonita Ranch," *Arizona Cattlelog* 15(4) (1949):32–36; Harwood P. Hinton, Jr., "John Simpson Chisum, 1877–84," *New Mexico Historical Review* 32(1) (1957):64; Gertrude Hill, "Henry Clay Hooker: King of the Sierra Bonita," *Arizoniana* 2(4) (1961):12–15; Jerry Weddle, *Antrim is My Stepfather's Name* (Tucson: Arizona Historical Society, 1993), 35, 62–63.

15. Gordon 1883, 93, 97; Haskett 1935, 25, 28; Peterson 1946, 25; John A. Rockfellow, *Log of an Arizona Trail Blazer* (Tucson: Arizona Silhouettes, 1955; re-

publication of 1933 ed.), 91. 103–4; Richard G. Schaus, "Jackson (Jack) Busenbark 1875–1948," *Arizona Cattlelog* 13(4) (1957): 51–56 and back cover.

16. Schaus 1957, 51; Joseph Bowyer, Galeyville A.T., to Hon. John J. Gosper, Acting Governor, A.T., September 17, 1881, National Archives, Interior Department Territorial Papers, Arizona, 1868–1913, Microcopy M429 Roll 3; Frank C. Lockwood, "Fifty Years in Paradise," *Progressive Arizona* 11(13) (1931):16, 21; Wagoner 1952, 104–5.

17. Cameron 1896, 224.

18. Cameron 1896.

19. Ibid., 224–26; Wagoner 1952, 45.

20. Cameron 1896, 225–26; Saunderson 1950, 127–31; Wagoner 1952, 54; Raymond E. Seltzer, "The Economic Value of the Arizona Cattle Industry," *Arizona Cattlelog* 14(5) (1959):26–30; Elmer L. Menzie, "Beef Production and Marketing in Arizona," *Arizona Cattlelog* 27(2) (1970):28–33; Gene M. Gressley, *Bankers and Cattlemen* (Lincoln: University of Nebraska Press, 1971; reprint of 1966 ed.), 155–57.

21. Peterson 1946; Wagoner 1952, 54–57; A. L. Spellmeyer, "Notes on Fifty Years of Cattle History 1867–1917," *Southwestern Stockman-Farmer* 32(55), February 15, 1917, p. 1; Jay J. Wagoner, *Arizona Territory 1863–1912: A Political History* (Tucson: University of Arizona Press, 1970), 373–75, 383.

22. Eulalia "Sister" Bourne, *Ranch Schoolteacher* (Tucson: University of Arizona Press, 1974), 217.

23. Will C. Barnes, *Western Grazing Grounds and Forest Ranges* (Chicago: Breeder's Gazette, 1913), 24.

24. Maurice Frink, W. Turrentine Jackson, and Agnes Wright Spring, *When Grass Was King* (Boulder: University of Colorado Press, 1956), 117–19.

25. Gressley 1971, 274.

26. Gressley 1971, 169–74.

27. Hooker 1949, 34. See also *Daily Arizona Citizen*, October 11, 1880, p. 1.

28. R. W. Clothier, *Dry-Farming in the Arid Southwest*, University of Arizona Agricultural Experiment Station, Bulletin no. 70 (Tucson: University of Arizona, 1913); O. E. Meinzer and F. S. Kelton, *Geology and Water Resources of Sulphur Spring Valley, Arizona*, U.S. Geological Survey, Water-Supply Paper 320 (Washington, D.C.: U.S. Government Printing Office, 1913); A. T. Schwennesen, "Ground Water in San Simon Valley, Arizona and New Mexico," in *Contributions to the Hydrology of the United States, 1917*, U.S. Geological Survey, Water-Supply Paper 425 (Washington, D.C.: U.S. Government Printing Office, 1919), 1–35; C. K. Cooperrider and R. W. Hussey, *Range Appraisal Report for the Coronado National Forest* (Tucson: Coronado National Forest, 1924).

29. Joseph H. Tudor, "The Development of the Fee System on Public Lands," *Arizona Cattlelog* 25(11) (1969):22–27.

30. Will C. Barnes, "The U.S. Forest Service," *Out West* 29(2) (1908):89–109; Will C. Barnes, "National Forests and the Public Domain," in *Hearings before a Subcommittee of the Committee on Public Lands and Surveys, United States Senate* . . . 69th Cong. 1st sess. Pursuant to S. Res. 347 (Washington, D.C.: U.S. Government Printing Office, 1926) 2:1586–88.

31. Anne E. Harrison, *The Santa Catalinas: A Description and History (Tucson: Coronado National Forest, 1972), 90.*

32. Richard G. Schaus, "Wiley Marion Morgan, 1864–1946," *Arizona Cattlelog* 18(4) (1961b): back cover.

33. Peterson 1946; Wagoner 1952, 58–62.

34. Saunderson 1950, 37–38, 48–53, 100–103.

35. Larry S. Allen, *Livestock and the Coronado National Forest: A Historical Perspective* (1987), unpublished manuscript located at Forest Supervisor's Office, Coronado National Forest, Tucson.

36. Gordon 1883, 97.

37. *Daily Arizona Citizen,* October 11, 1880, p. 1.

38. Meinzer and Kelton 1913, 214–15.

39. Hooker 1949; Forrest 1965, 142–43.

40. Gordon 1883, 95, 103.

41. Gordon 1883, 96. See *The Tombstone Epitaph,* January 10, 1881, p. 2, for the numbers of sheep and cattle reported at various ranches.

42. Bert Haskett, "History of the Sheep Industry in Arizona," *Arizona Historical Review* 7(3) (1936):20–22.

43. Ezra A. Carman, H. A. Heath, and John Minto, *Special Report on the History and Present Condition of the Sheep Industry of the United States,* U.S. Department of Agriculture, Bureau of Animal Industry (Washington, D.C.: U.S. Government Printing Office, 1892), 935–46; "Report of the Governor of Arizona [1895]," *Report of the Secretary of the Interior* . . . 54th Cong. 1st sess., House Doc. no. 5 (Washington, D.C.: U.S. Government Printing Office, 1895) 3:332; "Report of the Governor of Arizona [1896]," *Report of the Secretary of the Interior* . . . 54th Cong. 2d sess., House Doc. no. 5 (Washington, D.C.: U.S. Government Printing Office, 1896) 3:210; "Report of the Governor of Arizona [1897]," *Annual Reports of the Department of the Interior for the Fiscal Year Ended June 30, 1897,* Misc. Reports, 55th Cong. 2d sess., House Doc. no. 5 (Washington, D.C.: U.S. Government Printing Office; 1897), 284; "Report of the Governor of Arizona [1898]," *Annual Reports of the Department of the Interior for the Fiscal Year Ended June 30, 1898,* Misc. Reports, 55th Cong. 3d sess., House Doc. no. 5 (Washington, D.C.: U.S. Government Printing Office, 1898), 230.

44. Cameron 1896, 228; "Report of the Forester," in *Annual Reports of the Department of Agriculture for the Year Ended June 30, 1923* (Washington, D.C.: U.S. Government Printing office, 1924), 319; Marion Clawson, *The Western Range Livestock Industry* (New York: McGraw-Hill, 1950), 195.

45. Richard G. Schaus, "Samuel Benjamin Tenney, 1858–1949," *Arizona Cattlelog* 27(5) (1971):40 and back cover.

46. Barnes 1913, 11; Anonymous, "Goat Raising in Arizona," in *Arizona: The New State Magazine* 4(6–7) (1914):16; Mohair Council of America, *Mohair: Production and Marketing in the U.S.* (San Angelo, Tex.: Mohair Council of America, 1982[?]), 14.

47. "Report of the Governor of Arizona [1899]," *Annual Reports of the Department of the Interior for the Fiscal Year Ended June 30, 1899,* Misc. Reports, part II,

56th Cong. 1st Sess., House Doc. no. 5 (serial no. 3918) (Washington, D.C.: U.S. Government Printing office, 1899), 62; Le Grand Powers, *Agriculture Part 1: Farms, Live Stock, and Animal Products,* Twelfth Census of the United States, Taken in the Year 1900, Census Reports (Washington, D.C.: U.S. Census Office, 1902) 5:684; Diana Hadley, Peter Warshall, and Don Bufkin, *Environmental Change in Aravaipa, 1870–1970, An Ethnoecological Survey,* Cultural Resources Series no. 7 (Phoenix: Arizona State Office of the Bureau of Land Management, 1991), 182–83.

48. *Southwestern Stockman, Farmer and Feeder* 18(19), September 20, 1901, p. 5.

49. Gordon 1883, 101; *Arizona Daily Star,* April 30, 1910, p. 3, June 26, 1910, section II p. 4, August 25, 1911, p. 5; Bureau of the Census, *Thirteenth Census of the United States (1910), Abstract of the Census . . . with Supplement for New Mexico* (Washington, D.C.: U.S. Government Printing office, 1913), 333, 352; Mohair Council of America 1982, 14.

50. Haskett 1936, 44; Wagoner 1952, 55–56.

51. Barnes 1908, 94–95; Hadley 1991, 181–203; S. A. Frey, "Gila National Forest. Report on Area of 8160 Acres Recommended for Elimination," September 1, 1910 (3 pp.), Located at Forest Archeologist's Office, Gila National Forest, Silver City, N.M.; Rex King, "Land Classification of the Mt. Graham, Santa Teresa and Galiuro Division, Crook National Forest, Arizona," in *Extensive and Intensive Classification, Galiuro, Santa Teresa and Mt. Graham Divisions, Crook National Forest, Arizona, District 3* (Washington D.C.: U.S. Department of Agriculture, 1915b); W. R. Chapline, Jr., "General Progress Report on Study of Goat Management on National Forests in the Southwest," 1917, located at Forest Archeologist's Office, Gila National Forest, Silver City, N.M.; W. R. Chapline, *Production of Goats on Far Western Ranges,* U.S. Department of Agriculture, Bulletin no. 749 (Washington, D.C.: U.S. Government Printing Office, 1919); O. D. Knipe, "The Use of Angora Goats in Converting Arizona Chaparral to Grassland," and Miguel A. Galina et al., "Social Status of the Goat Industry in Mexico," both in *Proceedings of the Third International Conference on Goat Production and Disease* (Scottsdale, Ariz.: Dairy Goat Journal Publishing Co., 1982), 411–16 and 420–21; William D. Rowley, *U.S. Forest Service Grazing and Rangelands: A History* (College Station: Texas A&M University Press, 1985), 80.

52. Hadley 1991, 183–84; "Report of the Governor of Arizona [1909]," *Reports of the Department of the Interior for the Fiscal Year Ended June 30, 1909,* Administrative Reports (Washington, D.C.: U.S. Government Printing Office, 1910) 2:555; William Lane Austin, *United States Census of Agriculture, 1925, Part III, The Western States* (Washington, D.C.: U.S. Government Printing Office, 1927), 302.

53. Cooperrider and Hussey 1924; Barnes 1926, 1643–727; "Report of the Forester," in *Annual Reports of the Department of Agriculture for the Year Ended June 30, 1908* (Washington, D.C.: U.S. Government Printing Office, 1909), 428.

54. Lonnie E. Rawdon, comp., "History of Animas Valley—Bill Bercham Draw," n.d. (3 pp.), located at Forest Archeologist's Office, Coronado National Forest, Tucson.

55. Hadley 1991, 181–86; Richard G. Schaus, "Eugene Nelson Shepherd, 1873–1947," *Arizona Cattlelog* 21(1) (1964b):48 and back cover; Richard G. Schaus,

"Jacob Prospect Weathersby, 1874–1930," *Arizona Cattlelog* 25(3) (1968): 40 and back cover; Richard G. Schaus, "George Upshaw, 1882–1951," *Arizona Cattlelog* 26(9) (1970a):32 and back cover; Richard G. Schaus, "James Able White, 1887–1967," *Arizona Cattlelog* 26(12) (1970b):32 and back cover; Richard G. Schaus, "Samuel Benjamin Tenney, 1858–1949," *Arizona Cattlelog* 27(5) (1971):40 and back cover.

56. Junietta Claridge, "We Tried to Stay Refined. Pioneering in the Mineral Strip," *Journal of Arizona History* 16(4) (1975):415, 423–24.

57. Schaus, 1968, 1970a, 1970b.

58. *The Arizona Daily Star,* market reports for various dates, 1921; also *Arizona Daily Star,* June 14, 1921, p. 1, July 2, 1921, p. 2, and August 23, 1921, p. 2.

59. Jimmy M. Skaggs, *Prime Cut: Livestock Raising and Meatpacking in the United States, 1607–1983* (College Station: Texas A&M University Press, 1986), 134–36.

60. Wagoner 1952, 58; Skaggs 1986, 137–38.

61. Lawrence R. Borne, *Dude Ranching: A Complete History* (Albuquerque: University of New Mexico Press, 1983), 50–59, 182–85.

62. *Arizona Daily Star,* September 11, 1920, p. 3, September 16, 1920, p. 3.

63. Richard G. Schaus, "George Stone Wilson, 1887–1957," *Arizona Cattlelog* 16(9–10) (1961a): back cover; George Stone Wilson, "Saga of Oracle, Mountain Cow Town," Part X, *Arizona Cattlelog* 22(9) (1965):30–39.

64. Anonymous, "The History of Faraway Ranch," *Hoofs and Horns* 4(5), October 1934, 2, 16; Mark F. Baumler, *The Archeology of Faraway Ranch, Arizona* (Tucson: Western Archeological and Conservation Center Publications in Anthropology, no. 24, 1984), 7–8, 149–50; Chuck Milliken, "History Buffs Can Get 'Faraway' from the Fast Lane," *Arizona History* 6(3) (1989):4–5.

65. Lowell J. Arnold, "Dude Ranches of Southern Arizona," *Progressive Arizona* 1(3) (1925):13–16, 38–39.

66. Lowell J. Arnold, "Vacationing at Circle Z Ranch," *Progressive Arizona* 2(1) (1926):15–16; *Arizona Summerland Resort Directory,* fourth annual ed., 1927, located at Arizona Historical Society, Frederick Winn Collection, box 4.

67. Borne 1983, 54–55.

68. Harrison Burrall, *Forest Recreation Plan* (Tucson: Coronado National Forest, 1930), Located at Forest Supervisor's Office, Coronado National Forest, Tucson.

69. Burrall 1930, 9; Borne 1983, 54.

70. Anonymous, "Guest Ranches Abound Near Tucson," *Tucson* 5(10), October 1932, 1–4; Anonymous, "Hosts of the Open Spaces," *Tucson* 6(10), October 1933, 3–5, 8.

71. Borne 1983, 184; Dale Ann Deffer, "Flying V Ranch Still Soaring High," *Arizona History* 6(4) (1989):4–5.

72. Anonymous, *Arizona Summerland Resort Directory,* fourth annual ed., 1927, 19.

73. See n. 63; also Juanita Daniel Zachry, "Mining Adventures of Buffalo Bill Cody," *True West* 37(4) (1990):37–41.

74. Borne 1983, 226; Anonymous "Hosts of the Open Spaces," *Tucson* 6(10) October 1933, 3–5, 8.

75. Burrall 1930, 10–11; see also n. 72.

76. Burrall 1930, 10; see also n. 70.

77. Borne 1983, 225–26; Anonymous 1932; advertisement for Diamond C Ranch in *Tucson* 7(10), October 1934.

78. Arnold 1925; Burrall 1930, 11; Richard G. Schaus, "Frank Bennett Moson, 1878–1959," *Arizona Cattlelog* 23(2) (1965):48 and back cover.

79. Joseph Wood Krutch, "It's Carr Canyon for Birdwatchers," *Westways* 58, April 1966, 18–19; personal communication, Dr. Robert H. Weber, Socorro, N.M., June 26, 1987.

80. See n. 70; Anonymous, "News from the Ranges," *Tucson* 7(10), October 1934, 20.

81. Arnold 1925.

82. See n. 70; Borne 1983, 42, 55, 66, 206; advertisement for Triangle T Ranch in *Tucson* 7(10), October 1934; *Arizona Daily Star,* February 8, 1937 (clipping); Ervin Bond, *Cochise County, Arizona, Past and Present* (Douglas: privately published, 1984), 88–89; personal communication, Gloria J. Fenner, Tucson, July 4, 1987.

83. Anonymous, "Hosts of the Open Spaces," *Tucson* 6(10), October 1933, 3–5, 8.

84. Borne 1983, 225.

85. Burrall 1930, 11, appendix.

86. Anonymous 1927, 20.

87. Arnold 1925, 38.

88. Borne 1983, 225.

89. Burrall 1930, 12; *Benson News,* February 19, 1927 (clipping); *Arizona Daily Star,* January 19, 1984 (clipping); Anonymous 1927, 23.

90. Burrall 1930, 12; see also Anonymous 1927, 20.

91. Bond 1984, 46–47; personal communication, Richard Y. Murray, Tucson, July 13, 1987.

92. Burrall 1930, 13, appendix; see also Anonymous 1927, 23.

93. Burrall 1930, appendix E.

94. Catrien Ross Laetz, "San Bernardino Ranch," *Arizona Highways* 62(10) (1986):2–11.

Chapter 9

1. Fred Winn, Forest Supervisor, letter with enclosure to Forrest E. Doucette, General Manager, Arizona Year Book, Phoenix, Az., March 11, 1931, located at Forest Archeologist's Office, Coronado National Forest, Tucson; Mary Ellen Lauver, "A History of the Use and Management of the Forested Lands of Arizona, 1862–1936," (M.A. thesis, University of Arizona, 1938), 97; Conrad J. Bahre and Charles F. Hutchinson, "The Impact of Historic Fuelwood Cutting on the Semidesert Woodlands of Southeastern Arizona," *Journal of Forest History* 29(4) (1985).

2. H. C. Grosvenor, "Letter from Arizona," *Railroad Record,* August 12, 1858, 293; "Interesting from Arizona," *Los Angeles Star,* September 4, 1858, p. 2; Richard

H. Coolidge, *Statistical Report on the Sickness and Mortality in the Army of the United States* (Washington, D.C.: George W. Bowman, Printer, 1860), 208.

3. William A. Bell, *New Tracks in North America* (Albuquerque: Horn and Wallace, 1965; reprint of 1870 ed.), 526–27.

4. "Forestry of the Western States and Territories," in *Annual Report of the Commissioner of Agriculture for the Year 1878* (Washington, D.C.: U.S. Government Printing Office, 1879), 533–36.

5. Gifford Pinchot, *Breaking New Ground* (New York: Harcourt, Brace and Co., 1947), 40–41.

6. Royal S. Kellogg, *Report on an Examination of the Graham Mountains in Arizona*, 1902a, located at Forest Archeologist's Office, Coronado National Forest, Tucson; Royal S. Kellogg, "Forest Conditions in Southern Arizona," *Forestry and Irrigation* 8(12) (1902b):501–5; Rex King, "Land Classification of the Santa Catalina Division, Coronado National Forest, Arizona," in *Extensive Land Classification, Santa Catalina Division, Coronado National Forest, Arizona, District 3* (Washington, D.C.: U.S. Department of Agriculture, 1915a).

7. Richard G. Schaus, "William Hudson Kirkland, 1832–1920," *Arizona Cattlelog* 20(3) (1963): 48 and back cover.

8. Robert Lavesco Matheny, "The History of Lumbering in Arizona before World War II" (Ph.D. diss., University of Arizona, 1975), 12–13.

9. "Evidence for the Petitioner," in the Court of Claims, no. 1883, *William S. Grant vs. The United States*, October Term, 1863, p. 156, located at National Archives and Records Administration, Washington, D.C., Record Group 123, U.S. Court of Claims, G.J. Case no. 1883, Folder 1.

10. Matheny 1975, 12–13; David A. Clary, *These Relics of Barbarism: A History of Furniture in Barracks, Hospitals, and Guardhouses of the United States Army, 1800–1880* (Bloomington, Ind.: David A. Clary and Associates, Report DAC-7, March 1982), 311.

11. Schaus 1963; Matheny 1975, 16–17; Robert W. Frazer, *Forts and Supplies: The Role of the Army in the Economy of the Southwest, 1846–1861* (Albuquerque: University of New Mexico Press, 1983), 166–70.

12. *William S. Grant vs. The United States*, 133–34, 155, 167; Richard R. Willey, *La Canoa: A Spanish Land Grant Lost and Found, The Smoke Signal*, no. 38 (Tucson: Tucson Corral of the Westerners, 1979), 165–66.

13. *William S. Grant vs. The United States*, 150, 155, 168, 191.

14. Ibid., 132–33, 155; also William S. Grant, *A Concise Statement of the Prominent Facts and Grounds of Claim Made by Wm. S. Grant . . .* (Washington, D.C.: February 4, 1862), transcript provided by Dr. Martin H. Hall, University of Texas at Arlington.

15. *William S. Grant vs. The United States*, 131, 142, 148, 155–56, 159, 168; Grant 1862; Matheny 1975, 17; Frazer 1983, 178.

16. Carl B. Schoelfield, letter to Fred Winn, September 18, 1941, located at Arizona Historical Society, Frederick Winn Collection, Box 1.

17. Matheny 1975, 18–19; Robert H. Forbes, *The Penningtons: Pioneers of Early Arizona* (Tucson: Arizona Archaeological and Historical Society, 1919), 26–29.

18. "A Mistake Discovered," *Weekly Arizonan,* October 30, 1869, p.2.

19. Matheny 1975, 19–20; Frank D. Reeve, ed., "Albert Franklin Banta: Arizona Pioneer," *New Mexico Historical Review* 27(3) (1952):232–33.

20. See n. 18; *Weekly Arizonan,* February 26, 1870, p. 3.

21. "The Lumber Contract," *Weekly Arizonan,* November 6, 1869, p. 3.

22. Matheny 1975, 21–22; "The Santa Rita Saw-Mill," *Weekly Arizonan,* April 16, 1870, p. 3.

23. J. Richards, "A Treatise on the Construction and Operation of Woodworking Machines," (selections), *Forest History* 9(4) (1966):16–23; William G. Gove, "The Lane Sawmill, Vermont's Contribution of the Century," *Northern Logger and Timber Processor* 30(1982):18–20, 84–90; Richard C. Davis, ed., *Encyclopedia of American Forest and Conservation History* (New York: Macmillan, 1983) 1:724.

24. Matheny 1975, 22–24.

25. Anne E. Harrison, *The Santa Catalinas: A Description and History* (Tucson: Coronado National Forest, 1972), 81–82, 177.

26. T. F. Meagher, Supervisor, Santa Catalina Forest Reserve, letter to the Forester, Washington, D.C., July 28, 1905, located at Arizona Historical Society, Frederick Winn Collection, Box 1.

27. "Beautiful Scenic Road Leads to Mount Lemmon by Route of Oracle; Many Make Trip Today," *Arizona Daily Star,* May 29, 1921, Society Section, p. 1.

28. "Sawmill No Menace to Timber Supply," *Arizona Daily Star,* July 26, 1916, p. 8.

29. Pete Cowgill, "Mill Only One Left in Area," *Arizona Daily Star,* June 16, 1968. This article should be used with care, as it confounds the histories of three sawmills on the north slope of the Santa Catalinas.

30. "Progress in Building Rapid at Summerhaven This Year; Season Still in Full Swing," *Arizona Daily Star,* July 31, 1921, Society Section, p. 1; see also "Summer Colony in Catalinas is Growing Rapidly," *Arizona Daily Star,* June 20, 1920, first section, p. 7; and "Summerhaven," *Arizona Daily Star,* July 14, 1920, p. 4.

31. See n. 29; also Anthony J. Davis, "Catch a Buzz on Mt. Lemmon," *Tucson Citizen,* September 29, 1979.

32. A. M. Gustafson, ed., *John Spring's Arizona* (Tucson: University of Arizona Press, 1966), 58, 111.

33. Cornelius C. Smith, Jr., *Fort Huachuca, The Story of a Fronter Post* (Washington, D.C.: U.S. Government Printing Office, 1981), 26.

34. Matheny 1975, 35–36; Clary 1982, 305–6.

35. Matheny 1975, 35; "The Huachucas," *Tombstone Epitaph,* June 12, 1880, p. 2; see also advertisements in the 1880 issues of *Tombstone Epitaph* and the Tombstone *Daily Nugget.*

36. Matheny 1975, 36; "The Huachucas," *Tombstone Epitaph,* June 12, 1880, p. 2.

37. Matheny 1975, 38–42; Roberta (Biff) Lamma, *A Place Called Sunnyside* (Tucson: A and W Limited Editions, 1982), 21–23, 28.

38. Kellogg 1902b, 503–4.

39. "Report of Scout after Indians, by Capt. T. T. Tidball," *Santa Fe Weekly Gazette,* October 15, 1864, p. 2.

40. *War of the Rebellion: A Compilation of the Official Records of the Union and Confederate Armies,* Series I, vol. 50, pt. 2 (Washington, D.C.: U.S. Government Printing Office, 1897), 1134–35; Charles and Jacqueline Meketa, *One Blanket and Ten Days Rations* (Globe, Ariz.: Southwest Parks and Monuments Association, 1980), 17.

41. Meketa 1980, 19–20.

42. Matheny 1975, 37–38; Interview between Ben Erickson, S. R. Albert, and L. N. Rawdon, January 28, 1970 (extracts), copy at Forest Archeologist's Office, Coronado National Forest, Tucson; *A Proclamation . . . by the President of the United States of America* . . . Chiricahua Forest Reserve, Arizona (second proclamation), November 5, 1906, p. 1 + map.

43. Erickson interview; *Tombstone Epitaph,* December 13, 1880, p. 4; "Chiricahua News," *Tombstone Daily Nugget,* December 16, 1881, p. 3.

44. "From the Chiricahuas," *Tombstone Epitaph,* August 14, 1880, p. 1; "Morse Mill Items," *Tombstone Epitaph,* October 25, 1880, p. 3.

45. Erickson interview; Charles T. McGlone, Forest Officer's Report of Timber Cut, Public Timber Sale, B. B. Riggs, Chiricahua Forest Reserve, Arizona, Case no. 68, June 1, 1903, located at Arizona Historical Society, Frederick Winn Collection, Box 1; John A. Rockfellow, *Log of an Arizona Trail Blazer* (Tucson: Arizona Silhouettes, 1955; republication of 1933 ed., 77, 119; Richard G. Schaus, "William Monroe Riggs, 1861–1949," *Arizona Cattlelog* 20(11) (1964):40 and back cover; Richard G. Schaus, "James Lee Hudson, 1874–1931," *Arizona Cattlelog* 29(8) (1973):32 and back cover.

46. Kellogg 1902b.

47. *Coronado Bulletin,* December 15, 1939, May 3, 1941, November 18, 1941, located at Forest Supervisor's Office, Coronado National Forest, Tucson.

48. U.S. War Department, Surgeon-General's Office, *A Report on the Hygiene of the United States Army, with Descriptions of Military Posts* (Washington, D.C.: U.S. Government Printing Office, 1875), 535; Maj. Gen. Irvin McDowell, *Outline Descriptions of Military Posts in the Military Division of the Pacific* (San Francisco: Presidio of San Francisco, 1879), 10.

49. Eastern Arizona Museum and Historical Society, *Pioneer Town: Pima Centennial History* (Pima, 1979), 217–18; Wm. R. Ridgway, "$100 Reward for Can (and Contents)," *Eastern Arizona Courier,* September 5, 1984, section A, p. 8.

50. Alice Chesley Davis, "A Short History in Connection with Chesley Flat up top of Mount Graham," n.d., copy at Forest Archeologist's Office, Coronado National Forest, Tucson.

51. Eastern Arizona Museum 1979, 218–20, 227.

52. Ibid., 220.

53. Ibid., 224–26.

54. Kellogg 1902a, 6, 10.

55. Anonymous, "Arizona's Mountain Forests," *Forestry and Irrigation* 14(8) (1908):453–54; A. B. Recknagel, "Plan of Management for the Timber on the Mount Graham Division of the Crook National Forest, Arizona," U.S. Department of Agriculture, Forest Service, Circular (Washington, D.C.: U.S. Government Printing Of-

fice, 1911); Rex King, "Land Classification of the Mt. Graham, Santa Teresa and Galiuro Division, Crook National Forest, Arizona," in *Extensive and Intensive Classification, Galiuro, Santa Teresa and Mt. Graham Divisions, Crook National Forest, Arizona, District 3* (Washington, D.C.: U.S. Department of Agriculture, 1915), 7–8.

56. Kellogg 1902a, 4.

57. "The National Forests of Arizona," U.S. Department of Agriculture, Department Circular 318 (Washington, D.C.: U.S. Government Printing Office, August 1924), 11.

58. "Report of the Forester," in *Annual Reports of Department of Agriculture for the Year Ended June 30, 1913* (Washington, D.C.: U.S. Government Printing Office, 1914), 138–39.

59. Matheny 1975, 38–42.

60. Bahre and Hutchinson 1985.

Chapter 10

1. "Suggestions to Homesteaders and Persons Desiring to Make Homestead Entries," U.S. Department of the Interior, General Land Office, Circular no. 541 (Washington, D.C.: U.S. Government Printing Office; 1926); "Homesteads," U.S. Department of the Interior, Bureau of Land Management (Washington, D.C.: U.S. Government Printing Office, 1962); John P. Wilson, *The El Paso Electric Survey, Amrad to Eddy County, Southeastern New Mexico* (Las Cruces, N.M.: Report no. 34, 1984), 183–202.

2. George W. Woodruff, "Agricultural Settlement in Forest Reserves," *Forestry and Irrigation* 12(6) (1906):267–71; "Report of the Forester," in *Annual Reports of Department of Agriculture for the Year Ended June 30, 1910* (Washington, D.C.: U.S. Government Printing Office, 1911), 366–69; Fred Winn, "The Story of Lee Valley and Greer," *Arizona Cattlelog* 25(11) (1969):17.

3. Woodruff 1906; "Homesteads in the National Forests" (Washington, D.C.: U.S. Forest Service, 1917).

4. Henry S. Graves, "Agricultural Lands in National Forests," *American Forestry* 16(9) (1910):560–62; "Report of the Forester," in *Annual Reports of Department of Agriculture for the Year Ended June 30, 1912* (Washington, D.C.: U.S. Government Printing Office, 1913), 481–86; Samuel Trask Dana, *Forest and Range Policy: Its Development in the United States* (New York: McGraw-Hill 1956), 147; Harold K. Steen, *The U.S. Forest Service: A History* (Seattle: University of Washington Press, 1976), 79.

5. Dana 1956, 147–48; "Settlers are Relieved of Big Expense," *Arizona Daily Star*, October 13, 1911, p. 5.

6. Woodruff 1906; "Squatter Rights in National Forests," *American Forestry* 16(4) (1910):252–53; "Report of the Forester," in *Annual Reports of Department of Agriculture for the Year Ended June 30, 1909* (Washington, D.C.: U.S. Government Printing Office, 1910), 375–77.

7. "Report of the Forester," in *Annual Reports of Department of Agriculture for the Year Ended June 30, 1913* (Washington, D.C.: U.S. Government Printing Office, 1914), 136–44.

8. Dana 1956, 149; Rex King, *Extensive Land Classification; Whetstone, Santa Rita, Huachuca and Tumacacori Divisions* [Coronado National Forest] (Washington, D.C.: U.S. Department of Agriculture, 1915c) (pocket in back); "The National Forests of Arizona," U.S. Department of Agriculture, Department Circular 318 (Washington, D.C.: U.S. Government Printing Office, 1924), 10.

9. Dana 1956, 149; "Report of the Forester," in *Annual Reports of Department of Agriculture for the Year Ended June 30, 1923* (Washington, D.C.: U.S. Government Printing Office, 1924), 303; "The National Forests of Arizona."

10. Dana 1956, 149.

11. Homestead Entry Survey Plat Book, Forest Homesteads in Coronado National Forest, n.d., located at Forest Supervisor's Office, Coronado National Forest, Tucson.

12. Martyn D. Tagg, "Investigations at the Ratliff Property (AZ EE:12:34), An Early Homestead in Coronado National Memorial, Southeast Arizona," in *Miscellaneous Historic Period Archeological Projects in the Western Region,* Martyn D. Tagg, comp. (Tucson: Western Archeological and Conservation Center Publications in Anthropology no. 37, 1986), 21–40.

13. Chiricahua National Forest, Record of Settlement, Improvement and Cultivation of Forest Homesteads, 1913, located at Western Archeological and Conservation Center, Tucson, Faraway Ranch Papers (MS1), Series 8, Box 22, Folder 81.

14. Wilson 1984, 183–202.

15. R. R. Hill, "Grazing Administration of the National Forests in Arizona," *American Forestry* 19(9) (1913):581; "Report of the Forester," in *Annual Reports of the Department of Agriculture for the Year Ended June 30, 1914* (Washington, D.C.: U.S. Government Printing Office, 1914), 135.

16. Rex King, "Land Classification of the Santa Catalina Division, Coronado National Forest, Arizona," in *Extensive Land Classification, Santa Catalina Division, Coronado National Forest, Arizona, District 3* (Washington, D.C.: U.S. Department of Agriculture, 1915a), 6.

17. King, 1915c.

18. C. K. Cooperrider and R. W. Hussey, *Range Appraisal Report for the Coronado National Forest* (Tucson: Coronado National Forest, 1924). See also *Coronado-Garces Times,* March 1911, p. 2, located at Forest Archeologist's Office, Coronado National Forest, Tucson.

19. Cooperrider and Hussey 1924.

20. Ibid.

21. William D. Rowley, *U.S. Forest Service Grazing and Rangelands: A History* (College Station: Texas A&M University Press, 1985), 59.

22. Hill 1913, 581; Will C. Barnes, "The U.S. Forest Service," *Out West* 29(2) (1908):100–106.

23. Wilson 1984, 183–202.

24. Dana 1956, 148.

Chapter 11

1. Clarence C. Clendenen, *Blood on the Border: The United States Army and the Mexican Irregulars* (New York: Macmillan, 1969), 119–29.

2. Larry D. Christiansen, "Bullets across the Border," Part I, *Cochise Quarterly* 4(4) (1974):4–5; "Camp Stephen D. Little," in Records of U.S. Army Commands (Army Posts), National Archives Microfilm Publication T-912 (Washington, D.C.: National Archives and Records Service).

3. Christiansen 1974, 6; Reba B. Wells, "Slaughter Ranch Outpost," *Cochise Quarterly* 15(4) (1985):30–36; Catrien Ross Laetz, "San Bernardino Ranch," *Arizona Highways* 62(10) (1986):3–11.

4. John W. Kennedy, "Border Troubles, and Camp Stephen D. Little," *Periodical* no. 35 (1978):16.

5. "Field Return, Provisional Squadron 3d U.S. Cavalry for March 17, 1911," in Returns from U.S. Military Posts, 1800–1916; Douglas, Arizona, January 1911–December 1916, National Archives Microfilm Publication M617, Roll 323.

6. Clendenen 1969, 129–32; Christiansen 1974.

7. Larry D. Christiansen, "Bullets across the Border", Part II, *Cochise Quarterly* 5(1) (1975a):18–36; Cornelius C. Smith Jr., *Fort Huachuca, The Story of a Frontier Post* (Washington, D.C.: U.S. Government Printing Office, 1981), 160–66.

8. Larry D. Christiansen, "Bullets across the Border," Part III, *Cochise Quarterly* 5(4) (1975b):4–7; Major E. L. N. Glass, ed., *The History of the Tenth Cavalry, 1866–1921* (Tucson: printed by Acme Printing Company, 1921), 64–65; Barbara Tully, "Bullets for Breakfast in Naco, Arizona," *True West* 22(5) (1975):6–12.

9. Clendenen 1969, 187–88; Christiansen 1975b, 8–17; Carl H. Cole, "Douglas under Fire: An Account of Villa's Battle for Agua Prieta," *Cochise Quarterly* 14(3) (1984):3–12.

10. Christiansen 1975b; Kennedy 1978.

11. Glass 1921, 65; Jerome W. Howe, "Campaigning in Mexico, 1916," *Journal of Arizona History* 7(3) (1966):126–27.

12. Clendenen 1969, 189; Christiansen 1975b, 16, 21, 27.

13. Returns from U.S. Military Posts, 1800–1916: Douglas, Arizona, January 1911–December 1916, National Archives Microfilm Publication M617, Roll 323.

14. Glass 1921, 64.

15. Clendenen 1969, 346–49; Smith 1981, 214–18.

16. U.S. Army, *Order of Battle of the United States Land Forces in the World War (1917–19), Zone of the Interior,* vol. 3, pt. 1 (Washington, D.C.: U.S. Government Printing Office, 1949), 609–10, map no. 14.

17. Clendenen 1969, 275–76, 287; *War Department Annual Reports, 1916,* (Washington, D.C.: U.S. Government Printing Office, 1916) 1:187–89, 433–34; Henry J. Reilly, "The National Guard on the Mexican Border," in Frank Tompkins, *Chasing Villa* (Harrisburg, Pa.: Military Service Publishing Co., 1934), 222.

18. Reilly 1934, 221–28; Clendenen 1969, 288–97; *War Department Annual Reports, 1916* (Washington, D.C.: U.S. Government Printing Office, 1916) 1:187–89,

193, 433–34; *War Department Annual Reports, 1917* (Washington, D.C.: U.S. Government Printing Office, 1918) 1:196–98; Ronald Gardiner, *The History of AZ EE:9:109; A Military Camp in Nogales, Arizona, 1916 through 1918* (Tucson: Cultural Resource Management Division, Arizona State Museum, 1987).

19. Clendenen 1969, 296–97.

20. *Arizona Daily Star*, January 27, 1917, p. 1, January 28, 1917, p. 1, January 30, 1917, p. 2; Southern Department, 1913–1920, Entry 4442: General Correspondence, 1916–1920, Decimal #370.24, located at National Archives and Records Administration, Washington, D.C.: Record Group 393, Records of the U.S. Army Continental Commands, 1821–1920 (vol. 1).

21. Colonel H. B. Wharfield, "A Fight With the Yaquis at Bear Valley, 1918," *Arizoniana* 4(3) (1963):1–8.

22. Glass 1921, 83–86; Smith 1981, 214–18; Charles H. Harris III and Louis R. Sadler, "The Witzke Affair: German Intrigue on the Mexican Border, 1917–18," *Military Review* 59(2) (1979):36–50, reprinted in Charles H. Harris III and Louis R. Sadler, *The Border and the Revolution* (Las Cruces, N.M.: Center for Latin American Studies/Joint Border Research Institute, New Mexico State University, 1988), 115–29. See also Edwin A. Tucker, *The Early Days: A Sourcebook of Southwestern Region History, Book 1* (Albuquerque: USDA Forest Service, Southwestern Region, Cultural Resources Management Report no. 7, 1989), 151–52.

23. *Cavalry Journal*, October 1923, p. 494, January 1924, p. 117; "Camp Stephen D. Little; Camp Harry J. Jones," in Records of U.S. Army Commands (Army Posts), National Archives Microfilm Publication T-912 (Washington, D.C.: National Archives and Records Service); Christiansen 1975b, 26–27.

Chapter 12

1. U.S. War Department, Surgeon General's Office, *A Report on Barracks and Hospitals, With Descriptions of Military Posts* (Washington, D.C.: U.S. Government Printing Office, 1870), 466; William A. Bell, *New Tracks in North America* (Albuquerque: Horn and Wallace, 1965; reprint of 1870 ed.), 327; John G. Bourke, *On the Border with Crook* (Glorieta, N.M.: Rio Grande Press, 1969; reprint of 1891 ed.), 11, 35, 53; Sandra L. Myres, ed., "An Arizona Camping Trip; May Banks Stacey's Account of an Outing to Mount Graham in 1879," *Arizona and the West* 23(1) (1981):53–64.

2. George Stone Wilson, "Saga of Oracle, Mountain Cow Town," Parts I–X, *Arizona Cattlelog* 21(12) through 22(9) (1964–65); Anne E. Harrison, *The Santa Catalinas: A Description and History* (Tucson: Coronado National Forest, 1972), 82, 174.

3. Harrison 1972, 44.

4. *The Arizona Daily Star*, February 14, 1962 (clipping).

5. *Pioneer Town: Pima Centennial History* (Pima: Eastern Arizona Museum and Historical Society, 1979), 226–27, 230–33.

6. Royal S. Kellogg, *Report on an Examination of the Graham Mountains in*

Arizona, 1902a, located at Forest Archeologist's Office, Coronado National Forest, Tucson.

7. Rex King, "Land Classification of the Mt. Graham, Santa Teresa and Galiuro Division, Crook National Forest, Arizona," in *Extensive and Intensive Classification, Galiuro, Santa Teresa and Mt. Graham Divisions, Crook National Forest, Arizona, District 3* (Washington, D.C.: U.S. Department of Agriculture, 1915b), 5, 8.

8. Glen O. Robinson, *The Forest Service: A Study in Public Land Management* (Baltimore: Johns Hopkins University Press, 1975), 120–21; the law is 38 Stat. 1101.

9. *Arizona Daily Star,* July 10, 1910, section II, p. 1, August 10, 1910, p. 7, August 19, 1910, p.2, August 21, 1910, section II, p. 7, September 13, 1910, p. 7.

10. *Coronado Quarterly,* July 1911, p. 3, located at Forest Archeologist's Office, Coronado National Forest, Tucson; Harrison 1972, 55–56; John E. Myers, "The Catalina Mountains and Oracle As a Summer Resort," *Arizona: The New State Magazine* 3(7) (1913):4; *Arizona Daily Star,* June 21, 1911, p. 8, July 8, 1911, p. 2, September 7, 1911, p. 6, June 22, 1919, section II, p. 6, February 14, 1962 (clipping); *Arizona Republic,* May 21, 1977 (clipping).

11. *Arizona Daily Star,* September 2, 1916, p. 8, September 8, 1916, p. 6.

12. Stanley F. Wilson, "Development of a Mountain Summer Resort," *Coronado Almanac,* 1917, located at Western Archeological and Conservation Center, Tucson, Faraway Ranch Papers (MS1), Series 37, Box 60, Folder 4.

13. *Arizona Daily Star,* July 26, 1916, p. 8, September 26, 1916, p. 2, October 24, 1916, p. 6.

14. *The Arizona Daily Star,* February 21, 1917, p. 2, June 3, 1919, section I, p. 3, June 10, 1919, section I, p. 5, June 2, 1920, p. 8, July 14, 1920, p. 4, July 20, 1920, p. 8.

15. *The Arizona Daily Star,* June 2, 1920, p. 8, August 24, 1920, p. 3, August 16, 1921, p. 6.

16. Glenton G. Sykes, "First Mount Lemmon Road," n.d., located at Arizona Historical Society, ephemera file, Arizona Mountains—Mt. Lemmon; *Arizona Daily Star,* February 14, 1962 (clipping), September 11, 1981 (clipping).

17. *The Arizona Daily Star,* July 26, 1916, p. 8, July 9, 1920, p. 3, May 29, 1921, Society Section, p. 1; Harrison Burrall, *Forest Recreation Plan* (Tucson: Coronado National Forest, 1930), 8, located at Forest Supervisor's Office, Coronado National Forest, Tucson.

18. Anonymous, *Arizona Summerland Resort Directory,* fourth annual ed., 1927, 18.

19. *Coronado Bulletin,* January 13, 1928.

20. *Arizona Daily Star,* May 28, 1919, section I, p. 5, June 5, 1919, section I, p. 4, June 6, 1920, Society Section, p. 1, June 20, 1920, section I, p. 7, July 9, 1920, p. 3, May 15, 1921, Society Section, p. 1, May 31, 1921, section I, p. 2, June 5, 1921, p. 12, July 12, 1921, Society Section, p. 1, July 17, 1921, Society Section, p. 1, February 14, 1962 (clipping).

21. *Arizona Daily Star,* June 6, 1920, Society Section, p. 1.

22. *Arizona Daily Star,* June 20, 1920, section I, p. 7, June 22, 1920, p. 3, July 9, 1920, p. 3, July 14, 1920, p. 4, July 28, 1920, p. 3.

23. *Arizona Daily Star,* July 20, 1920, p. 8.

24. *Arizona Daily Star,* September 12, 1920, Society Section, p. 1.

25. Burrall 1930, 8. The decline may have occurred before 1926; see Fred G. Vickers, "Mt. Lemmon—An All-Year Resort," *Progressive Arizona* 2(6) (1926): 23–24.

26. Burrall 1930, 8.

27. *Arizona Daily Star,* September 15, 1974 (clipping).

28. *Arizona Daily Star,* April 24, 1932 (clipping).

29. *Arizona Daily Star,* May 20, 1910, p. 2, June 19, 1910, section II, p. 1, July 14, 1910, p. 7, August 7, 1910, section II, p. 9, August 20, 1910, p. 7, September 21, 1910, p. 7.

30. *Arizona Daily Star,* June 7, 1911, p. 5, June 18, 1911, section II, p. 1.

31. *Arizona Daily Star,* June 20, 1920, Society Section, p. 1, June 29, 1920, p. 3, August 1, 1920, section I, p. 3.

32. *Arizona Daily Star,* July 22, 1921, p. 3, August 25, 1921, Society Section, p. 1, August 30, 1921, Society Section, p. 1.

33. See nn. 18 and 28; Burrall 1930, 10; "Santa Rita Trails Resort" brochure, c. 1927–30, located at Arizona Historical Society, ephemera file, Mountains—Arizona—Santa Rita.

34. *Arizona Daily Star,* June 19, 1910, section II, p. 1, September 10, 1910, p. 5, August 2, 1959 (clipping); *Tucson Daily Citizen,* August 21, 1973 (clipping); March 25, 1976 (clipping).

35. *Arizona Daily Star,* June 11, 1916, section II, p. 2, September 10, 1916, section II, p. 2, August 27, 1919, p. 8 July 20, 1920, pp. 3, 8, September 7, 1921, Society Section, p. 1.

36. Anonymous 1927, 22.

37. Burrall 1930, 11, 13–14.

38. Folio, Plats of Summer Home Areas, Coronado National Forest, c. 1926–1975, and File, Turkey Flat Summer Home Area, Coronado National Forest, 1928–1940, both located at Forest Supervisor's Office, Coronado National Forest, Tucson.

39. U.S. Department of Commerce, Bureau of Public Roads, Division Seven, *Final Construction Report, Arizona Forest Highway Project 33, Catalina Highway; Coronado National Forest, Pima County, Arizona* (Tucson: Coronado National Forest [?], 1951); Lawrence W. Cheek, "Try a Drive up Mount Lemmon," *Arizona Highways* 66(7) (1990):38, 41–43.

40. U.S. Department of Commerce, *Catalina Highway,* (1951):7. "Echoes From Mt. Lemmon," *The Magazine Tucson* 1(6) (1948):34.

41. "The Story of Mt. Lemmon," *The Magazine Tucson* 1(5) (1948):18–25; "Echoes from Mt. Lemmon," *The Magazine Tucson* 1(6) (1948):34; *Arizona Daily Star,* May 30, 1954 (clipping), August 3, 1976 (clipping); *Tucson Citizen,* July 20, 1984 (clipping); *Arizona Republic,* August 4, 1985 (clipping).

Chapter 13

1. "The National Forests of Arizona," U.S. Department of Agriculture, Department Circular 318 (Washington, D.C.: U.S. Government Printing Office, 1924), 10. These figures apparently refer to lands patented under all homsteading entry systems, including the Act of June 11, 1906. See also Edwin A. Tucker, *The Early Days: A Source-book of Southwestern Region History, Book 1* (Albuquerque: USDA Forest Service, Southwestern Region, Cultural Resources Management Report no. 7, 1989), 88–89, 142–43, 164–65.

2. See *The Civilian Conservation Corps, Coronado National Forest, 1933–1942* (Albuquerque: USDA Forest Service, Southwestern Region, 1991).

REFERENCES

Authored Works

Aguirre, Yginio F.

1975 Echoes of the Conquistadores: Stock Raising in Spanish-Mexican Times. *Journal of Arizona History* 16(3):267–86.

Albert, S.R.

1974 History of Camp John A. Rucker. *Arizona Cattlelog* 30(10): 18–27, 30(11):24–27.

Allen, Larry S.

1987 *Livestock and the Coronado National Forest: A Historical Perspective.* Manuscript on file, Supervisor's office, Coronado National Forest, Tucson.

Alsop, J. T., T. J. Bidwell, and F. H. Goodwin [Indian Committee]

1964 *Memorial and Affidavits Showing Outrages Perpetrated by the Apache Indians, in the Territory of Arizona, for the Years 1869 and 1870.* Reprint of 1871 ed. Tucson: Territorial Press.

Altshuler, Constance Wynn

1973a The Case of Sylvester Mowry: The Charge of Treason. *Arizona and the West* 15(1):63–82.

1973b The Case of Sylvester Mowry: The Mowry Mine. *Arizona and the West* 15(2):149–74.

1983 *Starting with Defiance.* Tucson: Arizona Historical Society.

Altshuler, Constance Wynn, ed.

1969 *Latest from Arizona!* Tucson: Arizona Pioneers' Historical Society.

1984 Arizona in 1861: A Contemporary Account by Samuel Robinson. *Journal of Arizona History* 25(1):21–76.

Ames, Charles R.

1977 Along the Mexican Border—Then and Now. *Journal of Arizona History* 18(4):431–46.

Ames, George Walcott Jr., ed.

1942 A Doctor Comes to California. *California Historical Society Quarterly* 21(3):193–224.

Anonymous

1859 Silver and Copper Mining in Arizona, With a Map, *and* Processes for the Extraction of Silver, Followed at the Reducing Establishments of the Heintzelman Mines, Arizona, and the Real del Monte Mines, Mexico. *The Mining Magazine and Journal of Geology,* Second Series 1(1):1–18.

1897 Campaigning in Arizona and New Mexico, 1895–6. *Journal of the United States Cavalry Association* 10(36):25–28.

1908 Arizona's Mountain Forests. *Forestry and Irrigation* 14(8): 453–54.

1910a Squatter Rights in National Forests. *American Forestry* 16(4): 252–53.

1910b Marble Quarrying in Arizona. *Mine and Quarry,* October 1910:440–43.

1914 Goat Raising in Arizona. *Arizona: The New State Magazine* 4(6–7):16.

1927 *Arizona Summerland Resort Directory.* Fourth Annual Ed. 1927.

1932 Guest Ranches Abound Near Tucson. *Tucson* 5(10):1–4.

1933 Hosts of the Open Spaces. *Tucson* 6(10):3–5, 8.

1934a News from the Ranges. *Tucson* 7(10):20.

1934b The History of Faraway Ranch. *Hoofs and Horns* 4(5):2, 16.

1935 Col. John Finkle Stone and The Apache Pass Mining Company. *Arizona Historical Review* 6(3):74–80.

1948a The Story of Mt. Lemmon. *The Magazine Tucson* 1(5):18–25.

1948b Echoes From Mt. Lemmon. *The Magazine Tucson* 1(6):34.

Arizona Bureau of Mines

1950 *Arizona Zinc and Lead Deposits, Part I.* Arizona Bureau of Mines, Bulletin 156, University of Arizona Bulletin 21(2). Tucson: University of Arizona.

1951 *Arizona Zinc and Lead Deposits, Part II.* Arizona Bureau of Mines, Bulletin 158, University of Arizona Bulletin 22(3). Tucson: University of Arizona.

Arnold, Lowell J.

1925 Dude Ranches of Southern Arizona. *Progressive Arizona* 1(3): 13–16, 38–39.

1926 Vacationing at Circle Z Ranch. *Progressive Arizona* 2(1):15–16.

Austerman, Wayne R.

1985 *Sharps Rifles and Spanish Mules.* College Station: Texas A&M University Press.

Austin, William Lane

1927 *United States Census of Agriculture, 1925. Part III, The Western States.* Washington, D.C.: U.S. Government Printing Office.

Ayres, James E.

1984 *Rosemont: The History and Archaeology of Post-1880 Sites in the Rosemont Area, Santa Rita Mountains, Arizona.* Arizona State Museum, Cultural Resource Management Division, Archaeological Series no. 147, vol. 3. Tucson.

Bahre, Conrad J.

1977 *Land-Use History of the Research Ranch, Elgin, Arizona.* Journal of the Arizona Academy of Science 12 (Supplement 2).

Bahre, Conrad J., and Charles F. Hutchinson

1985 The Impact of Historic Fuelwood Cutting on the Semidesert Woodlands of Southeastern Arizona. *Journal of Forest History* 29(4):175–86.

Bailey, L.R., ed.

1963 *The A. B. Gray Report.* Republication of 1856 ed. Los Angeles: Westernlore Press.

Baldwin, Percy M., ed.

1926 *Discovery of the Seven Cities of Cibola by the Father Fray Marcos de Niza.* Historical Society of New Mexico Publications in History, vol. 1. Albuquerque: El Palacio Press.

Ball, Eve

1980 *Indeh, an Apache Odyssey.* Provo: Brigham Young University Press.

Bancroft, Hubert Howe

1883 *North Mexican States,* vol. 1, 1531–1800. (Vol. 10 of his *History of The Pacific States of North America).* San Francisco: A. L. Bancroft and Company.

1889 *History of Arizona and New Mexico, 1530–1888.* (Also published as vol. 15 of his *Works*). San Francisco: History Company.

Bandelier, Adolph F.

1890 *Final Report of Investigations Among the Indians of the Southwestern United States, Carried on Mainly in the Years from 1880 to 1885,* part 1. Cambridge, Mass.: John Wilson and Son.

1892 *Final Report of Investigations Among the Indians of the Southwestern United States, Carried on Mainly in the Years from 1880 to 1885,* part 2. Cambridge, Mass.: John Wilson and Son.

1929 The Discovery of New Mexico by Fray Marcos of Nizza. *New Mexico Historical Review* 4(1):28–44.

1969 *A History of the Southwest.* Supplement to volume 1. Rome: Jesuit Historical Institute.

Bandelier, Fanny, trans.

1972 *The Narrative of Alvar Núñez Cabeza de Vaca.* Barre, Mass.: Imprint Society.

Banning, Captain William, and George Hugh Banning

1930 *Six Horses.* New York: Century.

Bannon, John Francis

1955 *The Mission Frontier in Sonora, 1620–1687.* New York: United States Catholic Historical Society.

Barnes, Will C.
1908 The U.S. Forest Service. *Out West* 29(2):89–109.
1913 *Western Grazing Grounds and Forest Ranges.* Chicago: Breeder's Gazette.
1926 The Story of the Range, *and* National Forests and the Public Domain: Information Furnished by Will C. Barnes, Assistant Forester, Department of Agriculture. Hearings before a Subcommittee of the Committee on Public Lands and Surveys, United States Senate, 69th Cong. 1st sess., Pursuant to S. Res. 347. 2:1579–640, 1642–825. Washington, D.C.: U.S. Government Printing Office.

Barney, James M.
1933 *Tales of Apache Warfare.* N.p.; published by the author.

Barrett, S.M. (editor)
1971 *Geronimo, His Own Story.* Republication of 1906 ed. New York: Ballantine Books.

Bartlett, John Russell
1965 *Personal Narrative of Explorations and Incidents in Texas, New Mexico, California, Sonora, and Chihuahua, . . .* 2 vols. Reprint of 1854 ed. Chicago: Rio Grande Press.

Baumler, Mark F.
1984 *The Archeology of Faraway Ranch, Arizona.* Western Archeological and Conservation Center, Publications in Anthropology no. 24. Tucson.

Bell, William A.
1965 *New Tracks in North America.* Reprint of 1870 ed. Albuquerque: Horn and Wallace.

Bentz, Donald N.
1965 Sword of Revenge. *Golden West* 1(6):22–26, 58–59.

Bieber, Ralph P., ed.
1974 *Exploring Southwestern Trails, 1846–1854.* Reprint of 1938 ed. Philadelphia: Porcupine Press

Blake, William P.
1902 The Geology of the Galiuro Mountains, Arizona, and of the Gold-Bearing Ledge Known as Gold Mountain. *The Engineering and Mining Journal* 73:546–47 (April 2, 1902).
1910 Sketch of Pima Co., Ariz., Mining Districts, Minerals, Climate and Agriculture. *Arizona Daily Star,* June 19, 1910, 1st section, p. 6, section 2, p. 4; June 26, 1910, 1st section, p. 6, section 2, p. 4.

Bloom, Lansing B.
1940 Who Discovered New Mexico? *New Mexico Historical Review* 15(2):101–32.

Bloom, Lansing B., ed.
1934 Bourke on the Southwest, II. *New Mexico Historical Review* 9(1):33–77.

Bolton, Herbert Eugene

1919 *Kino's Historical Memoir of Pimería Alta,* vol. I. Cleveland: Arthur H. Clark.

1930 *Anza's California Expeditions,* vol. 2. Berkeley: University of California Press.

1964 *Coronado, Knight of Pueblos and Plains.* Reprint of 1949 ed. Albuquerque: The University of New Mexico Press.

1967 *Spanish Exploration in the Southwest, 1542–1706.* Reprint of 1908 ed. New York: Barnes and Noble.

Bond, Ervin

1984 *Cochise County, Arizona, Past and Present.* Douglas: published by the author.

Borne, Lawrence R.

1983 *Dude Ranching: A Complete History.* Albuquerque: University of New Mexico Press.

Bourke, John B.

1969 *On the Border with Crook.* Reprint of 1892 ed. Glorieta, N.M.: Rio Grande Press.

Bourne, Eulalia "Sister"

1974 *Ranch Schoolteacher.* Tucson: University of Arizona Press.

Bowden, Charles

1987 Frog Mountain Blues. (Tucson) *City Magazine* 2(4):29–34.

Brandes, Ray

1960 *Frontier Military Posts of Arizona.* Globe, Ariz.: Dale Stuart King.

Brandes, Ray, and Ralph A. Smith

1962 *The Scalp Business on the Border, 1837–1850. The Smoke Signal,* No. 6. Tucson: Tucson Corral of the Westerners.

Brinckerhoff, Sidney B.

1967 The Last Years of Spanish Arizona, 1786–1821. *Arizona and the West* 9(1):5–20.

Brinckerhoff, Sidney B., and Odie B. Faulk

1965 *Lancers for the King.* Phoenix: Arizona Historical Foundation.

Brophy, Frank Cullen

1966 San Ignacio del Babacomari. *Arizona Highways* 42(9):2–17.

Brown, David E., ed.

1982 Biotic Communities of the American Southwest—United States and Mexico. *Desert Plants* 4(1–4):37–39, 43–48, 59–65, 70–71.

Brown, David E., and Charles H. Lowe

1983 *Biotic Communities of the Southwest,* General Technical Report RM-78. Fort Collins, Colo.: Rocky Mountain Forest and Range Experiment Station.

Browne, J. Ross

1868 *Report of J. Ross Browne on the Mineral Resources of the States and Territories West of the Rocky Mountains.* Washington, D.C.: U.S. Government Printing Office.

1974 *Adventures in the Apache Country.* Reprint of 1950 ed. Tucson: University of Arizona Press.

Burrall, Harrison

1930 *Forest Recreation Plan.* Tucson: Coronado National Forest.

Burrus, Ernest J.

1971 *Kino and Manje: Explorers of Sonora and Arizona.* Rome: Jesuit Historical Institute.

Callender, J. F., Jan C. Wilt, and R. E. Clemons, eds.

1978 *Land of Cochise: Southeastern Arizona.* New Mexico Geological Society (in cooperation with the Arizona Geological Society), 29th Field Conference. Socorro: New Mexico Geological Society.

Calvin, Ross, ed.

1951 *Lieutenant Emory Reports.* Albuquerque: University of New Mexico Press.

Cameron, Colin

1896 "Report of Colin Cameron Esq." In "Report of the Governor of Arizona [1896]," *Report of the Secretary of the Interior . . .* 3:222–31. 54th Cong. 2d sess., House Doc. no. 5. Washington, D.C.: U.S. Government Printing Office.

Campbell, Albert H.

1969 *Report upon the Pacific Wagon Roads.* Reprint of 1859 ed. Fairfield, Wash.: Ye Galleon Press.

Carman, Ezra A., H. A. Heath, and John Minto

1892 *Special Report on the History and Present Condition of the Sheep Industry of the United States.* U.S. Department of Agriculture, Bureau of Animal Industry. Washington, D.C.: U.S. Government Printing Office.

Chamberlain, Samuel E.

1956 *My Confession.* Tucson: Arizona Silhouettes.

Chapel, William L.

1973 Camp Rucker: Outpost in Apacheria. *Journal of Arizona History* 14(2):95–112.

Chapline, W. R.

1919 *Production of Goats on Far Western Ranges.* U.S. Department of Agriculture, Bulletin no. 749. Washington, D.C.: U.S. Government Printing Office.

Cheek, Lawrence W.

1990 Try a Drive up Mount Lemmon. *Arizona Highways* 66(7): 38–43.

Christiansen, Larry D.
1974–75 Bullets across the Border, Parts I–III. *Cochise Quarterly* 4(4): 3–20, 5(1):18–36, 5(4):3–27.

Christiansen, Paige W.
1974 *The Story of Mining in New Mexico. Scenic Trips to the Geologic Past,* no. 12. Socorro: New Mexico Bureau of Mines and Mineral Resources.

Claridge, Eleanor
1989 *Klondyke and the Aravaipa Canyon.* Safford, Ariz.: published by the author.

Claridge, Junietta
1975 We Tried to Stay Refined: Pioneering in the Mineral Strip. *Journal of Arizona History* 16(4):405–26.

Clarke, Carol
1961 The Longoreña. *Arizoniana* 2(2):31–34.

Clarke, Dwight L., ed.
1966 *The Original Journals of Henry Smith Turner: With Stephen Watts Kearny to New Mexico and California 1846–1847.* Norman: University of Oklahoma Press.

Clarke, Mary Whatley
1984 *John Simpson Chisum.* Austin: Eakin Press.

Clary, David A.
1982 *These Relics of Barbarism: A History of Furniture in Barracks, Hospitals, and Guardhouses of the United States Army, 1800–1880.* Report DAC-7. Bloomington, Ind.: David A. Clary and Associates. Published in part under same title by National Park Service, Harpers Ferry Center, 1985.

Clawson, Marion
1950 *The Western Range Livestock Industry.* New York: McGraw-Hill.

Clendenen, Clarence C.
1969 *Blood on the Border: The United States Army and the Mexican Irregulars.* New York: Macmillan.

Clothier, R.W.
1913 *Dry-Farming in the Arid Southwest.* University of Arizona Agricultural Experiment Station, Bulletin no. 70. Tucson: University of Arizona.

Clum, John P.
1928 Geronimo. *New Mexico Historical Review* 3(1):1–40, 3(2); 121–44, 3(3):217–64.

Cole, Carl H.
1984 Douglas under Fire: An Account of Villa's Battle for Agua Prieta. *Cochise Quarterly* 14(3):3–12.

Colton, Ray C.
1959 *The Civil War in the Western Territories.* Norman: University of Oklahoma Press.

Colyer, Vincent
1872 *Peace with the Apaches of New Mexico and Arizona.* Washington, D.C.: U.S. Government Printing Office.

Conkling, Roscoe P. and Margaret B.
1947 *The Butterfield Overland Mail, 1857–1869.* 3 vols. Glendale, Cal.: Arthur H. Clark.

Coolidge, Richard H.
1860 *Statistical Report on the Sickness and Mortality in the Army of the United States.* Washington, D.C.: George W. Bowman, Printer.

Cooper, John R., and Leon T. Silver
1964 *Geology and Ore Deposits of the Dragoon Quadrangle, Cochise County, Arizona.* U.S. Geological Survey, Professional Paper 416. Washington, D.C.: U.S. Government Printing Office.

Cooperrider, C. K., and R. W. Hussey
1924 *Range Appraisal Report for the Coronado National Forest.* Tucson: Coronado National Forest.

Cozzens, Samuel W.
1967 *The Marvellous Country.* Reprint of 1874 ed. Minneapolis: Ross and Haines.

Cramer, Harry G., III
1976 Tom Jeffords—Indian Agent. *Journal of Arizona History* 17(3): 265–300.

Creasey, S. C., J. E. Jinks, F. E. Williams, and H. C. Meeves
1981 *Mineral Resources of the Galiuro Wilderness and Contiguous Further Planning Areas, Arizona.* U.S. Geological Survey, Bulletin 1490. Washington, D.C.: U.S. Government Printng Office.

Creasey, S. C., and George L. Quick
1955 *Copper Deposits of Part of Helvetia Mining District, Pima County, Arizona.* U.S. Geological Survey Bulletin 1027-F. Washington, D.C.: U.S. Government Printing Office.

Dana, Samuel Trask
1956 *Forest and Range Policy: Its Development in the United States.* New York: McGraw-Hill.

Darrow, Robert A.
1944 *Arizona Range Resources and Their Utilization: I. Cochise County.* Arizona Agricultural Experiment Station, Technical Bulletin no. 103. Tucson: University of Arizona.

Davis, Britton
1976 *The Truth about Geronimo.* Reprint of 1929 ed. Lincoln: University of Nebraska Press.

Davis, Richard C., ed.
1983 *Encyclopedia of American Forest and Conservation History.* Vol. 1. New York: Macmillan.

Deffer, Dale Ann
1989 Flying V Ranch Still Soaring High. *Arizona History* 6(4):4–5.

DiPeso, Charles C., John B. Rinaldo, and Gloria J. Fenner
1974 *Casas Grandes: A Fallen Trading Center of the Gran Chichimeca,* vol. 4. Dragoon, Ariz.: Amerind Foundation.

Dobyns, Henry F.
1962 *Pioneering Christians among the Perishing Indians of Tucson.* Lima, Peru: Editorial Estudios Andinos.
1963 Indian Extinction in the Middle Santa Cruz River Valley, Arizona. *New Mexico Historical Review* 38(2):161–81.
1964 *Lance, Ho! Containment of the Western Apaches by the Royal Spanish Garrison at Tucson..* Lima, Peru: Editorial Estudios Andinos.
1976 *Spanish Colonial Tucson.* Tucson: University of Arizona Press.
1981 *From Fire to Flood: Historic Human Destruction of Sonoran Desert Riverine Oases.* Socorro, N.M.: Ballena Press.

Dobyns, Henry F., ed.
1961 *Hepah, California! The Journal of Cave Johnson Couts from Monterey, Nuevo Leon, Mexico to Los Angeles, California during the years 1848–1849.* Tucson: Arizona Pioneers' Historical Society.

Donohue, John Augustine
1969 *After Kino: Jesuit Missions in Northwestern New Spain, 1711–1767.* Rome: Jesuit Historical Institute.

Drachman, S.H.
1899 Pioneer History of Arizona—Arizona Pioneers and Apaches. *Arizona Graphic* 1(10):3–4, 7 (November 18, 1899).

Drewes, Harald, and Frank E. Williams
1973 *Mineral Resources of the Chiricahua Wilderness Area, Cochise County, Arizona.* U.S. Geological Survey, Bulletin 1385-A. Washington, D.C.: U.S. Government Printing Office.

Duffen, William A., ed.
1960 Overland Via 'Jackass Mail' in 1858: The Diary of Phocion R. Way, parts I–IV. *Arizona and the West* 2(1):35–53, (2):147–64, (3):279–92, (4):353–70.

Dunne, Peter Masten
1955 *Jacobo Sedelmayr: Missionary, Frontiersman, Explorer in Arizona and Sonora; Four Original Manuscript Narratives, 1744–1751.* Tucson: Arizona Pioneers' Historical Society.
1957 *Juan Antonio Balthasar: Padre Visitador to the Sonora Frontier, 1744–1745.* Tucson: Arizona Pioneers' Historical Society.

Dunning, Charles H.
1966 *Rocks to Riches.* Pasadena, Cal.: Hicks Publishing Corporation.

Eastern Arizona Museum and Historical Society
1979 *Pioneer Town: Pima Centennial History.* Pima.

Emory, William H.
1848 *Notes of a Military Reconnoisance, from Fort Leavenworth, in Missouri, to San Diego, in California.* 30th Cong. 1st Sess., House Exec. Doc. no. 41 (serial no. 517). Washington, D.C.: Wendell and Van Benthuysen, Printers.
1857 *Report on the United States and Mexican Boundary Survey, Made under the Direction of the Secretary of the Interior.* 34th Cong. 1st Sess., Senate Exec. Doc. No. 108, vol. 1, pt. 1 (serial no. 832). Washington, D.C.: A. O. P. Nicholson, Printer.

Erickson, Neil
1931 Trailing the Apache. *Our Army* 3(11):6–7, 45–46.

Espinosa, J. Manuel
1942 *Crusaders of the Rio Grande.* Chicago: Institute of Jesuit History.

Ewing, Russell Charles
1945 The Pima Uprising of 1751: A Study of Spanish-Indian Relations on the Frontier of New Spain. In *Greater America: Essays in Honor of Herbert Eugene Bolton,* 259–80. Berkeley: University of California Press.

Farish, Thomas Edwin
1918 *History of Arizona.* Vol. 8. Cleveland: Arthur H. Clark.

Feil, Lin B.
1968 Helvetia: Boom Town of the Santa Ritas. *Journal of Arizona History* 9(2):77–95.

Fenneman, Nevin M.
1931 *Physiography of Western United States.* New York: McGraw-Hill.

Finch, Boyd
1969 Sherod Hunter and the Confederates in Arizona. *Journal of Arizona History* 10(3):139–206.

Fontana, Bernard L.
1958 The Mowry Mine: 1858–1958. *The Kiva* 23(3):14–16.
1963 *Biography of a Desert Church: The Story of Mission San Xavier del Bac. The Smoke Signal* (3). Tucson: Tucson Corral of the Westerners.

1971 *Calabazas of the Rio Rico. The Smoke Signal* (24): Tucson: Tucson Corral of the Westerners.

Fontana, Bernard L., and Daniel S. Matson

1987 Santa Ana de Cuiquiburitac: Pimería Alta's Northernmost Mission. *Journal of the Southwest,* 29(2):133–59.

Forbes, Jack D.

1957 The Janos, Jocomes, Mansos and Sumas Indians. *New Mexico Historical Review* 32(4):319–34.

1959 The Appearance of the Mounted Indian in Northern Mexico and the Southwest, to 1680. *Southwestern Journal of Anthropology* 15(2):189–212.

1960 *Apache, Navaho and Spaniard.* Norman: University of Oklahoma Press.

Forbes, Robert H.

1919 *The Penningtons, Pioneers of Early Arizona.* Tucson: Arizona Archaeological and Historical Society.

Forrest, Earle R.

1965 The Fabulous Sierra Bonita. *Journal of Arizona History* 6(3): 132–47.

Forsyth, George A.

1900 *Thrilling Days In Army Life.* New York: Harper and Brothers.

Frazer, Robert W.

1983 *Forts and Supplies: The Role of the Army in the Economy of the Southwest, 1846–1861.* Albuquerque: University of New Mexico Press.

Frink, Maurice, W. Turrentine Jackson, and Agnes Wright Spring

1956 *When Grass Was King.* Boulder: University of Colorado Press.

Gale, Jack C.

1977 Hatfield under Fire, May 15, 1886. *Journal of Arizona History* 18(4):447–68.

1981 Lebo in Pursuit. *Journal of Arizona History* 21(1):11–24.

Galina, Miguel A., Magdalena, Guerrero, Virginia Rojas, Ma. de Los Angeles Ruiz, and Vicente Vázquez

1982 Social Status of the Goat Industry in Mexico. In *Proceedings of the Third International Conference on Goat Production and Disease,* 420–21. Scottsdale, Ariz.: Dairy Goat Journal Publishing Co.

Gardiner, Arthur D.

1957 Letter of Father Middendorff, S.J., Dated from Tucson 3 March 1757. *The Kiva* 22(4):1–10.

Gardiner, Ronald

1987 *The History of AZ EE:9:109; A Military Camp in Nogales, Arizona, 1916 through 1918.* Tucson: Arizona State Museum, Cultural Resource Management Division.

Gatewood, Charles B., Lieutenant
1986 The Surrender of Geronimo. *Journal of Arizona History* 27(1): 53–70.

Gerald, Rex E.
1968 *Spanish Presidios of the Late Eighteenth Century in Northern New Spain.* Museum of New Mexico Research Records, no. 7. Santa Fe: Museum of New Mexico Press.
1974 The Suma Indians of Northern Chihuahua and Western Texas. In *Apache Indians III,* ed. David A. Horr, 67–114. New York: Garland Publishing.

Gilluly, James
1956 *General Geology of Central Cochise County, Arizona.* U.S. Geological Survey Professional Paper 281. Washington, D.C.: U.S. Government Printing Office.

Glass, E. L. N., Major
1921 *The History of the Tenth Cavalry, 1866–1921.* Tucson: Acme Printing Company.

Goetzmann, William H.
1959 *Army Exploration in the American West, 1803–1863.* New Haven: Yale University Press.

Gordon, Clarence W.
1883 "Arizona Territory." In Report on Cattle, Sheep, and Swine, *Report on the Productions of Agriculture As Returned at the Tenth Census* (June 1, 1880), 92–103. Washington, D.C.: U.S. Government Printing Office.

Gove, William G.
1982 The Lane Sawmill, Vermont's Contribution of the Century. *Northern Logger and Timber Processor* 30 (May 1982):18–20, 84–90.

Graeme, R.S.
1987 Bisbee, Arizona's Dowager Queen of Mining Camps; A Look at Her First 50 Years. In *History of Mining in Arizona,* ed. by J. Michael Canty and Michael N. Greeley, p. 51–76. Tucson: Mining Club of the Southwest Foundation.

Graham, Jeanne L.
1979 The Canyon Named for a Hero. *Cochise Quarterly* 9(2):3–17.

Granger, Byrd H.
1960 *Will C. Barnes' Arizona Place Names.* Tucson: The University of Arizona Press.

Granger, H. C., and R. B. Raup
1962 *Reconnaissance Study of Uranium Deposits in Arizona.* U.S. Geological Survey Bulletin 1147-A. Washington, D.C.: U.S. Government Printing Office.

Graves, Henry S.
1910 Agricultural Lands in National Forests. *American Forestry* 16(9):560–62.

Greeley, Michael N.
1987 The Early Influence of Mining in Arizona. In *History of Mining in Arizona,* ed. by J. Michael Canty and Michael N. Greeley, 13–50. Tucson: Mining Club of the Southwest Foundation.

Gressley, Gene M.
1971 *Bankers and Cattlemen.* Reprint of 1966 ed. Lincoln: University of Nebraska Press.

Griffen, William B.
1979 *Indian Assimilation in the Franciscan Area of Nueva Vizcaya.* Anthropological Papers of the University of Arizona, no. 33. Tucson: University of Arizona Press.
1985a Apache Indians and the Northern Mexican Peace Establishments. In *Southwestern Culture History: Collected Papers in Honor of Albert H. Schroeder,* ed. Charles H. Lange, 183–95. Santa Fe: Papers of the Archaeological Society of New Mexico, 10.
1985b Problems in the Study of Apaches and Other Indians in Chihuahua and Southern New Mexico During the Spanish and Mexican Periods. *The Kiva* 50(2–3):139–51.
1988 *Apaches at War and Peace: The Janos Presidio, 1750–1858.* Albuquerque: University of New Mexico Press.
1991 The Chiricahua Apache Population Resident at the Janos Presidio, 1792 to 1858. *Journal of the Southwest* 33(2):151–99.

Grosvenor, H. C.
1858 Letter from Arizona. *Railroad Record,* August 12, 1858, p. 293.
1973 Early Efforts on the Santa Rita and Salero. *Arizona Cattlelog* 29(7):10–20.

Gustafson, A. M., ed.
1966 *John Spring's Arizona.* Tucson: University of Arizona Press.

Hackett, Charles Wilson
1926 *Historical Documents Relating to New Mexico, Nueva Vizcaya, and Approaches thereto, to 1773.* vol. 2. Washington, D.C.: Carnegie Institution of Washington.

Hadley, Diana, Peter Warshall, and Don Bufkin
1991 *Environmental Change in Aravaipa, 1870–1970, An Ethnoecological Survey.* Cultural Resources Series no. 7. Phoenix: Arizona State Office of the Bureau of Land Management.

Hale, Duane Kendall
1981 Mineral Exploration in the Spanish Borderlands, 1513–1846. In *Mining in the West,* ed. by Alan Probert, 5–20. Manhattan, Kans.: Sunflower University Press.

Haley, J. Evetts, ed.
1932 A Log of the Texas-California Cattle Trail, 1854. *Southwestern Historical Quarterly* 35(3):208–37; 35(4):290–316; 36(1): 47–66.

Hall, Martin Hardwick
1960 *Sibley's New Mexico Campaign.* Austin: University of Texas Press.

Hamlin, Percy Gatling, ed.
1935 *The Making of a Soldier: Letters of General R. S. Ewell.* Richmond, Va.: Whittet and Shepperson.

Hammond, George P.
1929 Pimería Alta after Kino's Time. *New Mexico Historical Review* 4(3):220–38.

Hammond, George P., ed.
1949 *Campaigns in the West, 1856–1861.* Tucson: Arizona Pioneers' Historical Society.

Hammond, George P., and Edward H. Howes, eds.
1950 *Overland to California on the Southwest Trail, 1849.* Berkeley: University of California Press.

Hammond, George P., and Agapito Rey
1940 *Narratives of the Coronado Expedition 1540–1542.* Albuquerque: University of New Mexico Press.

Harris, Benjamin Butler
1960 *The Gila Trail: The Texas Argonauts and the California Gold Rush.* Norman: University of Oklahoma Press.

Harris, Charles H., III, and Louis R. Sadler
1979 The Witzke Affair: German Intrigue on the Mexican Border, 1917–18. *Military Review* 59(2):36–50.
1988 *The Border and The Revolution.* Las Cruces, N.M.: Center for Latin American Studies/Joint Border Research Institute, New Mexico State University.

Harrison, Anne E.
1972 *The Santa Catalinas: A Description and History.* Tucson: Coronado National Forest.

Haskett, Bert
1935 Early History of the Cattle Industry in Arizona. *Arizona Historical Review* 6(4):3–42.
1936 History of the Sheep Industry in Arizona. *Arizona Historical Review* 7(3):36–44.

Hastings, James Rodney
1961 People of Reason and Others: The Colonization of Sonora to 1767. *Arizona and the West* 3(4):321–40.

Haury, Emil W.
1984 The Search for Chichilticale. *Arizona Highways* 60(4):14–19.

Hedrick, Basil C.
1978 The Location of Corazones. In *Across the Chichimec Sea,* ed. by Carroll L. Riley and Basil C. Hedrick, 228–32. Carbondale: Southern Illinois University Press.

Herring, Patricia Roche
1978 The Silver of El Real de Arizonac. *Arizona and the West* 20(3): 245–58.

Hill, Gertrude
1961 Henry Clay Hooker: King of the Sierra Bonita. *Arizoniana* 2(4):12–15.

Hill, R. R.
1913 Grazing Administration of the National Forests in Arizona. *American Forestry* 19(9):578–85.

Hine, Robert V.
1968 *Bartlett's West: Drawing the Mexican Boundary.* New Haven: Yale University Press.

Hinton, Harwood P., Jr.
1956–57 John Simpson Chisum, 1877–84. *New Mexico Historical Review* 31(3):177–205; 31(4):310–37; 32(1):53–65.

Hodge, Frederick W., and Theodore H. Lewis, eds.
1971 *Spanish Explorers in the Southern United States, 1528–1543.* Reprint of 1907 ed. New York: Barnes and Noble.

Hooker, Mrs. Harry
1949 Five Generations of Hookers on the Sierra Bonita Ranch. *Arizona Cattlelog* 5(4):32–36.

Howe, Jerome W.
1966 Campaigning in Mexico, 1916. *Journal of Arizona History* 7(3):123–38.

Hufford, Kenneth
1967 Travelers on the Gila Trail, 1824–1850, part 2: An Annotated Bibliography. *Journal of Arizona History* 8(1):30–44.

Jackson, Robert H.
1981 The Last Jesuit Censuses of the Pimería Alta Missions, 1761 and 1766. *The Kiva* 46(4):243–72.

Jackson, W. Turrentine
1965 *Wagons Roads West.* New Haven: Yale University Press.

Jenkins, Jerry
1967 Ruby is All Alone. *Desert* 30(12):28–30.

Jones, Fayette
1968 *Old Mines and Ghost Camps of New Mexico.* Reprint of 1905 ed. Fort Davis, Tex.: Frontier Book Co.

Keith, Stanley B., Don E. Gest, Ed DeWitt, Netta Woode Toll, and Beverly A. Everson

1983 *Metallic Mineral Districts and Production in Arizona.* Arizona Bureau of Geology and Mineral Technology, Geological Survey Branch, Bulletin 194. Tucson: University of Arizona.

Keith, Stanton B.

1974 *Index of Mining Properties in Pima County, Arizona.* Arizona Bureau of Geology and Mineral Technology, Geological Survey Branch, Bulletin 189. Tucson: University of Arizona.

1975 *Index of Mining Properties in Santa Cruz County, Arizona.* Arizona Bureau of Mines Bulletin 191. Tucson: University of Arizona.

1985 *Index of Mining Properties in Cochise County, Arizona.* Reprint of 1973 ed. Arizona Bureau of Geology and Mineral Technology, Geological Survey Branch, Bulletin 187. Tucson: University of Arizona.

Kellogg, Royal S.

1902a *Report on an Examination of the Graham Mountains in Arizona.* Copy at Forest Archeologist's Office, Coronado National Forest, Tucson.

1902b Forest Conditions in Southern Arizona. *Forestry and Irrigation* 8(12):501–5.

Kennedy, John W.

1978 Border Troubles, and Camp Stephen D. Little. *Periodical* no. 35:14–25.

Kessell, John L.

1965 Father Eixarch and the Visitation at Tumacácori, May 12, 1775. *The Kiva* 30(3):77–81.

1966 The Puzzling Presidio: San Phelipe de Guevavi, Alias Terrenate. *New Mexico Historical Review* 41(1):21–46.

1969 Father Ramón and the Big Debt, Tumacácori, 1821–1823. *New Mexico Historical Review* 44(1):53–72.

1970 *Mission of Sorrows: Jesuit Guevavi and the Pimas, 1691–1767.* Tucson: University of Arizona Press.

1976 *Friars, Soldiers, and Reformers: Hispanic Arizona and the Sonora Mission Frontier 1767–1856.* Tucson: University of Arizona Press.

Kessell, John L., ed.

1964 San José de Tumacácori—1773. *Arizona and the West* 6(4): 303–12.

1968 Anza, Indian Fighter: The Spring Campaign of 1766. *The Journal of Arizona History* 9(3):155–63.

King, Rex

1915a Land Classification of the Santa Catalina Division, Coronado National Forest, Arizona. In *Extensive Land Classification, Santa Catalina Division, Coronado National Forest, Arizona.*

District 3. Washington, D.C.: U.S. Department of Agriculture.

1915b Land Classification of the Mt. Graham, Santa Teresa and Galiuro Division, Crook National Forest, Arizona. In *Extensive and Intensive Classification, Galiuro, Santa Teresa and Mt. Graham Divisions, Crook National Forest, Arizona. District 3.* Washington, D.C.: U.S. Department of Agriculture.

1915c Land Classification, Whetstone, Santa Rita, Huachuca and Tumacacori Divisions, Coronado National Forest, Arizona. In *Extensive Land Classification; Whetstone, Santa Rita, Huachuca and Tumacacori Divisions* [Coronado National Forest]. Washington, D.C.: U.S. Department of Agriculture.

Kinnaird, Lawrence

1958 *The Frontiers of New Spain: Nicolás de Lafora's Description, 1766–1768.* Berkeley: Quivira Society.

Klasner, Lily

1972 *My Girlhood among Outlaws.* Tucson: University of Arizona Press.

Knipe, O. D.

1982 The Use of Angora Goats in Converting Arizona Chaparral to Grassland. In *Proceedings of the Third International Conference on Goat Production and Disease,* 411–16. Scottsdale, Ariz.: Dairy Goat Journal Publishing Co.

Knox, Mertice Buck

1931 The Escape of the Apache Kid. *Arizona Historical Review* 3(4):77–87.

Krutch, Joseph Wood

1966 It's Carr Canyon for Birdwatchers. *Westways* 58 (April 1966): 18–19.

Lacy, John C.

1987 Early History of Mining in Arizona; Acquisition of Mineral Rights 1539–1866. In *History of Mining in Arizona,* ed. by J. Michael Canty and Michael N. Greeley, 1–12. Tucson: Mining Club of the Southwest Foundation.

Laetz, Catrien Ross

1986 San Bernardino Ranch. *Arizona Highways* 62(10):2–11.

Lamma, Roberta (Biff)

1982 *A Place Called Sunnyside.* Tucson: A and W Limited Editions.

Lane, Jack C., ed.

1970 *Chasing Geronimo: The Journal of Leonard Wood, May– September 1886.* Albuquerque: University of New Mexico Press.

Lang, Walter B., ed.

1940 *The First Overland Mail—Butterfield Trail.* N.p.: published by the author(?).

Lange, Charles H., and Carroll L. Riley, eds.
1970 *The Southwestern Journals of Adolph F. Bandelier, 1883–1884.* Albuquerque: University of New Mexico Press.

Lauver, Mary Ellen
1938 *A History of the Use and Management of the Forested Lands of Arizona, 1862–1936.* M.A. thesis, University of Arizona, Tucson.

Leckie, William H.
1967 *The Buffalo Soldiers.* Norman: University of Oklahoma Press.

Lockwood, Frank C.
1931 Fifty Years in Paradise. *Progressive Arizona* 11(13):15–16, 21–22.
1932 Fifty Years in Paradise. *Progressive Arizona* 12(1):13–14, 18.

Long, James A.
1965 Bloodstained Ghost Town. *Frontier Times* 39(2):24–25, 71–72.

Loomis, Noel M.
1962 Early Cattle Trails in Southern Arizona. *Arizoniana* 3(4): 18–24.

Manje, Juan Mateo
1954 *Unknown Arizona and Sonora, 1693–1721.* Harry J. Karns and Associates, trans. Tucson: Arizona Silhouettes.

Marsh, S. P., S. J. Kropschot, and R. G. Dickinson, eds.
1984 *Wilderness Mineral Potential: Assessment of the Mineral-Resource Potential in U.S. Forest Service Lands Studied 1964–1984.* U.S. Geological Survey Professional Paper 1300, vols. 1 and 2. Washington, D.C.: U.S. Government Printing Office.

Marshall, Thomas Maitland
1916 St. Vrain's Expedition to the Gila in 1826. *Southwestern Historical Quarterly* 19(3):251–60.

Martin, E. R.
1979 Old Camp Rucker: Its Place in History. *Periodical* 11(1)(no. 39):42–49.

Martin, W.P., and Joel E. Fletcher
1943 *Vertical Zonation of Great Soil Groups on Mt. Graham, Arizona, as Correlated with Climate, Vegetation, and Profile Characteristics.* University of Arizona Agricultural Experiment Station, Technical Bulletin no. 99. Tucson: University of Arizona.

Matheny, Robert Lavesco
1975 *The History of Lumbering in Arizona before World War II.* Ph.D. diss., University of Arizona, Tucson.

Matson, Daniel S., and Albert H. Schroeder, eds.
1957 Cordero's Description of the Apache—1796. *New Mexico Historical Review* 32(4):335–56.

Mattison, Ray H.
1946 Early Spanish and Mexican Settlements in Arizona. *New Mexico Historical Review* 21(4):273–327.

McBride, Darvil
1984 *The Evaders, Or Wilderness Shoot-Out.* Pasadena, Cal.: Pacific Book and Printing.

McCarty, Kieran
1976 *Desert Documentary.* Tucson: Arizona Historical Society, Historical Monograph No. 4.
1981 *A Spanish Frontier in the Enlightened Age: Franciscan Beginnings in Sonora and Arizona, 1767–1770.* Washington, D.C.: Academy of American Franciscan History.

McDowell, Irvin, Major General
1879 *Outline Descriptions of Military Posts in the Military Division of the Pacific.* San Francisco: Presidio of San Francisco.

Meinzer, O. E., and F. C. Kelton
1913 *Geology and Water Resources of Sulphur Spring Valley, Arizona.* U.S. Geological Survey, Water-Supply Paper 320. Washington, D.C.: U.S. Government Printing Office.

Meketa, Charles and Jacqueline
1980 *One Blanket and Ten Days Rations.* Globe, Ariz.: Southwest Parks and Monuments Association.

Menzie, Elmer L.
1970 Beef Production and Marketing in Arizona. *Arizona Cattlelog* 27(2):28–33.

Merwin, Nelle
1967 Tales of Paradise, Arizona. *The West* 6(6):36–41, 67–69.

Meyer, Carol Clarke
1974 The Rise and Fall of Ruby. *Journal of Arizona History* 15(1): 8–28.

Miller, Darlis A.
1989 *Soldiers and Settlers: Military Supply in the Southwest, 1861–1885.* Albuquerque: University of New Mexico Press.

Milliken, Chuck
1989 History Buffs Can Get "Faraway" from the Fast Lane. *Arizona History* 6(3):4–5.

Milton, Maxwell C.
1913 The Oro Blanco District of Arizona. *Engineering and Mining Journal* 96(22):1005–7 (November 29, 1913).

Mohair Council of America
1982[?] *Mohair: Production and Marketing in the U.S.* San Angelo, Tex.: Mohair Council of America.

Moore, Yndia, comp.
1958(?) *The Butterfield Overland Mail across Arizona.* Tucson: Arizona Pioneers' Historical Society.

Moorhead, Max L.
1975 *The Presidio: Bastion of the Spanish Borderlands.* Norman: University of Oklahoma Press.

Morrisey, Richard J.
1950 The Early Range Cattle Industry in Arizona. *Agricultural History* 24(3):151–56.

Mowry, Sylvester
1857 *Memoir of the Proposed Territory of Arizona.* Washington, D.C.: Henry Polkinhorn, Printer.

Mullane, William H., ed.
1963 *This Is Silver City 1882–1883–1884.* Volume I. Silver City, N.M.: Silver City Enterprise.
1968 *Indian Raids As Reported in the Silver City Enterprise, 1882–1886.* Silver City, N.M.: Silver City Enterprise.

Mulligan, Raymond A.
1958 Sixteen Days in Apache Pass. *The Kiva* 24(2):1–13.

Murbarger, Nell
1955 They Mine Marble in Apacheland. *Desert* 18(5):11–15.

Myers, John E.
1913 The Catalina Mountains and Oracle As a Summer Resort. *Arizona: The New State Magazine* 3(7):4.

Myres, Sandra L.
1969 *The Ranch in Spanish Texas, 1691–1800.* Social Science Series no. 2. El Paso: Texas Western Press.

Myres, Sandra L., ed.
1981 An Arizona Camping Trip; May Banks Stacey's Account of an Outing to Mount Graham in 1879. *Arizona and the West* 23(1):53–64.

Myrick, David F.
1980 *Railroads of Arizona. Vol. 2.* San Diego: Howell-North Books.

Navarro García, Luis
1964 *Don José de Gálvez y la comandancia general de las provincias internas del norte de Nueva España.* Sevilla: Escuela de Estudios Hispano-Americanos.
1967 *Sonora y Sinaloa en el siglo XVII.* Sevilla: Escuela de Estudios Hispano-Americanos.

Naylor, Thomas H., and Charles W. Polzer, eds.
1986 *The Presidio and Militia on the Northern Frontier of New Spain.* Vol. 1. Tucson: University of Arizona Press.

Nentvig, Juan
1980 *Rudo Ensayo: A Description of Sonora and Arizona in 1764.* Tucson: University of Arizona Press.

Noonan, Buddy
1980 Camp Rucker, the Army's Forgotten Outpost. *Desert* 43(10): 18–20.

North, Diane M. T.
1980 *Samuel Peter Heintzelman and the Sonora Exploring and Mining Company.* Tucson: University of Arizona Press.

O'Conor, Hugo de
1952 *Informe de Hugo de O'Conor sobre el estado de las provincias internas del norte.* Mexico City: Editorial Cultura.

Officer, James E.
1987 *Hispanic Arizona, 1536–1856.* Tucson: University of Arizona Press.

Ogle, Ralph H.
1958 The Apache and the Government—1870's. *New Mexico Historical Review* 33(2):81–102.
1970 *Federal Control of the Western Apaches, 1848–1886.* Reprint of 1940 ed. Albuquerque: University of New Mexico Press.

Opler, Morris E.
1983 The Apachean Culture Pattern and Its Origins. In *Handbook of North American Indians,* William G. Sturtevant, general ed., vol. 10, *Southwest,* edited by Alfonso Ortiz, pp. 368–392. Washington, D.C.: Smithsonian Institution.

Park, Joseph F.
1961 The Apaches in Mexican-American Relations, 1848–1861. *Arizona and the West* 3(2):129–46.

Pattie, James O.
1984 *The Personal Narrative of James O. Pattie.* Republication of 1831 ed. Lincoln: University of Nebraska Press.

Peirce, H. Wesley
1967 *Geologic Guidebook 2—Highways of Arizona. Arizona Highways 77 and 177.* Arizona Bureau of Mines, Bulletin 176. Tucson: University of Arizona.

Peters, Joseph P., comp.
1966 *Indian Battles and Skirmishes on the American Frontier 1790–1898.* New York: Argonaut.

Peterson, Charles S., John F. Yurtinus, David E. Atkinson, and A. Kent Powell
1972 *Mormon Battalion Trail Guide.* Western Trail Guide Series no. 1. Salt Lake City: Utah State Historical Society.

Peterson, Thomas H., Jr.
1963 *Fort Lowell, A.T., Army Post During the Apache Campaigns. The Smoke Signal,* no. 8. Tucson: Tucson Corral of the Westerners.
Peterson, Virgil V.
1946 Arizona Range Cattle. *American Cattle Producer* 28(3):9–10, 24–26.
Pfefferkorn, Ignaz
1949 *Sonora, a Description of the Province.* Albuquerque: University of New Mexico Press.
Pinchot, Gifford
1947 *Breaking New Ground.* New York: Harcourt, Brace and Company.
Polzer, Charles W.
1968 *Legends of Lost Missions and Mines. The Smoke Signal,* no. 18. Tucson: Tucson Corral of the Westerners.
1971 *Kino's Biography of Francisco Javier Saeta, S.J.* Rome: Jesuit Historical Institute.
1972 The Franciscan Entrada into Sonora, 1645–1652: A Jesuit Chronicle. *Arizona and the West* 14(3):253–78.
1976 Long before the Blue Dragoons: Spanish Military Operations in Northern Sonora and Pimería Alta. In: *Views on the Military History of the Indian-Spanish-American Southwest: 1598–1886,* ed. by Bruno J. Rolak, 6–19. Fort Huachuca, Ariz.
Porras Muñoz, Guillermo
1980 *La frontera con los indios de Nueva Vizcaya en el Siglo XVII.* Mexico City: Fomento Cultural Banamex.
Poston, Charles D.
1963 *Building a State in Apache Land.* Republication of 1894 ed. Tempe: Aztec Press.
Powers, Le Grand
1902 *Agriculture Part I: Farms, Live Stock, and Animal Products.* Twelfth Census of the United States, Taken in the Year 1900. Census Reports, vol. 5. Washington, D.C.: U.S. Census Office.
Preston, Douglas
1990 Following—Painfully—the Route of Coronado after 450 Years. *Smithsonian* 20(10):40–53.
Probert, Alan
1969 Bartolomé de Medina: The Patio Process and the Sixteenth Century Silver Crisis. *Journal of the West* 8(1):90–124.
Pumpelly, Raphael
1918 *My Reminiscences,* vol. 1. New York: Henry Holt and Company.
Quaife, Milo Milton
1935 *Kit Carson's Autobiography.* Chicago: Lakeside Press.

Radbourne, Allan
1980 Captain Hatfield and the Chiricahuas. In *"Ho, for the Great West!"* ed. by Barry C. Johnson, 70–81. Special Publication no. 6B. London: English Westerners' Society.

Ransome, F.L.
1913 The Turquoise Copper-Mining District, Arizona. In *Contributions to Economic Geology, 1911,* part I, 125–34. U.S. Geological Survey, Bulletin 530. Washington, D.C.: U.S. Government Printing Office.

Raymond, Rossiter W.
1877 *Statistics of Mines and Mining in the States and Territories West of the Rocky Mountains; . . . Eighth Annual Report.* 44th Cong. 1st Sess., House Exec. Doc. no. 159 (serial no. 1691). Washington, D.C.: U.S. Government Printing Office.

Recknagel, A. B.
1911 *Plan of Management for the Timber on the Mount Graham Division of the Crook National Forest, Arizona.* U.S. Department of Agriculture, Forest Service, Circular. Washington, D.C.: U.S. Government Printing Office.

Reeve, Frank D., ed.
1952 Albert Franklin Banta: Arizona Pioneer. *New Mexico Historical Review* 27(2):81–106; 27(3):200–252; 27(4):315–47.

Reff, Daniel T.
1981 The Location of Corazones and Señora: Archaeological Evidence from the Rio Sonora Valley, Mexico. In *The Protohistoric Period in the North American Southwest, AD 1450–1700,* ed. by David R. Wilcox and W. Bruce Masse, 94–112. Tempe: Arizona State University Anthropological Research Papers no. 24.

Reid, John C.
1935 *Reid's Tramp.* Reprint of 1858 ed. Austin: Steck Company.

Reilly, Henry J., Brig. General
1934 The National Guard on the Mexican Border. In *Chasing Villa,* by Frank Tompkins, 221–30. Harrisburg, Pa.: Military Service Publishing Co.

Richards, J.
1966 A Treatise on the Construction and Operation of Woodworking Machines. Selections from 1872 ed. *Forest History* 9(4):16–23.

Riley, Carroll L.
1985 The Location of Chichilticale. In *Southwestern Culture History: Collected Papers in Honor of Albert H. Schroeder,* ed. by Charles H. Lange, 153–62. Santa Fe: Papers of the Archaeological Society of New Mexico 10.

Roberts, Virginia Culin
1992 *With Their Own Blood: A Saga of Southwestern Pioneers.* Fort Worth: Texas Christian University Press.

Robinson, Glen O.
1975 *The Forest Service: A Study in Public Land Management.* Baltimore: Johns Hopkins University Press.

Rockfellow, John A.
1955 *Log of an Arizona Trail Blazer.* Republication of 1933 ed. Tucson: Arizona Silhouettes.

Rodack, Madeleine Turrell, ed.
1981 *Adolph F. Bandelier's The Discovery of New Mexico by the Franciscan Monk, Friar Marcos de Niza, in 1539.* Tucson: University of Arizona Press.

Ross, Clyde P.
1925 *Geology and Ore Deposits of the Aravaipa and Stanley Mining Districts, Graham County, Arizona.* U.S. Geological Survey, Bulletin 763. Washington, D.C.: U.S. Government Printing Office.

Rowland, Donald
1969 The Sonora Frontier of New Spain, 1735–1745. In *New Spain and the Anglo-American West,* 1:147–64. Reprint of 1932 ed. New York: Kraus Reprint.

Rowley, William D.
1985 *U.S. Forest Service Grazing and Rangelands: A History.* College Station: Texas A&M University Press.

Russell, Don
1936 *One Hundred and Three Fights and Scrimmages.* Washington, D.C.: United States Cavalry Association.

Sacks, B.
1965 The Origins of Fort Buchanan, Myth and Fact. *Arizona and the West* 7(3):207–26.

Sacks, Benjamin H., ed.
1962 New Evidence on the Bascom Affair. *Arizona and the West* 4(3):261–78.

Sauer, Carl O.
1932 *The Road to Cibola.* Ibero-Americana 3. Berkeley: University of California Press.
1935 A Spanish Expedition into the Arizona Apachería. *Arizona Historical Review* 6(1):3–13.
1937 The Discovery of New Mexico Reconsidered. *New Mexico Historical Review* 12(3):270–87.

Sauer, Carl, and Donald Brand
1930 *Pueblo Sites in Southeastern Arizona.* University of California Publications in Geography, vol. 3(7). Berkeley: University of California Press.

Saunderson, Mont H.
1950 *Western Stock Ranching.* Minneapolis: University of Minnesota Press.

Schaus, Richard G.
1957 Jackson (Jack) Busenbark 1875–1948. *Arizona Cattlelog* 13(4): 51–56 and back cover

1961a George Stone Wilson, 1887–1957. *Arizona Cattlelog* 16(9–10): back cover

1961b Wiley Marion Morgan, 1864–1946. *Arizona Cattlelog* 18(4): back cover

1963 William Hudson Kirkland, 1832–1920. *Arizona Cattlelog* 20(3):48 and back cover.

1964a William Monroe Riggs, 1861–1949. *Arizona Cattlelog* 20(11): 40 and back cover.

1964b Eugene Nelson Shepherd, 1873–1947. *Arizona Cattlelog* 21(1): 48 and back cover.

1965 Frank Bennett Moson, 1878–1959. *Arizona Cattlelog* 23(2):48 and back cover.

1968 Jacob Prospect Weathersby, 1874–1930. *Arizona Cattlelog* 25(3):40 and back cover.

1970a George Upshaw, 1882–1952. *Arizona Cattlelog* 26(9):32 and back cover.

1970b James Able White, 1887–1967. *Arizona Cattlelog* 26(12):32 and back cover.

1971 Samuel Benjamin Tenney, 1858–1949. *Arizona Cattlelog* 27(5): 40 and back cover.

1973 James Lee Hudson, 1874–1931. *Arizona Cattlelog* 29(8):32 and back cover.

Schellie, Don
1968 *Vast Domain of Blood.* Los Angeles: Westernlore Press.

Schnabel, Lorraine, and John W. Welty
1986 *Bibliography for Metallic Mineral Districts in Cochise, Graham, and Greenlee Counties, Arizona.* Arizona Bureau of Geology and Mineral Technology, Geological Survey Branch, Circular 24. Tucson: University of Arizona.

Scholes, France V.
1936 Church and State in New Mexico, 1610–1650. *New Mexico Historical Review* 11(1):9–76, (2):145–78, (3):283–94, (4): 297–349.

Scholes, France V., and H. P. Mera
1940 Some Aspects of the Jumano Problem. *Contributions to American Anthropology and History,* no. 34, 265–99. Washington, D.C.: Carnegie Institution of Washington.

Schrader, Frank C.
1915 *Mineral Deposits of the Santa Rita and Patagonia Mountains, Arizona.* U.S. Geological Survey, Bulletin 582. Washington, D.C.: U.S. Government Printing Office.

Schroeder, Albert H.
1952 Documentary Evidence Pertaining to the Early Historic Period of Southern Arizona. *New Mexico Historical Review* 27(2): 137–67.
1955–56 Fray Marcos de Niza, Coronado and the Yavapai. *New Mexico Historical Review* 30(4):265–296; 31(1):24–37.
1956 Southwestern Chronicle: The Cipias and Ypotlapiguas. *Arizona Quarterly* 12(2):101–11.
1974 A Study of the Apache Indians, Parts IV and V. In *Apache Indians IV,* general ed. David A. Horr. New York: Garland Publishing.

Schuetz, Mardith K.
1986 *Archaeology of Tom Jeffords' Chiricahua Indian Agency.* COAS Monograph no. 6. Las Cruces, N.M.: COAS Publishing and Research.

Schwennesen, A. T.
1919 Ground Water in San Simon Valley, Arizona and New Mexico. In *Contributions to the Hydrology of the United States, 1917,* comp. by Nathan C. Grover. U.S. Geological Survey, Water-Supply Paper 425, 1–35. Washington, D.C.: U.S. Government Printing Office.

Seltzer, Raymond E.
1959 The Economic Value of the Arizona Cattle Industry. *Arizona Cattlelog* 14(5):26–30.

Serven, James E.
1965 *The Military Posts on Sonoita Creek. The Smoke Signal,* no. 12. Tucson: Tucson Corral of the Westerners.

Seymour, Deni J.
1989 The Dynamics of Sobaipuri Settlement in the Eastern Pimería Alta. *Journal of the Southwest* 31(2):205–22.

Sherman, James E. and Barbara H.
1969 *Ghost Towns of Arizona.* Norman: University of Oklahoma Press.

Simons, Frank S.
1964 *Geology of the Klondyke Quadrangle, Graham and Pinal Counties, Arizona.* U.S. Geological Survey, Professional Paper 461. Washington, D.C.: U.S. Government Printing Office.

Skaggs, Jimmy M.
1986 *Prime Cut: Livestock Raising and Meatpacking in the United States, 1607–1983.* College Station: Texas A&M University Press.

Smith, Cornelius C., Jr.
1967 *William Sanders Oury, History-Maker of the Southwest.* Tucson: The University of Arizona Press.
1981 *Fort Huachuca, The Story of a Frontier Post.* Washington, D.C.: U.S. Government Printing Office.

Smith, Fay Jackson, John L. Kessell, and Francis J. Fox
1966 *Father Kino in Arizona.* Phoenix: Arizona Historical Foundation.

Smith, Ralph A.
1962a Apache Plunder Trails Southward, 1831–1840. *New Mexico Historical Review* 37(1):20–42.
1962b Apache "Ranching" below the Gila, 1841–1845. *Arizoniana* 3(4):1–17.
1964 The Scalp Hunter in the Borderlands, 1835–1850. *Arizona and the West* 6(1):5–22.

Spellmeyer, A. L.
1917 Notes on Fifty Years of Cattle History 1867–1917. *Southwestern Stockman-Farmer* 32(55):1 (February 15, 1917).

Steen, Harold K.
1976 *The U.S. Forest Service: A History.* Seattle: University of Washington Press.

Sweeney, Edwin R.
1991 *Cochise, Chiricahua Apache Chief.* Norman: University of Oklahoma Press.

Tagg, Martyn D.
1986 Investigations at the Ratliff Property (AZ EE:12:34), An Early Homestead in Coronado National Memorial, Southeast Arizona. In *Miscellaneous Historic Period Archeological Projects in the Western Region,* comp. by Martyn D. Tagg, 21–40. Western Archeological and Conservation Center, Publications in Anthropology no. 37. Tucson.

Tenney, James Brand
1927–29 *History of Mining in Arizona.* Copy at Library, Arizona Bureau of Geology and Mineral Technology, Geological Survey Branch, Tucson.

Tevis, James H.
1954 *Arizona in the '50's.* Albuquerque: University of New Mexico Press.

Texas Almanac
1859 Overland Mail Route between San Antonio, Texas, and San Diego, California. *Texas Almanac for 1859,* 139–50. Galveston, Tex.

Thomas, Alfred B.
1932 *Forgotten Frontiers.* Norman: University of Oklahoma Press.
1941 *Teodoro de Croix and the Northern Frontier of New Spain, 1776–1783.* Norman: University of Okahoma Press.
Thonhoff, Robert H.
1971 *San Antonio Stage Lines, 1847–1881.* Southwestern Studies, Monograph no. 29. El Paso: Texas Western Press.
Thorman, Charles H., Harald Drewes, and Michael E. lane
1981 *Mineral Resources of the Rincon Wilderness Study Area, Pima County, Arizona.* U.S. Geological Survey Bulletin 1500. Washington, D.C.: U.S. Government Printing Office.
Thrapp, Dan L.
1967 *The Conquest of Apacheria.* Norman: University of Oklahoma Press.
1974 *Victorio and the Mimbres Apaches.* Norman: University of Oklahoma Press.
Treutlein, Theodore E., trans.
1945 Document: The Relation of Philipp Segesser. *Mid-America* 27(3):139–87, (4):257–60.
1965 *Missionary in Sonora: The Travel Reports of Joseph Och, S.J., 1755–1767.* San Francisco: California Historical Society.
Tucker, Edwin A., comp.
1989 *The Early Days: A Sourcebook of Southwestern Region History, Book 1.* Albuquerque: USDA Forest Service Southwestern Region, Cultural Resources Management Report no. 7.
Tudor, Joseph H.
1969 The Development of the Fee System on Public Lands. *Arizona Cattlelog* 25(11):22–27.
Tully, Barbara
1975 Bullets for Breakfast in Naco, Arizona. *True West* 22(5):6–12.
Udall, Stewart L.
1984 In Coronado's Footsteps. *Arizona Highways* 60(4):3–12, 20–33.
Undreiner, George J.
1947 Fray Marcos de Niza and His Journey to Cibola. *The Americas* 3(4):415–86.
U.S. Army
1948 *The Medal of Honor of the United States Army.* Washington, D.C.: U.S. Government Printing Office.
U.S. Geological Survey, Arizona Bureau of Mines, and U.S. Bureau of Reclamation
1969 *Mineral and Water Resources of Arizona.* Arizona Bureau of Mines, Bulletin 180. Tucson: University of Arizona.

U.S. War Department, Surgeon General's Office

1870 *A Report on Barracks and Hospitals, with Descriptions of Military Posts.* Washington, D.C.: U.S. Government Printing Office.

1875 *A Report on the Hygiene of the United States Army, with Descriptions of Military Posts.* Washington, D.C.: U.S. Government Printing Office.

Utley, Robert M.

1962 *Historical Report on Fort Bowie, Arizóna.* 2d ed. U.S. Department of the Interior, National Park Service, Region Three. Santa Fe, N.M.

1967 *Frontiersmen in Blue.* New York: Macmillan.

1973 *Frontier Regulars.* New York: Macmillan.

1977 *A Clash of Cultures: Fort Bowie and the Chiricahua Apaches.* Washington, D.C.: National Park Service.

Valputic, Marian E., and Harold H. Longfellow

1971 The Fight at Chiricahua Pass in 1869, As Described by L. L. Dorr, M.D. *Arizona and the West* 13(4):369–78.

Varney, Philip

1980 *Arizona's Best Ghost Towns.* Flagstaff: Northland Press.

Vickers, Fred G.

1926 Mt. Lemmon—An All-Year Resort. *Progressive Arizona* 2(6): 23–24.

Wagner, Henry R.

1934 Fr. Marcos de Niza. *New Mexico Historical Review* 9(2): 184–227.

Wagoner, Jay J.

1952 *History of the Cattle Industry in Southern Arizona, 1540–1940.* Social Science Bulletin No. 20, University of Arizona Bulletin 23(2). Tucson, Az.: University of Arizona.

1970 *Arizona Territory·1863–1912: A Political History.* Tucson: University of Arizona Press.

1975 *Early Arizona: Prehistory to Civil War.* Tucson: University of Arizona Press.

Walker, Henry P., and Don Bufkin

1979 *Historical Atlas of Arizona.* Norman: University of Oklahoma Press.

Wallace, Edward S.

1955 *The Great Reconnaissance.* Boston: Little, Brown and Company.

Wallmo, Charles O.

1955 Vegetation of the Huachuca Mountains, Arizona. *American Midland Naturalist* 54:466–80.

Way, W. J. "Jack"

1966 *Ghosts and Ghost Towns.* N.p.: published by the author.

Webb, George W.

1939 *Chronological List of Engagements between the Regular Army of the United States and Various Tribes of Hostile Indians Which Occurred During the Years 1790 to 1898, Inclusive.* St. Joseph, Mo.: Wing Printing and Publishing.

Weber, David J.

1971 *The Taos Trappers: The Fur Trade in the Far Southwest, 1540–1846.* Norman: University of Oklahoma Press.

Weddle, Jerry

1993 *Antrim is My Stepfather's Name.* Tucson: Arizona Historical Society.

Wehrman, Georgia

1965 Harshaw: Mining Camp of the Patagonias. *Journal of Arizona History* 6(1):21–36.

Wells, Reba B.

1985 Slaughter Ranch Outpost. *Cochise Quarterly* 15(4):30–36.

Wharfield, H. B., Colonel

1963 A Fight With the Yaquis at Bear Valley, 1918. *Arizoniana* 4(3): 1–8.

Whittaker, R. H., and W. A. Niering

1964 Vegetation of the Santa Catalina Mountains, Arizona. I. Ecological Classification and Distribution of Species. *Journal of the Arizona Academy of Science* 3(1):9–34.

Willey, Richard R.

1979 *La Canoa: A Spanish Land Grant Lost and Found. The Smoke Signal,* (38). Tucson: Tucson Corral of the Westerners.

Williams, Jack

1986 *San Agustín del Tucson,* and *The Presidio of Santa Cruz de Terrenate: A Forgotten Fortress of Southern Arizona. The Smoke Signal* (47–48):129–48. Tucson: Tucson Corral of the Westerners.

Williamson, Dan R.

1931 Al Sieber, Famous Scout of the Southwest. *Arizona Historical Review* 3(4):60–76.

Wilson, Eldred D.

1962 *A Résumé of the Geology of Arizona.* Arizona Bureau of Mines, Bulletin 171. Tucson: University of Arizona.

1981 *Gold Placers and Placering in Arizona.* Arizona Bureau of Geology and Mineral Technology, Geological Survey Branch, Bulletin 168. Reprint of 1961 ed. Tucson.

Wilson, Eldred D., J. B. Cunningham, and G. M. Butler

1983 *Arizona Lode Gold Mines and Gold Mining.* Arizona Bureau of Geology and Mineral Technology, Geological Survey Branch, Bulletin 137. Reprint of 1967 rev. Tucson: University of Arizona.

Wilson, George Stone
1964–65 Saga of Oracle, Mountain Cow Town, Parts I–X. *Arizona Cattlelog* 21(12) through 22(9), inclusive (August 1964–May 1965).

Wilson, John P.
1975 Retreat to the Rio Grande: The Report of Captain Isaiah N. Moore. *Rio Grande History* 2(3–4):4–8.
1984 *The El Paso Electric Survey, Amrad to Eddy County, Southeastern New Mexico.* Report no. 34. Las Cruces, NM: published by the author.
1987 *Merchants, Guns and Money: The Story of Lincoln County and Its Wars.* Santa Fe: Museum of New Mexico Press.

Winfrey, Dorman H.
1969 The Butterfield Overland Mail Trail. In *Along the Early Trails of the Southwest,* contributions by Wayne Gard, Dean Krakel, Joe B. Frantz, Dorman Winfrey, H. Gordon Frost, and Donald Bubar, 15–44. Austin: Pemberton Press.

Winn, Fred
1969 The Story of Lee Valley and Greer. *Arizona Cattlelog* 25(11):4–20.

Winship, George Parker
1896 The Coronado Expedition, 1540–1542. *Fourteenth Annual Report of the Bureau of Ethnology to the Secretary of the Smithsonian Institution, 1892–93,* by J.W. Powell. Part 1, 339–613. Washington, D.C.: U.S. Government Printing Office.

Woodruff, George W.
1906 Agricultural Settlement in Forest Reserves. *Forestry and Irrigation* 12(6):267–71.

Wright, Lyle H., and Josephine M. Bynum, eds.
1962 *The Butterfield Overland Mail.* San Marino, Cal.: Huntington Library.

Wyllys, Rufus Kay, ed.
1931 Padre Luis Velarde's Relación of Pimería Alta, 1716. *New Mexico Historical Review* 6(2):111–57.

Young, Otis E., Jr.
1967 *How They Dug the Gold.* Tucson: Arizona Pioneers' Historical Society.

Zachry, Juanita Daniel
1990 Mining Adventures of Buffalo Bill Cody. *True West* 37(4):37–41.

Government Documents

1. Arizona—Reports of the Governor

Report of the Governor of Arizona [1895]. In *Report of the Secretary of the Interior* . . . Vol. III, 54th Cong. 1st Sess., House Doc. No. 5. Washington, D.C.: U.S. Government Printing Office (1895).

Report of the Governor of Arizona [1896]. In *Report of the Secretary of the Interior* . . . Vol. III, 54th Cong. 2nd Sess., House Doc. No. 5. Washington, D.C.: U.S. Government Printing Office (1896).

Report of the Governor of Arizona [1897]. In *Annual Reports of the Department of the Interior for the Fiscal Year Ended June 30, 1897,* Misc. Reports, 55th Cong. 2nd Sess., House Doc. No. 5. Washington, D.C.: U.S. Government Printing Office (1897).

Report of the Governor of Arizona [1898]. In *Annual Reports of the Department of the Interior for the Fiscal Year Ended June 30, 1898,* Misc. Reports, 55th Cong. 3d Sess., House Doc. No. 5. Washington, D.C.: U.S. Government Printing Office (1898).

Report of the Governor of Arizona [1899]. In *Annual Reports of the Department of the Interior for the Fiscal Year Ended June 30, 1899,* Misc. Reports, Part II, 56th Cong. 1st Sess., House Doc. No. 5 (Serial No. 3918). Washington, D.C.: U.S. Government Printing Office (1899).

Report of the Governor of Arizona [1909]. In *Reports of the Department of the Interior for the Fiscal Year Ended June 30, 1909,* Administrative Reports, Vol. II. Washington, D.C.: U.S. Government Printing Office (1910).

Report of the Governor of Arizona . . . for the year ended June 30, 1911. In *Reports of the Department of the Interior for the Fiscal Year Ended June 30, 1911,* Administrative Reports, Vol. II. Washington, D.C.: U.S. Government Printing Office (1912).

2. Bureau of the Census

Thirteenth Census of the United States (1910). Abstract of the Census . . . with Supplement for New Mexico. Washington, D.C.: U.S. Government Printing Office (1913).

3. Explorations and Surveys

Report of Explorations for That Portion of a Railroad Route, Near the Thirty-Second Parallel of North Latitude, Lying Between Doña Ana, on the Rio Grande, and Pimas Villages, on the Gila, by Lt. John G. Parke. In: *Reports of Explorations and Surveys, to Ascertain the Most Practicable and Economical Route for a Railroad from the Mississippi River to the*

Pacific Ocean, Vol. II. 33d Cong. 2nd Sess., Senate Exec. Doc. No. 78 (Serial No. 759). Washington, D.C.: Beverley Tucker, Printer (1855).

Itinerary, by Lieutenant A.W. Whipple. In *Reports of Explorations and Surveys, to Ascertain the Most Practicable and Economical Route for a Railroad from the Mississippi River to the Pacific Ocean,* Vol. III Part I. 33d Cong. 2nd Sess., Senate Exec. Doc. No. 78 (Serial No. 760). Washington, D.C.: Beverley Tucker, Printer (1854).

Report Upon the Indian Tribes, by A.W. Whipple, Thomas Ewbank, and Wm. W. Turner. In *Reports of Explorations and Surveys, to Ascertain the Most Practicable and Economical Route for a Railroad from the Mississippi River to the Pacific Ocean,* Vol. III Part III. 33d Cong. 2nd Sess., Senate Exec. Doc. No. 78 (Serial No. 760). Washington, D.C.: Beverley Tucker, Printer (1855).

Report of Explorations from Pimas Villages to Rio Grande (by Lt. John G. Parke?). In *Reports of Explorations and Surveys, to Ascertain the Most Practicable and Economical Route for a Railroad from the Mississippi River to the Pacific Ocean,* Vol. VII Part I No. 2. 33d Cong. 2nd Sess., Senate Exec. Doc. No. 78 (Serial No. 764). Washington, D.C.: Beverley Tucker, Printer (1857).

4. Indian Affairs

Annual Report of the Commissioner of Indian Affairs . . . for the Year 1868. Washington, D.C.: U.S. Government Printing Office (1868).

Report of the Commissioner of Indian Affairs . . . for the Year 1869. Washington, D.C.: U.S. Government Printing Office (1870).

Annual Report of the Commissioner of Indian Affairs . . . for the Year 1870. Washington, D.C.: U.S. Government Printing Office (1870).

Annual Report of the Commissioner of Indian Affairs . . . for the Year 1871. Washington, D.C.: U.S. Government Printing Office (1872).

Annual Report of the Commissioner of IndianAffairs . . . for the Year 1872. Washington, D.C.: U.S. Government Printing Office (1872).

Annual Report of the Commissioner of Indian Affairs . . . for the Year 1874. Washington, D.C.: U.S. Government Printing Office (1874).

Annual Report of the Commissioner of Indian Affairs . . . for the Year 1875. Washington, D.C.: U.S. Government Printing Office (1875).

Annual Report of the Commissioner of Indian Affairs . . . for the Year 1876. Washington, D.C.: U.S. Government Printing Office (1876).

5. Military

Report of the Secretary of War (1857). 35th Cong. 1st Sess., Senate Exec. Doc. No. 11, Vol. II (Serial No. 920). Washington, D.C.: William A. Harris (1858).

Report of the Secretary of War (1859). 36th Cong. 1st Sess., Senate Exec. Doc. No. 2, Vol. II Pt. 2 (Serial No. 1024). Washington, D.C.: George W. Bowman, Printer (1860).

War of the Rebellion: A Compilation of the Official Records of the Union and Confederate Armies:

Series I Vol. 4 (1882)
Series I Vol. 9 (1883)
Series I Vol. 34 Pt. 1 (1891)
Series I Vol. 34 Pt. 3 (1891)
Series I Vol. 41 Pt. 1 (1893)
Series I Vol. 50 Pt. 1 (1897)
Series I Vol. 50 Pt. 2 (1897)

War Department Annual Reports, 1916, Vol. I. Washington, D.C.: U.S. Government Printing Office (1916).

War Department Annual Reports, 1917, Vol. I. Washington, D.C.: U.S. Government Printing Office (1918).

Order of Battle of the United States Land Forces in the World War (1917–19), Zone of the Interior, Vol. 3 Pt. 1. Washington, D.C.: U.S. Government Printing Office (1949).

6. U.S. Forest Service

Forestry of the Western States and Territories. In *Annual Report of the Commissioner of Agriculture for the Year 1878,* pp. 533–536. Washington, D.C.: U.S. Government Printing Office (1879).

A Proclamation . . . By the President of the United States of America . . . Chiricahua Forest Reserve, Arizona (Second Proclamation), November 5, 1906 (with map).

Report of the Forester. In *Annual Reports of the Department of Agriculture for the Year Ended June 30, 1908.* Washington, D.C.: U.S. Government Printing Office (1909).

Report of the Forester. In *Annual Reports of the Department of Agriculture for the Year Ended June 30, 1909.* Washington, D.C.: U.S. Government Printing Office (1910).

Report of the Forester. In *Annual Reports of Department of Agriculture for the Year Ended June 30, 1910.* Washington, D.C.: U.S. Government Printing Office (1911).

The Coronado-Garces Times, March 1911. Copy at Forest Archeologist's Office, Coronado National Forest, Tucson.

Coronado Quarterly, July 1911. Copy at Forest Archeologist's Office, Coronado National Forest, Tucson.

Report of the Forester. In *Annual Reports of Department of Agriculture for the Year Ended June 30, 1912.* Washington, D.C.: U.S. Government Printing Office (1913).

Report of the Forester. In *Annual Reports of Department of Agriculture for the Year Ended June 30, 1913.* Washington, D.C.: U.S. Government

Printing Office (1914).

Report of the Forester. In *Annual Reports of Department of Agriculture for the Year Ended June 30, 1914.* Washington, D.C.: U.S. Government Printing Office (1914).

Coronado Almanac, 1917. Copy at Western Archeological and Conservation Center, Faraway Ranch Papers (MS1), Series 37, Box 60, Folder 4. Tucson.

Homesteads in the National Forests (12 pp.). Washington, D.C.: U.S. Forest Service (1917).

Report of the Forester. In *Annual Reports of the Department of Agriculture for the Year Ended June 30, 1923.* Washington, D.C.: U.S. Government Printing Office (1924).

The National Forests of Arizona. U.S. Department of Agriculture, Department Circular 318. Washington, D.C.: U.S. Government Printing Office (August 1924).

Coronado Bulletin. Issues for January 13, 1928; December 15, 1939; May 3 and November 18, 1941. Copies at Forest Archeologist's Office, Coronado National Forest, Tucson.

The Civilian Conservation Corps: Coronado National Forest, 1933–1942. U.S. Forest Service, Southwestern Region. Washington, D.C.: U.S. Government Printing Office (1991).

7. U.S. Department of the Interior

Suggestions to Homesteaders and Persons Desiring to Make Homestead Entries. U.S. Department of the Interior, General Land Office, Circular No. 541. Washington, D.C.: U.S. Government Printing Office (1926).

Homesteads. U.S. Department of the Interior, Bureau of Land Management. Washington, D.C.: U.S. Government Printing Office (1962).

Manuscript and Microfilmed Materials

1. Arizona Historical Society, Tucson.

Frederick Winn Collection, Boxes 1, 4, 6

Ephemera files: (1) Arizona Mountains—Mt. Lemmon
(2) Mining / Marble
(3) Mountains—Arizona—Chiricahua
(4) Mountains—Arizona—Dragoon
(5) Mountains—Arizona—Santa Rita
(6) Summerhaven

2. Arizona State Museum, Tucson.

General Juan Fernández de la Fuente—"Journal of the Pima Campaign of 1695." Copy courtesy of Dr. Thomas H. Naylor, Documentary Relations of the Southwest; original in Archivo de Hidalgo del Parral, Microfilm 1695.

3. The Bancroft Library, Berkeley, Cal.

Campaign diary of Francisco Salas Bohorques—"Diario de las Novedades ocurridas en la campaña acayado executar de orden del Teniente coronel Ayudante Inspector y comandante de las Armas, Don Roque de Medina," 1789 (copy). Original in Archivo General de la Nación, Provincias Internas, Tomo 193, Mexico City.

4. National Archives and Records Administration, Washington, D.C.

A. Civil Archives

Letters Received by the Office of Indian Affairs, 1824–1881.
Microcopy M234 Roll 581.
Interior Department Territorial Papers, Arizona, 1868–1913.
Microcopy M429 Roll 3.
Records of the New Mexico Superintendency of Indian Affairs, 1849–1880.
Microcopy T21 Rolls 4, 30.

Record Group 75, Records of the Bureau of Indian Affairs, Entry 310, I.S.P., Letters of General O. O. Howard, 1872.

Record Group 123, Records of the United States Court of Claims. In the Court of Claims, No. 1883, *William S. Grant vs. The United States*, October Term, 1863.

B. Military Archives

Returns from U.S. Military Posts, 1800–1916. Camp John A. Rucker, Ariz.; Douglas, Ariz.; Nogales, Ariz. Microcopy M617 Rolls 323, 556, 866.

Letters Received by the Office of the Adjutant General (Main Series), 1861–1870. Microcopy M619 Roll 737.

Letters Received by the Office of the Adjutant General (Main Series), 1871–1880. Microcopy M666 Roll 265.

Registers of Letters Received and Letters Received by Headquarters, Department of New Mexico, 1854–1865. Microcopy M1120 Rolls 9, 11.

Brief Histories of United States Army Commands (Army Posts) and Descriptions of Their Records. Microcopy T912.

Record Group 159, Records of the Office of the Inspector General, Entry 15: Letters Received #253–1879. Inspection Report, Camp John A. Rucker, A.T., January 17, 1879.

Record Group 393, Records of United States Army Continental Commands, 1821–1920. Department of New Mexico 1849–1866, Headquarters Records, Records of Staff Officers, Inspector, Letters Sent December 1863–May 1865 (Vol. I, Entry 3192 in Preliminary Inventory, RG 393).

Record Group 393, Post Records, Fort Bowie Az., Letters Sent, Vol. 18 (June 11, 1869–February 8, 1871).

Record Group 393, Order Book—To & From Troops in the Field, Southeastern Arizona, July 1878–November 1880.

Record Group 393, Post Records, Camp Supply [John A. Rucker] A.T., 1878–1880.

Record Group 393, Order Book–To & From Troops in the Field, Southeastern Arizona, heliograph communications, 1886.

Record Group 393, Southern Department, 1913–1920, General Correspondence 1916–1920, Decimal #370.24 (Vol. I, Entry 4442 in Preliminary Inventory, RG 393).

5. U. S. Forest Service

A. Coronado National Forest Offices, Tucson, Az.

Alice Chesley Davis—"A short history in connection with Chesley Flat up top of Mount Graham," n.d., 2 pp.

Ellen Predmore—"History of Black Diamond Historic Site, Black Diamond Smelter Historic Site, n.d., unpublished manuscript.

Lonnie E. Rawdon, comp.—"History of Animas Valley—Bill Bercham Draw," n.d., 3 pp.

File, Turkey Flat Summer Home Area, Coronado National Forest, 1928–1940.

Fred Winn, Forest Supervisor, to Forrest E. Doucette, General Manager, Arizona Year Book, Phoenix, Az., March 11, 1931, 3 pp.

U.S. Department of Commerce, Bureau of Public Roads, Division Seven, "Final Construction Report, Arizona Forest Highway Project 33, Catalina Highway. Coronado National Forest, Pima County, Arizona," 1951, unpublished manuscript.

Interview between Ben Erickson, S. R. Albert and L. N. Rawdon, January 28, 1970 (extracts), 17 pp.

B. Gila National Forest offices, Silver City, N.M.

S.A. Frey—"Gila National Forest. Report on Area of 8160 Acres Recommended for Elimination," September 1, 1910, 3 pp.

W.R. Chapline, Jr.—"General Progress Report on Study of Goat Management on National Forests in the Southwest," 1917, 31 pp.

6. Western Archeological and Conservation Center, Tucson.

"Manuscript Record, The Faraway Ranch Papers, 1873–1976. Manuscript Collection 1," 1983. 60 pp.

"Chiricahua National Forest. Record of Settlement, Improvement and Cultivation of Forest Homesteads, 1913," Faraway Ranch Papers, Series 8, Box 22, Folder 81.

Neil Erickson—"Some Facts About (Bigfoot) Massai," n.d., 7 pp. Faraway Ranch Papers, Series 4, Box 18, Folder 7.

7. U.S. Army Military History Institute, Carlisle Barracks, Pa.

Captain J. A. Sladen—"Making peace with Cochise, Chief of Chiricahua Indians, 1872," 54 pp.

8. Dr. Martin H. Hall, University of Texas at Arlington.

Transcript of William S. Grant—"A Concise Statement of the Prominent Facts and Grounds of Claim Made by Wm. S. Grant upon the United States, for Property Destroyed in Arizona by Order of the Military Authorities, and Captured by the Rebels in Texas," February 4, 1862. Original 13 pp.

9. Karl W. Laumbach, Human Systems Research Inc., Las Cruces, N.M.

"Massai (New Mexico's Apache Kid)." Paper presented to the Historical Society of New Mexico, April 23, 1993.

Maps

1784 Gerónimo de la Rocha's Map of the Gila Apache Country, March 18, 1784 (from Library of Congress).

1859 Territory and Military Department of New Mexico, compiled . . . under the authority of Hon. J.B. Floyd, Sec. of War, 1859 (from National Archives, RG 77, Records of the Office of the Chief of Engineers, Sheet W55[1]).

1867–1868 Map of the Route of the Southern Continental R.R. . . . Kansas Pacific Railway Co. (reproduced in *Arizoniana* 3(4), following p. 27).

c. 1872–1873 Map of Part of Arizona Showing the Chiricahua Reserve (from National Archives, RG 75, Records of the Bureau of Indian Affairs, Map 392).

1878 Parts of Southeastern Arizona, Atlas Sheet No. 10, 1878 (from National Archives, RG 77, Records of the Office of the Chief of Engineers, Sheet W275-10).

1880 Official Map of the Territory of Arizona . . . by E. A. Eckhoff and P. Riecker, Civil Engineers, 1880 (reproduction by Tucson Blueprint).

1886 Outline Map of the Field of Operations Against Hostile Chiricahua Indians (reproduction by Tucson Blueprint).

All maps and plats listed below with the exception of USGS Map MR-46 are located at the Forest Supervisor's office, Coronado National Forest, Tucson.

1910–1924 Homestead Entry Survey Plat Book; Forest Homesteads in Coronado National Forest.

1918 U.S. Forest Service, Map of Coronado National Forest

1926–1975 Plats of Summer Home Areas, Coronado National Forest (includes plats of summer home areas in the Santa Rita, Santa Catalina, Pinaleño, and Chiricahua mountains).

1940 U.S. Forest Service, Map of Coronado National Forest

1941 U.S. Forest Service, Map of Crook National Forest

1943 U.S. Geological Survey Galiuro Mts., Ariz. 15' Quadrangle

1950 U.S. Geological Survey San Simon Az.—N. Mex. 15' Quadrangle

1967 Reported Occurrences of Selected Minerals in Arizona. U.S. Geological Survey Mineral Investigations Resource Map MR-46 (South Half).

Current Plat folder—Summerhaven—Mt. Lemmon Leases

Newspapers

(The) Arizona Citizen, Tucson, May 20, 1871; February 5, 1876

(The) Arizona Daily Star, Tucson, 1879–1880, 1886, 1910–1911, 1916–1917, 1919–1921, 1931–1932, 1937, 1954, 1959, 1962, 1968, 1974, 1976–1977, 1981, 1984

The Arizona Republic, Phoenix, May 21, 1977; January 13, October 9, 1983; August 4, 1985

Arizona Weekly Citizen, Tucson, Ariz., October 9, 1875

Arizona Weekly Star, Tucson, July 24, 1879

The Benson News, Benson, Ariz., February 19, 1927
Daily Alta California, San Francisco, September 29, November 4, 1858; January 11, April 6, 1860; July 2, September 2, 29, December 17, 1861; June 11, July 10, August 10, 16, 1862
Daily Arizona Citizen, Tucson, July 15, September 16, October 11, 25, November 24, 1880.
Daily Evening Bulletin, San Francisco, November 19, 27, 1858
Daily Missouri Republican, St. Louis, Mo., February 22, March 10, 1859
(The) Daily Morning Chronicle, Washington, D.C., November 10, 1872
The Daily Nugget, Tombstone, Ariz., November 12, December 15, 1880
Eastern Arizona Courier, Safford, September 5, 1984
El Paso Daily Herald, May 18, 1896
The Herald, Silver City, N.M., September 23, 1876
Los Angeles Star, September 4, 8, November 20, 1858; May 21, 1859; July 20, September 7, 29, December 17, 1861; June 15, 1862
Oquawka Spectator, Oquawka, Ill., May 17, 1860
The Mesilla Times, Mesilla, Ariz. (N.M.), October 18, 25, November 1, 1860; May 11, 17, June 8, 1861
The Ranchero, Corpus Christi, Tex., November 3, 1860
The San Francisco Herald, August 21, December 27, 1860; January 1, 28, February 25, September 14, 21, 1861
Santa Fe Weekly Gazette, October 15, 1864
(The) Semi-Weekly Southern News, Los Angeles, Ca., August 30, September 6, 1861; June 4, 1862
Southwestern Stockman, Willcox, Ariz., May 31, 1890
Southwestern Stockman, Farmer and Feeder, Phoenix, Az., September 20, 1901
Sulphur Valley News, Willcox, Ariz., May 12, 1896
Sunday Morning Republican, St. Louis, Mo., June 26, 1859
Texas Republican, Marshall, February 18, 1859
Tombstone Daily Nugget, October 4, 5, December 16, 1881
(The) Tombstone Epitaph, June 12, August 14, October 25, December 6, 13, 1880; January 10, 1881
Tombstone Prospector, August 4, 1890
Tucson Citizen, September 4, 29, 1979; July 20, 1984
Tucson Daily Citizen, August 21, 1973; March 25, 1976
(The) Washington Union, Washington, D.C., September 16, October 17, 1857; October 21, 1858
(The) Weekly Arizonan, Tucson, October 30, November 6, 1869; February 26, April 16, 1870
(The) Weekly Arizonian, Tubac, March 3, 31, April 28, June 30, July 7, August 11, October 27, 1859

Personal Communications

Mr. Don Bufkin, Tucson, various dates

Miss Gloria J. Fenner, Western Archeological and Conservation Center, Tucson, October 30, 1986; July 4, 1987

Dr. Bernard L. Fontana, University of Arizona, August 26, 1986

Mr. Mike Granger, Fort Huachuca, Ariz., September 29, 1986

Mr. Conrad R. McCormick, Sierra Vista, Ariz., September 3, 1986

Mr. Richard Y. Murray, Western Archeological and Conservation Center, Tucson, July 13, 1987

Mr. Michael Shaughnessey, Fort Huachuca, Ariz., September 29, 1987

Mr. Robert B. Tippeconnic, Coronado National Forest, Tucson, October 2, 1986

Dr. Robert Weber, Socorro, N.M., June 26, 1987.

INDEX